JANE AUSTEN AND CHILDREN

Jane Austen and Children

David Selwyn

continuum

Published by the Continuum International Publishing Group

The Tower Building   80 Maiden Lane
11 York Road   Suite 704
London   New York
SE1 7NX   NY 10038

www.continuumbooks.com

First published 2010

British Library Cataloguing-in-Publication Data
A catalogue record for this book is available from the British Library.

ISBN 978-1847-25041-4

Designed and typeset by Pindar NZ, Auckland, New Zealand
Printed and bound by MPG Books Ltd, Cornwall, Great Britain

Contents

Acknowledgments		vi
Introduction		1
1	Confinement	5
2	Birth	15
3	Infancy	31
4	Childhood	59
5	Parents	95
6	The child in the family	119
7	Reading and writing	143
8	Education	163
9	Maturity	181
Notes		219
Bibliography		239
Index		245

Acknowledgements

Anyone who writes about Jane Austen owes a great debt to Deirdre Le Faye, whose scholarship has contributed so much to our knowledge about the Austen family and their circle; but I am particularly grateful for her unstinting help and advice, her kind provision of some of her own working notes and transcriptions of manuscripts, and her careful reading of the typescript and the invaluable comments she made on it.

I should also like to record my thanks to the following individuals, libraries and institutions: Pat Ballinger; Bristol Central Library; colleagues at Bristol Grammar School, among them Kate Maddock, Derrick Gale, Di Swain and the Library staff; the British Library; Mary Burkett; Tom Carpenter and the Trustees of the Jane Austen Memorial Trust; Ann Channon; David Gilson; the staff of the Hampshire Record Office; Maggie Lane; Joyce Morris; Timothy Mowl; Michael Richardson and Jamie Carstairs, University of Bristol Arts and Social Sciences Library, Special Collections; Brian Southam; Patrick Stokes; Chris Viveash.

I am most grateful to Christopher Harries and the registrar's Department of the University of Bristol for permission to reproduce the painting of Thomas Tyndall and his family on the dustcover.

Finally, to Martin Sheppard, formerly at Hambledon, who first discussed and planned the book with me, and to my editors at Continuum, Ben Hayes, Kim Pillay and Alice Eddowes, who took it on, I must also express my gratitude.

Introduction

In the eighteenth and early nineteenth centuries children came to be perceived as a species quite separate from adults, and historians are apt to interpret this as representing a beneficial development in their treatment by society. Roy Porter points out that not only were they regarded, under the influence of the philosophers John Locke and Jean-Jacques Rousseau, as natural innocents whose feelings and wishes were to be taken into account, but, in a period of rising consumerism, they commanded a market of their own, with toys, books and educational games aimed directly at them, and painters ready to take their portraits in return for the handsome fees that proud parents were willing to pay.[1] Instead of being merely untamed creatures, sinful from birth and consequently needing repeated chastisement to bring them to a state of reason, children were now allowed to be an autonomous group capable of rational thought and behaviour and possessed of rights that Enlightenment society was perfectly happy to acknowledge; Locke regarded the young mind as *tabula rasa*, something without innate ideas on which it was the responsibility of society to inscribe rational and moral precepts. But Porter indicates that this attention carried with it the danger of an intrusion of adult moralizers into their lives, as high-minded writers turned out 'prim learning books' intended to replace the traditional stories of the nursery with improving factual lessons. Furthermore, if they were considered to be capable of reasonable behaviour, it followed that any lapse would reduce them to the level of brute beasts – a warning that, as Andrew O'Malley has noted, such writers were quick to give them.[2]

In understanding the role that Jane Austen assigns to children in her novels, it is necessary to negotiate this contradiction. Unlike the writers of nursery primers, she is not of course concerned with the education of the young; rather, in a reversal of their methods, she is more inclined to make use of children to reveal aspects of her adult characters (a theme that will naturally be central to this book). Moreover, for her the dichotomy between the attention that is due to a child and the irrational behaviour that the child will all too often exhibit is both a welcome and a truthful source of comedy. The attention she pays it is that neither of the philosopher nor of the shopkeeper, but of the shrewdly observant novelist; and in her amused response to the idiosyncrasies of its behaviour, and the reactions to them of adults, she resolves the problem in her own way.

There are very few children in Jane Austen's work who could be said to live up to the idealized conceptions of Locke or Rousseau, and those who do, such as the little Gardiners and Harvilles, and perhaps the children of John and Isabella Knightley, are given fairly peripheral roles; the touching and beautifully drawn Charles Blake in *The Watsons* is an exception, but then he comes from a work that she was unable to bring to fruition. On the whole she prefers to create less satisfactory children: the spoilt young Middletons; the undisciplined Musgroves; the shy and vulnerable Fanny Price and her uncontrollable brothers and sisters in Portsmouth; and the wilful and selfish Julia and Maria Bertram – the latter a case, if ever there was one, of the child being mother to the woman. In references in her letters to children in her own family, she was similarly observant of, and amused by, their manners and foibles, though on occasion critical too of lapses on the part of their parents in exercising due restraint and discipline; but she and her sister Cassandra were devoted and proud aunts, and there is no doubt that their affection was amply repaid by their nephews and nieces.

The children Jane Austen describes, like the real ones in her own family, necessarily belong to the social world of the gentry in which her novels are set. They live in comfortable houses where there are servants and stables; some of them have governesses; and even the disorderly Price family in *Mansfield Park* are very much better off than a great many people lower down the scale. While she may occasionally provide a glimpse of the children of some sick cottager, or a little group eyeing the gingerbread in a baker's window, of the mass of poor, labouring children whose lives were led in the great factories of industrial England we see nothing. Pauper children who were not lucky enough to have an Emma Woodhouse to bestow her charity on them were often sent off by their parishes to work in the mills; and families who had no other resource sometimes consigned them there themselves. It is an astonishing fact that in 1793, nearly a fifth of Robert Owen's workers were under nine years old.[3] And it was not only in the north or the Midlands that masters employed juvenile labour. At Overton in Hampshire, there was a silk mill that employed 140 children to wind the skeins onto the bobbins or put the threads together to be twisted. They were well looked after and received a regular wage, and indeed the owner claimed to have set up the factory from motives of benevolence; younger children whose parents were working there were looked after by women appointed to care for them until they were six years old and big enough to be set to work themselves. Overton was only three miles from Jane Austen's home at Steventon; and her great friend Mrs Lefroy, wife of the rector of the neighbouring parish of Ashe, used to amuse her guests by taking them to see the mill in action.[4]

Though this book is largely concerned with the use that Jane Austen makes of children who are actually young, parent–child and sibling relationships also require some attention. To give too much consideration to this aspect of the novels would necessarily be to cover familiar ground, but one or two points are worth noting. In the three novels where the heroine is situated within her family, *Sense and Sensibility*, *Pride and Prejudice* and *Persuasion*, she is given no brothers, only sisters, one of whom, in the first two, acts as her confidante; the fact that for Anne Elliot neither Elizabeth nor Mary plays such a role is in itself very significant. Emma too has only a sister, though Isabella can hardly be considered a confidante; indeed it is in default of anyone better, after Miss Taylor's marriage, that she takes up Harriet Smith. In *Northanger Abbey* and *Mansfield Park* the heroines do have brothers; but since in the former case James Morland is included largely for the sake of the plot, it is only with Fanny and William Price that the brother–sister relationship is fully explored.

Beyond the use of children in the novels as a source of comedy or as a means of revealing attitudes and responses of the adults around them, on occasion they have an important function in the actual structure of a scene. An interesting and rather complex example can be found in *Emma*, when Mr John Knightley brings his two eldest boys, Henry and John, on a visit to Hartfield. They are to spend several weeks there, but he is staying only for one day, and it happens to be a day on which Emma has arranged to give a dinner party for Mr Elton and his new wife. The first effect is to play on two sustained strands of humour in the novel: one is Mr Woodhouse's dislike of large gatherings, since he considers 'eight persons at dinner together as the utmost that his nerves could bear – and here would be a ninth';[5] the other is Mr John Knightley's characteristic annoyance at interruptions to his quiet family life – 'it would be a ninth very much out of humour at not being able to come even to Hartfield for forty-eight hours without falling in with a dinner-party'.

But there are deeper purposes to be served. One is to have Mr John Knightley present for the conversation between Jane Fairfax and Mrs Elton about the post. It is in fact because he took the boys for a walk that he met Jane coming back from the post office as it began to rain ('and Henry and John had seen more drops than they could count long before');[6] and his kindly wish that the letters which mean so much to her now may at some time have less importance to her when she has everybody dearest to her always at hand produces 'a blush, a quivering lip, a tear in the eye'. Her vulnerability, perceived only in a general sense by him, will of course appear to the reader, as it does to Emma, to derive from the imagined relationship with Mr Dixon; but Jane Austen is preparing one of the most important (and at this stage entirely unperceived) clues about her real circumstances. As Mrs Elton officiously tries to insist on sending one of her own servants to collect the letters for the Bates household, Jane turns the discussion by speaking to Mr John Knightley about the remarkable efficiency of the post office:

> 'The post-office is a wonderful establishment!' said she. – 'The regularity and dispatch of it! If one thinks of all that it has to do, and all that it does so well, it is really astonishing!'
>
> 'It is certainly very well regulated.'
>
> 'So seldom that any negligence or blunder appears! So seldom that a letter, among the thousands that are constantly passing about the kingdom is even carried wrong – and not one in a million, I suppose actually lost! . . . '[7]

So protracted an encomium is surprising, and its purpose is by no means clear to the reader; but in fact it contains the key word 'blunder' that is to play such a crucial part in the game of anagrams in a later chapter. Frank Churchill is not of course present in this scene, and his subsequent use of the word in the game is not a conscious echo of hers. The only people who could make the connection, and who inevitably fail to do so, are we, the readers, who, as part of the extraordinary game that Jane Austen is playing with us, are immediately offered the answer, in the sure knowledge that we shall fail to recognize it. As the discussion turns to the different kinds of handwriting that postal officials have to decipher, Emma looks for an opportunity to introduce Frank's name into the conversation, and actually refers to a note that he has written her, thus deflecting our attention from any possible discovery of the true state of affairs by pointing to a quite different one. All this is made possible by Mr John Knightley's presence, which in turn is brought about by means of his children.

And there is something more. Emma's praise of Frank's handwriting provokes a sharp disagreement from Mr George Knightley; and the true state of his feelings is hinted at when later in the evening his brother tells Emma that if she finds the boys troublesome she must send them home: 'I hope I am aware,' he tells her, 'that they may be too noisy for your father – or even may be some incumbrance to you, if your visiting-engagements continue to increase as much as they have done lately.' As she protests, he insists that she is 'far more engaged with company' than she used to be; and he ascribes it to the activities of the Westons: 'The difference which Randalls, Randalls alone makes in your goings-on, is very great.' Mr Knightley, quick to reassure himself that this is indeed the cause, jumps in: '"Yes," said his brother quickly, "it is Randalls that does it all."' But he is thinking of Frank Churchill, and on his brother's repeating that if Henry and John are in the way they should be sent home, he says with a ruefulness that a casual reader may miss, 'No . . . that need not be the consequence. Let them be sent to Donwell. I shall certainly be at leisure.'[8]

This is only one example – albeit a subtle and important one – of the unobtrusive way in which Jane Austen can find in children a resource for her narrative strategies. In such instances the reader is hardly aware of the children at all, and certainly fails to see how important they are to the furthering of the plot; in fact, the casual reader may not even remember that there are any children in her novels, since, except for Fanny Price's fears when she arrives as a little girl at Mansfield Park, and the ironically charted development of Catherine Morland through her early years (which is done very much as a comic stereotype), they are rarely required to bear any of the emotional weight that Dickens, for example, would later give to David Copperfield or Pip. Yet for all that, they are distinctly seen as individuals, and their behaviour derives from their character just as much as it does in any adult in the novels; and while often what we enjoy is the reaction of other characters to them, there are occasional instances of sharply observed behaviour, for example little Walter in *Persuasion* coming into the room at Uppercross when his brother is ill and making a thorough nuisance of himself, that are delightful and memorable in their own right.

1

Confinement

To be in at the beginning of life, one must start at the end of the novel.

For although Jane Austen concludes her books with the marriage of hero and heroine to which the whole thrust of the narrative has been leading, and the reader rejoices in the perfect happiness of the union, in reality the best is yet to come: they will have children – procreation being not only the natural and desirable end of marriage, but also an economic and dynastic necessity. And those children will have their own stories, which we may make a reasonable guess at, since there were established ways of doing these things. What will become of the Darcy children? The eldest boy will inherit Pemberley, of course; one of his brothers may go into the army, perhaps joining Colonel Fitzwilliam's regiment, and another will probably enter the Church, no doubt enjoying that living to which Mr Wickham was so particularly unsuited. And among the girls there will surely be at least one pair of fine eyes to win the heart of a Bingley cousin. Meanwhile, Mr and Mrs Knightley will produce an heir to Donwell who will supplant little Henry, the 'heir expectant'[1] whose claims Emma is so quick to defend when Mrs Weston suggests that Mr Knightley may marry Jane Fairfax;[2] and the Revd and Mrs Edmund Bertram will fill Mansfield parsonage with children, just as the Revd and Mrs George Austen filled Steventon rectory. Jane Austen, who knew her Shakespeare, was well aware that 'the world must be peopled'.[3]

But it is neither her business nor that of the accepted structure of comedy to follow the hero and heroine beyond the church door; while it is true that at the end of *Sense and Sensibility* Marianne is foreseen as 'the mistress of a family'[4] (that is to say, of a whole household, comprehending children and servants), in *Mansfield Park*, where Jane Austen does permit her pen to speculate about her characters' future, there is only the most oblique of references to Fanny and Edmund having children. So in her novels there are only one or two minor characters who experience pregnancy during the course of the narrative; and as one might expect, any mention of their condition is of the most discreet kind.

In writing to her sister Cassandra about their friends and relations, however, Jane was prepared to be far more forthcoming, and over the years she reported frequently on the confinements of her sisters-in-law. 'Mary is quite well . . . "& uncommonly large", she quoted her brother James as saying, when in October 1798 his wife was expecting a baby.[5] Two days before the birth, she went to Deane parsonage with her father to see Mary, and reported that she was 'still plagued with the rheumatism, which she would be very glad to get rid of, and still more glad to get rid of her child, of whom she is heartily tired'.[6] A monthly nurse had been sent for, and Jane wrote that she had 'no particular charm either of person or manner'; but, she added, 'as all the Hurstbourne world pronounce her to be the best nurse that ever was, Mary expects her attachment to increase'. She also told Cassandra that two women had recently died in childbirth, and added cheerfully, 'We have not regaled Mary with this news'. By the time she got to the end of the letter, she was able to write: 'I have just received a note from James to say that Mary was brought to bed last night, at eleven o'clock, of a fine little boy, and that everything is going on very well.' The fine little boy was James Edward Austen-Leigh, destined eventually to be his aunt's first biographer.

At this time, Jane and her mother had not long returned from Godmersham in Kent, where another sister-in-law, Edward's wife Elizabeth, had also given birth, to her fifth child, and where Cassandra was staying on to lend assistance. Mrs Austen was still suffering from the fatigues of the journey; she was very close to both James and his wife, and if, as is probably the case, Mary had experienced a miscarriage the previous year,[7] it is not surprising that she was too anxious to wish to follow the last stages closely: 'My mother had desired to know nothing of it before it should be all over,' Jane wrote, 'and we were clever enough to prevent her having any suspicion of it, though Jenny, who had been left here by her mistress, was sent for home.' No doubt Jane too was relieved that all had gone well, and that after a second visit she was able to write to Cassandra that she had been 'really amazed at the improvement which three days had made' in her sister-in-law, that she 'looked well' and 'her spirits were perfectly good'.[8] Yet there is something curiously detached about the way in which, before she gives any account of mother and child, she begins this letter in a tone of high comedy:

> My dear Sister
> I expected to have heard from you this morning, but no letter is come. I shall not take the trouble of announcing to you any more of Mary's children, if, instead of thanking me for the intelligence, you always sit down and write to James. I am sure that nobody can desire your letters so much as I do, and I don't think anybody deserves them so well. Having relieved my heart of a great deal of malevolence, I will proceed to tell you that Mary continues quite well, and my mother tolerably so.

Mary's example did little to make Jane Austen feel that she herself would ever care to go through the experience of having a child, however. When she wrote again a week later, she could not help making comparisons between the two young mothers:

> I was at Deane yesterday morning. Mary was very well, but does not gain bodily strength very fast. When I saw her so stout on the third and sixth days, I expected to have seen her as well as ever by the end of a fortnight. . . . Mary does not manage matters in such a way as to make me want to lay in myself. She is not tidy enough in her appearance; she has no dressing-gown to sit up in; her curtains are all too thin, and things are not in that

comfort and style about her which are necessary to make such a situation an enviable one. Elizabeth was really a pretty object with her nice clean cap put on so tidily and her dress so uniformly white and orderly.[9]

There were times when, unmarried as she was, she clearly felt sympathy for those women who were forced to undergo a seemingly unending cycle of pregnancies. Some years later, in a letter from Godmersham announcing the arrival of Elizabeth's eleventh child, Cassandra passed on the news that Mrs Tilson, wife of Henry Austen's banking partner, was also about to have a baby; 'poor Woman!' Jane replied, 'how can she be honestly breeding again?'[10] Perhaps the general sense of over-production was too much for her; what could hardly be said, even to Cassandra, about the wife of their own brother, could be displaced onto a mere acquaintance. The child was Mrs Tilson's eighth. Five years later, Jane met Mrs Tilson in London; she was 'as affectionate & pleasing as ever', she told Cassandra, commenting ironically: 'from her appearance I suspect her to be in the family way. Poor Woman!'[11] She added that her niece Fanny prophesied 'the Child's coming within 3 or 4 days', and so it proved: shortly afterwards, the Tilsons' eleventh child, a little girl, was born.

A woman subjected to a series of thirteen pregnancies that came every two years with clockwork regularity was Mrs John Benn, wife of the rector of Farringdon, a mile to the south of the Austens' later home at Chawton. She was certainly well used to the routine; Jane wrote to Cassandra in September 1816: 'You left us in no doubt of Mrs Benn's situation, but she has bespoke her Nurse.'[12] And her thoughts turning to her brother Frank's wife, also Mary, then two months into her seventh pregnancy, she added: 'Mrs F. A. seldom either looks or appears quite well. – Little Embryo is troublesome I suppose.' There was a regularity in Mary's proceedings too; when Frank brought her to dinner at Chawton, six months later, Jane wrote to Fanny that it was 'the last visit of the kind probably, which *she* will be able to pay us for many a month; – Very well, to be able to do it so long, for she *expects* much about this day three weeks, & is generally very exact.'[13] At the same time, one of Fanny's aunts on her mother's side was expecting her eighteenth child; Jane wrote to her niece: 'Good Mrs Deedes! – I hope she will get the better of this Marianne, & then I w^d recommend to her & Mr D. the simple regimen of separate rooms.'[14] About twenty-four-year-old Fanny's own marriage prospects, she advised her not to be in a hurry; then, 'by not beginning the business of Mothering quite so early in life', she would be 'young in Constitution, spirits, figure & countenance', unlike Fanny's friend Mary Hammond, who, married at twenty, was 'growing old by confinements & nursing'.[15] Yet at that time, twenty-four was far from being considered 'early in life' for a woman to marry and begin the 'business of Mothering': Jane's sister-in-law Elizabeth Bridges, Fanny's mother, had been only 18 when she married Edward, and another sister-in-law, Fanny Palmer, was the same age when she married Charles Austen. Among her own heroines, Marianne Dashwood marries at nineteen, Fanny Price at eighteen and Catherine Morland at seventeen.

One has the feeling that in the last months of her life, the contemplation of this never-ending cycle of marrying and breeding seemed gradually to overwhelm her; and with her niece Anna Lefroy pregnant for the third time, it all became too much for her, almost as if her own ailing constitution could not withstand the thought of so much teeming new life. There is a palpable sense of disgust in her tone when she writes to Fanny:

> Anna has not a chance of escape; her husband called here the other day, & said she was *pretty well* but not *equal to so long* a walk; she *must come in* her *Donkey Carriage*. – Poor Animal, she will be worn out before she is thirty. – I am very sorry for her. – Mrs Clement too is in that way again. I am quite tired of so many Children. – Mrs Benn has a 13th.[16]

As it turned out, on this occasion Anna had a miscarriage. Her aunts had originally suspected her pregnancy partly because she was looking pale, but also because she had just weaned her previous child. Again, Jane's choice of words is interesting: 'We fear something else', she told Fanny.[17]

It was widely held that breastfeeding could prevent conception; a mother might delay becoming pregnant again too soon after giving birth by prolonging the period of suckling, but once she had ceased, falling pregnant again became a possibility. Mary Wollstonecraft actually advocated breastfeeding as a method of controlling the intervals between pregnancies, thus enabling a woman to manage her children herself rather than leaving them entirely to the care of servants, without wholly sacrificing her own needs to – in Jane Austen's phrase – the business of mothering:

> fulfilling the duties of a mother, a woman with a sound constitution, may still keep her person scrupulously neat, and assist to maintain her family, if necessary, or by reading and conversations with both sexes, indiscriminately, improve her mind. For nature has so wisely ordered things, that did women suckle their children, they would preserve their own health, and there would be such an interval between the birth of each child, that we should seldom see a houseful of babes.[18]

The frank discussion of pregnancy and its consequences was all very well in the letters that Jane wrote to her sister, but it is not something that would find its way into any of her novels, where, as we shall see, the stages of a woman's confinement are generally, though not quite always, charted at second-hand through the conversation of intermediary characters. There are novels by her contemporaries, Mary Wollstonecraft, Charlotte Smith and Mrs Opie among them,[19] in which not only does the heroine become pregnant but her condition plays an important part, functionally and psychologically, in the narrative; dealing as they do with the more extreme forms of pressure exerted on women's sensibilities, however, these narratives are not comedies.[20]

In the medical literature of the time a debate was taking place about the effects on women of the physiological changes brought about by pregnancy. Many physicians believed that at conception the womb was stimulated to a condition of excitement termed 'irritability', and that the other organs of the body were in 'consent' with it and were similarly excited; since this 'consent' could extend to the mind or emotions, a pregnant woman might often appear less calm and reasonable than she would normally be, and indeed might be subject to moods of extreme dejection or hysteria. Clare Hanson sees in this view a 'reworking of the Greek theory of the "wandering womb"'[21] – that is, the 'mother', a phenomenon most familiar to us, perhaps, from Lear's cry when he fears the onset of madness:

> O! how this mother swells up toward my heart;
> *Hysterica passio*! down, thou climbing sorrow!
> Thy element's below.[22]

The idea of the 'irritability' of the body in pregnancy, however, was dismissed by a female writer and midwife who took her stand in the controversy over the ascendancy of the man-midwife which was a matter of considerable importance in eighteenth-century obstetrics (and which will be discussed in the next chapter). Martha Mears, in *The Midwife's Candid Advice to the Fair Sex*, counters the term 'irritability' with the much more positive 'sensibility'; she rejects the idea of pregnancy as an illness, preferring to see it as a condition that confers blossoming health and increased charms on the woman who joyfully anticipates the state of motherhood.

This debate between authorities two hundred years ago might strike us as having little claim on our interest, except in terms of the history of obstetrics, were it not that something of it seems to have been rehearsed by Jane Austen. We have seen how she noted with pity the physical effects on the female body caused by repeated pregnancies; yet in the novels nothing of this is suggested. It is perfectly true, of course, that both Charlotte Palmer in *Sense and Sensibility* and Mrs Weston in *Emma* are undergoing their first pregnancy; and in fact, when Mr Weston comes to fetch Emma to Randalls so that his wife can break the news to her of Frank's engagement, her initial concern is that Mrs Weston is unwell.[23] But neither of these pregnancies is presented as a cause for undue worry; and in the case of Charlotte Palmer there is a marked cheerfulness, both in herself and in her mother, that shows little sign of her experiencing any 'irritation' of the womb, or indeed of any other part of her body with which it might be in 'consent'. When a character in Jane Austen experiences a serious illness – Marianne Dashwood or, in *Persuasion*, Louisa Musgrove, for example – it is usually as the result of some act of rashness or folly, and can therefore be regarded as an aberration; childbearing is altogether too much a natural and desirable part of human experience to be seen in such a light.

Yet there were many dangers in pregnancy, to both the mother and the child. The greatest risk was of having a miscarriage, or as it was medically termed, an abortion. Dr William Buchan, writing in *Domestic Medicine* in 1769, stated that every pregnant woman was 'more or less in danger of abortion', and that it was most common in the second or third month, though it sometimes happened in the fourth or fifth. He was very specific about the warning signs:

> a pain in the loins, or about the bottom of the belly; a dull heavy pain in the inside of the thighs; a slight degree of coldness or shivering; sickness; palpitation of the heart; the breasts become flat and soft; the belly falls; and there is a discharge of blood or watery humours from the womb.[24]

He offered equally specific recommendations for lessening the chance of having a miscarriage:

> To prevent abortion, we would advise women of a weak or relaxed habit to use solid food, avoiding great quantities of tea, and other weak and watery liquors; to rise early, and go soon to bed; to shun damp houses; to take frequent exercise in the open air, but to avoid fatigue; and never to go abroad in damp foggy weather, if they can shun it. Women of a full habit ought to use a spare diet, avoiding strong liquors, and every thing that may tend to heat the body, or increase the quantity of blood. Their diet should be of an opening nature, consisting principally of vegetable substances. Every woman with child ought to be kept cheerful and easy in her mind. All violent passions hurt the *foetus*, and endanger an abortion.

Should there nevertheless appear any of the danger signs,

> the woman ought to be laid in bed on a mattress, with her head low. She should be kept quiet, and her mind soothed and comforted. She ought not to be kept too warm, nor to take any thing of a heated nature. Her food should consist of broths, rice and milk, jellies, or gruels with a very little wine in them. If she be able to bear it, she should lose, at least, half a pound of blood from the arm . . . Sanguine robust women, who are liable to miscarry at a certain time of Pregnancy, ought always to be bled a few days before that period arrives.

For a normally active, busy woman, the period of enforced confinement before childbirth could become very tedious. 'I am determined,' wrote Bessy Ramsden, wife of the Usher of Charterhouse School, 'not to stay at home any Longer till I take to my bed.'[25] At Steventon, Mrs Austen kept going about the rectory, though she ruled out long journeys; in November 1772, two months before the birth of Cassandra, she wrote to her sister-in-law Susanna Walter that paying her a visit in Kent was 'not to be thought of', since she had all four of her boys at home and 'some time in January I expect a fifth, so you see it will not be in my power to take any journeys for one while'[26] – and she implied that it was looking after the other children quite as much as the pregnancy itself that deterred her. A little under three years later, in August 1775, when she was already six months pregnant with Jane, she told Mrs Walter: 'I am more nimble and active than I was last time, expect to be confined some time in November'; and she continued with news of the hay harvest ('we got the last load in yesterday'), and said that she would be 'sincerely glad' to see her sister-in-law should she be able to come to Hampshire.[27]

In November 1800, Jane Austen herself considered it worth commenting on when she saw the niece of James's first wife, well into her pregnancy and dancing at a ball: 'I was constrained to think [her] a very fine young woman,' she told Cassandra humorously, 'which I much regret. She has got rid of some part of her child, & danced away with great activity, looking by no means very large.'[28]

In *Sense and Sensibility* Charlotte Palmer shows a similar resilience and is equally willing to keep to her normal routine to the last possible moment. She is six months pregnant when she arrives with her husband on a surprise visit to Barton Park, and Mrs Jennings is not slow to explain her daughter's condition, even to comparative strangers, as the Dashwoods are:

> 'You may believe how glad we all were to see them . . . but, however, I can't help wishing they had not travelled quite so fast, nor made such a long journey of it, for they came all round by London upon account of some business, for you know (nodding significantly and pointing to her daughter) it was wrong in her situation. I wanted her to stay at home and rest this morning, but she would come with us; she longed so much to see you all!' Mrs. Palmer laughed, and said it would not do her any harm.[29]

Mrs Jennings's concern is understandable, since the Palmers have obviously travelled from their country house, Cleveland, near Bristol, to London and then down to Barton, near Exeter, a journey little short of three hundred miles that would indeed have been taxing for anyone less spirited. Mrs Jennings's insouciant discussion of the subject is too distasteful, however, for her other daughter, the refined Lady Middleton, who seeks to change the subject as soon as possible:

> 'She expects to be confined in February,' continued Mrs. Jennings. Lady Middleton could no longer endure such a conversation, and therefore exerted herself to ask Mr. Palmer if there was any news in the paper. 'No, none at all,' he replied, and read on.

But Mrs Jennings, whose cheerful forthrightness about such womanly matters derives partly perhaps from the Wife of Bath and partly from Jane Austen's own mother, is undaunted. When she arrives in London with Elinor and Marianne, she asks Colonel Brandon, who has been dining with the Palmers, 'How does Charlotte do? I warrant you she is a fine size by this time.'[30] And although it is only a month before she is due to give birth, Charlotte seems to have unbounded energy. Calling the next day, she comes 'laughing into the room; so delighted to see them all, that it was hard to say whether she received most pleasure from meeting her mother or the Miss Dashwoods again.'[31] After 'an hour or two spent in . . . comfortable chat', she invites them all to accompany her on a shopping expedition, which seems to take up most of the day as 'her eye was caught by every thing pretty, expensive, or new', and, 'wild to buy all', she 'could determine on none, and dawdled away her time in rapture and indecision'. But even after this she is anything but exhausted and joins in a dinner party, before leaving them 'soon after tea to fulfil her evening engagements'.

A week later, she and her husband attend Sir John Middleton's impromptu ball. Only after a further 'three or four days' following that does her 'indisposition' require her mother's presence on the evening in which Marianne meets Willoughby at the party to which she and Elinor are taken by Lady Middleton; and even this indisposition, though perfectly plausible so late in her pregnancy, is clearly a device by which Jane Austen is able to exclude Mrs Jennings's comic presence from a highly dramatic scene.[32] Nothing is subsequently made of Charlotte's suffering any illness, and Mrs Jennings does not see her the following day; when we do hear of her visiting again, it is to tell her all about Willoughby's desertion of Marianne for Miss Grey. In a later scene, when Jane Austen needs to have Elinor alone with Lucy Steele and subsequently Edward Ferrars, it is nothing more alarming than a 'message' from Charlotte that calls Mrs Jennings away.[33]

Charlotte Palmer's robust good health and bubbling spirits during her pregnancy throw Marianne Dashwood's simultaneously declining health into sharp relief. Clare Hanson has gone so far as to suggest that her narrative 'can be read in terms of the triumph of maternal *in*sensibility';[34] but if this is so, I feel that it is not necessarily in order to reflect well on Marianne: Charlotte's good-humoured ability to laugh her way through the difficulties of life is as much of a corrective to Marianne's uncontrolled sensibility as Elinor's more sober commonsense.

There is, however, another contrast to note here. When Charlotte finally presents Mr Palmer with his 'son and heir', her narrative, like her dynastic obligation, is satisfactorily accomplished. But the birth has taken place only a matter of months after another, far less desirable, one – that of the illegitimate child born to Eliza Williams; and Colonel Brandon's revelation of Willoughby's being the father is carefully placed between his desertion of Marianne and the announcement of the legitimate birth. The little knot of illegitimacy in the novel is tightly drawn: not only is Eliza herself illegitimate, having been 'the offspring of [her mother's] first guilty connection',[35] but she is widely spoken of – particularly by Mrs Jennings – as the Colonel's natural daughter.[36] Eliza's fate was the same as that which nearly overtook Miss Darcy at the hands of Wickham; fortunately she is saved by the intervention of her brother, but Colonel Brandon, having 'found her near her delivery', was unable to rescue Eliza in time.[37]

There had been a steady rise in the rate of illegitimate births in England between the end of the Puritan period in 1660 and the advent of the Evangelical movement towards the end of the eighteenth century. It has been argued that, at least among the poor, who had no property to be made secure by formal marriage, this was exacerbated by the Marriage Act of 1753, the effect of which was to remove the discretion of clergymen to register as legitimate children born in consensual, or common-law, marriages (that is to say, marriages that had not been formalized in church).[38] The aristocracy had often had children by mistresses, and continued to do so: the Duke of Clarence, later William IV, and Dorothea Jordan, had ten children who, under the name Fitzclarence, formed a recognized family; and in February 1807, looking for some cheerful news to tell Cassandra in a letter, Jane Austen wrote: 'Unluckily however I see nothing to be glad of, unless I make it a matter of Joy that Mrs Wylmot has another son & that Ld Lucan has taken a Mistress, both of which Events are of course joyful to the Actors.'[39] But for young women such as Eliza Williams and her daughter, seduction and its consequences were disastrous, unless there was a benevolent Colonel Brandon to save them – which, in the case of Eliza herself, he was unable to do, since, though when he found her, he 'saw her placed in comfortable lodgings, and under proper attendants', 'life could do nothing for her, beyond giving time for a better preparation for death'.[40] He cannot refrain from expressing (albeit hesitantly) what was by that period the conventional religious view: 'That she was, to all appearance, in the last stage of a consumption, was – yes, in such a situation it was my greatest comfort.'

It is worth noting that Jane Austen, while unreservedly condemning the seducer, takes a compassionate view of the woman's role, seeing her as a victim, and invariably a young one: Colonel Brandon's sister-in-law could have been eighteen at most when she gave birth; her daughter is seventeen; and Miss Darcy was fifteen when Wickham attempted to elope with her.[41] Of the illegitimate child itself Jane Austen gives no hint of disapproval, though in the case of Eliza she identifies in 'the unhappy resemblance between the fate of mother and daughter' an unfortunate tendency for history to repeat itself.

If in *Sense and Sensibility* both illegitimate children are relegated to a secondary narrative, in *Emma* Harriet Smith is complacently presented to the reader directly as 'the natural daughter of somebody'[42] and even invested by Emma herself with gentlemanly origins;[43] and when her parentage eventually becomes known, it provides material for considerable irony:

> She proved to be the daughter of a tradesman, rich enough to afford her the comfortable maintenance which had ever been her's, and decent enough to have always wished for concealment. – Such was the blood of gentility which Emma had been so ready to vouch for! – It was likely to be as untainted, perhaps, as the blood of many a gentleman: but what a connexion had she been preparing for Mr. Knightley – or for the Churchills – or even for Mr. Elton! – The stain of Illegitimacy, unbleached by nobility or wealth, would have been a stain indeed.[44]

It is significant, however, that the irony is directed at society, and perhaps a little at Emma; but it is certainly not at the expense of Harriet herself.

2

Birth

Three of Jane Austen's sisters-in-law died as a direct result of giving birth. Elizabeth, Edward's wife, died suddenly on 10 October 1808, a little over a week after the birth of her eleventh child. Fanny, the first wife of Charles, gave birth to her fourth child on board her husband's ship at Sheerness on 31 August 1814; complications set in, and she died six days later, the baby following a fortnight after that. And on 14 July 1823, Francis Austen lost his first wife, Mary, who had given birth to their eleventh child a week earlier; six months later the little boy died too. Childbirth could be a dangerous business.

Yet in the generation before, Mrs Austen had had eight children apparently with little difficulty. By the time her seventh child, Jane, was born, on Saturday 16 December 1775, both she and her husband seemed to take it all very much in their stride, even though the baby was a month overdue. Mr Austen wrote cheerfully to his sister-in-law, Susanna Walter, the day after the birth, to give her the rather long-delayed news:

> You have doubtless been for some time in expectation of hearing from Hampshire, and perhaps wondered a little we were in our old age grown such bad reckoners but so it was, for Cassey [*sic*] certainly expected to have been brought to bed a month ago: however last night the time came, and without a great deal of warning, everything was soon happily over. We have now another girl, a present plaything for her sister Cassy and a future companion. She is to be Jenny, and seems to me as if she would be as like Henry, as Cassy is to Neddy.[1]

He adds, 'Your sister thank God is pure well after it, and sends her love to you and my brother, not forgetting James and Philly' – and promptly turning to farming business gives news of a ploughing match the following Tuesday, 'Kent against Hants for a rump of beef'. It wouldn't be surprising to hear that Mrs Austen had attended the event.

Probably not too much should be read into the facial comparisons Mr Austen draws between his daughters and their brothers, as if they could hardly expect, or were entitled to, any independent physical identity; nor Jane's relegation to 'present plaything' and 'future companion' to her sister (though in asserting their mutual independence he was more prophetic than he could know); nor for that matter to the ploughing match – postage was expensive and people didn't leave empty space in their letters. Mr Austen loved his children, girls as well as boys;

though of course he must have realized that only by making better marriages than they would be likely to could they contribute to the family fortunes. Not so long before, however, and in a level of society only slightly above that of the Austens, there would have been a marked sense of disappointment at having only 'another girl', since she would have been unable to further the dynastic ambitions of the family – albeit that there were already five boys, four of them at least healthy and likely to make their way in the world. Jane Austen herself was coolly realistic about the matter in her novels; families of women such as the Dashwoods or the Bennets had little enough financial security unless proper care was taken to provide it; but if a man in Mr Bennet's position, with an estate entailed in the male line, and having only daughters, failed to make such provision, the outlook could be bleak unless those daughters happened to marry a Mr Darcy or a Mr Bingley – and such happy endings were apt to occur rather more often in novels than they did in real life.

And of course Mr Bennet had not made provision because neither he nor his wife faced up to the possibility of not having a son to inherit Longbourn until it was too late:

> When Mr. Bennet had first married, economy was held to be perfectly useless; for, of course, they were to have a son. The son was to join in cutting off the entail, as soon as he should be of age, and the widow and younger children would by that means be provided for. Five daughters successively entered the world, but yet the son was to come; and Mrs. Bennet, for many years after Lydia's birth, had been certain that he would. This event had at last been despaired of, but it was then too late to be saving.[2]

Families consisting entirely of daughters were not unknown in Jane Austen's circle. The three Lloyd sisters were among her closest friends, Mary becoming the second wife of James Austen, and, though Jane did not live to see it, Martha that of Francis. Elizabeth Chute, of the Vyne, came from a family of four sisters, one of whom would become the mother-in-law of James Edward Austen-Leigh. And in Jane's own family, her youngest brother, Charles, had only daughters by his first wife, though he subsequently married her sister and had more children after Jane's death. One of the reasons that people had large families was to ensure that there were one or more sons: the Bigg-Withers of Manydown Park, parents of Jane's friends Elizabeth, Catherine and Alethea, had had no fewer than six girls before eventually producing two boys; and of the seven children of Jane's niece Anna Lefroy, only one was male. This was quite typical of the period. Susan Sibbald, who in later life wrote memoirs of her childhood, was one of eleven children, of whom only the eighth and ninth were boys.

Child mortality in England was comparatively high across all levels of society, and the expectation that any family would lose a number of children meant that many women were subjected to almost annual pregnancy. Even then, an heir could not be guaranteed; after all, of Queen Anne's seventeen children, only one survived infancy, and he died at the age of eleven. These things were taken as a matter of course, even in the highest families, though naturally they still brought their due measure of grief. John Churchill, Marquess of Blandford, heir to the great Duke of Marlborough, died of smallpox at the age of sixteen in the winter of 1703. His parents were devastated; of seven children, two of whom had died in infancy, he was the only boy, and their dynastic ambitions ran very high. But their suffering was also profoundly human. Reeling from the shock of his loss, Marlborough spoke of retiring from his military campaigns, and Sarah temporarily became almost unbalanced. Even when the grind of work had begun to take his mind off his grief, Marlborough would suddenly be forcibly reminded of his son: the sight of a great procession made him think how much the boy would have enjoyed it, and these thoughts added to his suffering. He reflected sadly: 'Since it has pleased God to take him, I do wish from my soul I could think less of him.'[3]

Two of George III's children died in successive years. When little Prince Alfred, who had not reached his second birthday, died in August 1782, Queen Charlotte 'cried vastly at first, and ... though very reasonable' was 'very much hurt by her loss and the King also'.[4] She comforted herself with the fact that she had thirteen healthy children, and the King said that if it had been Alfred's three-year-old brother Octavius who had died, he himself would have died too. When in the following May Octavius did die, he was distraught: every morning he woke up he wished he were eighty, or ninety, or dead.[5] 'There will be no heaven for me,' he said, 'if Octavius is not there.'[6]

Nevertheless, towards the end of the eighteenth century, the death rate was beginning to decline. The physician Michael Underwood noted that while in 1770 60 per cent of children died, and of those 75 per cent were under two years, by the time of writing (1784), deaths under the age of two had fallen to 30 per cent; by 1805, he was able to record that while the average of deaths in the British Lying-in Hospital, in which he held the post of physician, had been one in thirty-four over the past forty years, during the last eight it had gone down to one in eighty-four.[7] Even so, it continued to be quite usual for death to occur in childhood. Of the seven children of Mrs Sibbald's sister, Margaret Pattison, only two survived into adulthood;[8] and Jane Austen's great friend Madam Lefroy lost one child in infancy as well as two older ones, and never really got over their deaths, as she expressed in some stanzas of a poem written for one of her surviving children:

Three times my breaking heart has bled,
When from my sight convey'd
My Darlings pressed th'untimely bier
And in the grave were laid.
Yet still for them affection glows,
And bids my soul aspire
To view once more their Angel forms,
Amidst the Heavenly Choir.
Tho' Faith and Hope their aid combine,

To sooth my sorrowing breast,
Yet oft the silent tear will fall
And rob my nights of rest.[9]

But since the death of children was quite usual, it was possible to be philo-sophical about the matter, especially if you were at a distance from those directly concerned. For Jane Austen, being philosophical often entailed a substantial degree of irony. When she read in June 1814 of the death of the Marquis of Granby, the six-month-old heir of the Duke of Rutland, whose godparents had been the Queen, the Prince Regent and the Duke of York, and the extravagant celebration of whose baptism had been reported in detail in the newspapers the previous January, she commented crisply to Cassandra: 'Only think of the Marquis of Granby being dead. I hope, if it please Heaven there should be another Son, they will have better Sponsors & less Parade.'[10] Nearer to home, in her Steventon days, a clergyman friend of the Austens, the Revd Henry Hall, vicar of the nearby parish of Monk Sherborne, had suffered a loss when his wife had a stillborn child. Jane observed, somewhat less than sympathetically: 'Mrs Hall of Sherbourn was brought to bed yesterday of a dead child, some weeks before she expected, owing to a fright. – I suppose she happened unawares to look at her husband.'[11]

But if stillbirths and infant deaths persisted, it was not for want of advice from the medical profession. Treatises for the benefit of those ministering to women undergoing childbirth proliferated. 'During actual labour', wrote Dr William Buchan in one of the best known,

nothing of a heating nature must be given. The woman may, now and then, take a little panada [bread boiled in water with sugar], and her drink ought to be toast and water, or thin groat-gruel. Spirits, wines, cordial-waters, and other things, which are given with a view to strengthen the mother, and promote the birth, for the most part tend only to increase the fever, inflame the womb, and retard the labour. Besides, they endanger the woman afterwards, as they often occasion violent and mortal haemorrhages, or predispose her to eruptive and other fevers.[12]

Two of the greatest dangers to the safe delivery of a child were a shrunken or distorted pelvis (a particular liability for women who had suffered from rickets in their youth) and obstructed labour. These difficulties were naturally quite beyond the capacity of the midwife, who would pull down the baby as far as she could, with the result that a limb might actually be ripped off; a surgeon would then have to complete the delivery, sometimes piecemeal, with the use of a hook-like instru-ment called a crotchet. Not surprisingly, women were terrified of the prospect of obstructed labour, and a considerable advance was made by the introduction of obstetric forceps, first introduced in the seventeenth century by the physician Peter Chamberlen. At this stage, it was a rather crude device, though it could be employed effectively; but the Chamberlen family kept it to themselves, and in

Britain it was not until the third decade of the eighteenth century that any text on midwifery included a description of forceps and their use, though by that time they were to be found in many European cities.

The proper scientific use of the forceps was pioneered by William Smellie, a Scottish apothecary who set up shop in Pall Mall, and not only practised midwifery himself but trained students, using poor women to whom he gave free treatment as clinical cases. He published his lectures and wrote an important treatise that appeared in print in 1752. The forceps he developed were considerably more sophisticated than anything that had been known before, as was his method of using them; he recommended that they should not be employed until after the baby's head had entered the pelvis, of which he would by then have made specific measurements that would enable him to control the deployment of the instrument. Caesarean section had lapsed and was not practised in Smellie's day; and although there are isolated cases of its being performed in the years leading to 1800, it was not generally successful until much later in the nineteenth century, when Joseph Lister introduced antiseptic surgery. But still, progress was rapidly being made; the eighteenth century saw the first obstetric hospital wards in London, which in 1752 became the General Lying In Hospital and eventually Queen Charlotte's Maternity Hospital.

There is no doubt that such progress was necessary. Cases of appalling deliveries in the early Georgian period abound. In 1739 Anne Gossip, suffering a transverse lie, had an agonizing labour lasting just under fifty hours, which necessitated the dead child's being torn in pieces in the womb and extracted by means of the crotchet over a very lengthy period.[13]

By the third quarter of the century it had become usual for genteel women to be attended by professional male midwives, rather than by the women of earlier times; and while historians contest the question as to whether this was a choice they had made for themselves sometimes with the disapproval of their husbands, or whether it put them in the position of helpless victims of a conspiracy of male professionals, there is little doubt that the change brought considerable obstetrical benefits. Furthermore, proper medical advice was available not just in London but in most provincial towns. Despite the occurrence of difficult cases requiring the forceps or the crotchet, the majority of births were uncomplicated. On the other hand, the old-fashioned system of midwifery could have advantages of its own in the conferral of a kind of womanly lore, without which a young wife giving birth for the first time might not always know what the experience would be like. In 1795 Lady Mary Talbot complained to her sister Harriot that their stepmother had not prepared her for what she would go through:

> Pray tell Maria she gave me but a poor idea of what I was to suffer at *the time*, and several things disapointed me very much, particularly as she told me it was not a sickening pain, but I was *dreadfully sick* for many hours before, every *paroxysm* brought on violent sickness.[14]

Since the second Lady Ilchester was only five years older than Lady Mary herself, and had no children, she probably knew as little about birth pains as her stepdaughter.

Unlike Lady Mary, Elizabeth Austen knew exactly what childbirth was like when at the end of September 1808 she had her eleventh child. Perhaps it was the sheer frequency of her deliveries that enabled Jane Austen to joke about it when she wrote to Cassandra, who had reached Godmersham just after the baby had arrived. Her tone from the very beginning of the letter is particularly playful:

> Your letter this morning was quite unexpected, & it is well that it brings such good news to counterbalance the disappointment to me of losing my first sentence, which I had arranged full of proper hopes about your Journey, intending to commit them to paper to day, & not looking for certainty till tomorrow. – We are extremely glad to hear of the birth of the Child, & trust everything will proceed as well as it begins; – his Mama has our best wishes, & he our second best for health & comfort – tho' I suppose unless *he* has our best too, we do nothing for *her*. – We are glad it was all over before your arrival . . .[15]

The priorities here are interesting: in such a large family, the survival of the mother (which, as it happened, was not to be) was of greater importance than the condition of the latest child, and, in those robust times, Jane Austen was sufficiently honest to say as much. In turning to family news, the jokes continue:

> About an hour & a half after your toils on Wednesday ended, ours began; – at seven o'clock, Mrs Harrison, her two daughters & two Visitors, with Mr Debary & his eldest sister walked in; & our Labour was not a great deal shorter than poor Elizabeth's, for it was past eleven before we were delivered.

She made a similar joke in a letter to Anne Sharp, in the spring of 1817, after she had been seriously ill in bed for five weeks. Frank's wife had given birth to her seventh child, and Jane commented: 'Mrs F. A. has had a much shorter confinement than I have – with a Baby to produce into the bargain. We were put to bed nearly at the same time, & she has been quite recovered this great while.'[16] The joke takes on a bleaker note when one realizes that less than two months later Jane Austen was dead.

Once a baby was safely born, it was considered that the coldness of everything, compared to the warmth of the womb, must cause it considerable shock. The surgeon William Moss thought that the whole experience of being born was so traumatic that it was surprising that more babies did not die instantly. Chills at birth, he said, brought on all sorts of ailments later, so the child should be wrapped warmly at once:

> A piece of flannel, commonly known by the name of a *Receiver*, is very properly made use of to wrap the child in before he is dressed; in which situation he ought to continue, very closely covered up, with the mouth and nose scarcely exposed, upon the knee of

some attendant, within the air of the fire, (even in summer) in a room apart from the mother, if convenient, to prevent her being disturbed or over-heated, for a quarter, or half an hour . . .[17]

Then there were the dangers to the mother herself. Bleeding and thrombosis could be fatal, and milk fever might set in if milk was withheld, as it often was, until the flow of colostrum had stopped. Puerperal fever, in which the initial symptoms were diarrhoea, pain in the bowels and hardening of the uterus, was often fatal; and in some years it reached epidemic status. It was not until the end of the eighteenth century that the physician Alexander Gordon of Aberdeen identified the connection with erysipelas, when he noticed simultaneous peaks in the occurrence of both diseases; and he realized that the fever only attacked women attended by a practitioner or nurse who had previously visited other patients suffering from the disease. 'It is a disagreeable declaration,' he admitted, 'for me to mention that I was myself the means of carrying the infection to a great number of women.'[18]

In view of the very serious risks to both mother and child, it is not surprising that the Church should have a special service of thanksgiving after childbirth, replacing the old Hebrew practice of Purification. In the Book of Common Prayer of the Church of England, it is called the Churching of Women. A woman who has given birth is instructed 'at the usual time of her Delivery' to come into the church 'decently apparelled', when the priest says: 'Forasmuch as it hath pleased Almighty God of his goodness to give you safe deliverance, and hath preserved you in the great danger of Child-birth: you shall therefore give hearty thanks unto God . . . ' After this comes either Psalm 116 ('I am well pleased: that the Lord hath heard the voice of my prayer') or Psalm 127 ('Except the Lord build the house: their labour is but lost that build it'). Then, following the Kyrie, The Lord's Prayer and special Responses, the service concludes with a prayer of thanksgiving, which again stresses the danger through which the woman has been safely brought:

O Almighty God, we give thee humble thanks for that thou hast vouchsafed to deliver this woman thy servant from the great pain and peril of Child-birth: Grant, we beseech thee, most merciful Father, that she, through thy help, may both faithfully live, and walk according to thy will, in this life present; and also may be partaker of everlasting glory in the life to come; through Jesus Christ our lord. Amen.

The service of Churching traditionally marked the end of what might almost be described as a ritual, according to which a woman remained at first lying in bed and then sitting up for a week after the birth, the monthly nurse looking after both her and the child; at the end of the second week she got up but kept to her room, only appearing downstairs after the third week; and finally, after four or five weeks, she emerged to go to church. It may be that the official ceremony was dying out by the second half of the eighteenth century; in *The Gentleman's Daughter* Amanda Vickery notes that she found only one specific reference to churching in the papers of the families she was studying and suggests that perhaps 'the dinner parties given after the christening were the polite equivalent'.[19] Lawrence Stone, however, in his book *The Family, Sex and Marriage in England 1500–1800*, cites the Revd William Cole of Bletchley, Bucks, who in a single day in 1766 'married a pair, baptized their newborn baby and churched the mother, the last two rituals being carried out in the privacy of his parlour, despite the incongruity of performing a "churching" in a private room'.[20] And Lady Mary Talbot is recorded as having gone to church a month after the birth of her third daughter in 1798, and as having intended to go on 18 October 1801, a month after the birth of her fifth, but being prevented on that occasion by bad weather;[21] since, however, the latter date was a Sunday, it may be that by then women on the whole simply attended a normal service to mark their re-entry into the outside world. This was certainly the case with Mary Lloyd, who went to church for the first time a month after the birth of James Edward, on Sunday 16 December 1798. But there may be some significance in the fact that Jane made a point of telling Cassandra about it in a letter:[22] it is hard to believe that in the Austen family either the Revd George or his son the Revd James would not have offered some kind of thanksgiving for their wives' safe delivery.

In preparation for the birth, one of the responsibilities of the mother-to-be was, as we have seen, to decide on what kind of medical attendance she would have. But other help was necessary to ensure the smooth running of the household and the well-being of her husband and of her other children, if there were any. As well as the monthly nurse, it was usual for a female member of the family, the woman's mother perhaps, or a sister, to come and stay during the later stages of lying-in, so that she would be on hand for the birth itself. When in 1798 Elizabeth Austen had her first child since the family moved to Godmersham, which was much larger than the house they had been living in previously, Mr and Mrs Austen and their two daughters were both able to go and stay during her confinement; and when, a fortnight after seeing the baby safely born, they returned to Steventon, Cassandra stayed on for another five months. Cassandra was there again for the births of Elizabeth's last two children, and it was she who helped to console the family after her sister-in-law's death. As we shall see in a later chapter, it was Cassandra, rather than Jane, who was the favourite at Godmersham.

In some families, there would already be a suitable person living in the house who could assist at a birth. Shortly after the Austens were married in 1764, Mrs Austen's widowed mother came to live with them in the parsonage at Deane; so she was there to help with the birth of their first child, James, in February 1765, and for those of the next two boys, George and Edward, both of whom were also born at Deane, in 1766 and 1767 respectively. Soon after they moved into the rectory at Steventon, however, in the summer of 1768, the old lady died. There followed a gap of four years before the birth of the next child, Henry, and Deirdre Le Faye suggests that during that period Mrs Austen may have suffered a miscarriage, possibly at the time of the move;[23] in his *Memoir* James Edward Austen-Leigh conjures up a vivid image of the journey down the rutted lane from one parsonage to the other, with Mrs Austen 'on a feather-bed, placed upon some soft articles of furniture in the wagon which held their household goods'.[24] The point is that he says that she was 'not then in strong health', which might indicate either that she had just suffered a miscarriage or that she was pregnant at the time, and being jolted on the ride resulted in her losing the child.

In between having her third and fourth sons, she was able to be of use at another birth. In July 1770, her elder sister Jane, wife of the Revd Dr Edward Cooper, at that time living at Southcote near Reading, was expecting her first child. The Coopers had decided to go to London for the birth, evidently still holding to the idea that medical advice was better in town than elsewhere. Mrs Austen went off to stay with them, but as it turned out, the child arrived early and she missed the birth itself, as Mr Austen informed Susanna Walter:

> The Day I received your kind Letter, for which accept my thanks, your sister set out for London to enter on her office of Nurse in Ordinary, & the same Post likewise brought me intelligence that she was too late for the Ceremony She intended being present at, for Mrs. Cooper was happily brought to Bed last Sunday morning of a Boy & both well; She came, it seems, rather before her time, & of course the Babe is a small one, but however very like to live.[25]

And rather disconsolately, the neglected rector added:

> I don't much like this lonely kind of Life, you know I have not been much used to it, & yet I must bear with it about three weeks longer, at which time I expect my Housekeeper's return.

When Mrs Austen eventually got back, she reported to Mrs Walter in her turn that she had had the pleasure of leaving her sister 'tolerably well & the Child quite so'; and she added: 'they are now moved into the Country; I hope change of air will enable her to pick up her Strength'.[26] The air of London certainly did nothing for Mrs Austen; she described it as 'a sad place' and told her sister-in-law that she 'would not live in it on any account: one has not time to do one's duty either to God or Man'.

The following summer, Mrs Cooper gave birth to a daughter, but then her sister was in no position to attend her, having just had her own fourth son, Henry. Again she wrote to Susanna Walter with news of the happy arrivals:

> Thank God I am quite stout again, had an extraordinary good time and Lying in, and am Bless'd with as fine a Boy as perhaps you ever saw, he is much the largest I ever had, and thrives very fast. Mr Austen and my other Boys are all well. I should rejoice to see you my Dear Sister, but it is not in my power to take any Journeys at present, my little family grows so numerous, there is no taking them abroad, nor can I leave them with an easy mind. My Sister Cooper has got a little Girl, not quite three weeks younger than my little Henry. She had a very good time and is pure well, and so is the Child, only remarkably

small, as I hear, the Boy wanted four days of being a year old when the Girl was born, so she seems to be making up for her lost time.[27]

It appears that childbirth gave both Mrs Austen and her sister a 'good time'; 'pure well', the phrase that Mr Austen would use to describe his wife after Jane's birth, seems to have been an expression in the family. The comment about making up for lost time suggests that Mrs Cooper was a little older than usual in having had her first child at the age of thirty-four; seeing her two years later, Mrs Austen commented that she had 'not been breeding since, so perhaps she has done' – a prognostication which proved to be correct.

With old Mrs Leigh no longer there, Mrs Austen had been looked after this time by another sister-in-law, Philadelphia Hancock, who came down from London to stay in the rectory, and who stood godmother to the baby. When in November 1772 Mrs Austen was expecting her next child, she told Susanna Walter that she hoped Mrs Hancock would come again; in true Austenian fashion, her letter shows her happily mixing discussion of her pregnancy with other snippets of family news:

> My little Boy is come home from Nurse, and a fine stout little fellow he is, and can run anywhere, so now I have all four at home, and some time in January I expect a fifth . . . so I hope you will come indeed so soon as the bad Winter Weather is over. We are very glad you have such accounts from Jamaica, and that you are all pretty well; and hope my Brother's Heel will not be bad again. Thank God we are all well in health; I begin to be very heavy & bundling as usual, I believe my Sister Hancock will be so good as to come and nurse me again, for which I am sure I shall be much oblig'd to her, as it will be a bad time of the year for her to take so long a Journey.[28]

Who but Mrs Austen would describe herself as 'heavy and bundling' – except perhaps Mrs Jennings?

And indeed something of the same matter-of-fact attitude to pregnancy is to be found in *Sense and Sensibility*. We learn of the birth of Charlotte Palmer's baby in the same way that the public does, as 'the newspapers announced to the world, that the lady of Thomas Palmer, Esq. was safely delivered of a son and heir', Jane Austen commenting on the notice that it was 'a very interesting and satisfactory paragraph, at least to all those intimate connections who knew it before'.[29] Foremost among those intimate connections, of course, is Mrs Jennings, Charlotte's mother, with whom Elinor and Marianne are staying at the time. She does not actually move into the Palmers' house – perhaps Mr Palmer would not quite have relished that – but the event,

> highly important to Mrs. Jennings's happiness, produced a temporary alteration in the disposal of her time, and influenced, in a like degree, the engagement of her young friends; for as she wished to be as much as possible with Charlotte, she went thither every morning as soon as she was dressed, and did not return till late in the evening . . .

The importance of the Palmers' child is essentially as a plot device. Mrs Jennings will not allow Elinor and Marianne to remain on their own in her house, but insists on their having what she regards as the convivial company of Lady Middleton and the Miss Steeles, which subsequently gives Fanny Dashwood an excuse for not inviting them as her guests, and asking the Steeles instead. The climactic consequence, when Anne Steele blurts out to Fanny the secret of Lucy's engagement to Edward, is therefore indirectly brought about by the fact of the baby's arrival; and it is also by means of the baby that Jane Austen contrives that Elinor – and the reader – should learn of it.

Jane Austen works it like this: at the end of a fortnight, Charlotte is well enough that 'her mother felt it no longer necessary to give up the whole of her time to her . . . contenting herself with visiting her once or twice a day'.[30] It is on Mrs Jennings's return from one of these visits that she brings the sensational news to Elinor and Marianne, who have settled back with her again. The child had not been well:

> When I got to Mr. Palmer's, I found Charlotte quite in a fuss about the child. She was sure it was very ill – it cried, and fretted, and was all over pimples. So I looked at it directly, and, 'Lord! my dear,' says I, 'it is nothing in the world but the red-gum;' and nurse said just the same. But Charlotte, she would not be satisfied, so Mr. Donavan was sent for; and luckily he happened to be just come in from Harley-Street, so he stepped over directly, and as soon as ever he saw the child, he said just as we did, that it was nothing in the world but the red-gum, and then Charlotte was easy. And so, just as he was going away again, it came into my head, I am sure I do not know how I happened to think of it, but it came into my head to ask him if there was any news.

The news is, of course, that Lucy has engaged herself to Edward Ferrars, and his family are in an uproar; Mr Donavan 'smirked, and simpered, and looked grave' and then 'it all came out'. The detail is perfect: the baby with a rash, fretful and crying; the anxious young mother; the gossiping older women offering reassurance; but only the authority of the medical man actually carrying weight. The whole shift in the pattern of childbirth attendance during the eighteenth century is caught in the passage; and it is interesting that there is no hint of resentment on the part of the nurse or Mrs Jennings when the apothecary confirms their own judgement: they are as willing as Charlotte herself to submit to male professional advice. Had there been a copy of Alexander Hamilton's *A Treatise of Midwifery* in Mr Palmer's library at Hanover Square, Charlotte might have reassured herself of the child's safety sooner, for she would have found the following information:

> *The red gum* – is an eruption of small red pimples, like a rash, which, in many children, appears all over the body soon after birth; it frequently disappears suddenly, without any inconvenience to the child, and comes and goes, while on the breast. It is distinguished from the measles by the absence of measly symptoms, and time of attack. Little

management is necessary, further than to attend to the state of the belly, and take care that the room or clothing of the child be not too warm.[31]

Mr Palmer is absent during all the commotion. Jane Austen might have allowed him to be present to express characteristic scepticism at his wife's alarm, or perhaps to have objected to Mr Donavan's being sent for; but she is preparing to reveal his true good nature in his kindness to Marianne when she is ill, and she tactfully makes no mention of him. His view of female fussing over his son and heir has in any case already been dealt with; it is the one thing that disturbs Mrs Jennings, who complains about it every day:

> Mr. Palmer maintained the common, but unfatherly opinion among his sex, of all infants being alike; and though she could plainly perceive at different times, the most striking resemblance between this baby and every one of his relations on both sides, there was no convincing his father of it; no persuading him to believe that it was not exactly like every other baby of the same age; nor could he even be brought to acknowledge the simple proposition of its being the finest child in the world.[32]

We are not told what name Mr Palmer's son is given, though we can make a guess that it is probably Thomas. A wealthy man generally gave his own name to his eldest son, as is the case, for example, with Sir Thomas Bertram – and according to Maggie Lane, Thomas was in any case the third most popular boy's name in the years between 1750 and 1799.[33] In a slightly less well-off family, however, a child might be named after a wealthy relation or friend from whom there were expectations of an inheritance. The Austens' eldest son, for example, was named after his rich uncle James Leigh Perrot, and only their second son after Mr Austen himself. In *Emma* the children of Mr and Mrs John Knightley also illustrate the point: Henry, the eldest boy – and heir to Hartfield until Emma marries – is named after his grandfather, and the second son after his father; the first daughter is then Bella, after her mother, and the other two children are named after their uncle and aunt, George and Emma: it is very neat. Often a child would be named after a godparent. In *Mansfield Park* Sir Thomas is godfather to Mrs Price's son Tom; and though Mrs Norris's Christian name is never revealed (she is the only one of the three Ward sisters not to be given a name), it is probably Elizabeth, since the youngest Price, Betsey, is her goddaughter. And of course, within the family, children would be called by shortened versions of their names, or by nicknames: Edward Austen was Neddy, Cassandra Cassy, Jane Jenny; and, from his liveliness as a young boy, Francis was known as Fly.

The giving of names at a public christening by no means always coincided with reception into the Church, which was usually done as early as possible. Mr Austen privately baptized his children either on the day they were born, or within a day or so of their birth (this practice was sometimes referred to as 'half baptism'); he then performed their full christening about a month later, when it would be possible to have at least some of the sponsors present. In Jane's case, her birth occurred during a particularly cold winter, so after her baptism at a day old, it was not until more than four months later, on 5 April 1776, that she was carried up the lane from the rectory to the church of St Nicholas for her christening. Her godmothers were Mrs Jane Austen, the wife of great-uncle Francis of Sevenoaks, and Mrs Jane Musgrave, a cousin by marriage of her mother; her godfather was the Revd Samuel Cooke, husband of another of Mrs Austen's cousins. Unlike her sister, Cassandra Elizabeth, she received only one Christian name; but at least she could claim to be named after two godmothers.

Childbirth marks a new stage in the continuous cycle of human existence. Although, given the constraints that comic form imposes on literature, the birth of a child to the hero and heroine is outside the scope of a novel (or for that matter a play), which must end with marriage, it would be unlikely for a writer so thoroughly imbued with Christian values as Jane Austen altogether to ignore such an important indicator of the blessings of Providence. It is significant, then, that towards the end of *Emma* there is a child born – little Anna Weston, who represents true maternal fulfilment for 'poor Miss Taylor' and a physical embodiment of the rejuvenation that has always been an aspect of Mr Weston's hearty character. She is also, of course, a replacement for Emma, as Emma herself has already reflected:

> The child to be born at Randall's must be a tie there even dearer than herself; and Mrs. Weston's heart and time would be occupied by it. They should lose her; and, probably, in great measure, her husband also.[34]

Emma is at the high point of her despondency, knowing that Frank Churchill and Jane Fairfax will be married and leaving Highbury, and bitterly aware that, as she thinks, she has lost Mr Knightley to Harriet; it may occur to the reader that what she needs is to have a child of her own. But by the time Mrs Weston's baby arrives, Mr Knightley has asked her to marry him, and the mood is very different; and in a way little Anna Weston foreshadows the little Knightley whose arrival must lie outside the scope of the narrative.

Emma will not give Mrs Weston the news of her engagement until she is safely delivered, and when she eventually breaks it to her, Jane Austen demonstrates the shift in her affections that Emma herself anticipated with characteristic comedy:

> Mrs. Weston, with her baby on her knee . . . was one of the happiest women in the world. If any thing could increase her delight, it was perceiving that the baby would soon have outgrown its first set of caps.[35]

And she deploys a somewhat deeper irony in allowing Emma to reflect that the child may even afford her the opportunity to practise a little matchmaking once again:

Mrs. Weston's friends were all made happy by her safety; and if the satisfaction of her well-doing could be increased to Emma, it was by knowing her to be the mother of a little girl. She had been decided in wishing for a Miss Weston. She would not acknowledge that it was with any view of making a match for her, hereafter, with either of Isabella's sons; but she was convinced that a daughter would suit both father and mother best. It would be a great comfort to Mr. Weston as he grew older – and even Mr. Weston might be growing older ten years hence – to have his fireside enlivened by the sports and the nonsense, the freaks and the fancies of a child never banished from home; and Mrs. Weston – no one could doubt that a daughter would be most to her; and it would be quite a pity that any one who so well knew how to teach, should not have their powers in exercise again.[36]

Mr Knightley, now licensed to speak more freely than ever to Emma, foresees that the little girl will be even more indulged than Emma was, while her mother will believe 'that she does not indulge her at all'. 'Poor child!' Emma cries; 'at that rate, what will become of her?' But happiness has driven all the censoriousness out of Mr Knightley, even if not quite all the irony, and his reply is tolerantly good-humoured:

Nothing very bad. – The fate of thousands. She will be disagreeable in infancy, and correct herself as she grows older. I am losing all my bitterness against spoilt children, my dearest Emma. I, who am owing all my happiness to *you*, would not it be horrible ingratitude in me to be severe on them?

Like Charlotte Palmer, Mrs Weston does have one brief moment of concern about her little girl, but unlike Charlotte, she reproaches herself with having been unduly worried; predictably, it is Mr Woodhouse who fusses:

The others had been talking of the child, Mrs. Weston giving an account of a little alarm she had been under, the evening before, from the infant's appearing not quite well. She believed she had been foolish, but it had alarmed her, and she had been within half a minute of sending for Mr. Perry. Perhaps she ought to be ashamed, but Mr. Weston had been almost as uneasy as herself. – In ten minutes, however, the child had been perfectly well again. This was her history; and particularly interesting it was to Mr. Woodhouse, who commended her very much for thinking of sending for Perry, and only regretted that she had not done it. 'She should always send for Perry, if the child appeared in the slightest degree disordered, were it only for a moment. She could not be too soon alarmed, nor send for Perry too often. It was a pity, perhaps, that he had not come last night; for, though the child seemed well now, very well considering, it would probably have been better if Perry had seen it.'[37]

It is richly comic, of course, to see Mr Woodhouse riding his hobbyhorse, but Jane Austen has another purpose in his constant reiteration of Perry's name. Frank Churchill catches it, and it reminds him of the blunder he made in nearly giving away the secret of his engagement to Jane Fairfax by revealing that he had heard of the possibility of Mr Perry's setting up his carriage – which of course could have come to him only in a letter from Jane. Now he laughs at the recollection, and in one last reversion to his conspiracy with Emma, laughs at, and of course with, Jane too. Though he speaks entertainingly, and all is now reconciled between them, Emma leaves Randall's feeling that

> pleased as she had been to see Frank Churchill, and really regarding him with friendship, she had never been more sensible of Mr. Knightley's high superiority of character. The happiness of this most happy day, received its completion, in the animated contemplation of his worth which this comparison produced.[38]

It is an extremely satisfying conclusion, and Jane Austen's happy means of bringing it about is Mrs Weston's newborn baby.

3

Infancy

Mrs Austen nursed her babies herself. She might have been expected to hire a wet-nurse, since breastfeeding was traditionally thought of as being practised by women of the lower classes, but she preferred for the first three months of their lives to give them her own milk. Many aristocratic women would not do so, possibly from weakness after childbirth or because they found it an uncomfortable procedure – or perhaps because it interfered with their social life or, worse still, impaired the appearance of their breasts. Mary Wollstonecraft laid the blame squarely on the husbands, of whom she said there were many 'so devoid of sense and parental affection, that during the first effervescence of voluptuous fondness they refuse to let their wives suckle their children'.[1] The sexual favours of a mother who was breastfeeding would not be available, and their husbands did not care for that: women were 'only to dress and live to please them: and love – even innocent love, soon sinks into lasciviousness when the exercise of a duty is sacrificed to its indulgence'. For her, breastfeeding was something natural and good that secured mutual love between mother and child; it also had other benefits for the mother, since, as we have seen, it was a way in which the interval between pregnancies could be controlled.[2] It was a theme she returned to on several occasions.

In many western European countries, particularly France, wet-nurses were commonly used by the upper classes; and in England wet-nursing constituted the major source of employment for women in some rural counties. The better sort of woman who undertook this work was respectable and well paid – wholly professional, in fact – and often well known to her employer. But there were also parish nurses, impoverished women on poor relief, who hardly made ideal substitute mothers for the babies they suckled; and in some cases suckling went on for anything up to three years – if the children did not die beforehand, given the relatively high mortality rate among children who were wet-nursed.

Mary Wollstonecraft was far from being alone in considering breastfeeding a wholly desirable practice for a mother. Seventeenth-century Puritan advisers on managing children had preached against the trend for employing wet-nurses, invoking moral as well as medical arguments: not only did babies run the risk of infection, but they might also absorb undesirable, lower-class characteristics; in their view, the use of wet-nurses was a wicked Roman Catholic custom. The *Spectator* inveighed against the practice as being inhuman and dangerous; Dr William Cadogan found a 90 per cent mortality rate among children who were fed pap or reared by slovenly wet-nurses;[3] and Richardson in *Sir Charles*

Grandison – a novel much loved in the Austen household – shows a woman's estranged husband being positively aroused by the sight of her with her baby at her breast. His enraptured exclamations, and the facial expressions that accompany them ('Dear-est, dear-est, dear-est Lady G. – shaking his head, between every dear and est, every muscle of his face working; how you transport me! – Never, never, never, saw I so delightful a sight!'),[4] as he all but crushes mother and child in his excitement, are undeniably grotesque. Mary Wollstonecraft presents an altogether more tender picture of reciprocal family love when she describes 'the chastened dignity with which a mother returns the caresses' that she and her child receive from a husband who would have a cold heart indeed if he 'did not feel more delight at seeing his child suckled by its mother, than the most artful wanton tricks could ever raise';[5] though it will be noticed that even here there is a tacit acknowledgment of the sexual attraction, albeit a restrained and wholly licit one, provoked in a man by the sight of his wife breastfeeding.

By the last quarter of the eighteenth century, aristocratic notables such as the Duchess of Devonshire were known to be breastfeeding their children, and the practice began to be spoken of as if it were something that society had a right to expect from its women; Thomas Gisborne, for example, gave it as his opinion that for a mother it was 'the first of parental duties . . . to be herself the nurse of her own offspring'.[6] The medical profession was wholly in favour, and advocated it strongly. Thus it gradually became not only the norm but almost a moral obligation, so that women felt pressure on them to conform. Some, of course, were unable to provide milk themselves, which meant that they had either to make use of a wet-nurse or bring the baby up by hand, or 'by the spoon'. They might become depressed about what they saw as their failure, and could even feel jealousy at seeing their infant turn to its nurse for nourishment. Sometimes a mother who had not been able to feed one child would succeed with subsequent ones. Surviving correspondence between women of the period reveals much discussion of the subject, often betraying considerable anxiety. Not only did a mother who could not breastfeed feel guilty, she also worried that she would not be able to establish a proper bond with her child; and she also had to contend with the tactless if well-meaning sympathy of grandparents or other relations. The fear of irresponsible, clumsy or unhygienic wet-nurses was, as the statistics suggest, justified. In his *Domestic Medicine* Dr William Buchan drew attention to many of their failings: in the daytime they would often leave the baby to cry unattended, and at night they would give it opiates to make it sleep. If it suffered an accident, they would conceal knowledge of it from the mother, especially if it was due to their own negligence; and they would also fail to disclose symptoms of possible illness or disease. On the other hand, if, instead of employing a wet-nurse, the mother ensured the child was given diluted cow's milk from the spoon or boat, there was the risk of contamination from water or other adulterations, or of mild poisoning from copper utensils.

Breastfeeding could cause problems of its own, however. One provable and all too frequent danger was the habit of withholding milk from a newborn baby for the first three or four days of its life, so that it should not drink the colostrum, or 'green milk'. If the child was not healthy, this could lead to starvation; and for the mother it often resulted in milk fever. Furthermore, physicians agreed that colostrum was a far more natural and satisfactory means of purging the meconium, or first faeces, from the intestine than the medical purges to which some mothers had recourse. If babies were to be fed before suckling was established, medical authorities agreed that it should not be on pap, which was a highly unsuitable food, especially as bread was often adulterated with alum; sugar was also unnecessary. In fact, since the griping and looseness caused by overfeeding were a common cause of neonatal death, it was considered best to leave the child alone, warm and dry, still and quiet, until the milk came. Once feeding began, ill effects might be felt by the mother, though whether they actually resulted from feeding may be open to doubt. One woman who suffered from headaches and impaired sight wrote:

> I have been almost Blind & am still dim sighted. It is Thought that suckeling is the occasion of it, but I don't care to give a hearing to that subject, as my little Tommy shall not Loose his comfort, Tho' his Mama's peepers suffer for it.[7]

The transition from wet-nursing to mothers breastfeeding their own children was not a linear, nor a particularly rapid, one; and throughout the eighteenth century both practices were to be found.

The time during which the child received breast milk alone could be quite short, and women might well seek advice on the matter from one another. When the wife of Jane Austen's brother Francis was expecting her first child, she wanted information about her sister-in-law Elizabeth Austen, who had just had her tenth: Jane wrote to Cassandra at Godmersham: 'Mary will be obliged to you to take notice how often Eliz[th] nurses her Baby in the course of the 24 hours, how often it is fed & with what.'[8] The little girl was three months old, and the question 'with what' suggests that Mary thought it likely that by then other foods were being added to the breast milk. This would accord with the advice given by Dr Buchan:

> If the mother or nurse has enough of milk, the child will need little or no other food before the third or fourth month. It will then be proper to give it, once or twice a-day, a little of some food that is easy of digestion; as water-pap, milk-pottage, weak broth with bread in it, or the like. This will ease the mother; it will accustom the child by degrees to take food, and render the weaning both less difficult and dangerous. All great and sudden transitions are to be avoided in nursing. For this purpose, the food of children ought to be simple, as near as possible resembling the properties of milk. Indeed milk itself should make a principal part of their food, not only before they are weaned, but for a long time after.[9]

Once a child was weaned, Buchan recommended a varied diet, but one that was kept plain and simple, with none of the rich foods that adults enjoyed. Butter, in particular salt butter, was very bad for children, as were unripe fruits, though ripe ones might be given in small quantities; root vegetables were indigestible, and alcohol should not be given in any form, since it induced fevers. A liquid or sloppy diet was likely to make a child rickety; however honey was very good, especially for curing or preventing worms. As for the frequency of feeding, Buchan suggested four or five times a day, though not during the night. However, since demand feeding was used for the breast, to make a rigid schedule after weaning was difficult and he had never known such a plan to succeed (though the surgeon William Moss asserted in his book on child management that it could sometimes be done, if the child would accept it).[10] Alexander Hamilton, in his *Treatise of Midwifery*, went further and positively recommended demand feeding, arguing that it produced happier and healthier children.

Moss stated that the usual time for weaning was eight to ten months, and that it was advisable to wean at teething.[11] But the period during which breastfeeding lasted was by no means consistent from one woman to another, or even between children of the same woman; while the usual duration was indeed somewhere between six months and a year, it could often be considerably less, particularly if a child was being wet-nursed away from home and its mother wanted it back. James Austen's daughter Caroline was nearly nine months old when Mrs Austen wrote to her daughter-in-law to say how pleased the family were to hear that she 'wean'd so much like a philosopher, and proceeds in the business of Tooth-cutting'.[12] Yet Mrs Austen herself had regarded three months as a sufficient time before her children were weaned and sent to be looked after by a woman in the village; writing to her sister-in-law Susanna Walter five months after Cassandra's birth, she told her, 'I suckled my little girl thro' the first quarter; she has been weaned and settled at a good woman's at Deane just eight weeks'.[13] And as she did for little Cassy so she did for her brothers, and for Jane.

In effect, therefore, the older Austens reversed the process followed by other families, in which children were put out to nurse until they were weaned, and were then taken back into the home. When James Edward Austen-Leigh comes to discuss Jane Austen's early years (about which he says he knows little) in his *Memoir*, he regards the fact that she was farmed out as something that needs explaining; while the custom was 'not unusual in those days', he writes, it 'seems strange to us'.[14] Some biographers detect a sense of embarrassment in the haste with which he adds that 'the infant was daily visited by one or both of its parents, and frequently brought to them at the parsonage' and go so far as to suggest that the early separation may have resulted in an emotional coldness towards her mother on Jane's part in adult life;[15] to others, this seems rather a twentieth-century way of looking at it.[16] Perhaps it was the fact that Mrs Austen put her babies out to be nursed in 'a cottage in the village' that James Edward thought would cause eyebrows to be raised by his Victorian readers; he is very quick to assert that 'the contrast between the parsonage house and the best class of cottages was not quite so extreme then as it would be now, that one was somewhat less luxurious, and the other less squalid'. Catherine Hubback, a daughter of

Francis Austen, commented on the 'simple style of living, homely dwelling, and out of door habits' that her father and the other Austen children would have experienced.[17]

In any case, it might have been worse; Cornish-born Susan Sibbald was fostered by a smuggler's wife.[18]

To which cottage exactly the Austen babies were sent, and who the 'good woman at Deane' actually was, we cannot know for certain. James Edward tells us that one of the family, 'in after life, used to speak of his foster mother as "Movie," the name by which he had called her in his infancy' (was this James, his father? – it seems likely). Deirdre Le Faye has suggested that the woman was probably Elizabeth Littleworth, who with her husband, John, lived at Cheesedown Farm, in the north of the parish of Steventon (to all intents and purposes in Deane), which was farmed by Mr Austen as an addition to his glebe.[19] The connections between the two families seem to have been close: the Littleworths' younger daughter, Bet, the particular playfellow of little Edward Austen, probably helped to look after the Austen infants; their son, John, was the Austens' coachman; and his daughter, Eliza Jane, was a goddaughter of Jane Austen. And the connection continued, since when in 1809 Mrs Austen and her daughters moved to Chawton, William Littleworth, from another branch of the family, became their manservant.

Until the end of the seventeenth century, during the period before a child was weaned, or at least for the first four months or so of its life, it was wrapped from head to foot in the tight swaddling bandages that caused it to be virtually immobile. The benefit to the child was that it supposedly kept the limbs straight and gave support to the spine; it also had notable advantages for the parents, however, in that the child could be left unattended for considerable periods without being able to do itself any overt harm. But Locke, Cadogan, Rousseau and other writers attacked swaddling in so comprehensive a manner as an assault on human liberty and furthermore as a means of depriving children of early affectionate contact (it is not easy to cuddle a child rigidly encased in layers of stiff linen) that by the second half of the century it was dying out in England.[20] In 1769 William Buchan found that 'the practice of rolling children with so many bandages' was 'now, in some measure laid aside';[21] though the practice persisted with mothers who thought that their child's physique depended on its being stiffly wrapped. He could see from the crying provoked by its discomfort that it was unnatural, and he furthermore believed that it deformed them and was likely to send them into convulsions. Fifteen years later, Michael Underwood noted that swaddling had been rapidly diminishing over the thirty years since Cadogan wrote, but that clothing was still not as loose as he would like to see it; furthermore, he strongly advocated strings for fastening rather than pins, and recounted the story of a pin sticking into a child's head and causing death by convulsions.[22] Oddly, one of the observations that had led to the condemnation of swaddling arose from a purely practical cause: at the newly created Foundling Hospital, since it became impossible for staff to cope with constantly changing a large number of heavily wrapped babies, the children were dressed in much lighter clothing, the so-called

'Foundling dress'; and it soon became obvious that they were thriving much better than the traditionally dressed babies of the wealthy. As a result, lighter clothing began to be adopted in most households; and by 1781 William Moss could record that the 'tight rolling and confining the limbs, which . . . must be very injurious, and must greatly impede and prevent the growth, strength and activity of the infant' was a 'former' practice.[23]

In poorer families the mother of a newborn child might expect to be provided with suitable garments by neighbouring gentry; no doubt such things were among the items worked for the poor basket that Mrs Norris reminds Fanny so sharply about.[24] In Steventon the Austens were prompt to help the villagers: in October 1798, Jane wrote to Cassandra, 'Dame Tilbury's daughter has lain-in – Shall I give her any of your Baby Cloathes?'[25]

The conflict between adherents of the old and new methods of dressing babies is dramatized in one of a pair of humorous little dialogues preserved in the Austen family and possibly written jointly by Jane and her sister-in-law Mary Lloyd. They concern the care of young children and may have been intended as advice for Francis's wife when she was expecting her first child.[26] At Christmas 1806 James, Mary and their little daughter Caroline visited Southampton, where the Francis Austens were sharing a house with Mrs Austen, Jane and Cassandra and Mary's sister Martha Lloyd, and the two little playlets may well have been composed and read as a festive entertainment in the household. There are only three speaking characters: the sensible Mrs Enfield, her friend Mrs Denbigh and the old-fashioned (and comically written) Irish nurse employed by the latter to look after her baby, Charles. On a visit with her own little baby, Julia, whom she is treating according to the latest, and obviously much healthier, methods, Mrs Enfield tries to encourage Mrs Denbigh and the patently ignorant nurse to adopt them too. Her first cause for concern is the way in which the boy's movements are completely restricted by his clothing; the nurse's defence of his overdressing (compared with the little girl's) reflects the almost superstitious nature of the earlier ideas.

Mrs E.   Pray how is Charles?

Mrs D.   Indeed he looks wretchedly tho' I have done every thing for him which the Doctor ordered. I wish you would look at him

Mrs. E.   With pleasure. But I have not much skill

Mrs D.   (rings the bell) I am sure you have skill, at least your child looks as if you had – Here comes my poor little creature – Nurse shew that angel to Mrs. E.

Mrs E.   (exchanges children with nurse) Dear! he has such a quantity of clothes on I can scarcely feel his limbs, nor he makes no attempt to stand.

Nurse   Oh ma'am if you set him to stand he'll surely have bandy legs – No wonder you think he has too much clothes for this poor creature has not a stitch upon her, & what little she has is only hanging on her shoulders ready to drop off. Oh ma'am see her poor little stumps of legs & feet quite bare & as blue & thick as a cabin [hovel] child, begging your pardon, only I pity the poor cratur

Mrs E.	No offence nurse – I don't wish her more tender than a cabin child, all the difference I wish to make is to keep her cleaner.
Nurse	And sure enough she is as clean as a new pin. I was advised not to change Master Charles' linen very often, on account of it drawing & wasting his little substance
Mrs E.	This great quantity of clothes won't draw him much now – Depend upon it that is all old women's talk – You see Julia is not wasted & I am far more exact about changing her shift than her frock

As Mrs Enfield undoes the child's clothes to examine a rash that the nurse has neglected to show his mother, she returns even more forcefully to the evils of restrictive dressing:

Mrs E.	Oh Nurse you dress him quite too tight, his clothes really burst open, & see he pants like a creature getting free – nor I don't like pins in any part of a childs clothing, strings & buttons answer the purpose as well, & without danger
Mrs D.	Mind Nurse.
Nurse	His little shape will be ruined for the pins are the only thing for making the shape all of an even tightness.
Mrs D.	No matter for a boy's shape.

And as she takes her leave Mrs Enfield urges her friend once more to 'make nurse change his linen every day & dress him much looser'.

A couple of months after Mrs Austen's children were sent to be fostered, they were taken out of the long gowns that they had worn instead of swaddling clothes and put into short washable dresses or frocks that enabled them to learn to walk and run about freely, and which also facilitated toilet training; Cassandra, she informed her sister-in-law in the letter written eight weeks after the little girl had been consigned to the family at Deane, 'is very healthy and lively, and puts on her short petticoats to-day'. There would have been little visible distinction between the appearance of the boys and their sisters at similar ages, except that boys might have higher necklines and buttons at the front of the dress, and their hair might well be cut in a straight fringe. This kind of dress might not necessarily improve a baby's appearance. One of Cassandra's own nieces, Lizzy Knight, described her ten-month-old cousin with the sharp eyes, and the honesty, of a girl of thirteen: 'I don't think little Fanny is quite so pretty as she was,' she wrote to her aunt; 'one reason is because she wears short petticoats, I believe.'[27]

The next stage in a boy's manner of dressing, which almost amounted to a rite of passage, was breeching, when he would put on breeches or trousers for the first time. In the seventeenth century this had usually occurred at about six or seven, when boys were removed from the charge of the women who had brought them up until then and put into the care of tutors; but during the eighteenth century breeching began to happen considerably earlier, generally by the age of four, and sometimes as early as three. Jane's brother Henry was just over four when his mother informed Susanna Walter: 'Henry has been in breeches some months and thinks himself near as good a man as his brother Neddy, indeed no one would judge by their looks that there was above three years and a half difference in their ages, one is so little and the other so great.'[28] In the next generation, Neddy's own eldest son was under two and a half when Jane cheerfully told Cassandra, 'Little Edward was breeched yesterday for good & all, and was whipped, into the Bargain.'[29] James's son, James Edward, was younger still when Jane sent a message from his mother to Cassandra, who was staying at Godmersham, asking for help with his clothes:

> She will be much obliged to you if you can bring her the pattern of the Jacket & Trowsers, or whatever it is, that Eliz[th].:'s boys wear when they are first put into breeches –; or if you could bring her an old suit itself she would be very glad, but that I suppose is hardly do-able.[30]

In earlier times, breeching meant assuming the style of clothing worn by men, just as small girls were dressed as miniature versions of women. But both Locke and Rousseau extended their disapproval of swaddling to an advocacy of natural and unrestricting clothing for older children; and from the middle of the eighteenth century, the general recognition of childhood as a period distinct from adulthood meant that dress appropriate to the young was developed. Boys started to wear skeleton suits – short jackets with looser fitting breeches or pantaloons which buttoned at the waist. Girls were permitted to abandon the tight-laced bodice for the kind of free, informal dresses that by the Regency were to become the style for adult women – light, short-sleeved frocks with a minimum of orna-ment, generally just a sash at the waist.

Like any mother, Mrs Austen recorded in family letters the various stages of her children's development. 'My last boy', she wrote of Francis, 'is very stout, and has run alone these two months, and he is not yet sixteen months old.' And she added of two-and-a-half-year-old Cassandra 'my little girl talks all day long, and in my opinion is a very entertaining companion.'[31] She liked small children.

Jane liked them too, and her own letters contain accounts of the progress of her various nieces and nephews, and in the case of her eldest niece, of her children too. 'Anna's eldest child just now runs alone,' she wrote in the last year of her life, 'which is a great convenience with a second in arms, & they are both healthy nice children.'[32] Many of her comments show that, like her mother, she found their manners and sayings entertaining; but she could be quite realistic about the duration of their attentions. Returning from a family visit to Godmersham in October 1798, she wrote to Cassandra, who had remained there, 'I flatter myself that *itty Dordy* will not forget me at least under a week. Kiss him for me.'[33] 'Itty Dordy' was George, Edward's second son, then aged just under three. Cassandra replied that he did indeed remember his aunt, and this provoked a characteristic piece of irony:

My dear itty Dordy's remembrance of me is very pleasing to me; foolishly pleasing, because I know it will be over so soon. My attachment to him will be more durable; I shall think with tenderness & delight on his beautiful & smiling Countenance & interesting Manners, till a few years have turned him into an ungovernable, ungracious fellow.[34]

At his present stage, however, he was all affection, and Jane told Cassandra to ask him if he had a new song for her. In a subsequent letter, written a few days after her birthday, she acknowledged his special greetings and was delighted to hear that he had been allowed to drink tea in her honour:

I am very much obliged to my dear little George for his messages, for his *Love* at least; – his *Duty* I suppose was only in consequence of some hint of my favourable intentions towards him from his father or Mother. – I am sincerely rejoiced however that I ever was born, since it has been the means of procuring him a dish of Tea. – Give my best Love to him.[35]

In Aunt Jane's absence he clearly devoted himself to Aunt Cassandra, who duly reported back to Steventon on his progress, much to Jane's amusement:

My sweet little George! – I am delighted to hear that he has such an inventive Genius as to face-making –. I admired his yellow wafer very much, & hope he will chuse the wafer for your next letter.[36]

Not only his pulling faces suggests that he may already have begun on the path towards ungovernability that Jane cheerfully foresaw for him, since she added that she had taken her white fan to a ball the previous evening and was 'very glad he never threw it into the River'. A couple of years later, the boy was deploying his energies in a more independent activity, and Jane wrote to Cassandra, who was again at Godmersham, 'Pray give my love to George, tell him that I am very glad to hear he can skip so well already, & that I hope he will continue to send me word of his improvement in the art.'[37]

Arriving at Godmersham on a visit in 1808, Jane provided for Cassandra a résumé of the appearance of their younger nephews and nieces, ranging in age from eight-year-old Lizzy down to Cassandra Jane at seventeen months. Lizzy, she wrote, had

gained in beauty in the last three years, though not all that Marianne has lost. Charles is not quite so lovely as he was. Louisa is much as I expected, and Cassandra I find handsomer than I expected, though at present disguised by such a violent breaking-out that she does not come down after dinner. She has charming eyes and a nice open countenance, and seems likely to be very lovable. Her size is magnificent.[38]

Jane was there with James and his family, and she commented on nine-year-old James Edward, at dinner on their first evening, that he 'was almost too happy, his happiness at least made him too talkative'. His sister Caroline, who had irritated her aunt by being 'fidgety' in the coach down to Kent, had her third birthday during their stay and wore a new brown hat with a feather.[39] It does not seem to have improved her appearance, however, since Jane told Cassandra: 'Little Caroline looks very plain among her Cousins, & tho' she is not so headstrong or humoursome as they are, I do not think her at all more engaging.'[40] Consigned with Caroline's nursemaid, Mary Smallbone, to the boys' attic, the two children seemed to Jane to be very happy. James Edward had 'nice playfellows in Lizzy and Charles';[41] he accompanied the adults on social visits, and his uncle Edward talked 'nonsense to him delightfully – more than he can always understand'.[42] But as far as Caroline was concerned, Edward's children were rather domineering; by the end of a fortnight Jane realized that she would be 'glad to go home; – her Cousins are too much for her'.[43] Years later, Caroline herself recalled her stay with mixed feelings:

> I remember the Godmersham visit well, in many little points; and I don't think I *was* very happy there, in a strange house. I recollect the model of a ship in a passage, and my cousins' rabbits out of doors, in or near a long walk of high trees. I have been told it was the lime-tree walk. As I never visited the place again, the very little that I *do* remember, must date from that time.[44]

At this time Jane seemed predisposed to judge the appearance of the various children she came across during her visit to Kent. Edward's sister-in-law, Harriot Mary Bridges, had been married for two years to the rector of Wrotham, the Revd George Moore, and Jane met them in Canterbury with their daughter, Eleanor; for Cassandra's benefit she compared the child's looks with those of their brother Francis's eldest daughter:

> I saw their little girl, & very small & very pretty she is; her features are as delicate as Mary Jane's, with nice dark eyes, & if she had Mary Jane's fine colour, she w^d be quite complete. – Harriot's fondness for her seems just what is amiable & natural, & not foolish.[45]

Mr Moore had an older child by his first marriage, and she too was with them; Jane thought her very plain.

While she was staying at Godmersham on another occasion several years later, in October 1813, the house was to be full of children, since apart from Edward's own, the Moores intended bringing one of their children, and Charles and Fanny Austen were due to arrive with two of theirs, the younger being a girl of ten months. Jane did not altogether view the prospect with relish:

> I hope Charles & Fanny may not fix the same time – but if they come at all in October they *must*. What is the use of hoping? – The two parties of Children is the cheif Evil. To be sure, here we are, the very thing has happened, or rather worse, a Letter from Charles this very morn^g which gives us reason to suppose they may come here to day . . . By her

own desire Mrs Fanny is to be put in the room next the Nursery, her Baby in a little bed by her; – & as Cassy is to have the Closet within & Betsey [the nursemaid] William's little Hole they will be all very snug together. – I shall be most happy to see dear Charles, & he will be as happy as he can with a cross Child or some such care pressing on him at the time. – I should be very happy in the idea of seeing little Cassy again too, did not I fear she w^d disappoint me by some immediate disagreeableness.[46]

Charles's party arrived rather late, when dinner was nearly over, because 'they did not set out earlier & did not allow time enough'; and they had a bad journey in the stormy October weather. Jane commented on the children's appearance:

poor little Cassy is grown extremely thin & looks poorly. – I hope a week's Country air & exercise may do her good . . . . The Baby does not appear so large in proportion as she was, nor quite so pretty, but I have seen very little of her. – Cassy was too tired & bewildered just at first to seem to know anybody – We met them in the Hall, the Women & Girl part of us – but before we reached the Library she kissed me very affectionately – & has since seemed to recollect me in the same way.

But the little girl's unappealing looks did not stem just from her poor health:

I talk to Cassy about Chawton; she remembers much but does not volunteer on the subject. – Poor little Love – I wish she were not so very Palmery – but it seems stronger than ever. – I never knew a Wife's family features have such undue influence.[47]

Charles was due to go back to his ship, the *Namur*, at Sheerness, and his wife was going with him; they had to decide whether or not to take Cassy:

Papa & Mama have not yet made up their mind as to parting with her or not – the cheif, indeed the only difficulty with Mama is a very reasonable one, the Child's being very unwilling to leave them. When it was mentioned to her, she did not like the idea of it at all. – At the same time, she has been suffering so much lately from Sea sickness, that her Mama cannot bear to have her much on board this winter. – Charles is less inclined to part with her. – I do not know how it will end, or what is to determine it.

It was not a problem that had to be faced by most parents.

When in *Mansfield Park* Fanny Price returns to her home in Portsmouth, the youngest of her brothers and sisters, is, she guesses, 'about five'; and the approximation underlines her estrangement from the family. Betsey, and the eldest sister, Susan, are 'both glad to see her in their way, though with no advantage of manner in receiving her'.[48] Advantage of manner is not something that has been instilled in any of the Price children, with the exception of Fanny herself (who as well as possessing natural modesty has been taught her manners at Mansfield) and, to a certain extent, William; but as she is the youngest, Betsey exhibits the deficiency most clearly. The delicacy with which Jane Austen builds up a portrait of this little girl demonstrates how well she had observed children, and how thoroughly she understood their behaviour. Betsey is still of an age to cling to her mother, and Mrs Price tells Fanny on her arrival that they have both been watching for her for the past half-hour. She is a 'very handy little messenger' and consorts with the recalcitrant Rebecca in the kitchen, where she is sent to find out if tea is ready (and reports back that it is not), and where she is familiar with the contents of the drawers. Accused by William as he puts on his uniform of 'having got at his new hat', she goes upstairs to defend herself, after which he tries in vain to send her down again, 'or keep her from being troublesome where she was'.[49] She cries 'at being allowed to sit up only one hour extraordinary in honour of her sister'.[50] Fanny is pained by the sight of her 'eating at table without restraint, and pulling every thing about as she chose',[51] and judges her 'a spoilt child, trained up to think the alphabet her greatest enemy, left to be with the servants at her pleasure, and then encouraged to report any evil of them'[52] – an opinion borne out by her mother's making a confidante of her:

> If I have spoke once to Rebecca about that carpet, I am sure I have spoke to her at least a dozen times; have I not, Betsey?[53]

In general, Mrs Price's daughters 'never had been much to her', and Betsey, 'her darling', is 'the first of her girls whom she had ever much regarded'.[54] Yet it is only by Susan's intervention, appreciated only by Fanny, that 'both her mother and Betsey were restrained from some excesses of very offensive indulgence and vulgarity'.[55]

Betsey's familiarity with Rebecca is one of the most significant indicators of Mrs Price's failure to manage her household. 'Familiarity between servants and children', declared Maria and Richard Lovell Edgeworth in *Practical Education*, 'cannot permanently increase the happiness of either party. Children, who have early lived with servants, as they grow up are notoriously apt to become capricious and tyrannical masters'.[56] While they recognized that very young children needed the help of a servant to dress themselves, the Edgeworths insisted that the mother or governess should 'make it a rule to be present when they are dressing' so that the servant 'would not talk to them, and could do them but little injury'. Specifically, they laid it down that 'children should never be sent with messages to servants, either on their own business, or on other people's; if they are permitted any times to speak to them, they will not distinguish what times are proper, and what are improper'.[57] Betsey Price is of course an incessant messenger between parlour and kitchen.

The Edgeworths also had strictures about the acquisition of good manners at table:

> patient care in feeding children neatly at first, will save many a bitter reprimand afterwards . . . Children should first be taught to eat with a spoon what has been neatly cut for them; afterwards they should cut a little meat for themselves towards the end of danger,

when the rage of hunger is appeased; they will then have 'leisure to be good'. The several operations of learning to eat with a spoon, to cut and to eat with a knife and fork, will become easy and habitual if sufficient time be allowed.[58]

Mrs Price, whose days are spent 'in a kind of slow bustle; always busy without getting on, always behindhand and lamenting it, without altering her ways,'[59] is unlikely to have found 'sufficient time' to teach her infants so patiently.

Perhaps the most striking aspect of the presentation of Betsey does not lie in the child herself but in the effect she has in bringing to Fanny's mind the memory of another child, now dead:

> As she now sat looking at Betsey, she could not but think particularly of another sister, a very pretty little girl, whom she had left there not much younger when she went into Northamptonshire, who had died a few years afterwards. There had been something remarkably amiable about her. Fanny, in those early days, had preferred her to Susan; and when the news of her death had at last reached Mansfield, had for a short time been quite afflicted. – The sight of Betsey brought the image of little Mary back again, but she would not have pained her mother by alluding to her, for the world.[60]

Jane Austen does something unique here in allowing Fanny's sensibility to perceive the shadow, almost the ghost, of a girl with whose gentle nature she had tenderly sympathized, because it had so closely resembled her own. In the noisy, uncontrolled family into which Fanny is so shocked to find herself thrust, the image of little Mary comes as a place of stillness and quiet, in which for a brief moment she can take refuge.

We have not heard of this sister before, the news of her death having arrived at Mansfield during the period between Fanny's ninth and fifteenth years which Jane Austen does not deal with; infant mortality is not something to have hanging over a novel. Now she is introduced for a very specific purpose. Fanny's meditation on the fused images of the two little girls is dispelled by the sudden resurfacing of the actual Betsey in a very characteristic vignette, as she sees her 'at a small distance ... holding out something to catch her eyes, meaning to screen it at the same time from Susan's'. It is the silver knife that Mary left to Susan as she lay dying, but which Mrs Price has never let her have. The reaction is immediate:

> Up jumped Susan, claiming it as her own, and trying to get it away; but the child ran to her mother's protection, and Susan could only reproach, which she did very warmly, and evidently hoping to interest Fanny on her side. 'It was very hard that she was not to have her *own* knife; little sister Mary had left it to her upon her death-bed, and she ought to have had it to keep herself long ago. But mamma kept it from her, and was always letting Betsey get hold of it; and the end of it would be that Betsey would spoil it, and get it for her own, though mamma had *promised* her that Betsey should not have it in her own hands.'

Fanny is 'quite shocked', by, we assume, both the insensitivity of her mother in withholding the knife from its rightful owner and the stridency of Susan's denunciation, expressed in the free indirect speech that Jane Austen always reserves for characters who do not have their tongues quite under control. Mrs Price's reply, which, like Susan's words, wounds 'every feeling of duty, honour, and tenderness' in Fanny, is unjust to the elder daughter and injudicious to the younger one, implying that the only reason that Betsey should not take the knife is that it makes Susan cross; yet at the same time, as she recalls the circumstances of Mary's leaving it to Susan, the warmth of her maternal feelings, so long thwarted by the demands of her life and her inadequacy to meet them, gives her dead child substance and brings her touchingly before the reader:

> Now, Susan . . . how can you be so cross? You are always quarrelling about that knife. I wish you would not be so quarrelsome. Poor little Betsey; how cross Susan is to you! But you should not have taken it out, my dear, when I sent you to the drawer. You know I told you not to touch it, because Susan is so cross about it. I must hide it another time, Betsey. Poor Mary little thought it would be such a bone of contention when she gave it me to keep, only two hours before she died. Poor little soul! she could but just speak to be heard, and she said so prettily, 'Let sister Susan have my knife, mamma, when I am dead and buried.' – Poor little dear! she was so fond of it, Fanny, that she would have it lay by her in bed, all through her illness.

The purpose of the knife is clear only when Fanny comes to what Michael Tatham has called a 'belated recognition' of Susan's merits,[61] and her purchase of a new knife ends the quarrel and is 'the means of opening Susan's heart to her'.[62] From then on, their intimacy grows and Fanny is able to begin her education and set her on the path that will lead to her eventual replacement of herself at Mansfield Park. Betsey, of course, is too young to have wanted the knife for anything but its own sake: the sentimental value it had for Susan meant nothing to her. So when the new one is bought for her it is 'accepted with great delight, its newness giving it every advantage over the other that could be desired', and Susan is 'established in the full possession of her own, Betsey handsomely declaring that now she had got one so much prettier herself, she should never want *that* again'.

Despite the death of little Mary Price, the second half of the eighteenth century saw, as was noted earlier, a marked fall in the rates of infant and child mortality. There were a number of contributory factors to this, among them better obstetrical practices, the wider availability of cow's milk in towns and cities, improvements in housing and sanitation, an increased awareness of personal hygiene and the effectiveness of inoculation against smallpox. Mrs Austen brought eight children into the world, all of whom, with the exception of Jane (and perhaps James, who died at fifty-three), were destined to live into old age. Only one child was not robust and healthy; this was her second son, George. He was mentally impaired and had fits; and there is a possibility that he may have been deaf and dumb, since we know that Jane Austen was able to converse

in sign language, and may have learnt it to be able to do so with her brother.[63]
Mr Austen was sad but resigned: thanking Susanna Walter for her 'kind wish of
George's improvement' in a letter written when the little boy was nearly four, he
said: 'God knows only how far it will come to pass, but from the best judgement
I can form at present, we must not be too sanguine on this head; be it as it may,
we have this comfort, he cannot be a bad or wicked child'.[64] They had tried to
keep him at home, but with other children to look after, as well as Mr Austen's
pupils, it was impossible for them to manage, and he was put out to board with
a local family and never thereafter lived in the rectory. He was brought to visit
his family, however, at least in his early years, and at times he seemed to be better; even so, his mother realized that there was little prospect of any long-term
improvement in his health, as she informed Mrs Walter: 'My poor little George
is come to see me to-day, he seems pretty well, tho' he had a fit lately; it was near
a twelvemonth since he had one before, so was in hopes they had left him, but
must not flatter myself so now.'[65]

The normal illnesses of childhood were, in Jane Austen's time as now, widespread through all levels of society. On her 1808 visit to Godmersham Jane told
Cassandra:

> There has been a cold & sorethroat prevailing very much in this House lately, the
> Children have almost all been ill with it, & we were afraid Lizzy was going to be very
> ill one day; she had specks & a great deal of fever. – It went off however, & they are all
> pretty well now.[66]

Even so, it spread to the visitors, as she reported the next week: 'Edward &
Caroline & their Mama have all had the Godmersham Cold; the former with
sorethroat & fever which his Looks are still suffering from.'[67] Among poor families such as the cottagers whom Emma visits with Harriet, however, they would
have been endemic, as Jane Austen recognizes in directly linking together the
concepts of poverty and illness: we are told that Emma has 'a charitable visit to
pay to a poor sick family', and, a few pages later, that 'it was sickness and poverty
together which she came to visit'.[68] Such people and their concerns are, however,
beyond Jane Austen's direct field of vision; they exist in *Emma* only because the
novel gives us a view of the complete village of Highbury, from the gypsy women
and 'great boy' that frighten Harriet to the 'stray letter-boy on an obstinate mule'
and the 'string of dawdling children round the baker's little bow-window eyeing
the gingerbread' that Emma sees from the door of Ford's shop.[69] In general, Jane
Austen's children are, to use the expression that Mrs Weston, in seeking a suitable
comparison for Emma, says is often used of a child, 'the picture of health'.[70]

Emma herself suffered the 'various illnesses of childhood', through which she
was nursed by Miss Taylor;[71] and her nieces and nephews, the children of Mr and
Mrs John Knightley, though clearly robust and healthy, have a sufficient number
of ailments to allow of a considerable amount of 'doctoring and coddling' by their
mother,[72] and to require the frequent attentions of the apothecary, Mr Wingfield,

who is as busily engaged in making as much money out of Isabella in London as Mr Perry is out of her father in Highbury.

Both apothecaries would have had a wide range of cures to administer, many of which are listed in Michael Underwood's *Disorders of Children*, published in 1784. When they were constipated, they might have been dosed regularly with manna (a mild laxative), caster oil, senna or aloes, rhubarb being given if there were gripes as well; if they had wind, magnesia and dill mixtures were the remedy.[73] Conversely, should they suffer from constant diarrhoea, Underwood did not think there was anything that could be done, except to wait for them to grow out of it.[74] Purging, he said, was not necessarily a bad thing, though the initial cause of the complaint should be discovered first; he advocated arrowroot and for the older child lightly cooked chicken, and Bates's Julep of Life was also to be recommended.[75] Worms could be found in any part of the body, though they were often more imaginary than real (a point with which Buchan agreed, though he reported the case of a three-month-old child passing real caterpillars with red heads).[76] While Underwood acknowledged that doctors did not know what caused them, he could not possibly agree with Dr Butter, who held the opinion that they were actually beneficial, since they were 'intended "as nature's remedy for destroying the superabounding morbid humours; and for stimulating the first-passages by their crawling motions, and thereby assisting the peristaltic motion of the guts to carry off what remains of the offending load." On the other hand,' Underwood conceded, 'children who are most troubled with worms are generally of a costive habit.'[77] Rickets, which since it was more prevalent in manufacturing towns than elsewhere was unlikely to afflict children in Jane Austen's novels, might come from unhealthy parents, but more often from bad nursing; starchy gruels were recommended for the young child, bread and meat, and wine, for the older one, though in fact children generally got better of their own accord.[78] For the treatment of ague, people would need to know the receipts of their country neighbours in order to be able to help the poor: these included bracelets of mustard seed and garlic worn on the ankles, and eating a rolled up spider's web accompanied by camomile tea. Underwood was naturally sceptical about such superstitions, and even more so about the charms and amulets worn at the time of teething, for which he advocated an altogether more scientific treatment: rubbing the gums with a hard teething ring and frequent lancing with a proper lancet (not a sharp sixpence, as was sometimes done), especially if the teething was accompanied by convulsions, in which case the application of leeches to the head was often also helpful.[79] Underwood was writing fifteen years after Buchan had published *Domestic Medicine*, and although in the matter of teething they agreed on several practices (dabbing the gums with honey and giving the child bread or liquorice to chew, for example), the earlier physician had not seen much advantage in the lancing by which the later one was to set such store, though he thought it might be tried in obstinate cases.[80]

In *Emma*, the children's health offers a subject of interest when Mr and Mrs John Knightley visit Hartfield, and the rival claims of the apothecaries and their respective advice becomes a subject of debate, which Emma has to use all her skills of tact and management to deflect. Mr Woodhouse has been rather put out that, rather than coming to Surrey, they spent their last holidays at Southend for the sea air, something of which he says he never had much opinion. Isabella protests:

> 'Mr. Wingfield most strenuously recommended it, sir – or we should not have gone. He recommended it for all the children, but particularly for the weakness in little Bella's throat, – both sea air and bathing.'
>
> 'Ah! my dear, but Perry had many doubts about the sea doing her any good; and as to myself, I have been long perfectly convinced, though perhaps I never told you so before, that the sea is very rarely of use to any body. I am sure it almost killed me once.'
>
> 'Come, come,' cried Emma, feeling this to be an unsafe subject, 'I must beg you not to talk of the sea. It makes me envious and miserable; – I who have never seen it! South End is prohibited, if you please. My dear Isabella, I have not heard you make one inquiry after Mr. Perry yet; and he never forgets you.'[81]

Emma's ruse does not quite do the trick, however, since Isabella's immediate interest in Mr Perry and his family gives Mr Woodhouse the opportunity to suggest that she should seek his advice:

> 'And Mrs. Perry and the children, how are they? do the children grow? – I have a great regard for Mr. Perry. I hope he will be calling soon. He will be so pleased to see my little ones.'
>
> 'I hope he will be here to-morrow, for I have a question or two to ask him about myself of some consequence. And, my dear, whenever he comes, you had better let him look at little Bella's throat.'
>
> 'Oh! my dear sir, her throat is so much better that I have hardly any uneasiness about it. Either bathing has been of the greatest service to her, or else it is to be attributed to an excellent embrocation of Mr. Wingfield's, which we have been applying at times ever since August.'
>
> 'It is not very likely, my dear, that bathing should have been of use to her – and if I had known you were wanting an embrocation, I would have spoken to – '
>
> 'You seem to me to have forgotten Mrs. and Miss Bates,' said Emma, 'I have not heard one inquiry after them.'

Isabella is delighted to hear about the Bateses, and says she will visit them the next day, since they 'are always so pleased to see my children'. But even this does not deflect the conversation for long, since she then asks her father how they are, and any such question is likely to lead Mr Woodhouse back to his favourite subject:

> 'Why, pretty well, my dear, upon the whole. But poor Mrs. Bates had a bad cold about a month ago.'

'How sorry I am! But colds were never so prevalent as they have been this autumn. Mr. Wingfield told me that he had never known them more general or heavy – except when it has been quite an influenza.'

'That has been a good deal the case, my dear; but not to the degree you mention. Perry says that colds have been very general, but not so heavy as he has very often known them in November. Perry does not call it altogether a sickly season.'

'No, I do not know that Mr. Wingfield considers it *very* sickly except –'

'Ah! my poor dear child, the truth is, that in London it is always a sickly season. Nobody is healthy in London, nobody can be. It is a dreadful thing to have you forced to live there! – and so far off! – and the air so bad!'

There then follows a discussion of the suitability of the air for the children, Isabella claiming that 'the neighbourhood of Brunswick Square' is quite different from the rest of London:

We are so very airy! I should be unwilling, I own, to live in any other part of the town; – there is hardly any other that I could be satisfied to have my children in; – but *we* are so remarkably airy! – Mr. Wingfield thinks the vicinity of Brunswick Square decidedly the most favourable as to air.'

It is of course the vicinity in which he is the apothecary.

Before the end of the evening, the subject of the seaside holiday is reopened, much to Emma's alarm. Mr Woodhouse says mournfully:

'I shall always be very sorry that you went to the sea this autumn, instead of coming here.'

'But why should you be sorry, sir? – I assure you, it did the children a great deal of good.'

'And moreover, if you must go to the sea, it had better not have been to South End. South End is an unhealthy place. Perry was surprized to hear you had fixed upon South End.'

'I know there is such an idea with many people, but indeed it is quite a mistake, sir. – We had all our health perfectly well there, never found the least inconvenience from the mud; and Mr. Wingfield says it is entirely a mistake to consider the place unhealthy; and I am sure he may be depended on, for he thoroughly understands the nature of the air, and his own brother and family have been there repeatedly.'

'You should have gone to Cromer, my dear, if you went any where. – Perry was a week at Cromer once, and he holds it to be the best of all the sea-bathing places. A fine open sea, he says, and very pure air . . .'[82]

Mr Woodhouse's insistence that they should have consulted Perry, who had considered going to Southend 'a very ill-judged measure', eventually leads to his son-in-law losing his temper, as Emma had feared:

'Mr. Perry,' said he, in a voice of very strong displeasure, 'would do as well to keep his opinion till it is asked for. Why does he make it any business of his, to wonder at what I do? – at my taking my family to one part of the coast or another? – I may be allowed, I hope, the use of my judgment as well as Mr. Perry. – I want his directions no more than his drugs.' He paused – and growing cooler in a moment, added, with only sarcastic dryness, 'If Mr. Perry can tell me how to convey a wife and five children a distance of an hundred and thirty miles with no greater expense or inconvenience than a distance of forty, I should be as willing to prefer Cromer to South End as he could himself.'

Good air was of course always considered important for health, for children and adults alike. Though William Moss recommended that extreme care should be taken with a baby's first introduction to cooler air, and that eight weeks was the earliest that it should be taken outside, even if before that 'the weather may be favourable',[83] there was no doubt that the young must be taken out for regular airings, as we see happening in Bath with the 'nursery-maids and children' whom Anne and Captain Wentworth are too preoccupied to notice during their walk up Belmont at the end of *Persuasion*.[84] William Buchan in his *Domestic Medicine* strongly recommended regular exercise for growing children: bad air kills the children of the poor in hospitals or workhouses, so it is the business of the rich

> to see that their children be daily carried abroad, and that they be kept in the open air for a sufficient time. This will succeed better if the mother goes along with them. Servants are often negligent in these matters, and allow a child to sit or lie on the damp ground, in place of leading or carrying it about.[85]

Fresh air could be found by the sea, but anywhere high and at a reasonable distance from the smoke and dirt of cities was a likely spot to attract visitors. Such a place was Clifton, the elegant eighteenth-century suburb built on the hill to the west of Bristol, where Jane Austen herself stayed with her mother and sister for a few weeks in the summer of 1806. It had the unusual advantage of combining the fresh air of its Downs with the waters of a spa, since a borehole had been sunk 250 feet to tap a hot spring; and it soon came to replace the old failing Hotwell at the bottom of the cliff by the River Avon. The city of Bristol itself was rough, squalid and industrial, with collieries and works of all kinds contributing their grime and fumes to the sewage-ridden waters of the port. If its radical reputation rested partly on a literary and intellectual culture that included Coleridge, Wordsworth and Southey, it was also reflected in the sporadic riots of its working people. James Malcolm, writing in the year after the Austens' visit, described the older parts of the city as 'inconceivably unpleasant, dark, and dirty' and its suburbs 'lined by houses inhabited by a wild race, whose countenances indicate wretchedness and affright'. These were 'the wives and offspring of the labourers at copper and ironworks, glass houses, and many other manufactories; and when released, sufficient leisure is denied to them to humanize themselves and families'.[86] It is the 'very heart' of this city that is the childhood home of Augusta Hawkins, before she marries Mr Elton.[87]

Clifton, elegant and airy, which Augusta Hawkins very specifically does not come from, was visited by a number of writers at the end of the eighteenth century, among them Maria Edgeworth, who stayed there in 1791 and again eight years later; her young brother Lovell suffered from consumption, and the family hoped that the air would be of help to him. Some of the stories she wrote there, which later appeared in her collection for children, *The Parent's Assitant*, were set in Clifton. For example, in 'The Mimic', Mr and Mrs Montague bring their children for the summer of 1795, and, having taken great care over their upbringing, they are 'particularly cautious in the choice of their acquaintances, as they were well aware that whatever passed in conversation before their children became part of their education'. For this reason, 'they wished to have a house entirely to themselves; but, as they came late in the season, almost all the lodging-houses were full, and for a few weeks they were obliged to remain in a house where some of the apartments were already occupied'.[88]

Jane Austen, who had no doubt visited Clifton prior to the visit of 1806, during visits to Bath, found it, like Maria Edgeworth, a useful setting for a story. When in 'Lesley Castle', one of the pieces of the *Juvenilia*, Eloisa Luttrell falls ill following the death of her fiancé, and her 'Physicians are greatly afraid of her going into a decline',[89] she is taken by her mother and her sister Charlotte to Bristol; this, of course, means Clifton, as is clear from the reference to 'the healthy air of the Bristol downs' – which, however, are not able, as it turns out, 'to drive poor Henry from her remembrance'. Their visit comes 'at so unfashionable a season of the year', in February, that they meet only 'one genteel family', whose own arrival is caused by the ill-health of their little boy; he too has been taken to Clifton in order to experience the benefits of the healthy air – and from the fact that he is soon back in London, we may conclude that it has done him good.

But in real life, the outcome was not always so happy. Lady Mary Talbot, daughter of the second Earl of Ilchester, had six healthy children who lived into old age, but two girls who died young. One of them, Christiana, known in the family as Tina, had a caustic substance applied to her face to remove a lump when she was only six; and three years later died, probably from tuberculosis. Lady Mary's former governess, Agnes Porter, who remained a lifelong friend and sometimes looked after her children, wrote blithely the next year: 'Your letters are indeed *refreshing* to me beyond description, and to hear that your lovely children are well. Six out of *seven*, is to me delightful. I suppose as to your dear Ellinor, *that is a case of time*, but in the meanwhile her being free from pain is a most consolatory circumstance.'[90] For poor little Ellinor, who had never been a very strong child, it was indeed a case of time, but not a very long one; even when the letter was written, she was already suffering from consumption, which she had possibly contracted from a governess.[91] Her fevers were treated with quinine and diluted vitriolic acid, but her mother was almost resigned to the inevitable, writing to her sister that she could not help dreading that 'the shade of an Ellinor, which is now all that is left, will soon depart for [a] mansion more suited to the innocence and patience of such little angels'.[92] In December 1809 her parents took her to Clifton, hoping that the air would do her good, but six weeks later she died. Lady Mary was obviously anxious about her other children, suspecting that consumption ran in the family; her fears proved groundless, however, and Agnes Porter waxed philosophical again:

> Afflictions which in general are regarded as common events in life, have been to you most poignant cause of sorrow. You have with-held all exterior signs of woe, and the impressions are the deeper. As you have never frittered your feelings away on trivial matters, they are the more condensed and heavier when there is real cause. But you have such *treasures* left – you have such *Christian consolation*, and such natural fortitude, that *time* and *pursued occupations*, and various scenes, will perform their due effect on your heart and understanding.[93]

Serious infectious diseases – tuberculosis, scarlet fever, diphtheria, typhus, all of which could prove fatal, and to a lesser extent whooping cough and measles – were feared by many parents, but they do not figure greatly among the 'various illnesses of childhood' in Jane Austen's novels, despite the fact that she herself very nearly died of typhus as a child, as we shall see in a later chapter. In *Sense and Sensibility*, Marianne Dashwood's fever is enough to give 'instant alarm to Mrs. Palmer on her baby's account', with the apothecary 'pronouncing her disorder to have a putrid tendency, and allowing the word "infection" to pass his lips';[94] and in *Sanditon* a family of children come from London to stay in the village 'for the sea air after hooping cough'.[95] Otherwise, children seem to stay robust and healthy. No doubt whenever Miss Taylor was called upon to deliver a report to Mr Woodhouse on little Isabella or Emma, she would have sounded much like Agnes Porter writing to Lady Mary Talbot in September 1810, while she was looking after some of the children at Great Malvern:

> My dear Lady Mary,
> Your children, I thank God, are *at least* as well as when you left them, and as happy as they can be in your absence. Little Christopher is really extremely well in health, and is one of the best children I ever knew . . . . Miss Emma, that darling star, sparkles yet in the better part, her intelligence, and as to her looks they are much mended in my opinion by her eyes being better. The ears I think are not so much enflamed as they were; she eats heartily, sleeps soundly, and plays as well as any of the party. Miss Isabella coughs a little, but they tell me it is no more than it was before you went, and is caused by a slight cold . . . .[96]

And again, three days later, of Miss Emma:

> My dear Lady Mary,
> Your little darling goes on improving very much indeed: her ears are less inflamed, her

eyes begin to recover their brightness, and her general health is encreasing. Accept a few minutes while disagreeables are performing in the morning, she scarcely ever cries. She eats hearty, her bowels are quite regular and well, and she is as blythe as a lark . . . .[97]

Mr Woodhouse would probably not have expected quite such a deferential tone from Miss Taylor, but he would have been very glad to hear about the disagreeables.

On the whole, preserving children's health depended very much on common sense, a quantity of flannel (something of which Miss Porter was a great advocate) and, for the newborn, a willingness to embrace the methods recommended by Mrs Enfield in the Austens' little playlets. Finding that Mrs Denbigh's baby has a 'breaking out' on his back, Mrs Enfield applies a 'mild plaister' which she orders the nurse to change night and morning, spreading it thin and keeping 'a few folds of soft linnen over it'.[98] She states, very sensibly, that she finds 'simple food & medicines & plaisters agree best with the tender frames of children', who 'not having lived long by art their complaints are seldom very complicated'. Finding that little Charles has an even worse eruption on his head, she again urges regular changing of his dressings, provoking another argument with the lazy nurse:

Mrs E.   Nurse we must dress his head the same as his back & I beg you will change these plaisters often, & while the parts are so tender wash them with warm water, but as soon as they are better, use plenty of cold water & soap.

Nurse   His poor head would be perished with the like

Mrs E.   I wash Julia's head with cold water & soap every morning; & once that the skin was a little tender behind her ears, I kept a rag constantly wet with cold water to the part, & found it cured her sooner than I could expect – Do you put a clean cap on him every night.

Nurse   Not myself indeed – he has but two in the world & I could not be washing them every minute

Mrs E.   I dare say your mistress would give you a supply, no matter how old or how plain, provided they are clean, & while his head is sore I assure you Mrs. D. it is absolutely necessary to have a clean one every night

When Mrs Enfield makes a second visit, Mrs Denbigh says that the child's back and head are better but his 'general health is rather worse'. When the nurse is told to bring him in, he is in a 'miserably dirty' state and 'looks very pale'; instead of changing his linen regularly, she has been giving him some potion to dry up the rash, so that Mrs Enfield, who 'thought a sucking child would require little or no medicine', now recommends 'small quantities of manna for a few days, which will sweeten his blood & is so mild a medicine that you need not apprehend danger from it'. He is in the course of being weaned, though very unsatisfactorily – it is difficult to say who is the more inadequate, the slovenly wet-nurse or his foolish mother. Mrs Enfield is ready with excellent advice, however:

Nurse	He wont eat a bit for me all day, nor does not care to suck either. What would you be pleased to order to bring him to his little stomach?
Mrs D.	You are very troublesome nurse, try him with a bit of plumb cake & go dress him.
Mrs E.	I assure you I don't think it any trouble to give advice nor should I think it troublesome to attend him myself if I had leisure & opportunity, for as nursing is my business & pleasure I take an interest in every child I see – but if you please Mrs. Denbigh, I would not recommend the plumb cake, which would cloy his stomach, & make him have no appetite for plain wholesome food.
Mrs D.	Surely when he eats one piece, I will give him more my little precious shall have plumb cake as long as I have any & it will melt so sweet in his mouth
Mrs E.	Perhaps you forget that such a quantity as his stomach ought to require would certainly make him sick, but if you only give him plain food, he will relish it & will not take it except he wants it.
Nurse	I never am without his bit of panado [boiled bread pulp] & makes it as sweet as sugar & offers it to him every minute of his life but he wont have it. I partly blame the cure Honour gave him for taking away his little stomach.
Mrs E.	It is better not to give him food immediately after any medicine, & always better not to be continually plying him even with suitable food such a plan makes children find eating their only business & they lose that relish which a degree of hunger gives to any food – a healthy child ought to eat or drink a little meal then play as it is capable, it then becomes hungry or sleepy & is refreshed by either – Constant eating sows the seeds of gluttony & peevishness & stupidity[99]

The stress placed in these passages on the importance both of washing with cold water and of plain food – and particularly the recommendation against rich or sweet things – is exactly in accordance with Dr Buchan's advice in *Domestic Medicine*, and suggests that Mary Lloyd had a copy of the book (it was very popular and frequently reprinted); she may even have taken it to Southampton for her sister-in-law's benefit. It is interesting to note, however, that in her opposition to constant feeding Mrs Enfield takes issue with Buchan's assertion that 'children thrive much better with small quantities of food frequently given'; and her reasons seem almost to be as much to do with morals as with health. Honour, onto whom the wet-nurse tries to shift the blame for the baby's lack of appetite, is presumably the assistant nursemaid, and no less ignorant than the nurse herself. Most sensible women would have tried to ensure that their nursery was better staffed than Mrs Denbigh's seems to be; at Godmersham, for example, Elizabeth Austen employed the beloved Susanna Sackree, known as 'Caky' by the children, who remained with the family for more than fifty years.

Even a parent with more sense than Mrs Denbigh, however, could on occasion act rashly with a newborn child, with potentially serious consequences. Elizabeth Ham, who wrote a memoir of her childhood during the last seventeen years of the eighteenth century (and of her subsequent life as a governess), attributed a tendency to suffer from inflamed eyes to her over-enthusiastic father:

> When I was but a few days old, my father, proud of his little girl, caught me up and ran down to the door with me to show me to a friend who called on horseback. The consequence of this early exposure was inflammation in the eyes, which made it necessary to confine me to a dark room for the first year of my life, and the effects of which I feel to this day. For this weakness, I was doomed to a daily immersion in a tub of cold water, then thought a very cruel remedy, but which, I have no doubt, tended greatly to strengthen my constitution, for the goodness of which I have all my life had great cause to be thankful.[100]

The 'cruel remedy' of cold water might have been approved of by Mrs Enfield, however much the infant Elizabeth Ham deplored it.

No child, of whatever age, would have relished a visit to the dentist, even when they were given money for the teeth they had extracted. In 1813, Lady Mary Talbot's ten-year-old son Christopher reported of a supposedly skilful practitioner that 'some of the boys whose teeth he has drawn say he had two or three tugs at it, and pulled out a piece of gum at last'.[101] In the same year, Marianne Knight (Edward Austen had by then taken the adoptive surname) celebrated her thirteenth birthday, 15 September, by visiting Mr Spence, a dentist in London. On that occasion, all seemed well enough with her, though rather worse for her sister Lizzy, as Jane Austen reported to Cassandra, conveying their apprehensions in the children's own voice:

> Going to Mr Spence's was a sad Business & cost us many tears, unluckily we were obliged to go a 2^d time before he could do more than just look: – we went 1st at $^1/_2$ past 12 and afterwards at 3. Papa with us each time – &, alas! we are to go again to-morrow. Lizzy is not finished yet. There have been no Teeth taken out however, nor will be I believe, but he finds *hers* in a very bad state, & seems to think particularly ill of their Durableness. – They have been all cleaned, *hers* filed, and are to be filed again. There is a very sad hole between two of her front Teeth.[102]

The next day, however, Marianne was in for a shock:

> The poor Girls & their Teeth! . . . we were a whole hour at Spence's, & Lizzy's were filed & lamented over again & poor Marianne had two taken out after all, the two just beyond the Eye teeth, to make room for those in front. – When her doom was fixed, Fanny Lizzy & I walked into the next room, where we heard each of the two sharp hasty Screams.[103]

The extended use that Jane Austen makes of a sick child in *Persuasion* is by far the most significant instance of childhood illness in any of the novels, though in fact it comes about not from any actual complaint but by an accident. Little Charles Musgrove suffers 'a bad fall'; we are not told how it happens, but it foreshadows Louisa's very serious fall on the Cobb at Lyme, which has even more important consequences for the plot. Both incidents are closely bound up with the renewal of Anne and Captain Wentworth's relationship: Louisa's accident eventually hastens their coming together; Charles's, on a smaller scale, initially delays it.

Shortly after Wentworth's return to Kellynch, Anne is about to set off with Mary from Uppercross Cottage to the Great House, where, she subsequently learns, he is at that moment calling, when the boy is brought home: 'The child's situation put the visit entirely aside, but she could not hear of her escape with indifference, even in the midst of the serious anxiety which they afterwards felt on his account.'[104] He has dislocated his collar-bone and received such injury in the back 'as roused the most alarming ideas'. In the emergency it is Anne who takes charge, again anticipating the scene at Lyme. She sends for the apothecary:

> Till he came and had examined the child, their apprehensions were the worse for being vague; – they suspected great injury, but knew not where; but now the collar-bone was soon replaced, and though Mr. Robinson felt and felt, and rubbed, and looked grave, and spoke low words both to the father and to the aunt, still they were all to hope the best, and to be able to part and eat their dinner in tolerable ease of mind . . .[105]

Anne again avoids the meeting she dreads with Captain Wentworth at dinner the next day by offering to stay with the child; and it is clear that he also wants to avoid meeting her, from the plans made for the next morning's shooting with Charles Musgrove:

> He was to come to breakfast, but not at the Cottage, though that had been proposed at first; but then he had been pressed to come to the Great House instead, and he seemed afraid of being in Mrs. Charles Musgrove's way, on account of the child; and therefore, somehow, they hardly knew how, it ended in Charles's being to meet him to breakfast at his father's.[106]

Captain Wentworth feels the same nervousness at the meeting (also coloured by the anger he has long been harbouring at Anne's rejection of him), but she misinterprets his motives and assumes he no longer loves her. When after breakfast Louisa and Henrietta want to visit Mary and the child, and Captain Wentworth therefore has to call at the Cottage, he insists on Charles's coming in first to give notice, 'though Charles had answered for the child's being in no such state as could make it inconvenient'. The notice, of course, is intended for Anne.

Anne and Wentworth are soon thrown regularly together, 'for the little boy's state could no longer supply his aunt with a pretence of absenting herself';[107] but she is able to make use of 'some return of indisposition' as a reason not to go to dinner at the Great House, where Mary subsequently tells her she would have been able to judge whether or not Wentworth favoured Henrietta over Louisa: she 'had thought only of avoiding Captain Wentworth; but an escape from being appealed to as umpire, was now added to the advantages of a quiet evening'.[108]

If the little invalid Charles is a means by which Anne and Wentworth are kept apart, he is also, in one of the most vividly imagined scenes of the novel, an unconscious means of bringing them into intimate contact. When Wentworth walks into the drawing-room at the Cottage one morning expecting Louisa and Henrietta to be there, he is embarrassed to find only Anne and the little boy, who is lying on the sofa. If 'the child had not called her to come and do something for him, she would have been out of the room the next moment, and released Captain Wentworth as well as herself';[109] as it is, while he looks out of the window 'to recollect himself, and feel how he ought to behave' she is 'obliged to kneel down by the sofa, and remain there to satisfy her patient', as he 'calmly and politely' says he hopes the little boy is better. It is a scene charged with emotion, underlined by a sense of helpless stasis: 'and thus they continued a few minutes'. But Jane Austen sees its potential for comedy, which she sets in motion with the addition of two more figures. First, as Anne hears 'some other person crossing the little vestibule' and hopes for relief in the form of her brother-in-law, Charles Hayter enters; and he, hoping to marry Henrietta, is 'probably not at all better pleased by the sight of Captain Wentworth, than Captain Wentworth had been by the sight of Anne'. Wentworth, however, 'came from his window, apparently not ill-disposed for conversation' (in reality, of course, pleased to have the opportunity to move nearer Anne and engage in talk in which she might join); repudiating his friendliness, however, Hayter sits down near the table to read the newspaper, and Wentworth returns to the window. Stasis is resumed, until Jane Austen makes her masterstroke:

> Another minute brought another addition. The younger boy, a remarkable stout, forward child, of two years old, having got the door opened for him by some one without, made his determined appearance among them, and went straight to the sofa to see what was going on, and put in his claim to any thing good that might be giving away.
>
> There being nothing to eat, he could only have some play; and as his aunt would not let him teaze his sick brother, he began to fasten himself upon her, as she knelt, in such a way that, busy as she was about Charles, she could not shake him off. She spoke to him – ordered, intreated, and insisted in vain. Once she did contrive to push him away, but the boy had the greater pleasure in getting upon her back again directly.
>
> 'Walter,' said she, 'get down this moment. You are extremely troublesome. I am very angry with you.'
>
> 'Walter,' cried Charles Hayter, 'why do you not do as you are bid? Do you not hear your aunt speak? Come to me, Walter, come to cousin Charles.'
>
> But not a bit did Walter stir.

Every detail is perfect: the invisibility, from inside the room, of whoever the child gets to open the door; the directness with which the little boy makes for the scene of interest – the sofa – and his assumption that there might be something to eat; his taking advantage of Anne's keeling position to jump on her back and, when at last pushed away, his 'greater pleasure' in getting straight back on again; and the four utterances of the word 'Walter' – Anne's, desperate; Charles Hayter's, both ineffectual; and the narrator's, expressive of the absolute immovability of a determined little boy of two.

Suddenly, from seeing the comic scene from, as it were, across the room (almost as Captain Wentworth might be seeing it, supposing that he too turned round at the moment of the child's entrance), we *feel* what happens next, as Anne feels it:

> In another moment, however, she found herself in the state of being released from him; some one was taking him from her, though he had bent down her head so much, that his sturdy little hands were unfastened from around her neck, and he was resolutely borne away, before she knew that Captain Wentworth had done it.

There is an extraordinary delicacy here. Wentworth's action is manly both in the 'resolute' way in which it is performed and in the chaste distancing effected by the mediating of his contact with her neck through the 'sturdy little hands' of the child; and this is reflected in the narrative itself, since the reader does not know who has performed the action until Anne herself knows. The moment is as much charged with emotion, however, as comparable moments in other novels – Elizabeth Bennet's seeing the portrait of Darcy in the picture gallery at Pemberley, or Emma's appreciation of the figure Mr Knightley cuts at the ball, for example – and considerably more than when, for example, at Hartfield Mr Knightley takes Emma's eight-month-old niece out of her arms 'with all the unceremoniousness of perfect amity':[110]

> Her sensations on the discovery made her perfectly speechless. She could not even thank him. She could only hang over little Charles, with most disordered feelings.

Again the invalid provides a means of escape, as she wrestles with, and seeks to analyse, the effect of Captain Wentworth's action:

> His kindness in stepping forward to her relief – the manner – the silence in which it had passed – the little particulars of the circumstance – with the conviction soon forced on her by the noise he was studiously making with the child, that he meant to avoid hearing her thanks, and rather sought to testify that her conversation was the last of his wants, produced such a confusion of varying, but very painful agitation, as she could not recover from, till enabled by the entrance of Mary and the Miss Musgroves to make over her little patient to their cares, and leave the room.

Captain Wentworth knows that if he has taken over little Walter, he must entertain him, and he does so robustly and noisily (much like Mr Knightley tossing his nephews up to the ceiling, to the consternation of Mr Woodhouse); no doubt he wishes to save both himself and Anne the embarrassment of her thanks, but she still misinterprets his reasons. Just before she leaves the room to 'arrange' her feelings, however, there is one last touch of humour as she has 'a strong impression' of Charles Hayter saying 'in a vext tone of voice, after Captain Wentworth's interference, "You ought to have minded *me*, Walter; I told you not to teaze your aunt".[111] Jane Austen maintains the comic and emotional balance of the scene to the end. What, after all, could be more irritating to a man than his rival in love getting the better of him in handling a recalcitrant infant?

4

Childhood

In writing of Jane Austen in his *Memoir* James Edward Austen-Leigh finds little to say of her childhood other than to express such amiable generalizations as that 'the home at Steventon must have been, for many years, a pleasant and prosperous one', that it was 'the cradle of her genius' and that 'in strolls along those wood-walks, thick-coming fancies rose in her mind, and gradually assumed the forms in which they came forth to the world' – forms which in the simple church she 'brought . . . into subjection to the piety which ruled her in life, and supported her in death'.[1] He briefly mentions her education, both at home and at school, and he does say that she was an observer of the family theatricals that took place during the summer holidays and at Christmas; but he confesses that he does not know much about her childhood.

Since for first-hand memories of her we are dependent on members of the next generation, her nephews and nieces, who of course did not know her until she was a woman, she fails to come into focus as a child, except perhaps for the odd glimpse recorded in a letter. There is, for example, a description of her by her older cousin Philadelphia (Phylly) Walter, who wrote that she was 'very like her brother Henry, not at all pretty & very prim, unlike a girl of twelve'.[2] Three years later, by contrast, Eliza de Feuillide reported to Phylly that her Austen cousins were apparently 'perfect Beauties & of course gain "hearts by dozens"';[3] and later that year she told her that she had heard they were 'two of the prettiest girls in England'.[4] Visiting Steventon the next year, when Jane was sixteen, Eliza informed Phylly that 'Cassandra & Jane are both very much grown (the latter is now taller than myself) and greatly improved in manners as in person, both of which are now much more formed than when you saw them'.[5] But of what girls could not such things be said or such developments through childhood into adolescence be traced? Jane Austen says them herself of Catherine Morland, whom 'no one who had ever seen [her] in her infancy, would have supposed . . . born to be a heroine':

> the Morlands were in general very plain, and Catherine, for many years of her life, as plain as any. She had a thin, awkward figure, a sallow skin without colour, dark lank hair, and strong features . . . she was moreover noisy and wild, hated confinement and cleanliness, and loved nothing so well in the world as rolling down the green slope at the back of the house. Such was Catherine Morland at ten. At fifteen, appearances were mending; she began to curl her hair and long for balls; her complexion improved, her features were softened by plumpness and colour, her eyes gained more animation, and her figure more

consequence. Her love of dirt gave way to an inclination for finery, and she grew clean as she grew smart; she had now the pleasure of sometimes hearing her father and mother remark on her personal improvement.[6]

We know of course of the particular closeness that existed between Jane and Cassandra, and of their mother's characteristically vivid remark years later to Anna Lefroy that 'if Cassandra's head had been going to be cut off, Jane would have her's cut off too'.[7] And Cassandra herself comes into view for a moment at the age of eleven, in a poem by their eldest brother James. As he sits one evening writing verses, Cassandra (whom he refers to by her second name as Eliza) leans over his chair and tries to see them; presumably not wishing to show them until they are finished, he prevents her, and she makes a 'rash resolution' that she will not go to sleep until he lets her read them:

> Exerting therefore all the power
> Which to subdue our tempers sour
> Fate gave to Woman's brain
> With all the Eloquence of eyes
> Her Brothers heart to move she tries
> But tries Alas! in vain[8]

Inevitably, as night comes on she cannot keep her eyes open, and eventually she has to be taken up to bed. The next morning, he shows her the completed verses, accompanying them with an apt moral:

> Your curiosity restrain,
> It may be done, tho' done with Pain,
> No rash resolves e're make:
> Sink in your mind this lesson deep,
> They may be very hard to keep,
> But easy still to break.

Thanks to another poem, in this case one by Jane Austen herself, we also have a picture of Francis in childhood. On the birth of his first son, in 1809, she wrote a congratulatory letter in verse in which she affectionately recalled his own early years, though since she was eighteen months younger than Francis, some of the detail must have been passed down as family lore. She hopes that his own son will resemble him and replicate his childish ways:

> May he revive thy Nursery sin,
> Peeping as daringly within,
> (His curley Locks but just descried)
> With, 'Bet, my be not come to bide.'
> Fearless of danger, braving pain,

And threaten'd very oft in vain,
Still may one Terror daunt his soul,
One needful engine of controul
Be found in this sublime array,
A neighbouring Donkey's aweful Bray![9]

The picture of the sturdy little boy, none too well behaved, braving the wrath of the nursery maid but terrified of a donkey braying, is appealing.

The delight that Jane Austen took in her nephews and nieces was of course an aspect of the lively interest she felt for all her family, and indeed that they felt for each other. But she observed them, as she observed everybody, and the characteristic behaviour of children allowed her to study people at a time of their lives that literature did not generally investigate. It amused her when they behaved in character. Writing to Anna shortly after her marriage to Ben Lefroy, she told her about the reaction of Charles's little girls to the news:

Cassy was excessively interested about your marrying, when she heard of it, which was not till she was to drink your health on the wedding day. She asked a thousand questions, in her usual way – What he said to you? & what you said to him? – And we were very much amused one day by Mary Jane's asking 'what Month her *Cousin Benjamin* was born in?'[10]

Equally she could be struck by a child's precocity, and by its priorities; of Francis's third son, then not quite four, she wrote to Cassandra, who was staying in Cheltenham, 'Little George could tell me where you were gone to, as well as what you were to bring him, when I asked him the other day.'[11] She could also be critical, however. She devoted an entire poem to her niece Anna in which, though ostensibly 'rehearsing' her 'charms', she hinted that her judgement, 'thick, black, profound, / Like transatlantic groves', was not always entirely sound – a fact which, given the rash engagement the girl had entered into at the time the poem was probably written, was fairly incontrovertible.[12] Even with younger children Jane felt that their characters could be judged quite firmly. 'How soon, the difference of temper in Children appears!' she wrote subsequently of the same niece Anna Lefroy's two eldest girls, respectively eighteen months and six months old at the time. 'Jemima has a very irritable bad Temper (her mother says so) – and Julia a very sweet one, always pleased & happy. – I hope as Anna is so early sensible of its' defects, that she will give Jemima's disposition the early & steady attention it must require.'[13]

Sometimes a child might give rise to a little speculative fiction-making. When six-year-old Cassy was staying at Chawton in September 1815, the fair was being held at Alton; Jane sent a note to Anna at Wyards:

We told M[r] B. Lefroy that if the weather did not prevent us, we should certainly come & see you tomorrow, & bring Cassy . . . but on giving Cassy her choice of the Fair or Wyards, it must be confessed that she has preferred the former, which we trust will not greatly affront you; – if it does, you may hope that some little Anna hereafter may revenge the insult by a similar preference of an Alton fair to her Cousin Cassy.[14]

It is interesting, incidentally, that little Cassy was given the choice, even though her decision meant altering plans already made by the grown-ups. The following year, when Cassy was again staying with her grandmother and aunts, she inspired a sentence that could well have found its place in a novel – indeed it would not have been inappropriate for the development of Catherine Morland's character. In another note to Anna, Jane wrote: 'Cassy desires her best thanks for the book. She was quite delighted to see it: I do not know when I have seen her so much struck by anybody's kindness as on this occasion. Her sensibility seems to be opening to the perception of great actions.'[15] If her aunt is amused by the disproportionate pleasure shown by the little girl, the irony is self-directed, lying as it does in the even more disproportionate terms employed to convey it.

A child who was lively and forthcoming might cause Jane Austen to look back on herself at a similar age, and with no very great satisfaction. When Francis brought the nine-year-old daughter of his friend Captain Foote to see her, she was pleased by the little girl's lack of self-consciousness. She told Cassandra:

> She is now talking away at my side & examining the Treasures of my Writing-desk drawer; – very happy I believe; – not at all shy of course. . . . What is become of all the Shyness in the World? . . . she is a nice, natural, openhearted, affectionate girl, with all the ready civility which one sees in the best Children of the present day; – so unlike anything that I was myself at her age, that I am often all astonishment & shame.[16]

Jane's memory of herself here seems to accord with cousin Phylly's impression of her. It also anticipates Emma's comment to Miss Bates on the generous salary that Jane Fairfax is to receive as governess to Mrs Smallridge's three little girls: 'Ah! madam,' she says, 'if other children are at all like what I remember to have been myself, I should think five times the amount of what I have ever yet heard named as a salary on such occasions, dearly earned.'[17] Emma was presumably not shy or awkward as a child, as her creator may have been: her fault was no doubt the reverse; but the sense of dissatisfaction with one's younger self, seen through the eyes of maturity, is the same with them both. It is possible of course that in Jane Austen's case her relative quietness may have been attributable to her closeness to an elder sister in whose shadow she was devotedly content to remain; her mother's remark about her having her head cut off certainly suggests that she sought to follow Cassandra rather than compete with her.

Part of her success with children was her imaginative ability to enter into their world, something that Cassandra did not perhaps have to the same degree. Evidence of this is found in many of the letters she wrote to them or in the messages that she included for them in letters to others. Caroline Austen, as she grew up, certainly came to delight her aunt. At the age of ten she became an aunt herself when her half-sister Anna Lefroy's first child was born, and Jane Austen entered into a jocular confederacy with her. She was staying at Chawton, where Jane wrote to her from London. She first admonished her to practise her music and to take care of the pianoforte, 'not letting it be ill used in any respect'. 'Do not allow anything to be put on it but what is very light,' she urged her, adding, perhaps in consideration of the other members of the household, 'I hope you will try to make out some other tune besides the Hermit.' Then, as one aunt to another, she told her: 'Now that you are become an Aunt, you are a person of some consequence & must excite great Interest whatever You do. I have always maintained the importance of Aunts as much as possible, & I am sure of your doing the same now.'[18] Having established a joke, she could keep it going happily; in a subsequent letter to Caroline she wrote: 'The Piano Forte often talks of you; – in various keys, tunes & expressions I allow – but be it Lesson or Country dance, Sonata or Waltz, *You* are really its' constant Theme.'[19] And again, at the end of another letter: 'The Piano Forte's Duty, & will be happy to see you whenever you can come.'[20] Sometimes a message was coded in childish language – 'Nunna Hat's Love to George. – A great many People wanted to mo up in the Poach as well as me';[21] sometimes, as in a New Year greeting to Cassy, a whole letter might be written backwards: 'Ym raed Yssac / I hsiw uoy a yppah wen raey . . .'[22] In these various ways she maintained with her nephews and nieces at a distance the playfulness that she enthusiastically engaged in when she was with them.

The theatricals that had been performed at Steventon in Jane's childhood were revived in the next generation by Edward's family at Godmersham, though not as elaborately as when James had presided over productions of full plays, with the rectory barn fitted up as a theatre. In the summer of 1805, when Fanny was twelve, Mrs Austen, Jane and Cassandra visited, taking Anna with them to relieve James and Mary at the time of Caroline's birth; this offered a splendid opportunity for some acting, and they all entered into the spirit of the thing thoroughly, as did another of Fanny's aunts, Harriet Bridges, her mother and her cousin Fanny Cage. As well as performing short playlets, they improvised scenes, for which they dressed up, as Fanny noted in her diary:

> Aunts and Grandmama played at school with us. Aunt Cassandra was Mrs. Teachum the Governess Aunt Jane, Miss Popham the Teacher Aunt Harriet, Sally the Housemaid, Miss Sharpe, the Dancing master the Apothecary and the Serjeant, Grandmama Betty Jones the Pie woman, and Mama the Bathing woman. They dressed in Character and we had a most delightful day – After dessert we acted a Play called 'Virtue Rewarded'. Anna was Duchess St. Albans, I was the Fairy Serena and Fanny Cage a Sheperdess 'Mona'.[23]

Even without their aunts and grandmother, the Godmersham family enjoyed such entertainments, especially at Twelfth Night, with the Christmas greenery still making the house festive (it is only more recently that decorations came to be taken down on 5 January: in earlier times they stayed up until Candlemas on 2 February). Everyone dressed up as a mythical or fairy-tale character, and they drew lots for King and Queen. In 1806 Fanny and her brother Edward were a shepherd king and queen, and with other characters such as Turk, Harlequin, Witch and Cupid, they were 'conducted into the Library, which was all lighted up, and at one end a throne surrounded with a Grove of Orange Trees and other Shrubs'.[24]

Caroline Austen also remembered dressing up when she was staying at Chawton, particularly if her cousins Cassy and Mary Jane were also staying, and it was always to Aunt Jane that they looked for help: 'She would furnish us with what we wanted from her wardrobe, and she would often be the entertaining visitor in our make beleive house'.[25] Jane Austen's gift for dialogue was also pressed into service when she made up a conversation between Caroline and her cousins, supposedly grown up, the day after a ball (it was, after all, 'absolutely necessary' to meet the next morning to discuss a ball, as the Miss Lucases and the Miss Bennets would agree).[26] The tradition of Austen theatricals continued well into the nineteenth century; in middle age James Edward wrote prologues and epilogues for his own family performances, often when visiting relations or friends, just as his father had at Steventon seventy years before.

If Jane Austen enjoyed large family events, she also liked to entertain children individually, and was resourceful in finding suitable games and toys for them. James Edward testifies to her own adroitness in playing:

> None of us could throw spilikins in so perfect a circle, or take them off with so steady a hand. Her performances with cup and ball were marvellous. The one used at Chawton was an easy one, and she has been known to catch it on the point above an hundred times in succession, till her hand was weary.[27]

As a child, James Edward played well himself, as a letter to his mother from Mrs Austen testified: 'Tell my little Edwd. I am rather mortified at his excelling me in the art of playing at Bilbocatch, I can catch in on the Cup *sometimes*, but on the point *never*'.[28] Besides spillikins and cup and ball (also known as bilbocatch or bilboquet), Jane enjoyed battledore and shuttlecock; playing with her nephew William at Godmersham, she told Cassandra, 'he and I have practised together two mornings, & improve a little; we have frequently kept it up *three* times, & once or twice *six*'.[29] She was not perhaps quite so expert at it as she was at the other games.

The vast increase in the production of consumer goods during the eighteenth century meant that there was a much greater variety of toys available to children than the simple wooden dolls, miniature animals or hobby-horses of earlier periods. As well as having more money to spend, parents, more aware than their forebears of the need for children to be themselves rather than miniature adults, were willing to buy them playthings with which to amuse themselves. Toy soldiers for boys, baby-houses for girls, model gardens or sets of animals imported from Germany, miniature ships, pull-along horses, tops, hoops, kites like the one Mr Weston flew for Emma's nephew, Noah's arks, dolls made of china or wax – all these became normal accessories of the nursery. Sometimes fathers made toys for their children themselves, as Francis Austen did, and as Captain Harville does in *Persuasion*; but for those who wished to buy, there was no shortage of them in establishments such as The Noah's Ark which William Hamley opened in High Holborn in 1760. The impoverished heroine of the early burlesque 'Henry and Eliza', after various misadventures, has to sell her fashionable clothes, and with the money she gets for them she buys 'others more usefull, some playthings for Her Boys and a gold Watch for herself'.[30] This of course is a light-hearted joke; the irony is more biting when the Steele sisters, using children's toys as a means of ingratiating themselves at Barton Park, arrive with the 'whole coach full of playthings for the children', as Sir John Middleton naively informs Elinor and Marianne.[31]

Many toys were expensive, but poor families bought cheap ones made out of paper – soldiers, dolls, rooms with figures to put in them, all engraved on flat sheets that would be cut out and made up by the children at home. A popular paper novelty – though one that was not actually very cheap – was *The History and Adventures of Little Henry*, produced by S. and J. Fuller in 1810; a set of hand-coloured costumes to which Little Henry's head could be attached, it was accompanied by a story in verse, the whole contained in a sturdy slip case. It was followed by *The History of Little Fanny* 'as a Companion to Little Henry'; and in each volume only one head was provided, so that, if it became damaged or lost, replacements had to be cut from coloured prints.

Toys with an obviously educational purpose were also much used. Board games, played on a track with markers and consisting of some kind of race, originated with the Game of Goose, dating from 1597; a new version called 'The Royall & Most Pleasant Game of the Goose' was published by H. Overton about 1750, setting a fashion for such games, some of them designed merely for amusement, others to afford instruction. There were geographical and historical games and later, no doubt in response to the Evangelical revival, games of moral improvement. The earliest of these was 'The New Game of Human Life', published by John Wallis in 1790, in which each panel on the board represented a year of life, depicting diverse human types such as 'The Gallant', 'The Coxcomb', 'The Glutton', 'The Miser', 'The Merry Fellow' and including specific occupations – 'The Poet', 'The Dramatist', 'The Romantic Writer' and so forth. As they moved their 'pillars', as the markers were called, along the board, young players were expected to take note of the lessons to be learned en route: the instructions directed parents to 'cause them to stop at each Character, & request their attention to a few moral and judicious observations, explanatory of each Character as they proceed, & contrast the happiness of a Virtuous & well spent life with the fatal consequences arising from Vicious & Immoral pursuits'.[32] A note on the board warned against one particular immoral pursuit: the purchaser was informed that 'the Totum must be marked with figures 1.2.3.4.5.6. & to avoid introducing a Dice Box into private Families, each Player must spin twice, which will answer the same purpose'. By the 1790s teetotums were used in games of chance in preference to dice, which were considered undesirable since they were liable to encourage gambling, as the young Jane Austen knew: the Johnsons, in another story in the *Juvenilia*, 'Jack and Alice', despite being 'a family of Love' and having 'many good Qualities', are 'a little addicted to the Bottle & the Dice'.[33]

A kind of early jigsaw puzzle (the term itself did not come into use until the middle of the nineteenth century, with the invention of the jig saw, or mechanical fretsaw) was the dissected map, which was very useful for teaching geography. John Spilsbury, a London engraver and map-maker, produced 'Europe, Divided into its Kingdoms, &c.' in 1766; mounted on thin mahogany board which was then cut into pieces round the borders of the kingdoms, it would be reassembled by the child. It is this puzzle that Fanny Price, newly arrived at Mansfield Park, cannot put together, to the astonishment of her cousins Maria and Julia.[34] Puzzle maps were subsequently made for the counties of Great Britain and for countries in other parts of the world. Perhaps the girls' scorn for their ten-year-old cousin's ignorance is not altogether unreasonable, since these maps were so successful that children made progress in their geographical learning at an astounding rate; the poet William Cowper cited a four-year-old boy who knew 'the situation of every kingdom, country, city, river and remarkable mountain in the world' as a result of playing with them.[35] The point is, of course, that Maria and Julia run to their mother with tales of Fanny's failings, rather than sociably playing with the maps with her and showing her how to put them together; the 'great deal of good advice' that Edmund gives her about playing with his sisters might perhaps have been better given to them.[36]

To help children learn to spell there were pictorial alphabet blocks or cards with letters on them. These might be bought, but they could quite easily be made at home, as are the ones that Emma has written out at Hartfield for her nephews, no doubt as one of the distractions from the serious reading that Mr Knightley thinks she ought to be doing. This game of alphabets was a simple one and its educational purpose equally simple and innocent; but in *Emma* we do not see the children playing it. It is the adults who amuse, or torment, each other with the letters, and there is a considerable irony in the observation that 'the quietness of the game made it particularly eligible for Mr. Woodhouse, who had often been distressed by the more animated sort, which Mr. Weston had occasionally introduced'.[37] Frank Churchill has already discovered the potential of the children's alphabets as a source of adult teasing: 'We had great amusement with those letters one morning,' he says. 'I want to puzzle you again.' Now, as Frank, playing his double game with Emma and Jane Fairfax, forms his words, the emotions of at least some of the players are anything but quiet. Mr Knightley, grasping for clues to a game whose rules he cannot understand but perceives to be duplicitous, rightly sees the letters to be 'but a vehicle for gallantry and trick', a 'child's play, chosen to conceal a deeper game on Frank Churchill's part'. Apart from the game of speculation in *Mansfield Park* (which is also made to bear the weight of serious adult concerns), this is the most sustained use of a game that Jane Austen makes in any of the novels. Since the letters, which are intended to enlighten a child, are here employed for purposes of obfuscation, the game both subverts an innocent purpose and serves to reflect badly on the heroine, thus matching the other games played in the book – Mr Elton's charade, which Emma solves but whose dedication she disastrously misinterprets; Mr Weston's conundrum, in which the perfection of 'M. and A. – Em – ma' comes too soon; and the invitation to say 'one thing very clever . . . two things moderately clever – or three things very dull indeed' that results in Emma's cruel remark to Miss Bates. And there is one further irony about the alphabets game: the letters almost fulfil their function, since by observing the words that Frank places on the table Mr Knightley comes very close to spelling out the central mystery of the novel.

Some games of an educational kind could be played without any materials at all. Agnes Porter, governess to Lord Ilchester's children at Redlynch in Somerset, used to test her pupils' memory for historic events by getting each of them in turn to think of some particular feature of a story from history which would then have to be guessed by the others. On 14 May 1791 she noted in her diary:

> With my pupils. Our studies successful – played at our old historic game. My thought was Cesar's robe when killed; Lady Elizabeth's Mahomet's shoulder of mutton which had announced itself poisoned; Lady Mary's the pigeon which was killed by a hawk and dropt some blood on Bernini's bust of Charles I.[38]

Card games were naturally a ready resource in entertaining children, just as they were for adults. At Eastwell Park, in Kent, Jane Austen played cribbage with fourteen-year-old George Finch-Hatton and his ten-year-old brother Daniel; 'George is a fine boy,' she told Cassandra, '& well behaved, but Daniel chiefly delighted me; the good humour of his countenance is quite bewitching. After tea we had a Cribbage Table, & he & I won two rubbers of his brother & [his aunt] Mrs Mary.'[39] With her nephew George she played speculation; 'it was so highly approved that we hardly knew how to leave off'.[40] This game, which is played by first bidding for cards before beginning to take tricks, was obviously a favourite of hers. In addition to the use she makes of it in *Mansfield Park*, she referred to it in several of her letters. Writing to Cassandra, who was staying at Godmersham, she said that she hoped speculation was 'generally liked';[41] and when she heard from her that another game, brag, was now being played by the family, she replied with some characteristic nonsense that was clearly meant to be relayed to her nephews:

> The preference of Brag over Speculation does not greatly surprise me I believe, because I feel the same myself; but it mortifies me deeply, because Speculation was under my patronage; – & after all, what is there so delightful in a pair-royal of Braggers? it is but three nines, or three Knaves, or a mixture of them. – When one comes to reason upon it, it cannot stand its' ground against Speculation – of which I hope Edward is now convinced. Give my love to him, if he is.[42]

A few days later she followed this up in another letter:

I have just received some verses in an unknown hand, & am desired to forward them to my nephew Edw[d] at Godmersham. – 'Alas! poor Brag, thou boastful Game! What now avails thine empty name? – Where now thy more distinguish'd fame? – My day is o'er, & Thine the same. – For thou like me art thrown aside, At Godmersham, this Christmas Tide; And now across the Table wide, Each Game save Brag or Spec: is tried.' – 'Such is the mild Ejaculation, Of tender hearted Speculation.' [43]

There were also plenty of sports and physical activities that children could take part in, either on their own or in teams. At the age of fourteen, we are told, Catherine Morland liked 'cricket, base ball, riding on horseback, and running about the country'.[44]

Cricket was predominantly, though by no means exclusively, a boy's game; and Jane Austen specifically says that as a little girl Catherine 'was fond of all boys' plays, and greatly preferred cricket not merely to dolls, but to the more heroic enjoyments of infancy, nursing a dormouse, feeding a canary-bird, or watering a rose-bush'.[45] But cricket was also regularly played by women, as is clear from an amusing print by Thomas Rowlandson recording a 'Cricket Match Extraordinary' that took place at Balls Pond, Newington on Wednesday 3 October 1811. The caption informs us that 'The Players on both sides were 22 Women, 11 Hampshire against 11 Surrey. The Match was made between The Amateur Noblemen of the respective Committees for 500 guineas stake [?]. The Performers in the Contest were of all Ages and Sizes.'[46] Rowlandson is of course making fun of an adult match, but another picture, a painting of the Tyndall family of Royal Fort House, Bristol, dating from 1800, shows several of the children holding cricket paraphernalia, among them one of the little girls.[47] Base ball, a kind of rounders, was played by the batsman hitting the ball and then trying to run to the next position before he could be caught out; John Newbery's *A Little Pretty Pocket-Book* of 1744, illustrating the game, has the rhyme:

The *Ball* once struck off,
Away flies the *Boy*
To the next destin'd Post,
And then Home with Joy.[48]

The *Pocket-Book* provides pictures and rhymes for all sorts of children's games. While some of them, such as marbles, flying the kite, leap-frog, blindman's buff or hopscotch, are still played today, others sound less familiar to our ears; hoop and hide, peg-farthing, stool-ball, trap-ball, tip-cat, hop-hay and all the birds in the air are unlikely to have been played within living memory.

Traditional games and sports, some of them rather rudimentary, were played in country areas, when the local squire provided entertainment for his tenants or farm workers. There was just such an occasion at Steventon on Saturday 17 July 1813, given by Francis Digweed, tenant of the manor, to his haymakers when all the hay had been cut. Twelve-year-old William Heathcote went with his friend

James Edward and later gave an account of the 'merry making' to his cousin Margaret Blackstone:

> There were donkey-races, merely for the sport; old women to wheel barrow blind folded, for two little ribbon bows, young women to run a race for a straw bonnet, girls for two pink ribbons, boys to run in sacks for harvest *gloves* not *bugs*, to roll down an hill for a plum pudding and to run a race for an handkerchief, & lastly to dip their heads into a bucket of water for some oranges. I got a donkey lent me to run, the one I used to ride [James] Edward Austen was my jockey, he was dressed in this manner; he had a black velvet cap, with a yellow button on the top, & a yellow band in front, & buff coat with black sleeves, we managed that in this manner, first he put on a black velvet spencer of Mrs Austen's, & over that, a buff waistcoat, it looked very well I assure you. I think you would be quite amused to see the two old women wheel their barrows, in one part of the field there was a rake, to which the prizes were hung, which was the goal, & another stick for the starting post, they did not run a race all at the same time, as perhaps you suppose, but one at a time & they (not seeing the goal) but go on as long as they liked & stop whenever they thought they were near the end of their journey, so that some women, by letting one hand lower than the other might turn their barrows completely round thinking that they were as straight as any of them all the time, when all had done they measured the distance of each woman's barrow from the goal, & that one which was the nearest obtained the prize.[49]

While some toys and games had an overtly instructive purpose and others were purely recreational, there was a view that all kinds of play could be educational in a moral sense. The Edgeworths, in *Practical Education*, discussed the attitudes that children took to their playthings, and what lessons a parent might draw from them. As a child stands 'idle and miserable, surrounded by disjointed dolls, maimed horses, coaches and one-horse chairs without wheels, and a nameless wreck of gilded lumber', his mother asks 'Why don't you play with your playthings, my dear? I am sure that I have bought toys enough for you; why can't you divert yourself with them, instead of breaking them to pieces?'[50] The answer is that he breaks them

> not from the love of mischief, but from the hatred of idleness; either he wishes to see what his playthings are made of, and how they are made, or whether he can put them together again if the parts be once separated. All this is perfectly innocent; and it is a pity that his love of knowledge and his spirit of activity should be repressed . . .

The nature of the toys that a child was given had to be carefully considered:

> A boy, who has the use of his limbs, and whose mind is untainted with prejudice, would in all probability prefer a substantial cart, in which he could carry weeds, earth, and stones, up and down hill, to the finest frail coach-and-six that ever came out of a toyshop: for what could he do with the coach after having admired, and sucked the paint, but drag it

cautiously along the carpet of a drawing-room, watching the wheels, which will not turn, and seeming to sympathize with the just terrors of the lady and gentleman within, who are certain of being overturned every five minutes. When he is tired of this, perhaps, he may set about to unharness horses which were never meant to be unharnessed; or to currycomb their woollen manes and tails, which usually come off during the first attempt.

This leads the Edgeworths to a rather surprising conclusion:

That such toys are frail and useless may, however, be considered as evils comparatively small: as long as a child has sense and courage to destroy the toys, there is no great harm done; but in general, he is taught to set a value upon them totally independent of all ideas of utility, or of any regard to his own real feelings . . .

Nor is it only destructive little boys who are deemed to be in greater danger from the imposition of a false sense of values than from being encouraged to give way to their 'real feelings':

A little girl, presiding at her baby tea-table, is pleased with the notion that she is like her mamma; and, before she can have any idea of the real pleasures of conversation and society, she is confirmed in the persuasion, that tattling and visiting are some of the most enviable privileges of grown people: a set of beings whom she believes to be in possession of all the sweets of happiness.

Dolls, boasting not only the 'right of ancient usage' but the approval of Rousseau, are allowed, somewhat reluctantly, to have their 'utility', since they are 'the means of inspiring girls with a taste for neatness in dress, and with a desire to make those things for themselves, for which women are usually dependent upon milliners'; nevertheless, 'a watchful eye should be kept upon the child to mark the first symptoms of finery and fashion'.[51] Baby-houses, however, are unreservedly condemned, for although 'an unfinished baby-house might be a good toy, as it would employ little carpenters and sempstresses to fit it up', a completely finished one

proves as tiresome to a child as a finished seat is to a young nobleman. After peeping, for in general only a peep can be had into each apartment, after being thoroughly satisfied that nothing is wanting, and that consequently there is nothing to be done, the young lady lays her doll upon the state bed, if the doll be not twice as large as the bed, and falls fast asleep in the midst of her felicity.

Mechanical toys, very popular at the time, come in for the same criticism: they fail to engage the child's interest after the initial pleasure gained from playing with them. Though they are 'ingenious in their construction, and happy in their effect,

that effect unfortunately is transitory. When the wooden woman has churned her hour in her empty churn; when the stiff-backed man has hammered or sawed till his arms are broken, or till his employer's arms are tired; when the gilt lamb has ba-ed, the obstinate pig squeaked, and the provoking cuckoo cried cuck-oo, till no one in the house can endure the noise; what remains to be done? – Woe betide the unlucky little philosopher, who should think of inquiring why the woman churned, or how the bird cried cuckoo; for it is ten to one that in prosecuting such an inquiry, just when he is upon the eve of discovery, he snaps the wire, or perforates the bellows . . .'

The Edgeworths consider useful, instructive pursuits to be the most desirable – prints, modelling in clay or wax, basket-making or weaving of cord for sash windows; toys must be ones that 'afford trials of dexterity and activity, such as tops, kites, hoops, balls, battledores and shuttlecocks, ninepins, and cup and ball', all of which are 'great and lasting favourites with children';[52] and they also recommend gardening, making model furniture and machinery, chemical toys, dye-making, fossils and microscopes.

For much of the time, children were expected to keep themselves amused and to find activities by which they could do so. Girls naturally had their 'work', or needlework, from an early age; Jane Austen sent some to Caroline from seven-year-old Cassy, telling her that she had 'had great pleasure working this – whatever it may be – for you', adding encouragingly, 'I beleive she rather fancied it might do for a quilt for your little wax doll, but you will find a use for it if you can I am sure'.[53] Boys also worked with a needle. At the age of ten, Edward's son William occupied himself with cross-stitch while he was ill; Jane commented that it must have been a comfort to him. Subsequently she learnt that he was working a footstool to be given as a present at Chawton, and she reacted with a certain wry amusement: 'I am sure his Grandmama will value it very much as a proof of his affection & Industry – but we shall never have the heart to put our feet upon it. – I beleive I must work a muslin cover in sattin stitch, to keep it from the dirt. – I long to know what his colours are – I guess greens & purples.'[54]

When Edward Austen's wife died in October 1808, there was naturally immediate concern for the young children she left behind her. Cassandra was already staying at Godmersham, where she had arrived just after the birth of the baby whose coming precipitated its mother's death. The two eldest boys, Edward and George, were at Winchester, and since it was too far for them to go home to Kent, they went to James and Mary at Steventon. Their Aunt Cassandra wrote to them at the college, and the letter was forwarded to them; and soon afterwards Edward had a letter from his father. Meanwhile, Mary wrote to Mrs Austen to ask whether she wished to have her grandsons at Southampton, but for the time being it was felt that they would be better off where they were, which, Jane told Cassandra, she hoped her brother would approve of:

I am sure he will do us the justice of beleiving that in such a decision we sacrificed inclination to what we thought best. – I shall write by the Coach tomorrow to Mrs J.A. & to Edward about their mourning . . . I shall certainly make use of the opportunity of addressing our Nephew on the most serious of all concerns, as I naturally did in my Letter to him before. The poor Boys are perhaps more comfortable at Steventon than they could be here, but you will understand *my feelings* with respect to it.[55]

The following week, however, they did go to Southampton on their way back to school. The letter Jane sent to Cassandra provides a touching picture of the bereaved boys, and of the care that was taken of them.[56] She began with a description of their arrival:

> Edward and George came to us soon after seven on Saturday, very well, but very cold, having by choice travelled on the outside, and with no great coat but what Mr Wise, the coachman, good-naturedly spared them of his, as they sat by his side. They were so much chilled when they arrived, that I was afraid they must have taken cold; but it does not seem at all the case; I never saw them looking better.

A letter from Edward had arrived and Jane knew that Cassandra would want to know – and to be able to tell him – how the boys had taken it.

> *They behave extremely* well in every respect, showing quite as much feeling as one wishes to see, and on every occasion speaking of their father with the liveliest affection. His letter was read over by each of them yesterday, and with many tears; George sobbed aloud, Edward's tears do not flow so easily; but as far as I can judge they are both very properly impressed by what has happened.

She saw that they had plenty to do, to take their minds off their sadness, as far as possible:

> We do not want amusement: bilbocatch, at which George is indefatigable, spillikins, paper ships, riddles, conundrums, and cards, while watching the flow and ebb of the river, and now and then a stroll out, keep us well employed . . .

Their mourning had to be sorted out; a letter arrived from Fanny, which Edward intended to answer soon; and on Sunday morning Jane took her nephews to church, where

> *Edward was much affected by the sermon, which, indeed I could have supposed purposely addressed* to the afflicted, if the text had not naturally come in the course of Dr Mant's observations on the Litany: 'All that are in danger, necessity, or tribulation,' was the subject of it. The weather did not allow us afterwards to get farther than the quay, where George was very happy as long as we could stay, flying about from one side to the other, and skipping on board a collier immediately.

In the evening they stayed at home and read the Psalms and Lessons for Evening Prayer, and a sermon, 'to which they were very attentive'; but, Jane added, 'you will not expect to hear that they did not return to conundrums the moment it *was over*. And with a fine novelist's eye she conveyed to Cassandra a description of the scene before her:

> While I write now, George is most industriously making and naming paper ships, at which he afterwards shoots with horse-chestnuts, brought from Steventon on purpose; and Edward equally intent over the 'Lake of Killarney,' [a novel by Anna Maria Porter] twisting himself about in one of our great chairs.

A less tranquil scene is described in *Persuasion*, when Anne and Lady Russell visit Uppercross at Christmas time:

> Immediately surrounding Mrs. Musgrove were the little Harvilles, whom she was sedu-lously guarding from the tyranny of the two children from the Cottage, expressly arrived to amuse them. On one side was a table, occupied by some chattering girls, cutting up silk and gold paper; and on the other were tressels and trays, bending under the weight of brawn and cold pies, where riotous boys were holding high revel . . . Mr. Musgrove made a point of paying his respects to Lady Russell, and sat down close to her for ten minutes, talking with a very raised voice, but, from the clamour of the children on his knees, generally in vain. It was a fine family-piece.[57]

It would have been perfectly possible for Jane Austen to be specific about who the various children are, but the lack of identification and the vagueness even as to number add to the sense of confusion and noise that leads Lady Russell to comment dryly when they leave that she hopes she will remember in future 'not to call at Uppercross in the Christmas holidays'. The 'tyranny' of Mary Musgrove's two children is amusing not only because it is directed at the little Harvilles whom they have been brought on purpose to play with, but also because it is so much in character.

The satirical delight which Jane Austen took in children behaving in character is evident in a number of places in the novels. In *Emma* when Harriet and Miss Bickerton have been frightened by the gipsies and the alarming news relayed to Hartfield so that 'poor Mr. Woodhouse trembled as he sat', long after 'the whole history' has 'dwindled . . . into a matter of little importance but to Emma and her nephews', 'Henry and John were still asking every day for the story of Harriet and the gipsies, and still tenaciously setting her right if she varied in the slightest particular from the original recital'.[58] Catherine Morland, whose unsuitability for the role of stock literary heroine is established by the ironic delineation of her entirely realistic childhood, is inattentive to lessons, picks flowers that she is told not to, hates music lessons and has no talent for drawing, 'though whenever she could obtain the outside of a letter from her mother, or seize upon any other odd piece of paper, she did what she could in that way, by drawing houses and trees, hens and chickens, all very much like one another'.[59] Julia Bertram torments her mother's pug and works a footstool so badly that it cannot be put in the drawing-room; Fanny's young brothers Tom and Charles are 'quite untameable by any means of address which she had spirits or time to attempt', every afternoon bringing 'a return of their riotous games all over the house', while her little sister Betsey is, as we have seen, a thoroughly 'spoilt child'.[60] If any general point can be made about Jane Austen's expectations of children, it is that if they are not kept under control they will behave in a very disorderly way and make a great deal of noise.

The person expected to control them, at least in well-to-do households, was the governess. For some, such as Agnes Porter, with the Earl of Ilchester's children at Redlynch, this seems to have been as much a pleasure as a duty: 'My lovely little girls well and happy', she wrote in her diary on 21 July 1791:

> Dear little Lady Susan grows much stronger, and every morning pays me a visit for the pleasure of thumping an old spinet in my room with her dear little hands. She will not go past my room door till she has had this satisfaction, and must have a book before her when she plays, to imitate her sisters . . . Looked in upon my dear children, as I constantly do the last thing before I go to bed. All well, thank God.[61]

Elizabeth Ham, engaged in 1822 by Charles Abraham Elton, son of the Revd Sir Abraham Elton, Bt of Clevedon Court, as governess to his daughters, was equally happy, though at first she felt rather overwhelmed by what she had taken on; as she wrote later in her memoir, 'seven girls of all ages is no trifle to undertake the finding of work for without confusion'.[62] Like Agnes Porter, she found herself loved by her young pupils, 'who', she remembered, 'all seemed to take to me very kindly'. There were two pairs of twins in the family, Caroline Lucy and Lucy Caroline, and Maria Catherine and Catherine Maria; the younger ones seemed to her to be particularly her children, since 'instead of getting away from their governess, like other children, when they could, they were always clinging to me'.[63]

Until the middle of the eighteenth century, the education of children was largely the responsibility of their mother, though their father might also have a hand in it. Up to the age of seven the elementary education of boys and girls was carried out at home; thereafter boys were generally sent to school (unless like Mr Austen their father himself took in pupils) and girls remained behind to be prepared for their future, which if they were from a wealthy family was the hope of a good marriage, and if they were not was probably some useful kind of work. From about the 1770s, people who could afford it began to employ governesses, who previously would have been brought in only where the mother had died or was an invalid; young unmarried women from respectable families in need of work and, later, émigrées fleeing from the French Revolution, ensured a ready supply. Wages varied considerably. While Nelly Weeton knew of someone who paid her governess only £12 a year, she herself asked and received 30 guineas;[64] Agnes Porter, when she became governess to the family of her own former pupil Lady Mary Talbot at Penrice Castle in 1799, was paid £100 a year – and even this was considerably less than the £300 recommended by the Edgeworths.[65]

The system did not always produce satisfactory results. Mary Wollstonecraft, who had, like her sisters, been a governess herself, testified in the *Vindication of the Rights of Woman* to its dangers if it was not carried out with a proper concern for the development of the intellect, or, as she describes it, 'the power of gaining general or abstract ideas', by reading:

> I have known several notable women, and one in particular, who was a very good woman – as good as such a narrow mind would allow her to be, who took care that her daughters (three in number) should never see a novel. As she was a woman of fortune and fashion, they had various masters to attend them, and a sort of menial governess to watch their footsteps. From their masters they learned how tables, chairs, &c. were called in French and Italian; but as the few books thrown in their way were far above their capacities, or devotional, they neither acquired ideas nor sentiments, and passed their time, when not compelled to repeat *words*, in dressing, quarrelling with each other, or conversing with their maids by stealth, till they were brought into company as marriageable . . . And these young ladies, with minds vulgar in every sense of the word, and spoiled tempers, entered life puffed up with notions of their own consequence, and looking down with contempt on those who could not vie with them in dress and parade.[66]

Mary Wollstonecraft was in many ways exceptional in her grasp of the desirability of developing the intellectual powers of young girls, and there were plenty of women whose own inferior education rendered them little better than 'menials' when they in turn became responsible for the education of the young. Nevertheless, she was not alone in understanding that growing minds needed something more to nourish them than the mere mechanical repetition of words in foreign languages. Governesses at their most ambitious saw to it that their pupils were stretched far more than is allowed for in this description, and the role remained crucial in the education of children right up to the First World War.

In the very highest circles, ample provision was made for governesses, and their duties were formally and efficiently laid down. George III and Queen Charlotte were intelligent and high-minded parents who wished to see their children subjected to a proper system which, though it inevitably depended on the efforts of those who carried it out, was intended to give them a balanced and rounded education. The two eldest princes were kept in the hands of their governess, Lady Charlotte Finch, for some time longer than was usual with boys before giving their education over to tutors; but when they were eventually taken away from her, their new regime was to prove considerably harsher than the one they were used to, since the tutors appointed to oversee their lessons were told by the King to beat them when they needed punishing. The princesses fared considerably better in this respect, and they became very fond of the succession of governesses who, under orders from the Queen and Lady Charlotte, read English, European and classical literature with them, so that they would learn something more than the accomplishments of music, dancing, drawing and needlework that were the sole proficiencies of so many young ladies. Lady Charlotte (whose daughter, Mrs Sophia Fielding, a Woman of the Bedchamber to the Queen, was an aunt by marriage of Edward Austen's wife Elizabeth Bridges, and was known to Jane Austen) was an intelligent and enlightened woman whose interests extended to natural sciences, in particular botany, which, with the encouragement of Sir Joseph Banks, director of the royal gardens at Kew, became a great enthusiasm of the Queen and her daughters.

Punishment for the princesses was more a matter of conscience-searching than the physical chastisement meted out to their brothers – and indeed to many children of both sexes in lesser families. Following a bout of bad behaviour to the sub-governess, Martha Gouldsworthy, and her assistant Mary Hamilton, a contrite Princess Augusta, aged nine, wrote to the latter:

> My dear Miss Hamilton, I am very sorry for the blow I gave to you the night before last. I am very sorry indeed, and promise I won't do so any more. I have written to Gouly and she has forgiven me, because I have been very good with every body and her too . . . I read very well, and I said my verses well also. I beg you will forgive me, for indeed I will be very good to you, and I will mind every thing you bid me. I am very sorry that I hurt Miss Gouldsworthy. I promise you I won't do so any more. But I hope I have not hurt you, and I was very sorry to find you put brown paper and arquebade upon your breast. I hope it will be of no consequence to you for I assure you that if it is, it will make me very unhappy. I am you affectionate Augusta Sophia.[67]

At the other end of the scale was Nelly Weeton. The daughter of a sea captain, who died when she was six, and a former lady's maid, Nelly chose to be a governess as a way of escaping from a life rendered lonely by the hostility of a younger brother whom she nevertheless doted on. She went to a family in the Lake District, where as well as being governess to a little girl who suffered epileptic fits, she was made responsible for the direction of the household, since her employer's wife, a former dairymaid, was very young and completely inexperienced. When in the course of a fit the child fell into the fire and subsequently died of her injuries, Nelly stayed on as companion to her mother, until the unpredictable temper of her father, exacerbated by drink, forced her to leave. She took up a new post with a family near Huddersfield, where despite long hours and a lack of interest on the part of her employers in what she was teaching the children, she was more or less happy; 'I am too comfortable here,' she told a friend, 'to have any thought of leaving . . . I love my little pupils, and receive many an affectionate embrace from them.'[68]

In one respect Nelly's situation was less awkward than that of other young women in her position. Not having been born into the world of the gentry, she did not suffer from the indignity experienced by many governesses who, driven by financial necessity into the only profession open to them, found themselves in a distinctly ambivalent position in the household. No longer accepted as being on the same level as the family who employed them, they were also distrusted, and often resented, by the servants, and thus found themselves isolated from everybody about them except the children. Elizabeth Ham, who came from a similar level of society to Nelly Weeton (though from a much happier family), was uneasy about this when she went to work for the Eltons:

> Mrs. Elton frightened me a great deal at first by her warnings about the Head Nurse, who, being an old and indulged servant, she said, liked to have her own way, and would, probably, be very jealous of anyone interfering with the children, but I was not to mind this. She likewise gently cautioned me against being too familiar with the servants, but this she might well have spared had she known me.
>
> Mrs. E's caution made me recall all the stories I had ever heard or read about the young ladies who had become obnoxious to lady's maids, and such like, having had jewels concealed in their drawers etc., so I always kept mine carefully locked, not to prevent anything being abstracted, but fearing that something might be unlawfully insinuated therein. But all undue apprehension soon ceased. After Mrs. Elton had shown her maternal care by making her wishes known to me, and her good sense enabled her, together with her experience, to give me many valuable hints, she left me the management of the children pretty much to myself. And as to Mrs. Mary, the formidable nurse, she was such a simple-minded, honest creature, that she soon came to consult me in all her difficulties about the children, instead of going to their mother. The whole family seemed to have become attached to me at once. No one could imagine the relief it was to me to find myself a *valued* inmate in a family of 'real gentlefolks', well informed and well bred. Intellectual conversation was such a treat to me, and I was treated with so much consideration that I cared nothing for my somewhat onerous duties.[69]

Elizabeth was fortunate to find herself in an unusually gifted and literary family. Charles Abraham Elton, described by Macaulay as 'the first of our minor poets',[70] was prominent in literary circles in Bristol; a contributor to the *London Magazine*, he was a friend of Charles Lamb and John Clare, he knew de Quincey, Hazlitt and Tom Hood, and his brother-in-law was the historian Henry Hallam, father of Tennyson's beloved friend Arthur. In 1824 the Bristol artist E. P. Rippingille depicted Elton and various members of his family among his literary friends and acquaintances in *The Travellers' Breakfast*, a painting of an imaginary scene taking place in a Bristol inn, in which as well as Lamb, Clare and himself, he depicted Southey, Joseph Cottle, the publisher of the *Lyrical Ballads*, and, for good measure (though they had long since left Bristol), Coleridge, Wordsworth and his sister Dorothy.[71] Having become a Unitarian, Elton had a difficult relationship with his High Church father, the Revd Sir Abraham, and with a large family to provide for, money was in short supply; furthermore, just before Elizabeth Ham came to them, the two eldest boys had been drowned when swimming off Birnbeck Island at Weston-super-Mare, a tragedy about which Mrs Elton talked to Elizabeth, since she seems to have made something of a confidante of her. Yet Elizabeth had no illusions about her position in the family, and she judiciously summed up her employers and their view of her:

Mrs. Elton was very amiable, with more worldly wisdom than her husband, and possessing a much better temper. But he had more good nature, was more impulsive, and open as day. I soon saw that Mrs. E. did not wish that I should be treated with quite so much consideration as he wished, and she was right. But it was natural, at that time, that my liking should preponderate where I seemed to be most valued.[72]

When Mrs Elton first interviewed Elizabeth Ham, she sensibly spelt out the extent to which the new governess would be expected, or permitted, to share the life of the family:

She spoke with perfect frankness of all that would be required, said that I should take my dinner with them, and that they should be happy with my company in the drawing room till after tea, when I might like to be alone myself, and Mr. Elton would prefer having his eldest daughters left without any restraint in their parents' company, that they should always be happy to have me with them when they had other company.[73]

Nelly Weeton was not so fortunate and suffered evenings of intense loneliness. 'I sit alone in the evening, in the schoolroom,' she wrote in her diary. 'Really I should be very glad of some society in an evening, it would be such an enjoyment, but there is nobody in the house with whom I can be on equal terms, and I know nobody out of it, so I must make myself contented.'[74]

The daily regime in the schoolroom was long and, if conscientiously carried out, quite demanding. The children would be heard saying their prayers at seven o'clock in the morning, and after breakfast and perhaps some play out of doors, lessons would last from nine until dinner between one and two; there would then possibly be walks, followed by more lessons until it was time for them to have their supper and say their prayers again before being put to bed. In more enlightened families, who employed knowledgeable governesses, history, geography, botany and arithmetic would be added to the reading and languages that were the academic staple of girls' education. Agnes Porter, beloved by two generations of the Fox-Strangways and Talbot families, kept her pupils on their toes, as she reported to their mother, Lady Mary Talbot: 'Miss Jane finds herself forced to lend her attention, as I frequently ask her the impertinent questions of "Who was this person? What was his motive? How did it succeed?" And so on.' But it would not do for the child (then aged fourteen) to dawdle in bed reading: 'Her delight is Shakespear, which I cruelly tore from her bosom in bed this morning, telling her that Shakespear loved *rising* early.'[75]

Though, as we know, children were generally discouraged from being on friendly terms with servants, governesses were another matter. Having had so much of their attention from an early age, it was inevitable that they should form a strong bond with them; and while the governess often observed a certain etiquette with her pupils (for example Agnes Porter writes of 'Miss Jane', rather than simply 'Jane'),[76] the fact that she was considered to belong to the gentry meant that a friendship was permitted to develop, and this could well continue into later life.

When a governess left, she was often much missed, particularly if her charges were still young. 'Poor dear Miss Laborde went away,' wrote the thirteen-year-old Sophia Baker in her diary in 1794. 'We were very sorry to part with Miss Laborde, as she was a good governess . . . and gave us all the little comforts she could think of. Oh when shall we get used to another governess?'[77] It was even more distressing to a child if a governess died; this happened to the six-year-old Susan Sibbald, and her grief was hardly lessened by the fact that the unfortunate woman's successor, Miss Kettle, was so inadequate that she had to be dismissed.

Eventually, of course, the time came when a pupil grew up, went out into the world, and the governess left anyway; and then, surprisingly often, they kept up the acquaintance. Such was the case with Jane Austen's niece Fanny Knight. Her early governess, Dorothy Chapman, was only eleven years older than she was, and after she left Godmersham, about 1803, when Fanny was ten, they started a regular correspondence that lasted for over fifty years, ending only with Miss Chapman's death in 1857. All Fanny's letters – more than 150 – were preserved by Miss Chapman, and after she died they were returned; together with Fanny's diaries, they provide an invaluable account of the Knight and Knatchbull families during the first half of the nineteenth century.[78]

The reason for Miss Chapman's leaving is unknown, but in January 1804 Fanny wrote to tell her of the arrival of a new governess, and one whom she clearly liked:

> I am happy to tell you that Miss Sharpe is come at last I say happy and mean so . . . I find her even more good-natured than I expected; . . . I think Miss Sharpe pretty but not strikingly so; she is in mourning & I think it becomes her.[79]

Anne Sharp was a kindly, sensitive and well-educated woman, but her health was delicate, and she stayed at Godmersham for only two years. During that time, however, she found kindred spirits in her employer's sisters when they came to visit. Jane and Cassandra Austen had not had a governess themselves, but they both came to know Miss Sharp extremely well, and they formed a lasting friendship. They wrote to each other, and she visited Chawton. It is not altogether easy, however, to form an objective view of her character. On a visit to Chawton in 1820, she was found by James Edward to be 'horridly affected but rather amusing';[80] and Jane relayed her constant complaints about her health to Cassandra with a characteristic hint of comedy: 'I have,' she told her in September 1816,

> a letter from Miss Sharp, quite one of her Letters; – she has been again obliged to exert herself – more than ever – in a more distressing, more harassed state – & has met with another excellent old Physician and his Wife, with every virtue under Heaven, who takes her & cures her from pure Love & Benevolence . . . I am happy to say however that the sum of the account is better than usual.[81]

Something of the affectedness that James Edward was to find is perhaps reflected in Jane's tone here, as well as a genuine concern for her welfare.

Yet there appears to have been a real intimacy between them, and she was among the people from whom Jane sought opinions of her work. When *Mansfield Park* was published, she sent her a copy, asking her to be 'perfectly honest' about what she thought of it, and there was certainly nothing affected about her reply: 'I think it excellent,' she wrote, '& of it's good sense & moral Tendency there can be no doubt. – Your Characters are drawn to the Life – so *very, very* natural & just – but as you beg me to be perfectly honest, I must confess I prefer P & P.'[82] Her views about *Emma*, as noted down by Jane, were equally firm: she liked it 'better than MP. – but not so well as P. & P. – pleased with the Heroine for her Originality, delighted with M^r K – & called Mrs Elton beyond praise. – dissatisfied with Jane Fairfax.'[83] *Pride and Prejudice* was clearly the book about which she was most enthusiastic: 'Oh! I have more of such sweet flattery from Miss Sharp!' Jane told Cassandra after its publication. 'She is an excellent kind friend.'[84] Eventually they were on Christian name terms, and Jane was willing to discuss delicate family matters with her. In a letter written less than seven weeks before she died, in which she calls her 'my dearest Anne', she makes critical remarks about Mary Lloyd, as well as referring to the disappointment of her uncle Mr Leigh Perrot's will, which Anne Sharp clearly already knew all about.[85] After Jane's death, Cassandra sent her a lock of her hair and some other mementoes, telling her: 'I know how these articles, trifling as they are, will be valued by you & I am very sure that if she is now conscious of what is passing on earth it gives her pleasure they should be so disposed of.'[86]

Miss Sharp was succeeded at Godmersham by Mrs Morris, a woman with children of her own then away at boarding school. Fanny took to her immediately, but after three years she left to go to Brazil in the service of the British Consul; no one was appointed for some time, since as Fanny observed in a letter to Miss Chapman 'it is such a bore changing and having new people.'[87] Following Elizabeth Austen's death in October 1808, the older girls were sent away to school, and she took on some of the responsibility for the younger ones herself. At last, on 27 April 1811, a new governess came. 'Miss Allen actually arrived just as we had done dinner!' she noted in her diary that day. 'I almost died of fright, and she seemed nearly as bad.'[88] The signs were not promising. In the same entry Fanny commented: 'Dull evening – she will not talk.' Interestingly, Cassandra, who was staying at Godmersham, must have formed a far more favourable impression, since three days later Jane wrote to her 'I like your opinion of Miss Allen much better than I expected, & have now hopes of her staying a whole twelvemonth.' And she added, 'By this time I suppose she is hard at it, governing away – poor creature! I pity her, tho' they *are* my nieces.'[89] But it was Fanny rather than Cassandra who proved to be right about her; she did in fact stay for more than a twelvemonth, but it was not a happy time and eventually, in November of the following year, 'after much vile behaviour', she 'treated Lizzy so ill that it was resolved she should go away on Wednesday next'.[90]

With four little girls in the family still under the age of thirteen, however, it was necessary to replace her, and by the beginning of February another governess had been found; in the event she was to prove longer-lasting than any of her predecessors, eventually staying with the Knights for seven years. Fanny described her as 'quite a treasure'.[91] Jane, writing to tell Cassandra the news, employed the humour that seems to have been her habitual tone when discussing governesses:

> Miss Clewes seems the very Governess they have been looking for these ten years; – longer coming than J. Bond's last Shock of Corn. – If she will but only keep Good & Amiable & Perfect! – Clewes . . . is better than Clowes. – And is not it a name for Edward to pun on? – is not a Clew a Nail?[92]

Despite Miss Clewes's satisfactory service at Godmersham, Jane did not make a particular friend of her as she had of Miss Sharp; but while she was staying there she was quite happy to dine with her when the rest of the family spent a day away from home ('I dare say I shall find her very agreeable,' she told Cassandra)[93] or to sit with her at a concert in Canterbury to which she has been invited to go in place of Edward. Yet there is a hint of mockery in Jane's tone when she relayed her good wishes to Cassandra: 'Miss Clewes begs me to give her very best respects to you; she is very much obliged to you for your kind enquiries after her';[94] and her real indifference to her emerges in a letter of March 1817 in reply to something that Fanny had reported to her, when she says crisply, 'Poor Miss C. – I shall pity her, when she begins to understand herself.' Probably Miss Clewes was more self-conscious than Miss Sharp about her subservient role in the family, and this must have made her ill at ease with Jane and Cassandra. On the sheet on which she collected her family's and friends' opinions of *Mansfield Park* Jane noted, 'Miss Clewes's objections much the same as Fanny's';[95] when she came to write down comments on *Emma* she did not trouble to quote her at all.

There seems to have been a degree of ambivalence in Jane Austen's attitude towards governesses. She clearly expected them to be employed in families who could afford them, and therefore must have thought that, for all their limitations, on balance they were of value; the ironic tone, however, that, as we have noticed, she habitually employed in referring to them, tends to obscure her real opinion. Writing to Fanny about her aunt Harriot Bridges, second wife of the Revd George Moore of Wrotham, Kent, who had a daughter, Caroline, by his first marriage, she said that she could not understand why she should part with the governess, Miss S,

> whom she seems very much to value, now that Harriot & Eleanor are both of an age for a Governess to be so useful to; – especially as when Caroline was sent to School some years, *Miss Bell* was still retained, though the others were then mere Nursery Children. – They have some good reason I dare say, though I cannot penetrate it, & till I know what it is I shall invent a bad one, and amuse myself with accounting for the difference of measures by supposing Miss S. to be a superior sort of Woman, who has never stooped to recommend herself to the Master of the family by Flattery, as Miss Bell did.[96]

One guesses that Miss Clewes, too, was quite adept at recommending herself to the family by flattery.

A similar ambivalence is found in Jane Austen's fictional treatment of governesses. Irony is present from the start. In one of the earliest pieces of the *Juvenilia*, 'Jack and Alice', Lady Williams recounts the story of the 'able handed Governess' procured to superintend her education:

> 'Miss Dickins was an excellent Governess. She instructed me in the Paths of Virtue; under her tuition I daily became more amiable, & might perhaps by this time have nearly attained perfection, had not my worthy Preceptoress been torn from my arms, e'er I had attained my seventeenth year. I never shall forget her last words. "My dear Kitty she said, Good night t'ye." I never saw her afterwards' continued Lady Williams wiping her eyes, 'She eloped with the Butler the same night.'[97]

Whether or not Elinor and Marianne Dashwood had a governess at Norland we are not told; it is very likely. In their impoverished state at Barton Cottage, however, it would be quite out of the question for the thirteen-year-old Margaret, and Mrs Dashwood takes responsibility for her education; when Elinor and Marianne are to go to London, their mother tells them that she and Margaret will 'go on so quietly and happily together with our books and our music! You will find Margaret so improved when you come back again!'[98] Mrs Dashwood is of course an incurable optimist, and it may well be that her faith in Margaret's improvement is a shade exaggerated.

On the other hand, her merits as a teacher must surely be superior to those of Mrs Bennet. Lady Catherine de Bourgh, conducting an officious and impertinent enquiry into Elizabeth's family, expresses astonishment that they had no governess: 'No governess! How was that possible? Five daughters brought up at home without a governess! – I never heard of such a thing.'[99] She assumes that their mother must have been 'quite a slave' to their education – an idea at which Elizabeth can 'hardly help smiling' as she assures her that 'had not been the case'. The reader smiles too; yet the way in which Elizabeth and Jane at least have received their education is not without interest, since they are both intelligent and well read and have certainly been instructed somehow in 'the Paths of Virtue'. When Lady Catherine persists – 'Then, who taught you? who attended to you? Without a governess you must have been neglected' – we, while deprecating her hectoring tone, are also keen to know. Elizabeth's answer reflects the laissez-faire approach to their upbringing that is all too characteristic of her father's direction of his family:

> Compared with some families, I believe we were; but such of us as wished to learn, never wanted the means. We were always encouraged to read, and had all the masters that were necessary. Those who chose to be idle, certainly might.

As in the old-fashioned way, their education had been in the hands of their mother, their father engaging masters to teach them the accomplishments of music and dancing and perhaps drawing, just as Mr Austen engaged George Chard, the assistant organist of Winchester Cathedral, to teach Jane the piano-forte.[100] In view of the stultifying effect of the system on the autodidactic Mary Bennet, and the almost total ignorance of Kitty and Lydia, we might perhaps have a certain sympathy for Lady Catherine's reply:

> but that is what a governess will prevent, and if I had known your mother, I should have advised her most strenuously to engage one. I always say that nothing is to be done in education without steady and regular instruction, and nobody but a governess can give it.

Yet the sheer assertiveness of her language – 'will prevent', 'strenuously', 'I always say', 'nothing is to be done', 'nobody but a governess' – holds us at arm's length, and makes us question whether such domineering certainty really articulates an opinion that the author could endorse. This reservation is intensified when Lady Catherine proceeds to demonstrate the extent to which her provision of governesses for other people provides an opportunity for self-congratulation:

> It is wonderful how many families I have been the means of supplying in that way. I am always glad to get a young person well placed out. Four nieces of Mrs. Jenkinson are most delightfully situated through my means; and it was but the other day, that I recommended another young person, who was merely accidentally mentioned to me, and the family are quite delighted with her. Mrs. Collins, did I tell you of Lady Metcalfe's calling yesterday to thank me? She finds Miss Pope a treasure. 'Lady Catherine,' said she, 'you have given me a treasure.'

Mrs Jenkinson was formerly governess to her own daughter, and like Miss Taylor in *Emma* has stayed on as a companion to Miss de Bourgh. As an example of the type she hardly bears out Lady Catherine's faith in governesses, since she seems to be a wholly ineffectual and colourless person whose fussing we see as she sits at dinner 'watching how little Miss De Bourgh ate, pressing her to try some other dish, and fearing she were indisposed',[101] or later at the card table expressing her fears 'of Miss De Bourgh's being too hot or too cold, or having too much or too little light'.[102] Whatever her former pupil's abilities may be, Mrs Jenkinson feels the need to make excuses for them, being quick to tell Mr Collins that her 'sickly constitution . . . has prevented her making that progress in many accomplishments, which she could not otherwise have failed of'.[103]

Scarcely more persuasive of the benefits of employing a governess is the presentation of Miss Lee in *Mansfield Park*. It would of course have been unthinkable for Sir Thomas not to engage one, since he would be only too well aware of the utter impossibility of expecting his wife to take any share in the responsibilities of the schoolroom. 'To the education of her daughters' Lady Bertram has paid 'not the smallest attention.'[104] Even if 'her days in sitting nicely dressed on a sofa, doing some long piece of needlework, of little use and no beauty' had allowed her 'greater leisure for the service of her girls, she would probably have supposed it unnecessary', for they are 'under the care of a governess, with proper masters, and could want nothing more'. Only at the end of the novel is Sir Thomas to realize how disastrously inadequate such a provision has been, yet the deficiency is spelt out to the reader as early as the visit to Sotherton, when Julia, separated from Henry Crawford, finds herself alone with Mrs Rushworth: while 'the politeness which she had been brought up to practise as a duty' makes it impossible for her to escape, 'the want of that higher species of self-command, that just considera-tion of others, that knowledge of her own heart, that principle of right which had not formed any essential part of her education, made her miserable under it'.[105] If we apply this equally to Maria as she moves about the grounds with Mr Crawford, the irretrievable damage that she will later do to herself, and the faults in her upbringing that allow her to do it, can be clearly understood. Yet for Mrs Norris, Maria and Julia are a model of what educated girls should be; as she discusses Fanny's coming to live at Mansfield she assures Sir Thomas that 'it will be an education for the child . . . only being with her cousins'; if the governess taught her nothing, 'she would learn to be good and clever from *them*'.[106]

Miss Lee never appears directly in the book, yet we can see that she represents the figure of the conventional governess, narrow, pedantic and wholly unimagi-native. Certainly not treated as a member of the family, she has a room up in the attics, near the housemaids; and Mrs Norris can say quite matter-of-factly when speaking of her teaching Fanny that 'it will be just the same to [her], whether she has three girls to teach, or only two – there can be no difference'.[107] The nature of her teaching is manifested in the leaden rote-learning to which Maria and Julia have been submitted, as they memorized 'the chronological order of the kings of England, with the dates of their accession, and most of the principal events of their reigns', along with those of 'the Roman emperors as low as Severus', besides 'a great deal of the Heathen Mythology, and all the Metals, Semi-Metals, Planets and distinguished philosophers'.[108] The girls are proud of having acquired all this redundant knowledge, and scornful of their cousin for not having done so – another lesson they have learnt from Miss Lee, who on Fanny's arrival 'wondered at her ignorance'.[109] Miss Lee teaches her French and hears her 'read the daily portion of History'; but her real education comes from Edmund, who 'recommended the books which charmed her leisure hours . . . encouraged her taste, and corrected her judgment . . . and made reading useful by talking to her of what she read, and heightened its attraction by judicious praise'.[110]

The essential selfishness of Maria and Julia, which is to determine their actions throughout the novel, goes hand in hand with a lack of interest in other people, as we see here with Fanny; in their anxiety to tell tales of their cousin's lack of knowledge, it never occurs to them to help her by imparting some of their own, even though it is a perfectly natural instinct in children to wish to teach what they themselves have just learnt. Susan Sibbald witnessed this enthusiasm in her little five-year-old niece Margaret Pattison, when her sister and brother-in-law returned from the Cape, bringing with them an Indian nanny called Theresa, whom the children called Mammy and were very fond of:

Whatever lesson Margaret learnt she immediately went to try to teach Mammy, who, although she always repeated it after her, never seemed in the least to improve, and to the day of her death 30 to 40 years after, never spoke better than she did at first when she arrived.[111]

Mrs Sibbald recalled that these lessons extended to the saying of prayers, and even embodied some wise little precepts, which she had caught from her mother:

After little Margaret had said her prayers to her Mamma in the bedroom of the latter, a door of which opened into the nursery, my sister would sometimes leave the door ajar that she might hear Margaret instruct Theresa. Once we had a dinner party, and the child had been enjoying much fun, with the ladies in the drawing-room. Her Mamma when she took her into her room had to talk to her a little before she said her prayers to make her attentive. As Margaret went into the nursery, some of the ladies listened to hear her speech to Theresa. She began, 'Now Mammy, if we were asking Papa and Mamma to take care of us, and at the time we were speaking to them we were restless, looking about and thinking of something else, they would suppose we were talking nonsense and did not mean what we said, and in the same way God would believe we were mocking Him, and then He would be angry with us and would not care about us. Now, Mammy, let us kneel down, attend to our prayers and think of what we are going to ask God for.' Then they knelt down side by side at the little bed, Theresa with all the simplicity of a little child repeating in her way after her, first the Lord's Prayer, and then even 'I pray to God to bless Papa and Mamma, and all kind friends &c, &c.'

It is in *Emma* that the governess question is most directly addressed, though the governesses themselves are not seen in action, since one, Miss Taylor, has exercised her duties long before the novel begins and the other, Jane Fairfax, is a governess only putatively. Nevertheless, Jane Austen's ambivalence about the profession is clearly demonstrated. Having lost her mother as a child, Emma was obviously in need of a governess, and Miss Taylor, the 'excellent woman' by whom 'her place had been supplied' had 'fallen little short of a mother in affection'.[112] A further elision of roles takes place as Emma grows up and Miss Taylor becomes 'less a governess than a friend' who shares with Emma the 'intimacy of sisters'. At most the office was only ever 'nominal', and before she ceased to hold it, 'the mildness of her temper had hardly allowed her to impose any restraint'; and as the novel begins, 'the shadow of authority being now long passed away, they had been living together as friend and friend very mutually attached, and Emma doing just what she liked'. This, inevitably, leads to 'the real evils' of her situation, which are 'the power of having rather too much her own way, and a disposition to think a little too well of herself'. The very closeness of Mrs Weston's friendship with Emma, the fact that she is good-natured, a lady (despite Mrs Elton's surprise at finding her so) and, with her husband, conspires always for Emma's happiness, should not make us forget that as a governess the former Miss Taylor is not shown to have been a complete success. She had 'taught' but also 'played with her from five years old', and she had 'devoted all her powers to attach and amuse her'.[113] When, later in the novel, she tries to convince Emma that Mr Knightley is in love with Jane Fairfax, she says that her matchmaking is the consequence of keeping Emma company;[114] at a deeper level, however, it may well be the other way round, and Emma's propensity for matchmaking is one of the results of the influence that Mrs Weston has had on her. The ambivalence of the relationship is touched on in the first conversation that Emma has with Frank Churchill, when he 'got as near as he could to thanking her for Miss Taylor's merits, without seeming quite to forget that in the common course of things it was rather to be supposed that Miss Taylor had formed Miss Woodhouse's character, than Miss Woodhouse Miss Taylor's'.[115]

Mr Knightley gets to the heart of the matter when at Randalls he and Mrs Weston discuss the fact that Emma has never read enough. 'You never could persuade her to read half so much as you wished. – You know you could not,' he tells her.[116] 'I dare say,' Mrs Weston replies, 'smiling', 'that I thought so *then*; – but since we have parted, I can never remember Emma's omitting to do any thing I wished.' Her sentiment cannot blind Mr Knightley to the real cause of the problem, however:

> Emma is spoiled by being the cleverest of her family. At ten years old, she had the misfortune of being able to answer questions which puzzled her sister at seventeen. She was always quick and assured: Isabella slow and diffident. And ever since she was twelve, Emma has been mistress of the house and of you all. In her mother she lost the only person able to cope with her. She inherits her mother's talents, and must have been under subjection to her.

Perhaps because our attention is on what this tells us about Emma's character, we may not immediately notice how strong a criticism Mr Knightely is making of her governess. Mrs Weston does, however; and her reply, which this time she does not make 'smiling', suggests that she is momentarily stung both by the reflection on her professional abilities and by the implication that she could not replace Emma's mother in her ability to control her:

> I should have been sorry, Mr. Knightley, to be dependent on *your* recommendation, had I quitted Mr. Woodhouse's family and wanted another situation; I do not think you would have spoken a good word for me to any body. I am sure you always thought me unfit for the office I held.

We may feel all this to be banter, but the very deftness of the way in which Mr Knightley turns his reply into a compliment (and this time it is he who is 'smiling') indicates the seriousness behind his words:

> Yes ... You are better placed *here*; very fit for a wife, but not at all for a governess. But you were preparing yourself to be an excellent wife all the time you were at Hartfield. You

might not give Emma such a complete education as your powers would seem to promise; but you were receiving a very good education from *her*, on the very material matrimonial point of submitting your own will, and doing as you were bid; and if Weston had asked me to recommend him a wife, I should certainly have named Miss Taylor.

If this seems to be an ironic deflection of the discussion of education into the rather more frivolous one of matchmaking with which the novel has much fun, we should perhaps pause to consider what the purpose of a girl's education was in the first place. Mrs Norris regards it as purely and simply to enable her to make a good marriage: 'Give a girl a good education, and introduce her properly into the world,' she tells Sir Thomas, 'and ten to one but she has the means of settling well, without farther expense to any body.'[117] But perhaps we should be a little wary of judging entirely by Mrs Norris's point of view. Mary Wollstonecraft wished women to be educated not so that they could 'have power over men; but over themselves' and that, if necessary, they might 'support a single life with dignity'.[118] Jane Austen, however, has nothing to say about this view, since the business of her novels is to lead neither to 'a single life' nor to a state in which the heroine has power over herself, but to a marriage of equals (though of course in her own life, it might have had some application). And she would hardly have endorsed another opinion of Mary Wollstonecraft's (presumably not meant ironically), that a 'mistaken education, a narrow, uncultivated mind' tends 'to make women more constant than men', and further that 'an unhappy marriage is often very advantageous to a family, and that the neglected wife is, in general, the best mother';[119] Mrs Bennet is surely an illustration of the fallaciousness of this. Perhaps the best idea that Jane Austen gives us of the use to which an intelligent woman can put her knowledge is to impart it wisely and gently to her children. When the little Gardiners stay at Longbourn, they are 'to be left under the particular care of their cousin Jane, who was the general favourite, and whose steady sense and sweetness of temper exactly adapted her for attending to them in every way – teaching them, playing with them, and loving them';[120] it is not difficult to foresee how, whatever the provision of governesses her husband will make, Jane will educate her own little Bingleys.

Miss Taylor has had the good fortune to escape from being a governess, or a companion, by marrying – and at an age when she is not too old to bear children. This, though it is necessary for the plot, is not what usually happened, since most governesses had insufficient means to attract a husband from their own class (the point is specifically made that Mr Weston, with 'an easy competence', and a son whose future is taken care of by his adoptive parents, is able to marry 'a woman as portionless even as Miss Taylor').[121] When occasionally a woman did find herself able to give up governessing for marriage, the consequences could be disastrous. This was the case with Nelly Weeton, who, at the age of thirty-seven, having some means of her own, married a factory owner; as it turned out, he was close to bankruptcy; possessed of a violent temper, once he had got his hands on her money he treated her with great cruelty, and the marriage ended in separation.[122]

Fantasies of marrying into the family by whom the governess was employed usually remained just that, since though she might not be ranked with the servants, she was unlikely to be accepted as a suitable wife for any young man belonging to it. Interestingly, the question arose in Jane Austen's own family. Her nephew William Knight, on a visit to his sister Fanny (by then Lady Knatchbull) formed an attachment with the governess in the household; the woman was instantly dismissed, and the family tried to hush it up, though word inevitably got out.[123] Jane Austen was dead by then, but one wonders if she would altogether have disapproved. When her friend Anne Sharp became governess to the daughters of a widowed Lady Pilkington, and in the summer of 1814 they went to the family seat of Chevet in Yorkshire, to stay with the children's bachelor uncle, Sir William Pilkington, Jane hoped, perhaps only half jokingly, that she might change her situation; 'I do so want him to marry her!' she told Cassandra, adding excitedly 'Oh! Sir W^m – Sir W^m how I will love you, if you will love Miss Sharp!'[124]

For Jane Fairfax becoming a governess offers no such hope; rather, it is her only recourse when it appears that her relationship with Frank Churchill has foundered. She is in many ways typical of the young women who became governesses. Born into a respectable family, she is orphaned and has no resources of her own; Colonel Campbell is able to take her into his family but, unlike Sir Thomas Bertram, he is not wealthy enough to make financial provision for her as well as for his own daughter, so in the normal course of events she would be unlikely to find herself in a position to make a good marriage. Fully aware of this, Colonel Campbell has had her educated with the plan that 'she should be brought up for educating others', thus 'supplying the means of respectable subsistence hereafter'.[125] Had it not been for the very fortunate meeting with Frank Churchill at Weymouth, this would undoubtedly have been her fate (and it is worth noticing that Frank's adoption by the wealthy Churchills eventually enables two governesses without independent means to marry). Having had, in London, 'the attendance of first-rate masters', she was 'at eighteen or nineteen . . . as far as such an early age can be qualified for the care of children, fully competent to the office of instruction'; but the Campbells, particularly their daughter, could not bear to part with her, and the 'evil day was put off'.

There can be no mistaking the distaste with which her destined future is regarded in the novel, by Jane herself, by other characters and undoubtedly by the author. When Miss Campbell marries, her 'less fortunate friend', with 'her bread to earn', now at the age of 21 has to enter 'on her path of duty'. The necessary withdrawal from the social world that she has enjoyed until now is seen as an irrevocable step leading her into the self-denying discipline of the cloister: with 'the fortitude of a devoted noviciate' she is 'resolved . . . to complete the sacrifice, and retire from all the pleasures of life, of rational intercourse, equal society, peace and hope, to penance and mortification for ever'.[126] The Campbells, willing to keep her with them indefinitely during their lifetime, nevertheless realize that 'what must be at last, had better be soon. Perhaps they began to feel it might have been kinder and wiser to have resisted the temptation of any delay, and spared her from a taste of such enjoyments of ease and leisure as must now be relinquished.' Their fears for her health, however, have given them an excuse for 'not hurrying on the wretched moment', since 'till she should have completely recovered her usual strength, they must forbid her engaging in duties, which, so far from being compatible with a weakened frame and varying spirits, seemed, under the most favourable circumstances, to require something more than human perfection of body and mind to be discharged with tolerable comfort'. Emma too, though she does not like Jane, feels compassion for her when she considers 'what all this elegance was destined to, what she was going to sink from, how she was going to live'.[127]

Later, Jane Fairfax's prospective position arises in a little exchange of dialogue that has complications of its own. The scene is Ford's shop, where Frank Churchill, newly arrived in Highbury, has come to show his patronage of the local tradesmen by buying gloves; Emma raises the subject of Jane's being destined for a governess periphrastically, as if to speak of it directly in a public place were not quite respectable:

> 'You know Miss Fairfax's situation in life, I conclude; what she is destined to be.'
> 'Yes – (rather hesitatingly) – I believe I do.'
> 'You get upon delicate subjects, Emma,' said Mrs. Weston smiling, 'remember that I am here. – Mr. Frank Churchill hardly knows what to say when you speak of Miss Fairfax's situation in life. I will move a little farther off.'
> 'I certainly do forget to think of *her*,' said Emma, 'as having ever been anything but my friend and my dearest friend.' He looked as if he fully understood and honoured such a sentiment.[128]

Frank's hesitation is really caused by his wondering for a moment whether Emma knows about his engagement; his ambiguous reply betrays caution – he is not yet sufficiently assured with Emma to enjoy the opportunity for game-playing that such an answer would afford him later on. It is only her reference to Mrs Weston's former position that explains what she meant; at that point the relief on his face must indeed make him look as if he 'fully understood'. The first-time reader, not yet in the secret, is of course unaware of any of this, and takes Frank's hesitant reply only as a sign of his concern for his stepmother's feelings.

The most devastating condemnation of the state of being a governess comes from Jane Fairfax herself. Mrs Elton, mistaking Jane's reserve for a weakness that will allow her to exercise the need to dominate that has been frustrated by Emma, takes it upon herself to find 'an eligible situation' for her among her 'very extensive' acquaintance;[129] and Jane, anxious for some resolution to the obstacles to her marriage, tries to fend her off by saying that she has not yet even begun any enquiries. Mrs Elton, however, insists on the necessity of beginning early:

> You do not know how many candidates there always are for the *first* situations. I saw a vast deal of that in the neighbourhood round Maple Grove. A cousin of Mr. Suckling,

Mrs. Bragge, had such an infinity of applications; every body was anxious to be in her family, for she moves in the first circle. Wax-candles in the school-room! You may imagine how desirable![130]

Jane, independent by nature, and with a reason here for wishing to remain so, has no intention of being committed by the interference of friends; if the time comes when she has to find employment she will visit one of the 'places in town, offices, where inquiry would soon produce something'. But the awfulness of that prospect, if she is not in the end able to marry Frank, perhaps brought out by the catalyst of the pressure that Mrs Elton is putting on her, induces her to qualify her description of these places as 'Offices for the sale – not quite of human flesh – but of human intellect'. Mrs Elton is both horrified and uncomprehending: 'Oh! my dear,' she exclaims, 'human flesh! You quite shock me; if you mean a fling at the slave-trade, I assure you Mr. Suckling was always rather a friend to the abolition.' Jane's explanation is equally beyond Mrs Elton's comprehension, but it is not beyond ours:

> I did not mean, I was not thinking of the slave-trade . . . governess-trade, I assure you, was all that I had in view; widely different certainly as to the guilt of those who carry it on; but as to the greater misery of the victims, I do not know where it lies.

The equation of governess trade and slave trade arises only from Mrs Elton's misunderstanding; but once raised, it impresses itself on the reader's mind, just as it evidently does on Jane's, to judge by the faltering manner of her denial as the image strikes her.

Finally saved by Mrs Churchill's death from accepting a position as governess to Mrs Smallridge's three 'elegant sweet children,'[131] and living 'only four miles from Maple Grove', Jane Fairfax is not destined to play the role which Mrs Elton tries to assign to her of the intelligent, passionate woman isolated in a dull and fashionable family, any more than she played that of the illicit lover of her friend's husband conceived for her by Emma. Novelists altogether different from Jane Austen would write about those kinds of heroine. But the language in which being a governess is spoken of in connection with Jane Fairfax, in contrast to the tactful description of Miss Taylor as hardly having been a governess at all, leaves us finally with little doubt about Jane Austen's views of the fate of young women condemned to live in such a way. Had she ever read A Vindication of the Rights of Woman, she might well have found herself in agreement with Mary Wollstonecraft:

> The few employments open to women, so far from being liberal, are menial; and when a superior education enables them to take charge of the education of children as governesses, they are not treated like the tutors of sons, though even clerical tutors are not always treated in a manner calculated to render them respectable in the eyes of their pupils, to say nothing of the private comfort of the individual. But as women educated

like gentlewomen, are never designed for the humiliating situation which necessity sometimes forces them to fill; these situations are considered in the light of a degradation; and they know little of the human heart, who need to be told, that nothing so painfully sharpens sensibility as such a fall in life.[132]

What Jane Austen would not have agreed with is the idea that clerical tutors might not always be treated with respect by their pupils or by their pupils' families. Her experience of clerical tutors was limited to her own father, who took pupils at the rectory; and by the end of the eighteenth century this was the usual way in which boys, at least from the kind of clerical families among whom the Austens moved, were taught, unless they were sent to school. But wealthier households might still employ a private tutor for their sons. Sir Thomas Bertram did not do so, having sent Tom and Edmund to Eton – though he obviously took an interest in their education himself, hearing them as schoolboys recite speeches from plays, so that they would learn to speak well.[133] Lord Osborne in *The Watsons*, however, did as a boy have a tutor; he is Mr Howard, now the clergyman of the local parish, having no doubt been presented to the living either by his grateful pupil when he inherited the estate or by his father. Cassandra Austen told her nieces after Jane's death that had the novel been completed, much of the interest was to arise from the widowed Lady Osborne's love for Mr Howard 'and his counter affection for Emma, whom he was finally to marry'.[134] While Mr Howard was destined to remain only an idea in his author's mind (and one that, presumably, she could not sufficiently bring to life to be able to go on with the work), we have in his ten-year-old nephew perhaps the most enchanting child that she ever created.

Charles Blake, with a 'fine Countenance & animated gestures', is 'uncommonly fond of dancing', and as they arrive in the ballroom, he is very excited about his partner, Lord Osborne's sister, who, as his mother tells someone standing near her, 'has been so very kind as to promise to dance the two 1st dances with him'.[135] 'Oh! yes,' the boy bursts out, 'we have been engaged this week . . . & we are to dance down every couple.' But as Emma Watson watches 'the smartest officer of the sett' that have gathered round the ladies from the castle 'walking off to the orchestra to order the dance', Miss Osborne says hastily to 'her little expectant Partner . . . "Charles, I beg your pardon for not keeping my engagement, but I am going to dance these two dances with Col^n Beresford. I know you will excuse me, & I will certainly dance with you after Tea."' And 'without staying for an answer', she goes off to lead the set.

Miss Osborne may not know how a ten-year-old child feels such a blow, but Jane Austen, a loving aunt to so many nephews and nieces, certainly does:

If the poor little boy's face had in it's happiness been interesting to Emma, it was infinitely more so under this sudden reverse; – he stood the picture of disappointment, with crimson'd cheeks, quivering lips, & eyes bent on the floor. His mother, stifling her own mortification, tried to sooth his, with the prospect of Miss Osborne's second promise; – but tho' he contrived to utter with an effort of Boyish Bravery 'Oh! I do not mind it' – it was very evident by the unceasing agitation of his features that he minded it as much as ever.

The observation is astute: the cheeks intensely red and the quivering of his lips depict the urgency of the boy's unhappiness, but he is embarrassed by his uncontrollable emotions, and, with 'eyes bent on the floor', cannot bring himself to look anyone in the face. The way children bear themselves, their movements and gestures, by which feeling is more directly visible than it is allowed to be in the controlled posture of adults, clearly touched and sometimes amused Jane Austen. We see this in *Mansfield Park* when Mary Crawford goes to rehearse in Fanny's East room, formerly the schoolroom. 'We must have two chairs at hand for you to bring forward to the front of the stage,' she says. 'There – very good school-room chairs, not made for a theatre, I dare say; much more fitted for little girls to sit and kick their feet against when they are learning a lesson.'[136]

There is something amusing too, of course, in Charles's 'effort of Boyish Bravery', but Jane Austen takes it seriously. She resists however any temptation to moralise, as her brother James was apt to do, for example in a poem written for James Edward when his pony died. James also captures succinctly the expressive actions of the child as, having kissed the horse for the last time, he

> ... slowly turned, & with a look,
> Which mingled grief & love bespoke,
> His Father's hand in silence took.[137]

His father comforts him with the thought that as he had never ill-treated the animal and that 'no quadraped / A kinder, milder master knew', he can cheer himself with the knowledge that he has nothing to blame himself for. But then, the sermon-writer perhaps getting the better of the poet, he warns him that this first loss is merely a preparation for all the others that he will suffer during his life:

> Each blessing that you now possess,
> Time's lapse itself will sure make less;
> And if you live, you'll love to mourn,
> Full many joys that ne'er return.
> Around, you now collected see
> Relations, friends, & family,
> Within a constant circle move,
> Endeared by bonds of mutual love:
> Yet these must all (nay do not start)
> From you – & from each other part:
> The time will come when every year
> Takes from you some one you held dear;
> Oh! then as now, may no remorse
> Increase affliction's native force;

No vain regrets for joys abused,
Neglected friends & time misused,
Imprint a sorrow in your breast,
More hard to bear than all the rest . . .

This is no doubt all very wise, but one wonders just how much of a comfort his son found it; it is hardly surprising, perhaps, that he should see the poor boy 'start'.

For Charles Blake, there is a happier source of consolation, when, foreshadowing Mr Knightley's rescue of Harriet Smith after Mr Elton refuses to dance with her, Emma Watson takes pity on the distraught child:

Emma did not think, or reflect; – she felt & acted –. 'I shall be very happy to dance with you Sir, if you like it.' said she, holding out her hand with most unaffected good humour. – The Boy in one moment restored to all his first delight – looked joyfully at his Mother and stepping forwards with an honest & simple Thank you Maam was instantly ready to attend to his new acquaintance.[138]

The very precise analysis of the behaviour of a child placed in an adult situation is a source of comedy, but it is touching, too. His emotions being the undirected ones of a child, it is merely the glamour of having a grown-up lady to dance with that matters to him, and the substitution of one for another restores him instantaneously 'to all his first delight'. Through the sophisticated medium of the dance, the innocent simplicity of childhood is reflected as Charles, 'being provided with his gloves & charged to keep them on', leads Emma towards the set:

It was a Partnership which c^d not be noticed without surprise. It gained her a broad stare from Miss Osborne & Miss Carr as they passed her in the dance. 'Upon my word Charles you are in luck, (said the former as she turned him) you have got a better partner than me' – to which the happy Charles answered 'Yes.' – Tom Musgrave who was dancing with Miss Carr, gave her many inquisitive glances; & after a time Ld Osborne himself came & under the pretence of talking to Charles, stood to look at his partner. – Tho' rather distressed by such observation, Emma could not repent what she had done, so happy had it made both the boy & his Mother; the latter of whom was continually making opportunities of addressing her with the warmest civility.

The scene was clearly intended to be crucial to the development of the plot, since Emma's kindly action endears her to Mrs Blake, and therefore presumably to her brother Mr Howard, and simultaneously brings her to the notice of Lord Osborne (and also of the rakish Tom Musgrave). Had the novel been completed it would have been unique in Jane Austen's work for having so much weight placed on the actions of a child.

As it is, we are left with Charles Blake to stand alone, in a fragment that affords him greater space proportionately than he would have enjoyed in the full-length book. He does so delightfully, and his conversation while they dance is, at least when Emma prompts him, as easy and frank as that of any gentleman in a Jane Austen ballroom:

> Her little partner she found, tho' bent chiefly on dancing, was not unwilling to speak, when her questions or remarks gave him anything to say; & she learnt, by a sort of inevitable enquiry that he had two brothers & a sister, that they & their Mama all lived with his Uncle at Wickstead, that his Uncle taught him Latin, that he was very fond of riding, & had a horse of his own given him by Ld Osborne; & that he had been out once already with Ld Osborne's Hounds.

As they sit in the tearoom, he now feels 'free enough to hazard a few questions in his turn':

> 'What o'clock was it?' – 'Eleven.' – 'Eleven! – And I am not at all sleepy. Mama said I should be asleep before ten. – Do you think Miss Osborne will keep her word with me, when Tea is over?' 'Oh! yes. – I suppose so.' – tho' she felt that she had no better reason to give than that Miss Osborne had *not* kept it before.[139]

For the plot to develop, Emma would have somehow to be introduced properly into the Osborne family; and it is at this moment, in Charles's next question, that we see how Jane Austen would have done it:

> 'When shall you come to Osborne Castle?' – 'Never, probably. – I am not acquainted with the family.' 'But you may come to Wickstead & see Mama, & she can take you to the Castle. – There is a monstrous curious stuff'd Fox there, & a Badger – anybody would think they were alive. It is a pity you should not see them.'

Social arrangements, so complicated among the etiquette and niceties of the adult world, are simple to a child. The whole course of Emma's life is to be altered by little Charles Blake, who, without having the least idea of what he is doing, beyond a wish of showing gratitude to the friendly lady who has been so kind to him, urgently wants her to go to Osborne Castle because he thinks that it would be a pity for her not to see the stuffed animals that look as if they are alive.

It is a charming portrait.

5

Parents

In Jane Austen's novels the parents best suited to bringing up children are dead. Mr Henry Dashwood, who hoped to compensate for the fact that the Norland estate was left to the son of his first marriage by 'living economically' and saving enough money to provide for his second wife and daughters, dies in the first chapter of *Sense and Sensibility*; Emma inherited 'her mother's talents' and when her mother died 'lost the only person able to cope with her';[1] Anne Elliot was sent to school at the age of fourteen 'grieving for the loss of a mother whom she had dearly loved';[2] and Eleanor Tilney, whose mother died when she was thirteen, has lost 'a constant friend' whose influence 'would have been beyond all other'.[3] Of the parents who survive only Catherine Morland's and, in *Sanditon*, Charlotte Heywood's are unexceptionable, and we do not see very much of them; for the rest, Mrs Dashwood is kind and loving but admits that she is imprudent; and most of the others are foolish (Mrs Bennet, Lady Middleton, Lady Bertram, Sir Walter Elliot), ill-judging (Mr Bennet, Sir Thomas Bertram), weak (Mr Woodhouse, Mary Musgrove), over-indulgent (Mrs Thorpe), incapacitated by circumstances (the Prices, Mr Watson) or downright poisonous (Mrs Ferrars, Lady Susan). They do not on the whole add up to an encouraging picture of parenthood, and in view of the fact that Jane Austen herself had exemplary parents, who loved their children and brought them up extremely well, we can only assume that as an author she found that bad parents made for richer drama and better comedy than good ones.

During the eighteenth century relations between parents and their children changed markedly. The formality of earlier periods was on the whole replaced by a more relaxed and affectionate kind of behaviour within the family. Children came to be regarded as individuals; their likes and dislikes, even their opinions, were taken into account; and they were brought down from the nursery and shown to visitors, not always only for short periods. They were no longer expected to stand in the presence of their parents; and their status was given visual testimony in the increasingly large number of family portraits, in which they were often depicted in very informal poses – seated, lying or crawling on the floor, frequently at play. The terms 'mamma' and 'papa' began to replace the earlier 'sir' and 'madam', though by the end of the century a return to the more formal terms was apparent in some families: thus among Jane Austen's characters, while it is not surprising that Mrs Ferrars should be addressed as 'ma'am' by Fanny, or Sir Walter Elliot as 'sir' by Anne, or Sir Thomas and Lady

Bertram as 'sir' and 'madam' by all their children, it is interesting that elsewhere there is considerable inconsistency. In *Sense and Sensibility*, *Pride and Prejudice* and *Emma* a mixture of forms of address is used within the same family; Elinor Dashwood, Jane and Elizabeth Bennet and Isabella Knightley all address their parents as 'madam', 'ma'am' or 'sir', while Marianne, Kitty and Lydia and Emma use 'papa' or 'mamma', the principle being, apparently, that the elder children in a family use the formal terms and the younger ones the informal.

Among the Austens there was an easy informality, as can be seen from some of the verses that the young James Edward, Jane's nephew, addressed to his parents. His very earliest poem, written when he was not more than six years old, contains a neat little squib directed at his father:

The Neck of Veal

Poor neck of veal, don't pity me
For pity more belongs to thee,
Though I've not tasted of thy meat
I've had the pleasure of seeing my Father eat.[4]

And when he was about to go away to his prep school in Ramsbury, he wrote something even more direct to his mother:

To Mamma

My grateful thanks, my Mother dear,
Accept for each box in the Ear
Which you have given to me.
I hope that I shall have as few
When I alas! away from you
At Ramsbury shall be.[5]

The boxes on the ear that James Edward had received were probably relatively few in number, since we have his aunt's testimony in several letters to his charm and good humour; on the other hand, as we shall see later, we also have the testimony of one of his nieces that he and his sisters sometimes suffered from their mother's sharp temper.

Some parents might not have spared the rod, but on the whole physical chastisement as a means of correcting children's behaviour was held to be brutal and undesirable. As one writer in the middle of the century argued, there were medical as well as social reasons for exercising moderation: 'Severe and frequent whipping is, I think, a very bad practice: it inflames the skin, it puts the blood in a ferment; and there is besides, meanness, a degree of ignominy attending it, which makes it very unbecoming.'[6] In 1751 Dr Johnson devoted a paper of the *Rambler* to the 'Cruelty of Parental Tyranny'. More interested, as might be expected, in the moral than the medical aspects of the subject, he declares the 'cruelties often exercised in private families' to be as 'dangerous' and 'detestable' as 'the perversion and exorbitance of legal authority'.[7] He seems to think that undue severity is still widespread: 'There are many houses,' he claims, 'which it is impossible to enter familiarly, without discovering that parents are by no means exempt from the intoxication of dominion.' Yet there is a profound and inescapable reason for such cruelty to be not only wrong but unnatural:

> If in any situation the heart were inaccessible to malignity, it might be supposed to be sufficiently secured by parental relation. To have voluntarily become to any being the occasion of its existence, produces an obligation to make that existence happy. To see helpless Infancy stretching out her hands and pouring out her cries in testimony of dependence, without any powers to alarm jealousy, or any guilt to alienate affection, must surely awaken tenderness in every human mind; and tenderness once excited will be hourly increased by the natural contagion of felicity, by the repercussion of communicated pleasure, by the consciousness of the dignity of benefaction ... We naturally endear to ourselves those to whom we impart any kind of pleasure, because we imagine their affection and esteem secured to us by the benefits which they receive.[8]

Johnson is thinking of parental tyranny in a form far more violent and extreme than any encountered in Jane Austen; yet there are instances in the novels of parents who exercise a kind of arbitrary control over their children which, if it does not exemplify itself in actual cruelty, is at best unfeeling and at worst unkind. The Tilneys are uneasy with their father, and are alert to the demands of his petty time-keeping. On her first evening at Northanger Abbey, Catherine is listening to him describing some of the rooms when

> taking out his watch, he stopped short to pronounce it with surprise within twenty minutes of five! This seemed the word of separation, and Catherine found herself hurried away by Miss Tilney in such a manner as convinced her that the strictest punctuality to the family hours would be expected at Northanger.[9]

The 'word' of separation almost seems to carry a weight of biblical authority, and indeed General Tilney is by far the most patriarchal father in any of the books, in zealous thrall to his own watch. Distracted by romantic speculations about the old chest in her room when she goes up to dress for dinner, Catherine is fetched by Eleanor, 'anxious for her friend's being ready'.

> Miss Tilney gently hinted at her fear of being late; and in half a minute they ran down stairs together, in an alarm not wholly unfounded, for General Tilney was pacing the drawing-room, his watch in his hand, and having, on the very instant of their entering, pulled the bell with violence, ordered 'Dinner to be on table *directly!*'[10]

The General deflects his irritation from his guest to his daughter, finding another reason to bully Eleanor in hypocritically displacing his own impatience on to her:

> Catherine trembled at the emphasis with which he spoke, and sat pale and breathless, in a most humble mood, concerned for his children, and detesting old chests; and the General recovering his politeness as he looked at her, spent the rest of his time in scolding his daughter, for so foolishly hurrying her fair friend, who was absolutely out of breath from haste, when there was not the least occasion for hurry in the world: but Catherine could not at all get over the double distress of having involved her friend in a lecture and been a great simpleton herself, till they were happily seated at the dinner-table, when the General's complacent smiles, and a good appetite of her own, restored her to peace.

Like many a tyrannical old widower, the General is not immune to the charms of a pretty girl: he recovers his politeness as he looks at his daughter's 'fair friend'; he sees that she is out of breath because he watches her bosom heaving.

Henry, like his sister, understands the true meaning that underlies his father's apparent complacency. When they are to visit him at Woodston, the General tells him, 'You are not to put yourself at all out of your way. Whatever you may happen to have in the house will be enough. I think I can answer for the young ladies making allowance for a bachelor's table.'[11] Catherine is surprised therefore to find Henry going away immediately to prepare for them. 'But how can you think of such a thing,' she exclaims, 'after what the General said? when he so particularly desired you not to give yourself any trouble, because *any thing* would do.' Reluctant to suggest that his father might have spoken insincerely, 'Henry only smiled', and Catherine goes on:

> I am sure it is quite unnecessary upon your sister's account and mine. You must know it to be so; and the General made such a point of your providing nothing extraordinary: – besides, if he had not said half so much as he did, he has always such an excellent dinner at home, that sitting down to a middling one for one day could not signify.

Henry's answer, brief as it is, is revealing – to the reader, if not to Catherine:

> I wish I could reason like you, for his sake and my own. Good bye. As to-morrow is Sunday, Eleanor, I shall not return.

The tone is light, but the anticipation of the General's tyrannical behaviour towards Catherine, and Henry's eventual permanent departure from Northanger when he marries her, is clear. Yet even at the end of the final chapter, Jane Austen draws back from dealing squarely with Johnson's problem of parental domination, instead taking refuge in irony – as is only right in a novel in which the reader has been taken into the author's ironic confidence all the way through. Her last sentence starts seriously enough, introducing the sensible ideas that 'to begin perfect happiness at the respective ages of twenty-six and eighteen, is to do pretty well' and that 'the General's unjust interference, so far from being really injurious to their felicity, was perhaps rather conducive to it, by improving their knowledge of each other, and adding strength to their attachment'; but it finishes by applying to *Northanger Abbey* itself the same amused scrutiny to which the Gothic novel has been submitted all the way through, as it is left 'to be settled by whomsoever it may concern, whether the tendency of this work be altogether to recommend parental tyranny, or reward filial disobedience'.[12]

It is possible that Jane Austen learnt something of the character of generals from the father of her brother James's first wife, Anne Mathew. In the family, General Mathew was regarded as something of a despot, though unlike General Tilney he was very generous. His great-granddaughter Fanny Caroline Lefroy wrote in her 'Family History' that although 'he always behaved very pleasantly' to James's second wife, 'Aunt Caroline says that she never got over her fear of him, a fear not peculiar to her for his own children & Grandchildren, my mother [Anna Lefroy] excepted quite shared it'.[13]

Johnson sums up the 'freaks of injustice which are sometimes indulged under the secrecy of a private dwelling' as 'capricious injunctions, partial decisions, unequal allotments, distributions of reward, not by merit but by fancy, and punishments regulated not by the degree of the offence but by the humour of the judge'. Mrs Ferrars, in *Sense and Sensibility*, seems to combine all these errors, not least in her response to the marriage between Robert and Lucy Steele. Having disinherited her elder son, Edward, for his intended marriage to Lucy, she is won round by her younger son, who procures her forgiveness 'by the simple expedient of asking it'; and the laughable unfairness of her behaviour is expressed in a passage of gleeful irony:

> The forgiveness at first, indeed, as was reasonable, comprehended only Robert; and Lucy, who had owed his mother no duty, and therefore could have transgressed none, still remained some weeks longer unpardoned. But perseverance in humility of conduct and messages, in self-condemnation for Robert's offence, and gratitude for the unkindness she was treated with, procured her in time the haughty notice which overcame her by its graciousness, and led soon afterwards, by rapid degrees, to the highest state of affection and influence. Lucy became as necessary to Mrs. Ferrars, as either Robert or Fanny; and while Edward was never cordially forgiven for having once intended to marry her, and Elinor, though superior to her in fortune and birth, was spoken of as an intruder, *she* was in every thing considered, and always openly acknowledged, to be a favourite child.[14]

Mrs Ferrars is treated as a comic autocrat, of a kind to be developed further in Lady Catherine De Bourgh; she is distanced from the reader by being introduced directly only at a late stage into the book, and, as we have seen, by being dealt with almost wholly ironically. Furthermore, she can be seen as a grotesque exaggeration, distorted by age, wealth and the petty exercise of power, of her own daughter, Fanny Dashwood. Her conduct towards her sons is too ludicrously illogical for even Jane Austen to take it seriously.

In *Lady Susan*, however, we see close to a mother who palpably loathes her own daughter. Whenever she refers to her to her confidante, Mrs Johnson, she speaks of her with undisguised contempt. Frederica, she says, is 'born to be the torment of my life'; she is 'the greatest simpleton on earth', 'a little Devil', 'a Chit, a Child, without Talent or Education'; she is 'a stupid girl, & has nothing to recommend her'; and she affords 'the most reasonable hope of . . . being ridiculed & despised by every Man who sees her'. In thanking Mrs Johnson for taking notice of her, she is grateful for such a mark of her friendship towards herself, but is 'far from exacting so heavy a sacrifice'. She herself has no pleasure in her daughter's company, and when she has her with her it is purely for tactical reasons in attempting to carry out her plan of forcing her into a marriage with a man she does not love. Irritated by her presence, even when she is bullying her, she bears out another observation in Johnson's *Rambler* paper:

> The unjustifiable severity of a parent is loaded with this aggravation, that those whom he injures are always in his sight. The injustice of a prince is often exercised upon those of whom he never had any personal or particular knowledge; and the sentence which he pronounces, whether of banishment, imprisonment, or death, removes from his view the man whom he condemns. But the domestic oppressor dooms himself to gaze upon those faces which he clouds with terror and with sorrow; and beholds every moment the effects of his own barbarities. He that can bear to give continual pain to those who surround him, and can walk with satisfaction in the gloom of his own presence; he that can see submissive misery without relenting, and meet without emotion the eye that implores mercy, or demands justice, will scarcely be amended by remonstrance or admonition; he has found means of stopping the avenues of tenderness, and arming his heart against the force of reason.

Such, precisely, is Lady Susan.

No other parent in Jane Austen is remotely comparable, nor does any come near to the kind of behaviour that Johnson condemns. The closest is Mrs Norris, a kind of surrogate mother, whose unreasoning partiality for Sir Thomas's children over Fanny leads her to compensate for her indulgence of the former by constant unkindness towards the latter. With Maria's disgrace, which in many ways is the result of the lack of restraint exercised over her by her aunt, her dislike of Fanny reaches its height, as she displaces the blame that should have been one niece's onto the other: Mrs Norris is 'but the more irritated by the sight of the person whom, in the blindness of her anger, she could have charged as the dæmon of the piece. Had Fanny accepted Mr. Crawford, this could not have happened.'[15]

In Jane Austen's own family there was no Lady Susan either. However, she and Cassandra were aware of the fact that their niece Anna did not get on very well with her stepmother, and they often had her to stay at Chawton. Mary Lloyd was James's second wife, and her relations both with him and with her own children, James Edward and Caroline, were affectionate and kindly; but whether from jealousy or perhaps because she found Anna less easy to manage than the younger children, she was never close to her; and James, 'his Opinions on many points too much copied from his Wife's', as Jane Austen wrote,[16] played safe and ignored her. Years later Anna's own daughter, Fanny Caroline Lefroy, wrote of Mary that she

> was a clever cheerful hospitable woman, generous where money was concerned though a careful & excellent manager. She was also warm hearted & would take any trouble for her friends. But her manner was abrupt & sharp, & she had a tartness of temper from which even her own children occasionally suffered. She did not love her stepdaughter, & she slighted her, she made her of no estimation, & the last & least in her father's house. She was very far indeed from being the cruel stepmother of fiction, & perhaps in truth of former times, but certainly it never entered into her imagination that she was to make no difference between her and her own children . . . I do not suppose her father was consciously unkind to her, but his heart was entirely absorbed in his two younger children, especially his son . . . for his motherless child with all her loveliness, intelligence and generosity of temper, he had not affection enough to care to do her justice. She was however a most dutiful daughter and she never spoke of him but with affection, and of her stepmother but with respect.[17]

If the last sentence is to be taken literally, this information must have come to Fanny Caroline in the form of family lore rather than directly from her mother.

It is not so much parental tyranny as lack of firm guidance from which most of Jane Austen's heroines suffer. Jane Austen herself believed that it was necessary to bring children up with a proper sense of what was expected of them. Writing to Anna Lefroy about a nephew of her husband's, she advised her: 'If You & his Uncles are good friends to little Charles Lefroy, he will be a great deal the better for his visit; – we thought him a very fine boy, but terribly in want of Discipline. – I hope he gets a wholesome thump, or two, whenever it is necessary.'[18] The wholesome thump may be a joke, but she was quite serious about the discipline. It was something that worried her about the way in which Charles and his wife brought up their children. After having two of them to stay at Chawton (one of them her god-daughter, Harriet), she wrote to Francis:

> Charles's little girls were with us about a month, & had so endeared themselves that we were quite sorry to have them go. We have the pleasure however of hearing that they are thought very much improved at home – Harriet in health, Cassy in manners. – The latter *ought* to be a very nice Child – Nature has done enough for her – but Method has been wanting; – we thought her very much improved ourselves, but to have Papa & Mama think her so too, was very essential to our contentment. – She will really be a very pleasing Child, if they will only exert themselves a little.[19]

Clearly, the childless Jane and Cassandra have no illusions about how parents ought to bring up children; they have subjected their naughty little niece to a little gentle discipline and it has had its effect. Francis's own bringing up of his children did not escape criticism, however: a few years later Jane was writing to her niece Caroline, 'I spent two or three days with your Uncle & Aunt lately, & though the Children are sometimes very noisy & not under such Order as they ought & easily might, I cannot help liking them & even loving them, which I hope may not be wholly inexcusable in their & [your affectionate Aunt].[20]

Jane Austen saw all too clearly where a lack of discipline in childhood would lead. Lydia Bennet, the subject of her mother's foolish indulgence and her father's wish for a quiet life, grows up to be, in Elizabeth's words, 'vain, ignorant, idle, and absolutely uncontrouled'.[21] In fact, it is Elizabeth, rather than her father, who understands the discipline she needs, and begs him to exercise it: 'If you,' she warns him, 'will not take the trouble of checking her exuberant spirits, and of teaching her that her present pursuits are not to be the business of her life, she will soon be beyond the reach of amendment. Her character will be fixed, and she will, at sixteen, be the most determined flirt that ever made herself and her family ridiculous.' Though the misbehaviour of young children, tolerated, permitted or actively encouraged by their parents, is a theme from which Jane Austen can draw considerable comedy, its primary purpose is to reveal the deficiencies of the parents rather than the wrongdoings of the children, since, as with little Cassy, she clearly held the view that on the whole a child would behave well if it was properly taught.

The faults of her brother Charles and his wife Fanny in bringing up their children are seen in an exaggerated degree in Lady Middleton. Self-consciously elegant, and stultifyingly dull, she matches her genial husband in 'that total want of talent and taste which confined their employments ... within a very narrow compass'.[22] They are both crisply defined, the irony falling on her:

> Sir John was a sportsman, Lady Middleton a mother. He hunted and shot, and she humoured her children; and these were their only resources. Lady Middleton had the advantage of being able to spoil her children all the year round, while Sir John's independent employments were in existence only half the time.

The extent to which she humours her children is not seen until the arrival of the Steele sisters; and it is to convey their determined toadying that Jane Austen introduces the little Middletons into the drawing-room. The tactics of the visitors is clear from the outset; they know precisely how to ingratiate themselves with Lady Middleton: 'With her children they were in continual raptures, extolling their beauty, courting their notice, and humouring all their whims.'[23] She is completely taken in, and it is natural that she would be, as Jane Austen ironically observes:

> Fortunately for those who pay their court through such foibles, a fond mother, though, in pursuit of praise for her children, the most rapacious of human beings, is likewise the most credulous; her demands are exorbitant; but she will swallow any thing; and the excessive affection and endurance of the Miss Steeles towards her offspring, were viewed therefore by Lady Middleton without the smallest surprise or distrust.

There follows a catalogue of the indignities to which the sisters allow themselves to be subjected, and which are coolly observed by the clear-seeing eyes of Elinor and Marianne:

> [Lady Middleton] saw with maternal complacency all the impertinent incroachments and mischievous tricks to which her cousins submitted. She saw their sashes untied, their hair pulled about their ears, their work-bags searched, and their knives and scissars stolen away, and felt no doubt of its being a reciprocal enjoyment. It suggested no other surprise than that Elinor and Marianne should sit so composedly by, without claiming a share in what was passing.

There is a scene of comparable juvenile licence in *A Christmas Carol*, when Scrooge is shown the home of the woman he might have married. She is sitting with her eldest daughter in the parlour:

> The noise in this room was perfectly tumultuous, for there were more children there, than Scrooge in his agitated state of mind could count; and, unlike the celebrated herd in the poem, they were not forty children conducting themselves like one, but every child was conducting itself like forty. The consequences were uproarious beyond belief; but no one seemed to care; on the contrary, the mother and daughter laughed heartily, and enjoyed it very much; and the latter, soon beginning to mingle in the sports, got pillaged by the young brigands most ruthlessly. What would I not have given to be one of them! Though I never could have been so rude, no, no! I wouldn't for the wealth of all the world have crushed that braided hair, and torn it down; and for the precious little shoe, I wouldn't have plucked it off, God bless my soul! to save my life. As to measuring her waist in sport, as they did, bold young brood, I couldn't have done it; I should have expected my arm to have grown round it for a punishment, and never come straight again.[24]

The fun becomes more boisterous still when their father comes home, 'attended by a man laden with Christmas toys and presents':

> Then the shouting and the struggling, and the onslaught that was made on the defenceless porter! The scaling him, with chairs for ladders, to dive into his pockets, despoil him of brown-paper parcels, hold on tight by his cravat, hug him round the neck, pommel his back, and kick his legs in irrepressible affection! The shouts of wonder and delight with which the development of every package was received! The terrible announcement that the baby had been taken in the act of putting a doll's frying-pan into his mouth, and was more than suspected of having swallowed a fictitious turkey, glued on a wooden platter! The immense relief of finding this a false alarm! The joy, and gratitude, and ecstacy! They are all indescribable alike. It is enough that by degrees the children and their emotions got out of the parlour and by one stair at a time, up to the top of the house; where they went to bed, and so subsided.

Dickens, quick as always to identify with the world of childhood, indeed to see the world itself from a child's point of view, presents this as an enviable picture – the happy rough and tumble of domestic life that might have been Scrooge's, had he not chosen instead to pursue the acquisition of wealth. There is a moral here, and a very firm one, but it has nothing to do with the children's behaviour. It is worth noting, incidentally, that the children are by implication boys; there are no doubt girls among them, but the various activities of infant assault seem to be male, as if Dickens does not quite like to suggest that little girls would behave with such a lack of decorum.

Jane Austen is more realistic; if John and William Middleton are bad, their sister Annamaria is infinitely worse, adding cunning to the simple naughtiness of her brothers:

> 'John is in such spirits to-day!' said [Lady Middleton], on his taking Miss Steele's pocket handkerchief, and throwing it out of window – 'He is full of monkey tricks.'
>
> And soon afterwards, on the second boy's violently pinching one of the same lady's fingers, she fondly observed, 'How playful William is!'
>
> 'And here is my sweet little Annamaria,' she added, tenderly caressing a little girl of three years old, who had not made a noise for the last two minutes; 'And she is always so gentle and quiet – Never was there such a quiet little thing!' But unfortunately in bestowing these embraces, a pin in her ladyship's head dress slightly scratching the child's neck, produced from this pattern of gentleness, such violent screams, as could hardly be outdone by any creature professedly noisy. The mother's consternation was excessive; but it could not surpass the alarm of the Miss Steeles, and every thing was done by all three, in so critical an emergency, which affection could suggest as likely to assuage the agonies of the little sufferer. She was seated in her mother's lap, covered with kisses, her wound bathed with lavender-water, by one of the Miss Steeles, who was on her knees to attend her, and her mouth stuffed with sugar plums by the other. With such a reward for her tears, the child was too wise to cease crying. She still screamed and sobbed lustily, kicked her two brothers for offering to touch her, and all their united soothings were ineffectual till Lady Middleton luckily remembering that in a scene of similar distress last week, some apricot marmalade had been successfully applied for a bruised temple, the same remedy was eagerly proposed for this unfortunate scratch, and a slight intermission of screams in the young lady on hearing it, gave them reason to hope that it would not be rejected. – She was carried out of the room therefore in her mother's arms, in quest of this medicine, and as the two boys chose to follow, though earnestly entreated by their mother to stay behind, the four young ladies were left in a quietness which the room had not known for many hours.[25]

The detail here is masterly. The child is seated in majesty on her mother's lap, while the Miss Steeles minister to her, one of them at least on her knees before her; thus supported, Annamaria is free to use her legs to kick her brothers, who try to help. This is not the first incident of its kind, since Lady Middleton 'luckily' remembers that apricot marmalade worked last week; and it is presumably one that will be repeated frequently. It is hoped that the 'medicine' will not be 'rejected'; and, still sovereign, the child is carried out of the room, with, as a final touch, the boys following, 'though earnestly entreated by their mother' not to do so. If the Miss Steeles choose to abase themselves before her, for their own ends, her mother seems really incapable of exerting any authority whatsoever. It is left to Marianne, outspoken as ever, to cut through the pretence:

> 'Poor little creature!' said Miss Steele, as soon as they were gone. 'It might have been a very sad accident.'
>
> 'Yet I hardly know how,' cried Marianne, 'unless it had been under totally different circumstances. But this is the usual way of heightening alarm, where there is nothing to be alarmed at in reality.'

Elinor is perhaps a little more tactful in her response to Anne Steele's enthusiasm:

> 'And what a charming little family they have! I never saw such fine children in my life. – I declare I quite doat upon them already, and indeed I am always distractedly fond of children.'
>
> 'I should guess so,' said Elinor with a smile, 'from what I have witnessed this morning.'

Lucy, more devious than her sister, probes Elinor further:

> 'I have a notion,' said Lucy, 'you think the little Middletons rather too much indulged; perhaps they may be the outside of enough; but it is so natural in Lady Middleton; and for my part, I love to see children full of life and spirits; I cannot bear them if they are tame and quiet.'
>
> 'I confess,' replied Elinor, that while I am at Barton Park, I never think of tame and quiet children with any abhorrence.'

Lady Middleton is anything but naive, however, in her indulgence towards her children; she is perfectly willing quite brazenly to exploit her guests' anxiety to ingratiate themselves. On a subsequent occasion, as they settle to cards, when the children have finally left the drawing-room after dinner, she says to Lucy

> 'I am glad . . . you are not going to finish poor little Annamaria's basket this evening; for I am sure it must hurt your eyes to work fillagree by candlelight. And we will make the dear little love some amends for her disappointment to-morrow, and then I hope she will not much mind it.'[26]

Lucy, of course, responds just as Lady Middleton expects her to:

> This hint was enough, Lucy recollected herself instantly and replied, 'Indeed you are very much mistaken, Lady Middleton; I am only waiting to know whether you can make your party without me, or I should have been at my fillagree already. I would not disappoint

the little angel for all the world, and if you want me at the card-table now, I am resolved to finish the basket after supper.'

'You are very good, I hope it won't hurt your eyes – will you ring the bell for some working candles? My poor little girl would be sadly disappointed, I know, if the basket was not finished to-morrow, for though I told her it certainly would not, I am sure she depends on having it done.'

Lucy directly drew her work table near her and reseated herself with an alacrity and cheerfulness which seemed to infer that she could taste no greater delight than in making a fillagree basket for a spoilt child.

Even from a distance Annamaria exerts her tyranny.

There is a double criticism here. For one thing, it would be of much greater use to the development of both the child's skill and her character if she were taught to make the basket for herself. More importantly, however, a question needs to be asked about the value of the article by which she sets such store. In 'The Birthday Present', one of the children's stories in Maria Edgeworth's *The Parent's Assistant*, which appeared in 1796, the spoilt little Bell is given just such a filigree basket made by her cousin Rosamond, who has spent a half-guinea given to her by her godmother on the papers to complete it. The fragility of the delicate item is stressed by Rosamond's father when, on the way to Bell's birthday dinner, he inspects her handiwork:

> 'Let us look at this basket,' said he, taking it out of her unwilling hands, for she knew of what frail materials it was made, and she dreaded its coming to pieces under her father's examination. He took hold of the handle rather roughly; when, starting off the coach seat, she cried, 'Oh, sir! father! sir! you will spoil it indeed,' said she, with increased vehemence, when, after drawing aside the veil of silver paper, she saw him grasp the myrtle-covered handle. 'Indeed, sir, you will spoil the poor handle.'
>
> 'But what is the use of *the poor handle,*' said her father, 'if we are not to take hold of it? And pray,' continued he, turning the basket round with his finger and thumb, rather in a disrespectful manner, 'pray, is this the thing you have been about all this week? I have seen you all this week dabbling with paste and rags; I could not conceive what you were about. Is this the thing?' 'Yes, sir. You think, then, that I have wasted my time, because the basket is of no use . . .'

When the basket is delivered, to be given to Bell after dinner as a surprise, the petulant child persuades her deceitful maid to let her look at it in advance and, in snatching at it, 'a struggle ensued, in which the handle and lid were torn off, and one of the medallions crushed inwards'; later, in trying to conceal their guilt, the child and the maid attempt to put the blame onto a poor girl who has delivered some lace to the house. The basket, though expensive and pretty (the maid describes it as 'the most *beautifullest* thing you ever saw in your life'), is actually useless; furthermore it is morally worthless, since it is the cause of both dishonesty and unkindness in its recipient.

Maria Edgeworth makes the filigree basket the centre of her story, and uses its gaudy insubstantiality to embody her moral. In the episode in *Sense and Sensibility*, Jane Austen has another purpose, and one for which she has been elaborately preparing. The child and her work-basket are amusing, of course, both in themselves and in what they bring out in Lucy and Lady Middleton; and any reader of *The Parent's Assistant* would have caught the ironic allusion. But Annamaria's basket has a more structural function in the scene. Elinor is very anxious for the opportunity to hear Lucy speak about her feelings for Edward, and she is now not above a little subterfuge of her own. 'Perhaps,' she says,

> if I should happen to cut out, I may be of some use to Miss Lucy Steele, in rolling her papers for her; and there is so much still to be done to the basket, that it must be impossible I think for her labour singly, to finish it this evening. I should like the work exceedingly, if she would allow me a share in it.'
>
> 'Indeed I shall be very much obliged to you for your help,' cried Lucy, 'for I find there is more to be done to it than I thought there was; and it would be a shocking thing to disappoint dear Annamaria after all.'
>
> 'Oh! that would be terrible indeed,' said Miss Steele – 'Dear little soul, how I do love her!'
>
> 'You are very kind,' said Lady Middleton to Elinor . . .

Sitting next to Lucy, while Marianne plays the pianoforte, Elinor is able to have one of the most important conversations of the book. Jane Austen has characteristically made use of a child to enable her to further the concerns of her adult characters.

Lady Middleton's indulgence of her children is presented as so palpably wrongheaded that there can be little doubt that we are expected to find it quite abnormal; commonsense – which Jane Austen always pays her readers the compliment of having – will suggest that such behaviour is unusual, and indeed no doubt depicted in the novel as much out of a spirit of comedy as anything else. But a writer who took a more radical view of the deficiencies of the situation of women might see the failure of mothers to bring up their children properly as a more widespread, and indeed inevitable, outcome of their lack of independence. Mary Wollstonecraft certainly took this view. Woman, she wrote,

> a slave in every situation to prejudice, seldom exerts enlightened maternal affection; for she either neglects her children, or spoils them by improper indulgence. Besides, the affection of some women for their children is, as I have before termed it, frequently very brutish: for it eradicates every spark of humanity. Justice, truth, every thing is sacrificed by these Rebekah's, and for the sake of their *own* children they violate the most sacred duties, forgetting the common relationship that binds the whole family on earth together. Yet, reason seems to say, that they who suffer one duty, or affection, to swallow up the rest, have not sufficient heart or mind to fulfil that one conscientiously. It then loses the venerable aspect of a duty, and assumes the fantastic form of a whim.[27]

This passage, though of course intended to have a wide social (and indeed economic and political) application, could almost serve as a direct commentary on Lady Middleton's willingness to sacrifice everybody's comfort to the whims of Annamaria.

Mary Wollstonecraft shared with Johnson a hatred of parental tyranny; but with respect to girls she went beyond him in her analysis of its effect on their position in life: 'more kept down by their parents, in every sense of the word, than boys', having been 'thus taught slavishly to submit to their parents', they are 'prepared for the slavery of marriage'.[28] On the other hand, where 'the indolent parent of high rank' may 'extort a shew of respect from his child', as she claims is particularly the case on the continent, 'the consequence is notorious; these dutiful daughters become adulteresses, and neglect the education of their children, from whom they, in their turn, exact the same kind of obedience'. Again, without looking as far as the continent, twenty years after she wrote this she might have applied it to the system of parental authority at Mansfield Park. While it is highly unlikely that Jane Austen ever read a word of Mary Wollstonecraft (though she did read the novels of her radical husband, William Godwin), she would hardly have disagreed with her view of the mutually dependent nature of the affection between parent and child:

> it is not the parents who have given the surest proof of their affection for their children, or, to speak more properly, who by fulfilling their duty, have allowed a natural parental affection to take root in their hearts, the child of exercised sympathy and reason, and not the over-weening offspring of selfish pride, who most vehemently insist on their children submitting to their will merely because it is their will. On the contrary, the parent, who sets a good example, patiently lets that example work; and it seldom fails to produce its natural effect – filial reverence.

The four little Gardiners in *Pride and Prejudice* – 'two girls of six and eight years old, and two younger boys' – provide an illustration of the connection made by Mary Wollstonecraft between the example set by parents and the behaviour of their children. Mr and Mrs Gardiner treat them with affection and kindness, and they are among the most attractive children in the novels. When Elizabeth arrives at Gracechurch Street on her way to Hunsford, they are crowding on the stairs: their 'eagerness for their cousin's appearance would not allow them to wait in the drawing-room', and their shyness, 'as they had not seen her for a twelvemonth, prevented their coming lower'.[29] Jane has been staying there, and they have obviously made friends with her; when subsequently they are left at Longbourn during the Gardiners' tour to Derbyshire, they are to be 'under the personal care of their cousin Jane, who was the general favourite, and whose steady sense and sweetness of temper exactly adapted her for attending to them in every way – teaching them, playing with them, and loving them'. These three functions, teaching, playing and loving, might almost sum up the necessary requirements as Jane Austen saw them for bringing up children, and certainly their welcoming of them from their cousin shows that they are what they receive at home. When Elizabeth returns with her uncle and aunt from Derbyshire to a Longbourn in tumult after Lydia's elopement, the Gardiner children in their innocence seem to represent a still centre of a household in great distress:

> The little Gardiners, attracted by the sight of a chaise, were standing on the steps of the house, as they entered the paddock; and when the carriage drove up to the door, the joyful surprise that lighted up their faces, and displayed itself over their whole bodies, in a variety of capers and frisks, was the first pleasing earnest of their welcome.[30]

Elizabeth gives each of them 'an hasty kiss' before hurrying to talk to Jane, and the point is then specifically made that Mr and Mrs Gardiner occupy themselves with their children before anything else. It is interesting, however, that they are never individualized: seen only as a group, and never even given names (they are referred to only as 'the little Gardiners'), it appears that such affectionate, well-behaved children do not quite offer the opportunities for satire that naughtier, less manageable ones do; though the engaging picture of their gathering to welcome newcomers with a characteristic mixture of eagerness and timidity is not without humour.

While disapproving of parents who indulged their children to the extent of spoiling them, Jane Austen was certainly sympathetic to those who, like the Gardiners, made them central to their happiness. When the Revd Richard Buller, a former pupil at Steventon rectory, was visiting Bath for his health in 1805, during the period when the Austens were living there, she wrote to Cassandra: 'The Children are not come, so that poor Mrs Buller is away from all that can constitute enjoyment with her. – I shall be glad to be of any use to her, but she has that sort of quiet composedness of mind which always seems sufficient to itself.'[31] It has been suggested that there is a hint here of the relationship between Jane Fairfax and Emma – that Mrs Buller may have been a little jealous of Jane Austen's friendship with her husband;[32] but the phrase 'quiet composedness of mind', suggesting calm resignation in the face of being parted from her children, since it cannot be helped, might be just as appropriate for Mrs Gardiner.

A similar lack of fuss and nonsense is found in Mrs Harville. 'Perfectly comfortable,' as Mrs Croft knows she would have been when Captain Wentworth took her in his ship from Portsmouth to Plymouth, crowded in with her three children, her sister and her cousin,[33] she is practical, adaptable and entirely unworried by anything; even the prospect of accommodating Louisa after her fall from the Cobb in their tight little cottage – and more too if necessary – leaves both her and her husband completely unperplexed: they are 'only concerned that the house could accommodate no more; and yet perhaps by "putting the children away in the maids' room, or swinging a cot somewhere," they could hardly bear to think of not finding room for two or three besides'.[34] When nieces or nephews visited Chawton Cottage, similar ad hoc arrangements had to be made. If Jane was away, her bed would be pressed into service. Writing home from a visit to London in

1814, she sent her love to her five-year-old niece, Cassy, Charles's eldest child, but added: 'I hope she found my Bed comfortable last night & has not filled it with fleas';[35] and in another letter a week later, she commented, 'If Cassandra has filled my Bed with fleas, I am sure they must bite herself'.[36]

Jane Austen often allows a reflection of parents' virtues, or more usually their faults, to appear in the children. Mr Bennet's wit and powers of amused observation (though not his irresponsibility) have been inherited by Elizabeth, just as Mrs Bennet's foolishness characterizes her younger daughters; in Anne Elliot Lady Russell 'could fancy the mother to revive again',[37] and the inheritance of Sir Walter's pride in his eldest daughter is too obvious to mention. Edmund Bertram has something of his father's solemnity – though it is properly directed towards the seriousness of conscience in a young man who knows that his calling is for the Church – and Tom perhaps something of his mother's idleness in a more active form; and in *Sense and Sensibility* the two qualities reflected in Elinor and Marianne were no doubt derived respectively from their father's cautious practicality (unavailing, as it turned out) and their mother's romantic optimism.

Emma Woodhouse, we might guess, takes after her mother; Mr Knightley's comment, noted earlier, that 'in her mother she lost the only person able to cope with her'[38] suggests that it was from her that she inherited her capacity for managing people. To her father, on the other hand, she seems on the surface to bear little resemblance. Her utter devotion to him is of course one of her better qualities; indeed, she is almost as protective of him as he wishes to be of everybody else. Considerable attention is paid in the narrative to the precise cause of her criticism of her brother-in-law, Mr John Knightley, whom Mr Woodhouse's 'peculiarities and fidgettiness' sometimes provoked to 'a rational remonstrance or sharp retort equally ill bestowed'.[39] The fact that he is not 'a great favourite with his fair sister-in-law', that 'nothing wrong in him escaped her', is partly attributed to her feeling 'the little injuries to Isabella, which Isabella never felt herself' and partly – with characteristic Austenian irony – because his manners are 'not flattering to Isabella's sister'; yet the true source of her reservations about him is unambiguously altruistic: 'hardly any degree of personal compliment could have made her regardless of that greatest fault of all in her eyes which he sometimes fell into, the want of respectful forbearance towards her father'. Her natural expectation that everyone should see her father as she does closely resembles Mr Woodhouse's uncritical view of her. At the beginning of the novel Mr Knightley suggests that it must be better for Miss Taylor, now that she is married, to have only one person to please, rather than two:

'Especially when *one* of those two is such a fanciful, troublesome creature!' said Emma playfully. 'That is what you have in your head, I know – and what you would certainly say if my father were not by.'

'I believe it is very true, my dear, indeed,' said Mr. Woodhouse with a sigh. 'I am afraid I am sometimes very fanciful and troublesome.'

'My dearest papa! You do not think I could mean *you*, or suppose Mr. Knightley to mean *you*. What a horrible idea! Oh, no! I meant only myself. Mr. Knightley loves to find fault with me you know – in a joke – it is all a joke. We always say what we like to one another.'

Mr. Knightley, in fact, was one of the few people who could see faults in Emma Woodhouse, and the only one who ever told her of them: and though this was not particularly agreeable to Emma herself, she knew it would be so much less so to her father, that she would not have him really suspect such a circumstance as her not being thought perfect by every body.[40]

In her 'playful' banter with Mr Knightley, Emma has forgotten for the moment that her father is likely to misunderstand her words. When she realizes that he has applied them to himself, she is genuinely anxious; her cry that the idea is 'horrible' is heartfelt – she is no Isabella Thorpe to use the word lightly; but then she has inadvertently opened up another unpleasant thought to him, that it might be possible for someone to find fault with her – hence her insistence that it is 'all a joke'. Some recent critics, notably Richard Jenkyns in his otherwise fine and judicious study of Jane Austen, *A Fine Brush on Ivory*, have been rather hard on Mr Woodhouse, regarding him as a deliberate obstructer of the heroine's happiness, like Mrs Norris. For Jenkyns he is 'the stealthiest of the villains', an 'active force of malignancy', a 'bloodsucker, fastened upon his daughter's flesh', an 'incubus' whose 'crime is to use his daughter's love for himself in a plot to blight her life, if he can'.[41] Yet *Emma* is a novel in which unconditional love for people who may, consciously or unconsciously, require sacrifices to be made for them is a recurring theme. Miss Bates lives out her restricted life with her elderly mother, not as a duty, but as an act of joyful and loving devotion; and all the love and pride which, in other circumstances, might have been given to children of her own, she invests unquestioningly in her niece (it is surely one of Jane Austen's greatest achievements to have made the principal comic character in the novel also the most radiant emblem of Christian goodness). Mr Woodhouse is to be seen in the same light: like Miss Bates he takes genuine pleasure in the company of his old friends, though the pleasure of his hospitality may be limited by his fastidiousness as hers is by her volubility; and his inability to see faults in Emma springs from the same love and generosity as Miss Bates has for Jane Fairfax.

This seems to be essentially a very serious aspect of what is being explored in the novel. More overt fun is had with Mr Woodhouse and his elder daughter. Isabella is a valetudinarian, like her father, with whom indeed she shares more characteristics than Emma does; and Jane Austen points the resemblance clearly:

Mrs. John Knightley was a pretty, elegant little woman, of gentle, quiet manners, and a disposition remarkably amiable and affectionate; wrapt up in her family; a devoted wife, a doating mother, and so tenderly attached to her father and sister that, but for these higher ties, a warmer love might have seemed impossible. She could never see a fault in any of them. She was not a woman of strong understanding or any quickness; and with this resemblance of her father, she inherited also much of his constitution; was delicate in her own health, over- careful of that of her children, had many fears and many nerves, and was as fond of her own Mr. Wingfield in town as her father could be of Mr. Perry. They were alike too, in a general benevolence of temper, and a strong habit of regard for every old acquaintance.[42]

As soon as she arrives on their visit to Hartfield she sympathizes with her father and sister for Miss Taylor's marriage: 'what a dreadful loss to you both!' she says. 'I have been so grieved for you.'[43] And she speaks in 'the plaintive tone which just suited her father'. But her over-anxious nature has its corrective in her husband, and if she 'coddles' her children and fills them with Mr Wingfield's patent medicines, Mr John Knightley ensures that they get a good country run, so that their 'healthy, glowing faces' seem to ensure 'a quick dispatch of the roast mutton and rice pudding' they hurry home for.[44] Like the Gardiners, they are fond and attentive parents: as they sit comfortably together at Hartfield, Mr Woodhouse takes Isabella's hand, 'interrupting, for a few moments, her busy labours for some one of her five children';[45] and faced with the prospect of spending the evening at Randalls, Mr John Knightley resents 'the sacrifice of his children after dinner'.[46] Yet they do not allow the children's behaviour to disturb the quiet pace of life of their grandfather's house; even Isabella's concern for the instant gratification of their wishes is subjugated to it:

> the ways of Hartfield and the feelings of her father were so respected by Mrs. John Knightley, that in spite of maternal solicitude for the immediate enjoyment of her little ones, and for their having instantly all the liberty and attendance, all the eating and drinking, and sleeping and playing, which they could possibly wish for, without the smallest delay, the children were never allowed to be long a disturbance to him, either in themselves or in any restless attendance on them.[47]

Having established the respective preoccupations of the elderly hypochondriac and the devoted young mother, Jane Austen is happy to deploy a little good-natured irony over their conjunction.

But as with so much in *Emma*, the irony, and the criticism it embodies, is tolerant and good-humoured. When on a subsequent occasion Mr John Knightley brings his two eldest children, John and Henry, to Hartfield, where they are to stay for several weeks with their grandpapa and aunt, he gives Emma a letter from Isabella, the contents of which he can guess, and on which he comments wryly:

> Well, Emma, I do not believe I have any thing more to say about the boys; but you have your sister's letter, and every thing is down at full length there we may be sure. My charge would be much more concise than her's, and probably not much in the same spirit; all that I have to recommend being comprised in, do not spoil them, and do not physic them.[48]

Emma's reply combines irony with a realistic understanding of the characters of both her sister and her brother-in-law:

> I rather hope to satisfy you both ... for I shall do all in my power to make them happy, which will be enough for Isabella; and happiness must preclude false indulgence and physic.

Perhaps the most incapable mother portrayed in the novels is Mary Musgrove. Without being in any way malign, as Lady Susan is, she seems quite unable to cope with her children, and is certainly unwilling to be put to any inconvenience or to forgo any pleasure on their account. When little Charles dislocates his collarbone, Anne has to manage everything – 'the apothecary to send for – the father to have pursued and informed – the mother to support and keep from hysterics – the servants to control – the youngest child to banish, and the poor suffering one to attend and soothe'.[49] Mary, as in any difficult situation, is able to do nothing. Invited to meet Captain Wentworth at the Great House, she and Charles are at first 'in much too strong and recent alarm to bear the thought' of leaving the child; but when, as he is clearly going on well, Charles decides that he will go, she is full of resentment – not at having to look after the child, but, as she makes clear to Anne, because she is left out:

> So, here he is to go away and enjoy himself, and because I am the poor mother, I am not allowed to stir; – and yet, I am sure, I am more unfit than any body else to be about the child. My being the mother is the very reason why my feelings should not be tried. I am not at all equal to it. You saw how hysterical I was yesterday.[50]

The conflicting claims to a mother's feelings and the right not to have them tried is at once comic and sad; and as usual it is Anne who resolves them by offering to stay and look after the boy herself; in happily accepting, Mary's reply is again couched in ironies of which she is altogether unaware:

> Dear me! that's a very good thought, very good indeed. To be sure I may just as well go as not, for I am of no use at home – am I? and it only harasses me. You, who have not a mother's feelings, are a great deal the properest person. You can make little Charles do any thing; he always minds you at a word.

The greatest irony, however, is Anne's, since, as we have seen, she is exploiting Mary's unwillingness to miss out on the visit to avoid having to go herself and meet Wentworth.

Mary's attitude towards her children is not judged only by the reader, but by other characters too. After Louisa's fall on the Cobb, Captain Wentworth proposes that Anne should stay in Lyme to assist Mrs Harville; 'Mrs. Charles Musgrove,' he says, 'will, of course, wish to get back to her children.'[51] But Mary is determined not to be made to go home, and her behaviour is described in terms that make it sound positively childish:

She was so wretched, and so vehement, complained so much of injustice in being expected to go away instead of Anne; – Anne, who was nothing to Louisa, while she was her sister, and had the best right to stay in Henrietta's stead! Why was not she to be as useful as Anne? And to go home without Charles, too – without her husband! No, it was too unkind!

Even Anne for once judges her (though not aloud) as she reluctantly submits to her 'jealous and ill-judging claims'. And Mary is again quite unconscious of the irony when she writes to Anne while the Harville children are staying at Uppercross: 'The house was cleared yesterday, except of the little Harvilles; but you will be surprised to hear that they have never gone home. Mrs. Harville must be an odd mother to part with them so long. I do not understand it.'[52] Anne in fact has no doubt about the relative merits of her sister and brother-in-law as parents:

> As to the management of their children, his theory was much better than his wife's, and his practice not so bad. – 'I could manage them very well, if it were not for Mary's interference,' – was what Anne often heard him say, and had a good deal of faith in; but when listening in turn to Mary's reproach of 'Charles spoils the children so that I cannot get them into any order,' – she never had the smallest temptation to say, 'Very true.'[53]

In one of her fits of nervous exhaustion, Mary herself admits that 'they are so unmanageable' that they do her more harm than good: 'Little Charles does not mind a word I say and Walter is growing quite as bad.'[54] As so often, Jane Austen makes use of the children and their management to reveal failings or virtues in their parents.

Anne in some ways almost seems to be a surrogate mother to her sister's two little boys, since she is so much better at dealing with them than Mary is; and this reciprocated affection is made very clear: 'in the children, who loved her nearly as well, and respected her a great deal more than their mother, she had an object of interest, amusement, and wholesome exertion.'[55] At a period when she is resigning herself to lifelong spinsterhood, two little nephews on whom to expend the affection that would in other circumstances have been devoted to children of her own must be of especial comfort to her. Other childless women in Jane Austen also find an outlet for their affection in nephews and nieces, sometimes to beneficial effect, sometimes not. As we have noted, no one could be more disinterestedly kind than Miss Bates is to Jane Fairfax; on the other hand, the lasting harm that Mrs Norris's indulgence causes Maria is considerably greater than the effect of her dislike on Fanny.

Fanny is not formally adopted by Sir Thomas, and she never thinks of him and Lady Bertram as anything other than her uncle and aunt, despite the fact that Mansfield Park becomes her home – something she never feels more strongly than when she returns to the noise and bustle of her father's overcrowded house in Portsmouth. Fanny's feelings for her own family, whom, apart from William, she has not seen for nine years, are unequivocal: 'Would they but love her, she should be satisfied.'[56] Yet such a long separation is bound to have had an effect on her relations with them, even if it is experienced subconsciously. When, on her arrival in Portsmouth, her mother meets her 'with looks of true kindness', Fanny loves her features 'the more, because they brought her aunt Bertram's before her'. It is a telling observation that reveals a recognition on Jane Austen's part of the complex and ambivalent feelings that may arise from a shift in the normal child–parent relationship.

It was not uncommon for children of a large family to be removed by a relation who was better able to provide for them, sometimes permanently, as in the case of Edward Austen, who was adopted by his father's wealthy cousin Thomas Knight and his wife (and as, in *Emma*, Frank Churchill is by his uncle and aunt). Such arrangements might be made only for a certain period. Elizabeth Ham, born some seven years after Jane Austen in the village of North Perrott in Somerset, was taken at the age of eighteen months to stay in the family of a great uncle, a mile or so away, when her mother was about to give birth to her next child. But the old man's daughter became so fond of her that she was kept on in the household, and it was only when this cousin married and had a child herself that Elizabeth was returned to her own parents, by which time she was ten years old. She seems to have accepted this long period of separation as quite normal and was apparently unaffected by it, recalling the return home in her memoir with perfect equilibrium:

> Here then began my acquaintance, as it were, with my own family, for before this time we had met only for short periods. My two elder brothers, and a large Newfoundland dog called Caesar, were now my play-fellows. My third brother, William, had, like myself, been abstracted from the family circle, and, after the death of my grandfather, continued to reside with his youngest son, still a bachelor.[57]

A more permanent arrangement was made by the Austens' friends the Chutes, of The Vyne, Basingstoke. William John Chute was the MP for Hampshire and Master of the Vine Foxhounds. In 1793 he married Eliza Smith (whose niece Emma would become the wife of James Edward Austen-Leigh); but they had no children and in 1803 they took to live with them the daughter of a cousin, the Revd James Wiggett, who had just been widowed and left with seven children. Caroline was only three at the time; they did not formally adopt her, but The Vyne was to become her home. Though she had a happy childhood, in later life she was to recall of her uncle and aunt 'though they were very kind to me, I ever felt I did not belong to them'.[58] She got on well with her uncle William and his good humoured brother Tom, but she never really felt quite at ease with Mrs Chute. Yet it was evident that the childless woman was very fond of her. Caroline often suffered from poor health, and during a particularly serious bout when she was seventeen, Jane Austen wrote 'I am sorry to hear of Caroline Wiggetts being so ill. Mrs Chute I suppose would almost feel like a Mother in losing her.'[59]

It is difficult to say whether children in such circumstances regarded themselves as lucky or not. On the whole it must have been better to be the sole object of affection of a childless couple than to be lost among the members of a large family. If, like the Churchills or, in Edward Austen's case, the Knights, the adopted child stood to inherit their estate, the advantage would have been seen to be considerable, especially since there was no reason for him to cut himself off from his own parents. Jane Austen presents an idealized, if nonsensical, version of the idea of adoption in 'Henry and Eliza', written when she was about fourteen, with her own brother already adopted by Mr and Mrs Knight. In the story, Sir George and Lady Harcourt are 'superintending the Labours of their Haymakers' and 'rewarding the industry of some by smiles of approbation, & punishing the idleness of others, by a cudgel', when they come upon a beautiful little girl, 'not more than 3 months old', lying 'closely concealed beneath the thick foliage of a Haycock':

> Touched with the enchanting Graces of her face & delighted with the infantine tho' sprightly answers she returned to their many questions, they resolved to take her home &, having no Children of their own, to educate her with care & cost. Being good People themselves, their first & principal care was to incite in her a Love of Virtue & a Hatred of Vice, in which they so well succeeded (Eliza having a natural turn that way herself) that when she grew up, she was the delight of all who knew her.[60]

Unfortunately, their teaching turns out not to have been quite as thorough as they might have wished:

> Beloved by Lady Harcourt, adored by Sir George & admired by all the World, she lived in a continued course of uninterrupted Happiness, till she had attained her eighteenth year, when happening one day to be detected in stealing a banknote of 50£, she was turned out of doors by her inhuman Benefactors.

A more general matter of luck for a child lay in its godparents, particularly if there was the expectation that it might receive presents or be left money in their will. Rich Uncle Francis was one of James Austen's godfathers and rich Uncle James Leigh-Perrot one of Edward's. Jane's own godparents were her great-aunt, Uncle Francis's wife Jane, Jane Musgrave, the wife of a clerical cousin of her mother, and the Revd Samuel Cooke, vicar of Great Bookham in Surrey, and another of her mother's cousins by marriage. Jane visited the Cookes on several occasions, and was fond of them, though perhaps more of Mrs Cooke (some of whose letters she preserved) than of her godfather: writing to Cassandra of a former manservant of the family in Bath when there was a question of his going to the Cookes, she commented: 'The Cookes' place seems of a sort to suit Isaac, if he means to go to service again, & does not object to change of Country. He will have a good Soil, & a good Mistress ... The only doubt which occurs to me is whether Mr Cooke may not be a disagreeable, fidgety Master, especially in matters concerning the Garden.'[61] Be that as it may, she was very pleased with his opinion of *Mansfield Park*, which they both greatly admired: 'Mr Cooke says "it is the most sensible Novel he ever read" – and the manner in which I treat the Clergy, delights them very much.'[62]

It is in *Mansfield Park* that we find a sharply contrasted pair of godparents – godmothers to two of Fanny's sisters. Mrs Price tells Fanny that the silver knife about which Susan and Betsey quarrel was originally given to Mary, now dead, by her 'good godmother, old Mrs. Admiral Maxwell'. She adds to Betsey: '*you* have not the luck of such a good godmother. Aunt Norris lives too far off, to think of such little people as you.'[63] Characteristically, when she knows that Fanny is going to Portsmouth, Mrs Norris considers sending her god-daughter a Prayer Book, but in finding that neither of the old ones belonging to her husband is suitable, 'the ardour of generosity went off', and all Fanny has to convey to the little girl is 'a message to say she hoped her god-daughter was a good girl, and learnt her book'. The greeting, cold and impersonal, bespeaks a false sense of duty. Where the admiral's wife shows love, the rector's widow fails in her obligation as a godparent, not only in a lack of kindness, but, since the gift in question is a Prayer Book, in contributing to the religious upbringing of the child entrusted to her spiritual care.

Jane Austen makes a severe indictment.

6

The child in the family

Jane Austen grew up in a happy, well-regulated family, in which the children were given a comfortable home, a good education and a firm understanding of sound moral principles. When the time came, careers were found for the boys, and in her widowhood Mrs Austen kept her daughters with her and warmly welcomed visits from her numerous grandchildren. Jane herself could, with Miss Bates, justly have misquoted the Psalms and claimed that 'our lot is cast in a goodly heritage';[1] and indeed the phrase has been used as the title of a biography of the Austen family.[2] Such a background undoubtedly shapes a contented, well-adjusted human being, but it does not necessarily make a good setting for a novel; and of Jane Austen's heroines only one, Catherine Morland, has a family that is equally sensible, loving and reliable. Yet this was the norm for the people among whom Jane grew up, many of whom came, like Catherine, from clerical families. She is unlikely to have come across many examples of a Mrs Bennet or a Sir Walter Elliot in her immediate circle, and though, as we have seen, she may at times have been somewhat critical of, for example, the lack of firmness with which Charles and Fanny Austen brought up their little girls, her brothers and their wives were kind and affectionate parents and as much interested in the well-being of each other's children as Jane and Cassandra were in their nephews and nieces.

An idea of the warm impression that the family had always made on other people is given by their cousin Eliza de Feullide, niece of Mr Austen, and subsequently the wife of Henry. Writing to Philadelphia Walter in October 1792, she reported that Cassandra and Jane were 'equally sensible, and both so to a degree seldom met with' and that Henry was 'endowed with uncommon Abilities, which indeed seem to have been bestowed, tho' in a different way, upon each Member of this Family'.[3] That there was a sense of ease among them, that they got on well together, was attested by Phylly herself when four years earlier she met Mr and Mrs Austen and their daughters; though little drawn to Jane on a first meeting, she nevertheless noted that they were 'all in high spirits & disposed to be pleased with each other'.[4] This was to prove an enduring quality. Years later Caroline Austen remembered Chawton Cottage as 'a cheerful house', and, also quoting the Psalms, laid emphasis on the closeness of her uncles and aunts and their enjoyment of each other's company:

> my Uncles, one or another, frequently [came] for a few days; and they were all pleasant in their own family – I have thought since, after having seen more of other households,

wonderfully, as the family talk had much of spirit and vivacity, and it was never troubled by disagreements as it was not their habit to argue with each other – There always was perfect harmony amongst the brothers and sisters, and over my Grandmother's door might have been inscribed the text, 'Behold how good – and joyful a thing it is, brethren, to dwell together in unity.' There was firm family union, never broken but by death . . .[5]

Fanny Caroline Lefroy, James Austen's granddaughter, wrote that

a great deal of intercourse was kept up between Steventon & Chawton. Our Grandfather was a most attentive son & one of the pleasures of my mothers youth was sometimes riding with him to see her Grandmother & Aunt through the pretty cress roads & rough lanes inaccessible to wheels which lay between the two places.[6]

Her mother, Anna Lefroy, had always had a second home with her grandmother and aunts; during the widowhood of her father, before he married Mary Lloyd, she was sent to live at Steventon rectory (then of course still inhabited by her grandparents) and 'could remember being noticed and played with by the pupils, and having "Pride and Prejudice" (begun 1796) read aloud by it's youthful author to her sister'. Anna was 'a very intelligent quick witted child and she caught up the names of the characters and talked about them so much downstairs, that her Aunts feared she would provoke enquiry, for the story was still a secret from the elders'.[7]

Henry, Frank, Charles, Cassandra and Jane frequently visited Edward and his growing family at Godmersham, and relations between them all were equally friendly, for Edward's children were similarly good-natured and also benefited from an upbringing by sensible and affectionate parents. Jane, however, may not always have felt altogether at home amid the comparative luxury of the wealthy household, and equally there is some evidence that they were not entirely at ease with her. In a letter written many years later to James Edward Austen-Leigh when he was preparing the *Memoir*, Anna Lefroy recalled that while 'the young people of Godmersham' liked Aunt Jane 'as a playfellow, & as a teller of stories', they were 'not really fond of her'. Anna believed that their mother, Elizabeth Bridges, was not, and that 'she very much preferred the elder Sister', ascribing this to a feeling that Jane was too clever for them. 'A little talent went a long way with the Goodneston Bridgeses,' she wrote, '& *much* must have gone a long way too far'.[8] Elizabeth certainly does not seem to have relished the kind of literary games at which Jane (and for that matter Mrs Austen) excelled. A surviving poem of hers, written as part of a game in which the participants each had to contribute a verse with all the lines rhyming with a given word (in this case 'rose'), reveals her reluctance to compete with her clever in-laws:

Never before did I quarrel with a Rose
Till now that I am told some lines to compose,
Of which I shall have little idea God knows!–

But since that the Task is assign'd me by those
To whom Love, Affection & Gratitude owes
A ready compliance, I feign would dispose
And call to befriend me the Muse who bestows
The gift of Poetry both on Friends & Foes . . .[9]

Though Jane thought it worth copying out on the same sheet on which she preserved her own, her mother's and Cassandra's offerings, it is not really very good (nor, for that matter, is Cassandra's); one cannot help feeling that Anna was right, and that Edward's family were perhaps a little intimidated by the brilliance of Jane's mind.

Yet these feelings about her were certainly not shared by nephews and nieces in other branches of the family, and when contrasted with their memories, Anna Lefroy's remark that the young people at Godmersham were not really fond of her seems surprising. Jane Austen took being an aunt seriously, and was only half in jest when, as we have seen, she wrote to the ten-year-old Caroline, 'Now that you are become an Aunt, you are a person of some consequence', and signing off 'Beleive me my dear Sister-Aunt . . . '[10] Years later, Caroline herself recalled that of the two aunts, Aunt Jane was by far her favourite:

I did not *dislike* Aunt Cassandra – but if my visit had at any time chanced to fall out during *her* absence, I don't think I should have missed her – whereas, *not* to have found Aunt Jane at Chawton, *would* have been a blank indeed.[11]

Caroline's view is certainly very different from that of the Godmersham children, if Anna was correct; and although, like them, she responded to her aunt's readiness to tell stories and play games, there was much more to it than that:

My visits to Chawton . . . were very pleasant to me – and Aunt Jane was the great charm – As a very little girl, I was always creeping up to her, and following her whenever I could, in the house and out of it – I might not have remembered this, but for the recollection of my mother's telling me privately, I must not be troublesome to my aunt – Her charm to children was great sweetness of manner – she seemed to love you, and you loved her naturally in return – *This* as well as I can now recollect and analyse, was what I felt in my earliest days, before I was old enough to be amused by her cleverness – But soon came the delight of her playful talk – *Every*thing she could make amusing to a child – Then, as I got older, and when cousins came to share the entertainment, she would tell the most delightful stories chiefly of Fairyland, and her Fairies had all characters of their own – The tale was invented, I am sure, at the moment, and was sometimes continued for 2 or 3 days, if occasion served –

The cousins – children of Francis and Charles Austen – all felt the same, or so Caroline remembered: 'I beleive we were all of us, according to our different ages and natures, very fond of our Aunt Jane – and that we ever retained a strong impression of the pleasantness of Chawton life.' She recalled that one of Francis's sons, Henry Edgar Austen,

> after he was grown up, used occasionally to go and see Aunt Cass – *then* left sole inmate of the old house – and he told me once, that his visits were always a disappointment to him – for that he could not help expecting to feel particularly happy at Chawton and never till he got there, could he fully realise to himself how all its peculiar pleasures were gone.[12]

Anna Lefroy herself testified to Jane Austen's popularity with her other nephews and nieces: 'Aunt Jane,' she wrote in the same letter to James Edward,

> was the general favorite with the children; her ways with them being so playful, & her long circumstantial stories so delightful! These were continued from time to time, & begged for of course at all possible or impossible occasions; woven, as she proceeded out of nothing, but her own happy talent for invention. Ah! if but one of them could be now recovered![13]

James Edward, himself a great favourite with his aunt when a boy, endorsed all this evidence and included it in his *Memoir*.

Anna stated that the preference among the Godmersham family for Cassandra 'lasted for a good while' and that indeed it never diminished. Furthermore, she suggested that the great friendship with the eldest child, Fanny, dated only from when Fanny was older:

> Time . . . brought, as it always does bring, new impressions or modifications of the old ones. Owing to particular circumstances there grew up during the latter years of Aunt Jane's life a great & affectionate intimacy between herself & the eldest of her nieces . . .[14]

The 'particular circumstances' to which she refers were presumably the death of Elizabeth Austen in October 1808 and the fact that Fanny had to take her mother's place as mistress of Godmersham thereafter. But it was earlier that year that Jane had first been struck by Fanny, who was then fifteen; and in a letter to Cassandra she recalled something of the surprise that she evidently felt at finding her so congenial:

> I am greatly pleased with your account of Fanny; I found her in the summer just what you describe, almost another Sister, & could not have supposed that a neice would ever have been so much to me. She is quite after one's own heart; give her my best Love, & tell her that I always think of her with pleasure.[15]

If there had been a certain reserve in Elizabeth's feelings towards Jane, after her death it was certainly not shared by her eldest daughter.

Perhaps inevitably in so close-knit a family, relations with sisters-in-law could sometimes be strained. Though Jane was fond of Eliza de Feuillide and was quite

Title page, *Domestic Medicine*

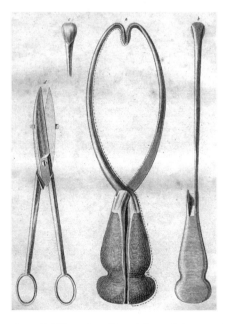

Crotchets, from William Smellie, *A Sett of Anatomical Tables*

Isaac Cruikshank, *A Man-Mid-Wife*

A

T R E A T I S E

OF

M I D W I F E R Y,

COMPREHENDING THE

MANAGEMENT OF FEMALE COMPLAINTS,

AND THE

TREATMENT OF CHILDREN IN EARLY INFANCY.

TO WHICH ARE ADDED

PRESCRIPTIONS FOR WOMEN AND CHILDREN,

AND

DIRECTIONS FOR PREPARING A VARIETY OF FOOD
AND DRINKS, ADAPTED TO THE CIRCUMSTANCES
OF LYING-IN WOMEN.

DIVESTED OF TECHNICAL TERMS AND ABSTRUSE THEORIES.

BY ALEXANDER HAMILTON,

PROFESSOR OF MIDWIFERY IN THE UNIVERSITY OF EDINBURGH,
AND MEMBER OF THE ROYAL COLLEGE OF SURGEONS.

L O N D O N:

PRINTED FOR J. MURRAY, NO. 32, OPPOSITE ST. DUN-
STAN'S CHURCH, FLEETSTREET; J. DICKSON, W.
CREECH, AND C. ELLIOT, AT EDINBURGH.

M DCC LXXXI.

Title page, *A Treatise of Midwifery*

James Gillray, *A Fashionable Mother*

John Spilsbury, Europe Divided into its Kingdoms

Base ball, John Newbery, *A Little Pretty Pocket-Book*

PRACTICAL EDUCATION;

BY

MARIA EDGEWORTH,

AUTHOR OF LETTERS FOR LITERARY LADIES, AND THE PARENT'S ASSISTANT;

AND BY

RICHARD LOVELL EDGEWORTH,

F.R.S. and M.R.I.A.

VOL. I. & II.

LONDON:

PRINTED FOR J. JOHNSON, ST. PAUL'S CHURCH-YARD.

1798.

Title page, *Practical Education*

Maria Edgeworth

Edward Austen as a child, English school, c. 1782 (Jane Austen Memorial Trust)

Miniature of Elizabeth and Marianne Austen, c. 1805. Caroline Austen said that Marianne bore a resemblance to Jane Austen. (Jane Austen Memorial Trust)

Frontispiece, *The History of Little Goody Two-Shoes*

Richard Lovell Edgeworth

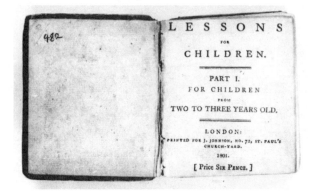

Title page, *Lessons for Children*

S. H. Grimm, *Reading Abbey Gateway* (late 18th century), in Sir William Dugdale, *Monasticon Anglicarum*, Enriched edn, 1817–1830)

Cassandra Esten and Frances Palmer, daughters of Admiral Charles Austen, English School, c. 1830 (private collection)

happy to share a house with Frank and his wife for a time, she found James's second wife, Mary Lloyd, difficult. This is odd, since they had been great friends before the marriage, as Eliza told her cousin Phylly at the time: 'Miss Mary Floyd ... is not either rich or handsome, but very sensible & good humoured ... Jane seems much pleased with the match, and it is natural she should having long known & liked the Lady.'[16] Furthermore Jane was very close to Mary's sister Martha, who, on Mrs Lloyd's death, took up permanent residence with Mrs Austen and her daughters. Jane's opinion of Mary, that she took no pleasure in books, that she was not 'a liberal-minded Woman',[17] has often been quoted. Yet when Jane lay dying in Winchester, it was Mary who helped Cassandra nurse her, having joined them, as Caroline said, 'to make it more cheerful for them'; and Caroline also recalled that Jane thanked her for being there, telling her 'You have always been a kind sister to me, Mary'.[18]

But whatever she might have felt at one time or another about her brothers' wives, there is no doubt at all about her closeness to her brothers themselves; that fraternal love which, famously, in *Mansfield Park* is said to be 'sometimes almost every thing ... at others worse than nothing'[19] was for her strong, affectionate and loyal, though of course none of her brothers occupied quite the central place in her life that Cassandra did. Since all but one of them were older than she was, as a child she must have felt herself to stand in the same relation to them, as regards her position in the family, as Fanny Price does to her Bertram cousins. Only the youngest, Charles, 'our own particular little brother',[20] was known to her from his earliest days, affording her direct evidence of how very young children behave. But, as we have seen, she also had a very clear picture of Frank, a year and a half older than herself, as a toddler, and recalled his fear of the braying of a neighbouring donkey, and his appearing in the living room or kitchen at an hour when he should have been in bed and saying to the nursery maid 'Bet, my be not come to bide';[21] she could hardly have found this in her own memory – it was family lore, and the little boy's 'be not come to bide' had become an affectionate catchphrase.

The passage in *Mansfield Park* in which she steps back and analyses the feelings between brothers and sisters is worth remarking:

> Children of the same family, the same blood, with the same first associations and habits, have some means of enjoyment in their power, which no subsequent connections can supply; and it must be by a long and unnatural estrangement, by a divorce which no subsequent connection can justify, if such precious remains of the earliest attachments are ever entirely outlived. Too often, alas! it is so.[22]

The purpose here is to show how close the attachment between William and Fanny has remained, despite their long separation during her time at Mansfield; and perhaps also to prepare us for the affectionate relation she is able to make with Susan when she eventually returns to Portsmouth. The exclamation 'Too often, alas! it is so', which is immediately followed by the statement that fraternal love can be 'less than nothing', is therefore intended, by contrast, to sharpen the reader's sense of Fanny and William's feelings for each other. Yet the effect of the sentence is rather odd. It arises out of no situation in the novel, and nor, for that matter, does it reflect any brother–sister relationship (or non-relationship) anywhere else in Jane Austen's writing; and it could certainly not be said of her own family. So it comes over as a piece of rather baleful moralizing, quite detached from the context, and stylistically as something of a lapse.

Of the heroines in the six novels, Catherine Morland and Fanny Price have brothers, and Elinor and Marianne Dashwood a half-brother whose preoccupation with money places him at a clear distance from them. Catherine has several: George must be quite young, since he waits with his sister Harriet to catch the first glimpse of her when she returns home from Northanger, and Richard is old enough for her to make cravats for him. It is only her eldest brother, James, who figures much in the novel; but although she is fond of him, and very much concerned about the way he is treated by Isabella, their feelings for each other are not explored like those of Fanny and William; in fact he seems to be there largely as a device in the plot.

The relationship between Fanny and William in some ways stands in for the one more usually found in Jane Austen, that between sisters. Like Elinor and Marianne Dashwood or Jane and Elizabeth Bennet (or for that matter Kitty and Lydia), they are adjacent in position in the family; indeed, like the first two pairs, they are the two eldest. Their trust in each other is absolute, and to a certain extent they are each other's confidante, though in this respect they are beautifully, and amusingly, differentiated as boy and girl, as we shall see. But Fanny's position is unlike that of the heroines of *Sense and Sensibility* or *Pride and Prejudice* in that she is separated from the member of her own family to whom she is closest; and it is further complicated by the fact that his place is taken by the cousin, a kind of surrogate brother, whom she will eventually marry. The double displacement here is unusual in terms of the emotional balance of the novel. Jane and Elizabeth, and Elinor and Marianne, can confide in each other about their feelings, in particular about the men with whom they are in love: indeed, this is one of the primary functions of the sister's role (and it is disastrous that Marianne does not discuss Willoughby more openly with Elinor); it is only at the end of the books that this sibling intimacy is replaced by that between the heroines and the heroes – at the point, in fact, at which the marriages take place. The pattern is different in *Mansfield Park*, since the introduction of the hero is, as it were, premature, and the distinction between confidant and lover is blurred.

During her childhood at Mansfield, Fanny sees William 'once, and once only in the course of many years',[23] and in his absence she turns to Edmund, who is 'always true to her interests, and considerate of her feelings . . . giving her advice, consolation and encouragement'[24] – in other words, he fulfils the role that Elinor has for Marianne, or that Jane and Elizabeth have for each other. He does not, however, replace William; while her love for him is still that of a child, once she has grown out of the kind of trust and dependence that a younger sister has for a brother (and as she no doubt did have for him at home in Portsmouth), she loves them equally – her heart is 'divided between the two'.[25] When gradually this quasi-sibling love for Edmund begins to turn into romantic love – when, in other words, the emotional dynamic is no longer held in a triangular balance – which of course is the very point at which a heroine can relieve her feelings by confiding them to her sister, Fanny has no one to talk to; and by Edmund's quite unconsciously, indeed inevitably, depriving her of that all-important comfort which, in a sister, would have been the culmination of all the earlier comforts she needed, she becomes completely isolated. The only other person who comes near to being a confidante is Mary Crawford, and from time to time she does indeed show a genuine sisterly consideration for Fanny. But it is an irony of Fanny's situation, and of the workings of the novel, that, as the object of his affections, Mary is the last person in whom she could confide her feelings for Edmund; nor, as Henry Crawford's sister, can she be the recipient of Fanny's woes about his unwelcome attentions to her.

Pairs of sisters in the novels (excepting *Persuasion*, which is a separate case) speak on more or less equal terms of the matters that concern them – much as one can see Jane Austen and Cassandra doing in the letters. However their characters may vary, they take a warm interest in each other's affairs, though in the case of pairs where neither is the heroine, their relationship may be fractured by jealousy, as with the rivalry between Maria and Julia Bertram over Henry Crawford, or Kitty Bennet's resentment of Lydia's going to Brighton without her. The simple fact that they are women means that they must necessarily share an interest in the daily events of their relatively limited domestic existence. But when one of the pair is a young man, and that young man a midshipman, bringing into his sister's consciousness a sense of the excitement of a life very different from her own, it is impossible that his interests and concerns should not predominate. It must have been so when Frank and Charles Austen returned on leave from their ships to Steventon or Chawton; it is certainly the case when William comes to Mansfield after being at sea for seven years. While Fanny is 'the first object of his love', the 'unchecked, equal, fearless' talks that they have together, which bring her so much 'felicity', consist in Jane Austen's summary first of his own preoccupations, as he is described 'opening all his heart to her, telling her all his hopes and fears, plans, and solicitudes respecting that long thought of, dearly earned, and justly valued blessing of promotion'.[26] Only after this are we told that he gives her news of their family, that he interests himself in the details of her life at Mansfield and that they reminisce about their earliest years together. Similarly when she goes back to Portsmouth, he is understandably keen to show off his newly acquired lieutenant's uniform to her. This is all perfectly natural, and it does not for one minute diminish the sense of his tender and protective love for her (the last thing he does before sailing away again is to charge their mother to take care of her); but as a young man, and a lively, adventurous and ambitious one at that, his relation with her cannot be the same as that of an equally affectionate sister would have been. This is amusingly demonstrated during the game of speculation at the parsonage. While Henry Crawford tries to make Fanny play more aggressively against her brother, William, naturally competitive, is 'driving as hard a bargain and imposing on her as much as he could'; and when, directing her hand, Crawford tells her that the game will be hers, Edmund comments with a smile that she 'had much rather it were William's'.[27] In an interesting reversal of a sister's sympathetic understanding of the heroine's feelings for her lover, Edmund shows his pleasure in the love that Fanny has for her brother.

Fanny is the only heroine except Emma to have been brought up from a child with the man she eventually marries; and the fact that they occupy the same house, and are not far apart in age, means that Fanny's childhood relationship with Edmund is the closer of the two. When, at an early age, her heart is 'divided' between him and William, her feelings might be regarded as sisterly; but by the time she is fifteen, and the possibility of her going to live with Mrs Norris is raised, there can be no mistaking the latent passion in her exclamation 'Oh! Cousin, if I am to go away, I shall remember your goodness, to the last moment of my life'.[28] The phrase may seem to be a hyperbole justified by the emotion of the moment; but it actually points to the outcome of the novel – indeed, by indicating the only term that can ever be put on Fanny's love, it goes far beyond it. Furthermore, while *Mansfield Park* presents an unchanging love on the part of the heroine, it balances it with the same on the part of the hero, the only difference between them being that he is unaware of its nature. When he inspects her dress before she goes to dinner at the parsonage, looking at her 'with the kind smile of an affectionate brother', he tells her 'as well as I can judge by this light, you look very nicely indeed',[29] and then asks if Miss Crawford hasn't got rather a similar gown. But the brotherly smile should not deceive us: he is looking at her as a woman, not as a sister, and the deflection of his thoughts away towards another woman confirms only that he has not yet found the true focus of his emotional regard.

By way of comparison, the genuine, uncomplicated voice of an affectionate brother can be heard in a verse that Jane Austen's nephew James Edward wrote in 1812 from his preparatory school to his elder half-sister Anna:

> Whilst I am toiling here in vain
> Some Verses from my scanty brain
> Upon a subject hard, to write
> My Sister, with a heart so light
> Returning from the busy Race
> (Forgetful of my harder case)
> Is now preparing wth. due Care
> The Dress which she intends to wear
> When at the ball wth. joyful heart
> She'll sport some fashion new & smart
> Forgetful did I say? Oh! No
> I'm sure it never will be so
> There can I'm certain be no fear
> She'll ere forget her Brother Dear[30]

In *Mansfield* Park the possibility of a relationship developing between Fanny and Edmund is foreseen from the beginning of the novel. In the very first chapter, when Mrs Norris first proposes bringing Fanny to Mansfield, Sir Thomas, deliberating with himself, considers the possibility of 'cousins in love', his objection, of course, being a financial one;[31] and he is only persuaded by Mrs Norris, who, wrong about people as she always is, reassures him with an argument that goes precisely counter to what will actually happen:

> You are thinking of your sons – but do not you know that of all things upon earth *that* is the least likely to happen; brought up, as they would be, always together like brothers and sisters? It is morally impossible. I never knew an instance of it. It is, in fact, the only sure way of providing against the connection. Suppose her a pretty girl, and seen by Tom or Edmund for the first time seven years hence, and I dare say there would be mischief. The very idea of her having been suffered to grow up at a distance from us all in poverty and neglect, would be enough to make either of the dear sweet-tempered boys in love with her. But breed her up with them from this time, and suppose her even to have the beauty of an angel, and she will never be more to either than a sister.[32]

The idea of a marriage between cousins who have been brought up 'like brothers and sisters' being 'morally impossible' is of course nonsense; as the wife of a clergyman Mrs Norris must surely remember that no bar to such a relationship is ordered in the Table of Kindred and Affinity. And of course cousins do marry, as Jane Austen knew well from instances in her own family. The picture painted by Mrs Norris of Tom and Edmund meeting an older Fanny, attractive and made interesting by her background, is not dissimilar to that of James and Henry Austen, who were both fascinated by their romantic cousin Eliza, widow of a French army captain guillotined in the Revolution; more Mary Crawford than Fanny, Eliza flirted with both cousins and eventually married Henry.

Eliza is sometimes taken to have been the model for Mary Crawford, and it is not only her bright, lively personality and her involvement in the Austen family theatricals that give weight to the supposition. There is something in her tone of voice, captured in her letters to Phylly Walter, that has a hint of the mixture of capriciousness and self-knowledge that Jane Austen was to depict in Mary. At the period when Eliza was considering the possibility of marrying James Austen, she wrote to Phylly:

> I am glad to find you have made up your mind to visiting the [Steventon] *Rectory*, but at the same time, and in spite of all your *conjectures and belief*, I do assert that Preliminaries are so far from settled that I do not believe *the parties* ever will come together, not however that they have quarrelled, but one of them cannot bring her mind to give up dear Liberty, and yet dearer flirtation – After *a few months* stay in the Country She sometimes thinks it possible to undertake sober Matrimony, but a few weeks stay in London convinces her how little the state suits her taste . . .[33]

Almost this precise situation is seen from the other point of view – the young clergyman's – when Edmund talks to Fanny with increasing gloom about the likelihood of his marrying Mary:

> She does not *think* evil, but she speaks it – speaks it in playfulness – and though I know it to be playfulness, it grieves me to the soul. . . . The time will never come. No such time as you allude to will ever come. I begin to think it most improbable: the chances grow less and less.[34]

The distinction implied by Eliza between London and the country as the location for a differing moral view is also reflected in *Mansfield Park*, though in this case it is Edmund who makes it; Mary Crawford, in her failure to have grasped it (and by extension the effect that London has had on her own character), shows herself to be less aware of her moral nature, perhaps, than Eliza. The discussion is about Edmund's intended ordination, to which Mary is opposed, since in her opinion a clergyman 'is nothing' socially:

> 'How can two sermons a week [asks Mary], even supposing them worth hearing . . . do all that you speak of? govern the conduct and fashion the manners of a large congregation for the rest of the week? One scarcely sees a clergyman out of his pulpit.'
>
> '*You* are speaking of London, *I* am speaking of the nation at large.'
>
> 'The metropolis, I imagine, is a pretty fair sample of the rest.'
>
> 'Not, I should hope, of the proportion of virtue to vice throughout the kingdom. We do not look in great cities for our best morality. It is not there, that respectable people of any denomination can do most good; and it is certainly not there, that the influence of the clergy can be most felt . . .'[35]

In *Mansfield Park* Jane Austen portrays, rather unusually, two contrasting pairs of brothers and sisters, and the innocence of the one is something of a foil to the worldliness of the other. While William and Fanny's conversation is characterized by the 'tête-à-tête, which Sir Thomas could not but observe with complacency, even before Edmund had pointed it out to him,'[36] Henry and Mary's is of an altogether more subtle and less innocuous kind. When he informs her of his intention of amusing himself on the days when he is not hunting by 'making a small hole in Fanny Price's heart,'[37] the language of their dialogue is that of two people who know each other intimately, who share exactly the same outlook and are united in putting their own (and perhaps each other's) pleasure before any other consideration. 'Fanny Price!' Mary replies. 'You ought to be satisfied with her two cousins.' And his frank admission that the challenge of Fanny's refusal to like him is his motive (for he is, in a sense, hunting) elicits nothing more condemnatory from his sister than an indulgent 'Foolish fellow! And so this is her attraction after all! This is it – her not caring about you – which gives her such a soft skin and makes her so much taller, and produces all these charms and graces!' She warns him against 'making her really unhappy', but she makes no very great effort to restrain him; to his protesting that he wants Fanny only 'to think as I think, be interested in all my possessions and pleasures, try to keep me longer at Mansfield, and feel when I go away that she shall be never happy again', Mary replies 'Moderation itself! . . . I can have no scruples now' and she '[leaves] Fanny to her fate'.[38] The culmination of this misplaced loyalty is the utterly amoral letter that she writes to Fanny after Henry's seduction of Maria.

There are few opportunities in the novels, outside *Mansfield Park*, for hearing the tone of private speech between brothers and sisters, though Jane Austen clearly knew that it would be different from that between sisters. In her own letters we occasionally catch it. Writing to Francis Austen from Godmersham, for example, while he was serving in the Baltic, she begins:

> The 11th of this month brought me your letter & I assure you I thought it very well worth its 2[s]/3[d]. – I am very much obliged to you for filling me so long a sheet a [*sic*] paper, you are a good one to traffic with in that way, You pay most liberally; – my Letter was a scratch of a note compared with yours – & then you write so even, so clear both in style & Penmanship, so much to the point & give so much real intelligence that it is enough to kill one.[39]

The affectionate raillery here may not be quite what Fanny would have written to William at sea, but it shows Jane Austen's capacity to adapt to a correspondent she knows so well, almost perhaps adopting his own voice in a kind of conspiratorial mimicry. She is even able to conspire with him in what was probably quite a well-worn joke about the expensive way of living that their brother Edward enjoyed:

> Rostock Market makes one's mouth water, our cheapest Butcher's meat is double the price of theirs; – nothing under 9[d] all this Summer, & I believe upon recollection nothing under 10[d]. – Bread has sunk & is likely to sink more, which we hope may make Meat sink too. But I have no occasion to think of the price of Bread or of Meat where I am now; – let me shake off vulgar cares & conform to the happy Indifference of East Kent wealth. – I wonder whether You & the King of Sweden know that I *was* to come to G[m] with my B[r].[40]

Brothers and sisters in the novels, other than William and Fanny, are encountered generally only when grown up, and therefore their dialogue, like that of any other characters, must primarily act as a vehicle for wit or reflection, as of course must much of the dialogue in comedy; and the childhood origin of the relationship is consequently sunk in the concerns of adult conversation. Occasionally a marked difference in age results in virtually a negation of the normal equality between brothers and sisters: Georgiana Darcy, for example, is twelve years younger than her brother and this, combined with her natural shyness, means that though she admires him and defers to him in everything, there is little opportunity, or need, for her to be given much to say to him.

Yet sometimes the kinship that privileges a woman to speak to her brother in a way that she could not do to any other man is acknowledged even in the most decorous characters. In *Northanger Abbey*, it might be expected that the coarse John Thorpe would show little gallantry to a sister when there are other women to pay attention to ('I did not come to Bath to drive my sisters about; that would be a good joke, faith!');[41] but even the impeccably mannered Eleanor Tilney can tease her brother, particularly in defence of a young lady to whom she realizes he is attracted: 'Henry,' she says, when he has criticized Catherine for her use of the word 'nicest',

> you are very impertinent. Miss Morland, he is treating you exactly as he does his sister. He is for ever finding fault with me, for some incorrectness of language, and now he is taking the same liberty with you. The word 'nicest', as you used it, did not suit him; and you had better change it as soon as you can, or we shall be overpowered with Johnson and Blair all the way.[42]

Eleanor's gentle mockery of her brother is as tender as is her kindly defence of their friend, and thus she is delightfully conspiring with each simultaneously; this is very different from Mary Crawford's endorsing of her brother's callous intentions towards Fanny. It will be noticed, too, that here the subject of the teasing is an appropriately light one – the loose meaning of a word. Yet it is not trivial: in a novel in which wrong reading is a central theme, Jane Austen's use of an amusing dispute over language to demonstrate a sister's pleasure in her brother's new-found affection is both apt and stylistically economical.

It would not perhaps be quite accurate to say that Eleanor is being protective exactly towards Henry here; but having had no one since their mother's death, which occurred during their childhood, to shield them from their father's petty tyrannies (they can seldom, after all, have found common cause with their elder brother), they have probably relied on each other from time to time for a degree of protection. In other novels there is certainly sometimes a sense that sisters, particularly if there is more than one of them, have a tendency at least to attempt to act protectively towards their brother. In *Pride and Prejudice* this is exemplified unpleasantly in the behaviour of Mrs Hurst and Miss Bingley, of whom the latter, in trying to separate her brother from Jane, is of course acting entirely in her own interest; and it provides comedy in *Sanditon* when Arthur Parker's bossy sisters do their best to stop him eating too much. We see it, however, altogether more amiably with Henrietta and Louisa Musgrove in *Persuasion*.

The Musgroves are one of the longest and most straggling families in any of Jane Austen's novels, only to be outdone in extensiveness, perhaps, by the Prices, or the Heywoods in *Sanditon*; they are also rather indeterminate, since we are not told exactly how many of them there are. Charles must be at least twenty-four, since his brother the late unlamented Dick would have been nearly twenty-two when the story takes place; and he is probably more, as he has been married for four years and proposed to Anne at least a year before that. Louisa and Henrietta are twenty and nineteen respectively, and their relationship with

Charles rings true throughout the book. But then there is an unknown number of younger boys, all the way down to 'the lingering and long-petted master Harry', who seems only recently to have been 'sent to school after his brothers';[43] and there are girls, too, also at school.[44] Quite what their function is, other than to contribute to the general noise and confusion that determines Lady Russell not to visit Uppercross again in the Christmas holidays, it is difficult to say; in fact it is hard to keep them in mind as brothers and sisters of Charles, Louisa and Henrietta, especially when one has to envisage all of them, even Harry, as uncles or aunts of Charles's two little boys.

The fact of their numerousness is not itself, apparently, intended to be comic, as in the case of the children of Mr and Mrs Willmot in 'Edgar and Emma', who are 'too numerous to be particularly described', and whose family 'being too large to accompany them in every visit, they took nine with them alternately'.[45] Some of these are named later, and the comedy lies in the very profusion of names unconnected with the story itself (which in any case staggers to a halt at the end of the subsequent paragraph):

> Our children are all extremely well but at present most of them from home. Amy is with my sister Clayton. Sam at Eton. David with his Uncle John. Jem & Will at Winchester. Kitty at Queen's Square. Ned with his Grandmother. Hetty & Patty in a Convent at Brussells. Edgar at college, Peter at Nurse, & all the rest (except the nine here) at home.[46]

Jane Austen could make comic use of such deliberate vagueness in real life in what might be considered the rather important matter of how many children someone has. Writing in a letter from Bath about some acquaintances, a Mrs Busby and her nephew, she informed Cassandra 'I am prevented from setting my black cap at Mr Maitland by his having a wife & ten Children', only to add in a postscript 'We drink tea tonight with Mrs Busby. – I scandalized her Nephew cruelly; he has but three Children instead of Ten.'[47] But with the string of Musgrove children it is different; no effect of comedy is intended, except perhaps in the rowdy Christmas scene (to which the little Harvilles, as well as Charles and Mary's boys contribute); and they seem less significant than, for example, the young Perrys in *Emma*, who, as the anonymous children of a character who never directly appears in the book, deftly serve both to exemplify a prosperously rising family and to flesh out the junior population of Highbury.

Be that as it may, Charles Musgrove and his two eldest sisters form a group that is as distinct as in any family in Jane Austen. Though Henrietta and Louisa are both younger than Charles, there are occasions when he hardly appears older, nor indeed seems to behave altogether like a married man and father. For one thing, his preoccupation with shooting, though perfectly usual in a gentleman at any stage of his life, is treated comically, rather like John Thorpe's obsession with horses and curricle gigs. And there is a decidedly boyish tone to his excited outburst after booking seats at the theatre:

Well, mother, I have done something for you that you will like. I have been to the theatre, and secured a box for to-morrow night. A'n't I a good boy? I know you love a play; and there is room for us all. It holds nine. I have engaged Captain Wentworth. Anne will not be sorry to join us, I am sure. We all like a play. Have not I done well, mother?[48]

It is possible that Charles has something of poor Richard's immaturity, though in a much less hopeless way. In fact, given Louisa's impetuousness on the Cobb, and Mr and Mrs Musgrove's delight in the noisy behaviour of their younger children, there seems to be a degree of childishness running through the whole family. Louisa, however, seems almost to be speaking as an elder sister when she tells Captain Wentworth of their regret that Charles had married Mary, and that they 'do so wish that Charles had married Anne instead'.[49] It is the fact that she is reflecting the family view that gives the appearance of reversing their positions.

Relations between the various sets of sisters in the novels are distinguished in various ways: there are the confidantes – Elinor and Marianne, Jane and Elizabeth, Kitty and Lydia and, to a certain extent, Maria and Julia Bertram; there are younger sisters, such as Margaret Dashwood or Susan Price, whom the elder ones look after, or over whom in the case of Kitty and Lydia they are able to exercise only a partial control; and in *Emma* there are two sisters who, though certainly not confidantes, have a happily mutual affection which both reflects and is absorbed in a more general affection for their family.

Some girls seem to be somewhat isolated even within the circle of the family. Mary Bennet is one such: the middle sister of the five, she belongs neither with Jane and Elizabeth nor with Kitty and Lydia, and her unsocial nature has caused her to erect a barrier between herself and the others which takes the form of the self-absorbed copying of improving extracts or redundant and unproductive piano practice. She is on the whole a figure of fun, though there is perhaps something in Jane Austen's treatment of her that anticipates the more overtly cruel handling of Richard Musgrove.

A more obviously isolated figure is the heroine of *The Watsons*. The sickly widower Mr Watson is unable to provide for his daughters, and Emma has been brought up by an aunt, returning as the novel begins to find herself virtually a stranger to her sisters. This necessitates some explanation on the part of the eldest, Elizabeth, who in describing their characters in answer to Emma's questions presents the picture of a family that does not seem to be particularly close:

'Has Penelope much wit?' – 'Yes – she has great spirits, & never cares what she says.' – 'Margaret is more gentle I imagine?' – 'Yes – especially in company; she is all gentleness & mildness when anybody is by. – But she is a little fretful & perverse among ourselves . . .'[50]

Of all the heroines, however, the one who has least emotional connection with her sisters, or indeed with anyone else in her family except her dead mother, is Anne Elliot. An obvious Cinderella, it perhaps comes as something of a surprise to remember that she is not actually the youngest of Sir Walter's daughters but the second; but then, there cannot even be said to be a pair of ugly sisters, since Elizabeth and Mary, unconcerned though they may be with Anne, are certainly no more interested in each other, each being absorbed by her own particular kind of selfishness. In the Elliots Jane Austen created a family further removed from her own than those in any other of her books. The notion of a happy home life such as was lived at Steventon rectory, and such as is depicted to a greater or lesser degree in all her earlier novels, is impossible to imagine at Kellynch. We are given no indication as to what their childhood was like, their early existence being reduced to the cold, impersonal formality of their entries in the *Baronetage*: 'he has issue Elizabeth, born June 1, 1785; Anne, born August 9, 1787; a still-born son, Nov. 5, 1789; Mary, born Nov. 20, 1791'.[51] The language with which Jane Austen presents them is altogether reductive and limiting. They were 'an awful legacy for a mother to bequeath' – a mother who while she lived had been 'anxiously' giving them 'good principles and instruction' (anxiously perhaps because she knew that they would get none from their 'conceited, silly father', or perhaps because she could not be sure that they would all follow them). Seen from Sir Walter's point of view, the language becomes even more negative. While Elizabeth is now distinguished by being 'his dear daughter', as if he had no others, the cause is immediately revealed with terse irony: she is 'very handsome, and very like himself'. For her 'he would really have given up any thing', which however he has 'not been very much tempted to do'. Consequently her influence with him has 'always been great'. But as far as his other children are concerned, they are 'of very inferior value'. Mary has 'acquired a little artificial importance, by becoming Mrs. Charles Musgrove', and in the formal nomenclature we note the persistent tone of the *Baronetage*, by which his whole thinking seems to be conditioned. As for his second daughter:

> Anne, with an elegance of mind and sweetness of character, which must have placed her high with any people of real understanding, was nobody with either father or sister: her word had no weight; her convenience was always to give way; – she was only Anne.[52]

The vocabulary of status is ironically kept up in the authorial aside which at this point denotes Anne as the heroine of the novel: though she would have been 'placed high' with people of understanding, in a consciousness governed by the hierarchy of the *Baronetage* she is powerless, has no influence and is in fact reduced – in a sentence of progressively diminishing clauses – to nothing more than her name (a name which, incidentally, does not figure among 'all the Marys and Elizabeths' that the earlier generations of baronets are listed as having married; she is isolated even in that – though she might take comfort from the fact of at least sharing with her sisters the only three names of the queens of England up to Jane Austen's day, even if together those names were given to more than half the girls christened at that time).[53] Furthermore, it is not only she who is reduced. She 'was nobody with either father or *sister*': the word is in the singular – Mary's 'little artificial importance' has not lasted long, since she has already been forgotten, anticipating a more conscious act of forgetfulness when, in Bath, Sir Walter introduces Anne to her cousin: '"Mr. Elliot must give him leave to present him to his youngest daughter" – (there was no occasion for remembering Mary) . . . .'[54]

Sir Walter's behaviour in regarding Elizabeth as the only one of his daughters who matters is seen from the first as both wrong and absurd – an illogical outcome of his snobbery; all three are after all his issue, each has her place in the family entry in the *Baronetage*. The status to be accorded a child who is taken into a family, however, may be a little less clear cut. This is a problem that worries Sir Thomas Bertram when he agrees to Mrs Norris's proposal that they should receive Fanny at Mansfield:

> There will be some difficulty in our way . . . as to the distinction proper to be made between the girls as they grow up; how to preserve in the minds of my *daughters* the consciousness of what they are, without making them think too lowly of their cousin; and how, without depressing her spirits too far, to make her remember that she is not a *Miss Bertram*. I should wish to see them very good friends, and would, on no account, authorize in my girls the smallest degree of arrogance towards their relation; but still they cannot be equals. Their rank, fortune, rights, and expectations, will always be different.[55]

Sir Thomas intends his arguments to be judicious and well weighed; he balances the natural assumptions of privilege accorded by rank and lineage with the demands of kindness and humanity. Judged by the system of the time, his conclusion is perfectly right. But his vocabulary, like that reflecting Sir Walter Elliot's views, is worth examining.

A language of inflexible personal authority – 'preserve', 'make', 'authorize' – is embedded in an equally unchallengeable socio-legal one which dictates that 'they cannot be equals' and that their 'rank, fortune, rights, and expectations, will always be different'. In speaking in this way, he is quite unconscious of any harshness in his assessment of Fanny's situation in relation to her cousins; and he is equally unaware of the readiness with which Mrs Norris will ensure that Fanny is never allowed to forget her inferior position, when he finishes his observations by telling her 'It is a point of great delicacy, and you must assist us in our endeavours to choose exactly the right line of conduct'. In contrast to Sir Walter, his thinking is logical and free from vanity – but then, in artistic terms, he does not have to carry the burden of providing a considerable portion of the comedy in the novel. What he fails to judge correctly is either his inability or that of Mrs Norris to choose 'the right line of conduct'. The threat to his household does not come from Fanny, who is the last person to think of setting herself up against her cousins, but from his own family and the influence on it of himself and his sister-in-law; and his earlier fear, 'of cousins in love', is resolved not by being proved wrong but by being proved triumphantly right, and bringing him the only happiness to redeem all the other catastrophic consequences of his misjudgments.

One of the earliest of these is a financial one. Though the Bertrams are among the wealthier families in the novels, Sir Thomas is painfully aware that Tom, 'with all the liberal dispositions of an eldest son, who feels born only for expense and enjoyment,'[56] has incurred debts large enough to cause genuine concern for the economy of the family. His extravagance – we know he goes to Newmarket and no doubt he gambles at cards too – makes it necessary for Sir Thomas to present a stranger to the Mansfield living, rather than putting someone in to hold it until Edmund is old enough to take orders; but though, in Tom's view, his father makes 'a most tiresome piece of work' of his rebuke, the fact remains that he seems to have been unable to exercise any restraint over his son's recklessness. Furthermore, in contrast to the security enjoyed by Mr Darcy, Mr Knightley or Emma, he finds that the very income that supports Mansfield Park is at risk as a result of losses on his West Indian plantations, presumably caused by the drying up of the supply of slaves following the abolition of the trade in 1807. Until now he has been very generous not just to Fanny but to other members of Mrs Price's family, and has 'assisted her liberally in the education and disposal of her sons as they became old enough for a determinate pursuit';[57] but at this point he hopes that Mrs Norris will take charge of Fanny, since it has become 'not undesirable to himself to be relieved from the expense of her support, and the obligation of her future provision.'[58] Bringing up children – one's own, quite apart from anyone else's – was expensive, particularly if they were girls who needed to be provided with a dowry; and in most of Jane Austen's novels (the exception of course being *Emma*) the heroines come from families whose future seems somewhat precarious. Such things are relative: when Mrs Norris makes it clear that she has never had any intention of having Fanny to live with her, Sir Thomas is obviously quite able to sustain the cost of keeping her at Mansfield, and no suggestion is given that he has to make any particular economies to be able to do so.

In a household such as the rectory at Steventon, it was a very different matter. When Mr Austen married in 1764, the living was worth no more that £100 a year, supplemented by the income from the 200-acre Cheesedown Farm, and he was not able to repair the house for some time, occupying instead the parsonage of the neighbouring parish of Deane, whose wealthy rector lived elsewhere.[59] Here his first three sons were born, and it was not until four years later, when he had inherited a sum of £1,200 from his stepmother, that he was able to move his wife and children into his own rectory at Steventon.[60] With the birth of the fourth son, Henry, living expenses continued to rise, and Mr Austen was obliged to progressively sell off his holding in Old South Sea Annuities; and it was only after the birth of the fifth child, Cassandra, in 1773, and a payment of £300 from Mrs Austen's wealthy brother and Trustee, James Leigh Perrot, that the living of Deane became free and Mr Austen was able to increase his income by £110 a year.[61] Even so, it became necessary to take in pupils as boarders in the rectory, and he continued to do so for the next twenty-three years, until long after his sons had all left home and he was supporting only his wife and two daughters.[62] Jane Austen's analysis of money matters in *Sense and Sensibility* is famously astute;

and when Colonel Brandon tells Elinor that the living to which he will present Edward Ferrars is not capable of being augmented much above the £200 that the previous incumbent made, and that the smallness of the rectory can do no more than make him 'comfortable as a bachelor; it cannot enable him to marry',[63] Jane must have been perfectly aware of the fact that her father had married and started a family in even less favourable circumstances.

The adoption of Edward Austen by Mr and Mrs Knight no doubt came as a relief to Mr Austen financially, as well as being seen as holding out a promise of future wealth for Edward himself. This was a time when, as the older members of the family grew up, the number of those living at the rectory was undergoing periodic changes. In fact, for a period in 1786, with James at Oxford, Edward in Kent and then on the Grand Tour, Francis entered at the Royal Naval Academy in Portsmouth and Jane and Cassandra at school in Reading, only Henry and Charles were at home. Indeed, holidays aside, there was altogether only one period of ten days, between the birth of the youngest son, Charles, on 23 June 1779 and the matriculation at St John's of his eldest brother, James, on 3 July, when all the Austen children (discounting George) were actually living with their parents.

In the Musgrove family, there cannot have been a long period during which Charles, Richard and the youngest children were all living at Uppercross together, before Charles married and Richard went to sea; but Jane Austen does not suggest any particular significance in this – indeed it could be said to be an aspect of the vagueness with which the younger Musgroves are treated generally. But among the Prices, Charles and Betsey have both been born after Fanny left Portsmouth for Mansfield; and it is not the brother and sister she has never seen that Fanny feels drawn to, but the next eldest, whom she remembers:

> Charles had been born since Fanny's going away, but Tom she had often helped to nurse, and now felt a particular pleasure in seeing again. Both were kissed very tenderly, but Tom she wanted to keep by her, to try to trace the features of the baby she had loved, and talk to him of his infant preference of herself.[64]

The inevitable separation brought about by marriage does not lessen the feelings that brothers and sisters have for each other in Jane Austen's novels, any more than it did in her own family. Sometimes the continuing closeness is realized in geographical proximity: Elinor and Marianne at Delaford, and Mr Bingley buying an estate in the next county to Derbyshire, so that Jane and Elizabeth are 'within thirty miles of each other'[65] (and Lydia visits them both). And even when they live further apart (as of course the various Austens did), the relationship is happily resumed whenever they meet; thus in *Emma* Isabella, despite being 'a devoted wife' and 'a doating mother', is 'so tenderly attached to her father and sister that, but for these higher ties, a warmer love might have seemed impossible'.[66] Occasionally affection can even grow after marriage, as is the case with Fanny and Susan, both brought together at Mansfield, and Susan surely coming to know her sister even better as she takes her place as companion to their aunt. Only when there has been no genuine closeness in the first place are divergent lives driven further apart: Maria and Julia Bertram irrevocably separated by the terrible outcome of the infatuation they had both jealously experienced; Anne Elliot physically removed by the uncertain vagaries of a naval life from two sisters who had never really valued her.

With the exception of Fanny and Edmund, whose relationship, as we have seen, is a special and complex one, cousins do not figure largely in the novels. Yet in the Austen family they figured extensively. They visited, they were friends, they married. On Mr Austen's side, his niece Eliza de Feuillide, lively and flirtatious, visited the rectory, took part in the family theatricals and eventually married her cousin Henry. At the end of the year in which so many of the family had been away (1786), though with Jane and Cassandra back from school and Francis on holiday from Portsmouth, Mrs Austen was cheered by the visits of two sets of relations during the Christmas holidays: first Eliza, her mother and her six-month-old son Hastings; then the two children of her late sister, Jane Cooper; and her happiness in having the rectory full is caught in a letter to Phylly Walter, describing the merry gathering:

> We are now happy in the company of our Sister Hancock Madame de Feuillide & the little Boy; they came to us last Thursday Sennet & will stay with us till the end of next Month. They all look & seem to be remarkably well, the little Boy grows very fat, he is very fair & very pretty . . . Madame is grown quite lively, when a child we used to think her too grave. We have borrowed a Piano-Forte, and she plays to us every day; on Tuesday we are to have a very snug little dance in our parlour, just our own children, nephew & nieces, (for the two little Coopers come tomorrow) quite a family party, I wish my *third niece* [i.e. Phylly] could be here also . . .[67]

On one of Eliza's subsequent visits Jane dedicated 'Love and Freindship' to her, writing in gleeful imitation of the pomposity of eighteenth-century literary tributes: 'To Madame La Comtesse De Feuillide This Novel is inscribed by Her obliged Humble Servant The Author'.[68] Jane and Cassandra had been at school with Jane Cooper; on a Christmas visit to the rectory in 1788 she took part in the theatricals, being given the leading role of Roxalana in Isaac Bickerstaffe's *The Sultan*, and speaking the epilogue specially written for her by James (it is one of his best light verses, and suggests that she was capable of lively and witty verbal delivery).[69] She was also the dedicatee of Jane's 'Henry and Eliza'.

In the next generation, with so many cousins in the family, it is not surprising that they all saw a good deal of each other. James Edward was very friendly with his Knight cousins, two of whom overlapped with him at Winchester; and his half-sister Anna was very fond of Fanny Knight, whom she used to visit at Godmersham. When Anna entered into the engagement that her father and step-mother disapproved of, she was sent off to Kent, where Fanny was a sympathetic listener; Fanny having lost her mother the year before, and Anna's mother having died when she was an infant, they now had a stronger reason than ever to confide in each other. Anna wrote poems, Fanny making copies of her cousin's to keep when she had gone; and she urged to Fanny to write too, which she did. In one of hers, written on the last day of 1809, she looks back over the past year, which has brought such troubles to both of them, and dedicates her wistful lines to Anna:

>   *To Anna Eliza Austen*
>
> This Year is done
> Its course is run
> Its pleasures & its pains
> Alike are o'er
> And they no more
> Shall fill our anxious brains.
>
> But may I ask
> Who can the task
> Of introspection bear?
> And turn their eye
> Without a sigh
> Back on the closing Year?
>
> Anna can you
> Look back & view
> This chequered scene of Woes
> And not lament
> The short time spent
> In thinking of its close?[70]

When cousins appear in the novels, on the whole their relationship is not made much of, except in the case of Darcy and Anne De Bourgh, whose 'tacit engagement', according to Lady Catherine, had been planned by their respective mothers while the children were in their cradles and was their 'favourite wish'. The absurdity of thinking that such a wish could give any kind of authority to the union is expressed succinctly by Elizabeth:

> You both did as much as you could, in planning the marriage. Its completion depended on others. If Mr. Darcy is neither by honour nor inclination confined to his cousin, why is not he to make another choice?[71]

In one of her earliest pieces of writing Jane Austen had expressed the absurdity of such notions in another way. The opening of 'Frederic and Elfrida' presents so patently exaggerated a picture of cousinly affinity as to undermine any possible claims of the relationship to an inevitable outcome:

The Uncle of Elfrida was the Father of Frederic; in other words, they were first cousins by the Father's side.

Being both born in one day & both brought up at one school, it was not wonderfull that they should look on each other with something more than bare politeness. They loved with mutual sincerity but were both determined not to transgress the rules of Propriety by owning their attachment, either to the object beloved, or to any one else.

They were exceedingly handsome and so much alike, that it was not every one who knew them apart. Nay even their most intimate friends had nothing to distinguish them by, but the shape of the face, the colour of the Eye, the length of the Nose & the difference of the complexion.[72]

Elsewhere, rather than being drawn together, cousins are seen as something of a necessary evil. When Mrs Jennings meets the Steele sisters and discovers that they are relations of hers, she tries to reassure her daughter as to their acceptability as guests, the hospitable Sir John having immediately invited them to stay:

Lady Middleton was thrown into no little alarm on the return of Sir John, by hearing that she was very soon to receive a visit from two girls whom she had never seen in her life, and of whose elegance, – whose tolerable gentility even, she could have no proof; for the assurances of her husband and mother on that subject went for nothing at all. Their being her relations too made it so much the worse; and Mrs. Jennings's attempts at consolation were therefore unfortunately founded, when she advised her daughter not to care about their being so fashionable; because they were all cousins and must put up with one another.[73]

The Steeles themselves have other cousins, who seem to treat them with a degree of cosy familiarity: they plague Anne about the doctor she is supposedly in love with (or so she likes to say), so that sometimes she does not know 'which way to look before them'; and cousin Richard does not believe that Edward will turn down the wealthy Miss Morton in favour of Lucy, and that 'when it came to the point, he was afraid Mr. Ferrars would be off'.[74] The only marriages that do take place between cousins are those of Henrietta Musgrove and Charles Hayter, and, in *Lady Susan*, Frederica and Reginald De Courcy – who is in any case not exactly a cousin, being her mother's brother-in-law.

The various relationships within the family are on the whole more important to Jane Austen's characters than friendships outside it. In some ways this was probably true of many young people in Georgian England, since independent life outside the family, at least for girls, was virtually impossible. Boys made friends at school, and if girls were sent to school they obviously could do so as well. But only one of the heroines in the novels, Anne Elliot, goes to school, and she indeed does have an old school friend – one who is crucial in the development of the plot. When she is told by her former governess of the invalid Mrs Smith's being in Bath, she has not seen her since her schooldays; but at that time they had been close, and her fondness for her, characteristically of Anne, was founded on the appreciation of her goodness:

> Miss Hamilton, now Mrs. Smith, had shewn her kindness in one of those periods of her life when it had been most valuable. Anne had gone unhappy to school, grieving for the loss of a mother whom she had dearly loved, feeling her separation from home, and suffering as a girl of fourteen, of strong sensibility and not high spirits, must suffer at such a time; and Miss Hamilton, three years older than herself, but still from the want of near relations and a settled home, remaining another year at school, had been useful and good to her in a way which had considerably lessened her misery, and could never be remembered with indifference.[75]

Despite the age difference, they must have felt an innate sympathy from the similarity of their situations; no doubt the elder girl's loneliness made her sensitive to Anne's, and natural goodness prompted her to look after her. Possibly some element of the kindliness and dependability in Anne's own character was developed by this early experience; and as she in her turn is able to bring comfort to Mrs Smith (a comfort given a practical dimension by Captain Wentworth's putting her affairs to rights), the re-established friendship flourishes to become an important constituent of Anne's married life.

Of the other heroines, the only significant friendship of longstanding is that of Elizabeth Bennet and Charlotte Lucas. We know nothing of how they got on when they were children, and their friendship, described as 'intimate', is in any case rather surprising, since they are seven years apart in age; that, along with the comparative seriousness of Charlotte's character, might have made it more natural for her to have been Jane's friend rather than Elizabeth's. It is of course necessary for the working of the novel that Charlotte should be old enough to feel that it is better to marry Mr Collins than wait any longer, and sober enough in temperament to believe that she could manage to live with him; even so, to be seven years older than Elizabeth and to be her 'intimate friend' may well strike us as surprising. But it may not have seemed so to Jane Austen. Among her friends, though some, like the Bigg sisters at Manydown, were her own age, others were older. Indeed, Madam Lefroy belonged to the generation above her, and was only ten years younger than Mrs Austen; though she could not perhaps be described as Jane's 'intimate friend', they were certainly very close, particularly intellectually – she is often referred to as her 'mentor'.

More analogous perhaps to the friendship between Elizabeth and Charlotte is that of Jane and Cassandra with the Lloyd sisters, particularly Mary and Martha. The daughters of a clergyman, on his death they moved with their mother into Mr Austen's rectory at Deane, when Jane and Cassandra became very friendly with them. Jane was then thirteen, Cassandra sixteen, Mary eighteen and Martha twenty-three. Though they moved to Ibthorpe three years later, the close friendship continued; and since eventually Martha shared their home at Chawton, it is obvious that despite the age difference of ten years, she and Jane (and for that matter Cassandra) were obviously very close friends.

The third Lloyd sister, Eliza, was already married when the rest of her family came to Deane. Her husband was a cousin, Fulwar Craven Fowle, son of the vicar of Kintbury and a childhood friend of James Austen. Fulwar had been one of Mr Austen's pupils, living in the rectory as he, like James, was prepared for his entrance to Oxford; like James too, he was entered for St John's, though not until three years later, since James went up at the unusually early age of fourteen. During his first year at the university, James wrote a verse epistle to Fulwar in which, in language reminiscent of Milton's *Lycidas* (also a tribute to a friend), he imagined him in future years as a great statesman, and urged him to look back on the days of their youth and to recall 'Each tranquil hour, each happy scene' when they were in their 'own converse blest'; then he would remember how

> Together often have we strayed
> Thro' many a daisy-dappled mead,
> And flower-enamelled vales;
> Or haply thro' some leafy grove
> Caught the soft plainings of the dove,
> Who her lost mate bewails.

He would be reminded of their swims in the river on hot summer days, of the sound of the huntsman's horn in autumn, and in winter of congenial pleasures indoors:

> When frosts that rise, & winds that pierce
> And snows descending foul & fierce
> Forbade the sylvan toil;
> The genial feast we'd then prolong;
> With festive mirth and jocund song
> The weary hours beguile.

Characteristically, James allows himself to indulge in a little moralizing, with just a hint of the future parson:

> What though those days can ne'er return
> Twere folly sure for that to mourn;
> 'Twere wise to be content;
> With what the Gods to us allow,
> And thank them with unclouded brow,
> For all the blessings sent.

And, in a testimony to an idealized view of friendship, he ends without any suspicion of envy as he draws a comparison between the great public career that he imagines for Fulwar and his own humbler calling as a poet of nature:

To different men the fates assign
A different part to act; 'twas thine,
To bask in glory's blaze;
Twas mine to woo in lowly strain
The nymphs of fountain, wood or plain
To bless my peaceful lays.[76]

Far from becoming a great statesman, Fulwar Craven Fowle took orders and eventually followed his father as vicar of Kintbury, dying in the rectory in which he had been born. When *Emma* was published, Jane Austen noted that he 'read only the first & last Chapters, because he had heard it was not interesting'.[77]

7

Reading and writing

One of the treasures passed down in the Austen family is a battered and much used copy of *The History of Little Goody Two-Shoes*. The title page and many others are missing, and those that remain are torn and ragged. The frontispiece, depicting the little heroine, has been pasted down onto the inside of the cover; it is not the rather attractive woodcut used for the first edition of the book but a simpler, less sophisticated one, and it has been crudely coloured in by hand. In the top left corner, above the picture, it bears the name of Jane Austen.[1]

'For fifty years,' commented a writer in the *Athenaeum* in 1871, *The History of Little Goody Two-Shoes* 'was the delight of every child in England that could read';[2] and indeed Goody's name passed into the language as a perhaps not entirely complimentary epithet for a virtuous child. The original Goody is very virtuous indeed. Orphaned with her little brother Tommy at an early age, and so poor that she has only one shoe, she is rescued by the wealthy relation of a worthy clergyman; this kindly gentleman takes Tommy to London to 'make him a little sailor' and orders a new pair of shoes for Goody. It is only the pleasure she takes in these new shoes that supports her in the loss of her brother, and she is so excited about them that she shows them to everybody she meets, crying out 'Two Shoes . . . see Two Shoes', and 'by that means obtained the name of Goody Two-Shoes, though her play-mates called her Old Goody Two-Shoes'.[3] Concluding that the goodness and wisdom of the clergyman are the result of his great learning (an irony not commented on in the story), she teaches herself to read and write by borrowing books from the children as they come home from school, and soon starts to teach other children who are 'more ignorant than herself'. Eventually she becomes principal of a local college 'for instructing little gentlemen and ladies in the science of A, B, C',[4] and after various adventures such as seeing the school roof fall in, and being accused of witchcraft, she marries a wealthy widower; at which point her brother, who has made his fortune at sea and is now as wealthy as she is, makes a dramatic reappearance just in time for the wedding.

Goody is a model of patience and Christian self-denial. She never rails against her fate, however hard it may be; her lessons are humane, enlightened and enjoyed by all her pupils; and, far from resenting the cruelty that led to her initial destitution, when she overhears a gang of thieves planning to rob the house of the landowner, Sir Timothy Gripe, who dispossessed her father, she immediately goes to inform him, thereby saving his life. In her will, she makes generous bequests to the villagers, among them several acres of land to be planted with potatoes every year for the benefit of the poor. It is not surprising that after her death, as people pass her gravestone they 'weep continually, so that the stone is ever bathed in tears'.[5]

Little Goody Two-Shoes is the very essence of the moral tale, which by the end of the eighteenth century became the principal kind of reading matter for children. Like all such works, it obviously seeks to instil notions of good behaviour in its young readers; but it also has a more specifically didactic purpose in that it is concerned with reading and with learning to read – 'the science of A, B, C' itself. The education of children was considered vital to the inculcation in society of the values that J. H. Plumb defined as 'sobriety, obedience, industry, thrift, benevolence and compassion';[6] and while the belief that a carefully designed system of pedagogy would offer a route to success might originate in such dissenting scientists as Erasmus Darwin and Joseph Priestley, it soon came to be generally held by a middle class that saw itself in opposition to both the extravagance of the aristocracy and the profligacy and ignorance of the labouring classes. At the very base of such a system must be an effective way of teaching children to read and write.

The anonymous author of *Little Goody Two-Shoes* is very specific about her system:

> She found that only the following letters were required to spell all the words; but as some of these letters are large, and some small, she with her knife cut out several pieces of wood, ten sets of each of these:
>
> a b c d e f g h i j k l m n o p q r s t u v w x y z.
> And six sets of these:
> A B C D E F G H I J K L M N O P Q R S T U V W X Y Z.
>
> And having got an old spelling-book, she made her companions set up all the words they wanted to spell, and after that she taught them to compose sentences.
>
> You know what a sentence is, my dear, 'I will be good,' is a sentence; and is made up, as you see, of several words.
>
> The usual manner of spelling, or carrying on the game, as they called it, was this: suppose the word to be spelt was plum-pudding, (and who can suppose a better?) the children were placed in a circle, and the first brought the letter p, the next l, the next u, the next m, and so on till the whole word was spelt; and if any one brought a wrong letter, he was to pay a fine, or play no more. This was their play; and every morning she used to go round to teach the children with these rattle-traps in a basket, as you see in the print.[7]

At this stage, before she is in her school, she is still an itinerant instructress of children not much younger than herself, and it is clear that she, and they, treat learning as a game, just as Emma Woodhouse must have intended the box of letters that she made in the same way for her nephews both to instruct and to amuse them.[8] The dual purpose of Goody's method, to teach and to play – indeed, to teach *through* play – is embodied in the book itself. Its huge popularity throughout the second half of the century and well into the next was testimony to children's enjoyment of it. At the same time, any young reader would be learning even as he read, or more pertinently, was read to, for at an early age children would have had the book read to them as they turned the pages and looked at the pictures, as is evident from the words 'as you see in the print'; and there is a tacit acknowledgment of the two roles of reader and auditor in the authorial assumption of the voice of mother or nurse, for example in 'You know what a sentence is, my dear.'

The History of Little Goody Two-Shoes; Otherwise called, Mrs. Margery Two-Shoes, 'With The Means by which she acquired her Learning and Wisdom, and in consequence thereof her Estate', was, so the original title-page informed its readers, 'set forth at large for the Benefit of those, *Who from a State of Rags and Care,/And having Shoes but half a Pair;/Their Fortune and their Fame would fix,/And gallop in a Coach and Six.*' If the promise of material reward for application to learning, both in Goody's case and in that of the aspiring reader, appears to fit the serious project of middle-class education, the balance of fun is restored by the note that follows the rhyme:

> See the Original Manuscript in the *Vatican* at *Rome*, and the Cuts by *Michael Angelo*. Illustrated with the Comments of our great modern Critics.

A literary joke about publications that boast of textual authority, improbably superior illustrations and elaborate critical apparatus might be thought to go rather above the heads of the intended audience of *Little Goody Two-Shoes*; and in the Introduction there is an extended passage which is similarly, and avowedly, aimed at adults rather than children. Describing the ways in which the tenantry have been impoverished by Sir Timothy and the avaricious Farmer Graspall, who has taken all the small farms of the parish into his own hands when their leases expired, there is an apostrophe to a reader who could not possibly be the little child learning his 'A, B, C':

> Judge, O kind, humane, and courteous reader, what a terrible situation the poor must be in, when this covetous man [Graspall] was perpetual overseer, and every thing for their maintenance was drawn from his hard heart and cruel hand. But he was not only perpetual overseer, but perpetual churchwarden; and judge, O ye Christians, what state the church must be in, when supported by a man without religion or virtue. He was also perpetual surveyor of the high-ways, and what sort of roads he kept for the convenience of travellers, those best know who have had the misfortune to be obliged to pass through that parish. – Complaints indeed were made; but to what purpose are complaints, when brought against a man who can hunt, drink, and smoke with the Lord of the Manor, who is also a Justice of the Peace?[9]

There then follows an account of the attempts by Goody's father to seek legal redress for actions by Sir Timothy designed to intimidate him into giving up his lease, the result of which is that the poor man is ruined. This provokes another indignant rhetorical outburst:

> Ah! my dear reader, we brag of liberty, and boast of our laws; but the blessings of the one, and the protection of the other, seldom fall to the lot of the poor; and especially when a rich man is their adversary. How, in the name of goodness, can a poor wretch obtain redress, when thirty pounds are insufficient to try his cause? Where is he to find money to fee counsel, or how can he plead his cause himself, (even if he was permitted,) when our laws are so obscure, and so multiplied, that an abridgement of them cannot be contained in fifty volumes folio?

The tone here is heavily political, and the writer, clearly realizing that no child is going to be interested in what amounts to a radical pamphlet, concludes with a humorous disclaimer:

> 'But what (says the reader) can occasion all this? Do you intend this for children?' Permit me to inform you, that this is not the book, Sir, mentioned in the title, but an introduction to that book; and it is intended, Sir, not for those sort of children, but for children of six feet high, of which, as my friend has justly observed, there are many millions in the kingdom; and these reflections, Sir, have been rendered necessary by the unaccountable and diabolical scheme which many gentlemen now give into, of laying a number of farms into one, and very often a whole parish into one farm; which in the end must reduce the common people to a state of vassalage, worse than that under the barons of old, or that of the clans in Scotland, and will in time depopulate the kingdom. But as you are tired of the subject, I shall take myself away, and you may visit little Margery.[10]

This presupposes an adult reader for the Introduction quite separate from the child who would read the book itself. On the other hand, without the background to little Margery's poverty, her story would not make sense; and in particular, the episode in which she warns Sir Timothy about the planned robbery would lose much of its significance. Presumably the Introduction is intended for whoever is reading the story with the child; this of course would almost certainly be the mother or nurse, and the use of the term 'Sir' to address her ironically draws attention to the public and masculine concerns that the writer has been drawn into, which are so self-evidently outside the sphere of both child and woman. Nevertheless, she would be able to supply the infant with a résumé of the cruel treatment suffered by the family at the hands of the farmer and the squire, while herself appreciating the more general political points that the writer wished to convey.

Who, then, was this radical author who introduced a children's story with so outspoken a denunciation of social injustice? *Little Goody Two-Shoes* first appeared in 1765; it was produced by John Newbery, the first British publisher of children's books, and the man who can be said to have created, or at least perceived, the market for them. Its political views, particularly as expressed in the Introduction, have led some authorities to believe that the author was Oliver Goldsmith, who published several works with Newbery; but whereas for those books his name can be found in the firm's accounts, there is nothing there to connect him with *Goody*, and in the absence of further evidence it is reasonable to conclude that the likeliest author was John Newbery himself.

Newbery had wide business interests, but eventually came to concentrate on two: publishing and patent medicines. While most of his books were for adults, it is for his children's books that he is now remembered; and from the appearance of *A Little Pretty Pocket Book* in 1744, also probably written by himself, he issued a series of entertaining and instructive works avowedly influenced by Locke's idea, set out in *Some Thoughts Concerning Education*, that learning is most effective when it is made into a game; *Little Goody Two-Shoes*, it will be noted, simultane-ously illustrates and enacts this pedagogical method. But as a shrewd man of business, Newbery was well aware of the advantage to his firm of the proliferation of reading among a public with money to spend on his products; and he lost no opportunity of publicizing them, to the extent that he would work a reference to one into the text of another. When Goody begins giving spelling lessons with games and songs, the author promptly notes that they 'may be found in the Little Pretty Pocket Book, published by Mr Newbery'. Even his medicines get a puff, for example in the very opening of the story:

> Care and discontent shortened the days of Little Margery's father. – He was forced from his family, and seized with a violent fever in a place where Dr James's powder was not to be had, and where he died miserably.

Dr James's Powder was one of Newbery's best-selling lines.

Chapter 7 of *Little Goody Two-Shoes*, which is headed 'Containing an Account of all the Spirits or Ghosts she saw in the Church', describes Goody falling asleep one night in church, following a funeral she has attended, and thinking that she has seen a ghost, which turns out to be nothing more alarming than a neighbour's dog, Snip. The chapter ends with this 'Reflection', in a reassuring intervention of the authorial voice:

> After this, my dear children, I hope you will not believe any foolish stories that ignorant, weak, or designing people may tell you about ghosts; for the tales of ghosts, witches, and fairies, are the follies of a distempered brain. No wise man ever saw either of them. Little Margery was not afraid; no, she had good sense, and a good conscience, which is a cure for all these imaginary evils.[11]

This at first sight rather surprising attack on fairy stories and other ghostly tales indicates that Newbery was distancing himself from the supernatural content so often found in the old popular chapbooks, and redirecting his publications towards middle-class aspirations of a rationalist and educative upbringing for children. Fairy tales had been subjected to harsh criticism from writers such as

Sarah Trimmer and Maria Edgeworth, and denounced by Madame de Genlis in *Adelaide and Theodore* (a book, incidentally, that Emma has read) as containing ridiculous ideas and bringing no moral benefits. By the end of the century they had been largely replaced as the dominant form of children's literature by the moral tale, of which *Little Goody Two-Shoes* is an example; meanwhile, for the children of the poor, Hannah More used the cheap and simple chapbook form for her Cheap Repository Tracts, in which she provided lively and entertaining stories, all with a strong moral, religious and essentially conservative purpose. By 1798, Maria Edgeworth and her father could write in *Practical Education* that fairy tales 'are not now much read';[12] and the objections they make to them, apart from their rationalist basis, stem from the association of the genre with the lower classes. Referring to a story called 'The Hobgoblin', in which a little girl has been told 'a hundred foolish stories by her maid', among them one about a black-faced goblin which results in her being terrified by the sudden appearance of a chimney sweep, they comment:

> For children who have had the misfortune to have heard the hundred foolish stories of a foolish maid, this apparition of the chimney-sweeper is well managed . . . By children who have not acquired the terrors of the black faced goblin, and who have not the habit of frequenting the kitchen and the pantry, this story should never be read.[13]

The class theme is expressed even more emphatically in their criticism of another story, in which 'the part of the spectre is played by the groom'. This, they observe primly, 'is ill contrived in a drama for children; grooms should have nothing to do with their entertainments . . . .'[14] In a way, Jane Austen transfers the debate about fairy tales on to the Gothic novel in *Northanger Abbey*; seen as a narrative about reading, it opposes the truth of rationalist writers such as Fanny Burney and, significantly, Maria Edgeworth, to the more sensational authors that Catherine is encouraged to read by the foolish Isabella, only to discover finally that

> Charming as were all Mrs. Radcliffe's works, and charming even as were the works of all her imitators, it was not in them perhaps that human nature, at least in the midland counties of England, was to be looked for.[15]

If the supernatural element of traditional children's literature had been largely eradicated by the end of the century, the animal fable escaped censure, and retained its popularity. Jane Austen owned a copy of *Fables Choisies*, a volume of ninety-nine prose fables in French, which was possibly one of the books she had at the Abbey House School, Reading; it has been preserved in the family and bears both her name and that of her brother Francis.[16] There is an element of the fable too in *Little Goody Two-Shoes*, where Goody has as her teaching assistants Ralph the raven, Tom the pigeon, a skylark, a lamb and a little dog called Jumper. The raven can talk, spell and read and the pigeon can also spell and read, though the writer makes it clear that they can do so only because Goody has taught them to. Similarly, when Sarah Trimmer published her *Fabulous Histories* (later republished as *The History of the Robins*), in which four young robins, Robin, Dicky, Flapsy and Pecksy, are given human characteristics and have conversations, she spelt out in her Introduction that she had ensured that the stories should be understood by her own children, for whom they were written, 'not as containing the real conversations of Birds, (for that it is impossible we should ever understand,) but as a series of FABLES, intended to convey moral instruction'.[17] John Gay wrote a collection of fifty animal fables in verse, which was published in 1727, and many of these would have been well known in the Austen family from their inclusion in the popular anthology *Elegant Extracts*, of which Jane owned a copy. One of them, 'The Hare and Many Friends', was brought out separately as a children's book, and it is quite possible that Jane herself had a copy of that too as a child and learnt it, like Catherine Morland, 'as quickly as any girl in England'.[18]

Conveying a moral about false friends, it concerns a hare who, being pursued by the hounds, attempts to persuade the other animals to save her. They all make some excuse, however; the bull, for example, has a romantic engagement:

> Since ev'ry beast alive can tell
> That I sincerely wish you well;
> I may, without offence, pretend
> To take the freedom of a friend.
> Love calls me hence; a fav'rite cow
> Expects me near yon barley mow;
> And when a lady's in the case,
> You know, all other things give place.
> To leave you thus might seem unkind;
> But see, the Goat is just behind.[19]

This fable is referred to twice in *Emma*. Harriet tells Emma that Mr Perry had met Mr Elton setting off for London 'on business which he would not put off for any inducement in the world' and concluded that 'there must be a *lady* in the case'.[20] The phrase, which of course bears considerable weight in the context since *which* lady will only become apparent later, had become proverbial; but it is likely that Jane Austen had in mind its use by Gay, since towards the end of the book Mrs Elton quotes the two lines exactly. Sitting in Miss Bates's parlour with Jane Fairfax and Emma, and delighted to be in possession of what she thinks is still the secret knowledge of Jane's engagement, she speaks ostentatiously in riddles, to exclude Emma. In fact, though, the quotation is rather awkward, as she dimly perceives:

> Let us be discreet – quite on our good behaviour. – Hush! – You remember those lines – I
> forget the poem at this moment:
> 'For when a lady's in the case,

'You know all other things give place.'
Now I say, my dear, in *our* case, for *lady*, read – mum! a word to the wise.[21]

The most famous fables, those of Aesop, had long been a favourite with children, and there were several editions published during the eighteenth century by, among others, Samuel Richardson and the publisher Robert Dodsley. The Aesop approach was adopted by Thomas Mozeen for a two-volume edition of verse fables; he dedicated them to Viscount Cobham, declaring that they had been written 'on the Principles of LIBERTY, HONESTY, and OPENNESS of HEART', which he said were 'the well known and approved Characteristics of the ENGLISH in general', and for which his Lordship was 'particularly eminent'.[22] Though written in jogging octosyllabics, they are fairly solemn affairs, each ending with its moral, or 'Application'. Much more appealing to children was John Newbery's version of Aesop, also written in octosyllabic verse, and amusingly attributed to 'Abraham ÆSOP Esq.'; though they were stipulated as being 'For the Improvement of the Young and the Old', they were produced in the usual small format with pretty Dutch paper covers intended for the younger end of the market.

As well as stories and poems, Newbery included among his output for children overtly educational books, ranging from *A Museum for Young Gentlemen and Ladies: or, A Private Tutor for Little Masters and Misses* and *A Pretty Book of Pictures for Little Masters and Misses: or, Tommy Trip's History of Beasts and Birds*, to *Grammar Made Familiar and Easy, to Young Gentlemen and Ladies*. The deliberate inclusion of 'misses' or 'young ladies' in his target readership was both historically significant – education in the Enlightenment was intended for girls as well as for boys – and economically astute. Adept at seeing that children could be brought to grasp quite difficult concepts if their interest was once aroused, he devised such titles as *The Philosophy of Tops and Balls; or, The Newtonian System of Philosophy adapted to the Capacity of Youth, and familiarized and made entertaining by Objects with which they are intimately acquainted.*

The popularity of serious multi-volume history books in the eighteenth century was reflected in the production of shorter and simpler versions for children. Newbery published Goldsmith's two-volume *History of England in a Series of Letters from a Nobleman to His Son*, while later the rival firm of John Marshall brought out Sarah Trimmer's *A Description of a Set of Prints of English History*, which she modestly claimed to be an abridgement of 'the excellent work of the celebrated Historian Hume' (whose six-volume *History of England* is read with pleasure by Eleanor Tilney, as it presumably was by Jane Austen, since she owned a set).[23] Mrs Trimmer's account of Mary Queen of Scots would no doubt have pleased Jane, if she read it. Commenting on her return from France in her nineteenth year, she observes that 'the bloom of her youth and beauty were still farther recommended, by the affability of her address, the politeness of her manners, and the elegance of her genius'.[24] While the murder of Darnley and her subsequent marriage to Bothwell brought 'a great stain on her character', her dignity and courage at the end of her life were not in doubt, when on the arrival of her death warrant she 'received this awful summons with a cheerful and smiling countenance, and welcomed the approach of death as the end of all her miseries'.[25] Jane Austen would also have relished the irony in the remark that 'Elizabeth was, or affected to be, extremely grieved at the death of Mary'.

There were thus plenty of books explaining factual material to children who were capable of reading essentially adult works; but despite the devotion of Goody Two-Shoes and her avian assistants to the alphabet in a story that emphasized the material rewards of learning, there was no simple primer designed expressly to teach younger ones to read in the first place. This need came to the notice of Anna Laetitia Barbauld, wife of a Dissenting minister with whom she ran a boys' boarding school in Suffolk, when, having no children themselves, they adopted her nephew Charles. Finding nothing suitable to use with the little boy, she wrote a series of four books of her own for teaching children from two to four years old, which she published in 1787–8. They were issued in tiny volumes, perfectly suited to being held in small hands, but with large print; and Mrs Barbauld set out her intentions clearly in the Advertisement to the first one:

> The eye of a child and of a learner cannot catch, as ours can, a small, obscure, ill-formed word, amidst a number of others all equally unknown to him. – To supply these deficiencies is the object of this book. The task is humble, but not mean; for to lay the first stone of a noble building, and to plant the first idea in a human mind, can be no dishonour to any hand.[26]

The opening lesson is concerned with the act of reading itself:

> Come hither Charles, come to mamma.
> Make haste.
> Sit in mamma's lap.
> Now read your book.
> Where is the pin to point with?
> Here is a pin.
> Do not tear the book.
> Only naughty boys tear books.
> Charles shall have a pretty new lesson.
> Spell that word. Good boy.
> Now go and play.[27]

The kindly adult voice that obtrudes from time to time in *The History of Little Goody Two-Shoes* ('This lamb she called Will, and a pretty fellow he is; do but look at him in the next page')[28] is here adopted for the whole book; not only is it phrased in simple language such that the child will be able to spell, but it is also synonymous with the voice of the mother herself, so that the lessons constitute the written form of her actual words, thus providing a familiar and reassuring textual presence. Attention is then turned to the child's play:

> Where is puss?
> Puss is got under the table.
> You cannot catch puss.

Apparently, Charles can, and the lesson ends on a surprisingly robust note:

> Do not pull her by the tail, you hurt her.
> Stroke poor puss. You stroke her the wrong way. This is the right way.
> But puss, why did you kill the rabbit?[29]

Adopting the question-and-answer form that Newbery had used for his instruction books, *The Circle of the Sciences*, Mrs Barbauld can soon progress to the imparting of actual knowledge, though the opportunity to insert a moral is rarely resisted:

> Charles, what are eyes for?
> To see with.
> What are ears for?
> To hear with.
> What is tongue for?
> To talk with.
> What are teeth for?
> To eat with.
> What is nose for?
> To smell with.
> What are legs for?
> To walk with.
> Then do not make mamma carry you. Walk yourself. Here are two good legs.
> Will you go abroad?
> Fetch your hat.[30]

This lesson, like the first in the book, enacts its own termination.

As the child works his way through the next volume (he is now three years old), he learns more about the world in lessons on the days, months, parts of the body, features of various animals; and there are also a number of stories, all of course with the purpose of encouraging good conduct and dedication to learning. Occasionally she ends on a somewhat lame, though undoubtedly well-meaning, note, as in the story of a little boy, 'not higher than the table', who, instead of going to school, asks the wild creatures to play with him; but the bee is gathering honey, the dog is catching a hare for his master's dinner, the bird is getting hay to build a nest and the horse is ploughing:

Then the little boy thought with himself, what, is no body idle? Then little boys must not be idle neither. So he made haste, and went to school, and learned his lesson very well, and the master said he was a very good boy.[31]

Yet, again, there is a striking honesty about the natural world, which serves both to teach the child compassion and to remind him of his moral superiority to the animals:

As soon as you have breeches you must learn to climb trees. Ask puss to teach you; she can climb. See, how fast she climbs! She is at the top. She wants to catch birds. Pray puss do not take the little birds that sing so merrily! She has got a sparrow in her mouth. She has eaten it all up. No, here are two or three feathers on the ground all bloody. Poor sparrow![32]

In the third volume there are more advanced lessons on natural history and minerals, and by the time the child has reached the fourth, he can learn about quadrupeds and the sun and moon; furthermore, he is encouraged to think for himself about moral questions, 'for', he is told, 'you know what it is to be good now'.[33] A rather laboured tale about three schoolboys and the cakes they are sent manages to combine morality with dietary advice. Harry eats all his cake, which is 'very large, and stuffed full of plums and sweetmeats, orange and citron' and 'iced all over with sugar' so that it is temptingly 'white and smooth on the top like snow'. Naturally he is ill:

So they sent for Dr. Camomile, and he gave him I do not know how much bitter stuff. Poor Harry did not like it at all, but he was forced to take it, or else he would have died, you know.[34]

His friend Peter Careful hoards his cake, and it is nibbled by mice and eventually goes mouldy. But the third boy, Billy, not only shares his, but gives what is left to a blind fiddler who is very hungry:

And the Fiddler thanked him, and Billy was more glad than if he had eaten ten Cakes. Pray which do you love best? do you love Harry, or Peter, or Billy best?[35]

Mrs Barbauld's *Lessons for Children* were hugely successful, and showed what could be done in educational books even for the very youngest readers. Although the Romantics might rail against a system that filled the young with facts instead of feeding their imagination ('Hang them!' wrote Charles Lamb '– I mean the cursed Barbauld crew, those blights and blasts of all that is human in man and child'),[36] the widespread popularity of her work was recognized, and largely endorsed, by the Edgeworths in *Practical Education*:

The first works which are now usually put into the hands of a child are Mrs. Barbauld's Lessons; they are by far the best books of the kind that have ever appeared; those only who know the difficulty, and the importance of such compositions in education, can sincerely rejoice, that the admirable talents of such a writer have been employed in such a work . . .[37]

They were not altogether without criticism, however. For one thing, they considered that Mrs Barbauld was wrong in writing for children quite so young: 'Lessons for children from three to four years old should, we think, have been lessons from four to five years old; few read, or ought to read, before that age.' Then there were reservations about the implications of certain phrases in the book. Quoting the sentence 'Charles shall have a pretty new lesson', they take exception to the conjunction of ideas on moral grounds:

> In this sentence the words pretty and new are associated; but they represent ideas which ought to be kept separate in the mind of a child. The love of novelty is cherished in the minds of children by the common expressions that we use to engage them to do what we desire . . .[38]

They also disapprove of some of the strategies by which rules of conduct are instilled:

> 'Little boys don't eat butter.'
>   'Nobody wears a hat in the house.'
>   This is a very common method of speaking, but it certainly is not proper towards children. Affirmative sentences should always express real facts. Charles must know that some little boys do eat butter; and that some people wear their hats in their houses. This mode of expression, 'Nobody does that!' 'Every body does this!' lays the foundation for prejudice in the mind. This is the language of fashion, which, more than conscience, makes cowards of us all.

What the Edgeworths object to is the linguistic dishonesty embodied in the very tone of voice that is the hallmark of Mrs Barbauld's teaching method. The reply to Charles's demand for wine is couched in the tone of astonished indignation that many a mother would use with her child, and it will not do:

> 'I want some wine.'
>   Would it not be better to tell Charles in reply to this speech, that wine is not good for him, than to say 'Wine for little boys! I never heard of such a thing!' If Charles were to be ill, and it should be necessary to give him wine; or were he to see another child drink it, he would lose confidence in what was said to him. We should be very careful of our words, if we expect our pupils to have confidence in us; and if they have not, we need not attempt to educate them.[39]

When in *Practical Education* the Edgeworths come to consider the more advanced stories to which children progress, they are concerned that they undergo a greater danger from the powerful influences to which they may be exposed, particularly if they lead sheltered lives:

> The less children associate with companions of their own age, the less they know of the world, the stronger their taste for literature, the more forcible will be the impression that will be made upon them by the pictures of life, and the characters and sentiments which they meet with in books.[40]

The solution is a system of censorship, whereby books for such children would be '*sifted* by an academy of enlightened parents'. The examples they proceed to give, which include their strictures quoted earlier on 'The Hobgoblin' and the story in which the spectre is played by a groom, are from *L'ami des enfans*, a collection of moral tales for children in twelve volumes by Arnaud Berquin published in Paris in 1782–3 and reissued in London, also in French, with an English translation following in 1786. Jane Austen was given a copy (in French) for her eleventh birthday, and she later acquired its three-volume successor, *L'ami de l'adolescence*.[41] The Edgeworths pronounced *The Children's Friend* 'a work we much admire', and assured their readers that they did not 'mean to criticise this work as a literary production, but simply to point out to parents, that, even in the best books for children, much must still be left to the judgment of the preceptor, much in the choice of stories, and particular passages suited to different pupils'.[42] Their singling out of the book was indeed an acknowledgment of its success:

> We have chosen M. Berquin's work because of its universal popularity; probably all the examples which have been selected are in the recollection of most readers, or at least it is easy to refer to them because 'The Children's Friend' is to be found in every house where there are any children. The principles by which we have examined Berquin may be applied to all books of the same class.[43]

One further type of literature gave them cause for concern and suggested the need for a similar kind of discrimination among those who might be permitted to read it. This was stories of voyages and travels, which, they admitted, 'interest young people universally'. Citing *Robinson Crusoe* and *Gulliver's Travels* among others, they warn:

> this species of reading should not early be chosen for boys of an enterprising temper, unless they are intended for a seafaring life, or for the Navy. The taste for adventure is absolutely incompatible with the sober perseverance necessary to success in any other liberal professions.[44]

Such books were fairly safe for girls, however, since they 'must very soon perceive the impossibility of their rambling about the world in quest of adventures'.

Nevertheless, the choice of books for girls in general should be a matter for careful thought on the part of their parents; and in particular the Edgeworths saw it as the responsibility of their mother to ensure that anything they read would encourage them to enjoy literature while at the same time developing in them a sense of what was proper for them to read. It was a difficult balance:

> Much prudence and ability are requisite to conduct properly a young woman's literary education. Her imagination must not be raised above the taste for necessary occupations, or the numerous small, but not trifling pleasures of domestic life; her mind must be enlarged, yet the delicacy of her manners must be preserved: her knowledge must be various, and her powers of reasoning unawed by authority; yet she must *habitually* feel that nice sense of propriety, which is at once the guard and the charm of every feminine virtue. By early caution, unremitting, scrupulous caution in the choice of the books which are put into the hands of girls, a mother, or a preceptress, may fully occupy, and entertain their pupils, and excite in their minds a *taste* for propriety, as well as a taste for literature. It cannot be necessary to add more than this general idea, that a mother ought to be answerable to her daughter's husband for the books her daughter had read, as well as for the company she had kept.[45]

It is difficult to imagine such 'unremitting, scrupulous caution' being practised at Steventon rectory when Cassandra and Jane were beginning to read, since from an early age they would have shared books with their brothers, and no doubt like them they would have been allowed to choose books from their father's library.

Mrs Austen taught her children their letters, and learning would not necessarily have come as easily as Newbery and Mrs Barbauld might suggest. Perhaps Jane Austen recalled something of her mother's struggles when in *Northanger Abbey* Catherine defends to Henry Tilney her use of the word 'torment' for instruction:

> You think me foolish to call instruction a torment, but if you had been as much used as myself to hear poor little children first learning their letters and then learning to spell, if you had ever seen how stupid they can be for a whole morning together, and how tired my poor mother is at the end of it, as I am in the habit of seeing almost every day of my life at home, you would allow that to *torment* and to *instruct* might sometimes be used as synonimous words.[46]

Some of the teaching was done orally; learning poetry was considered important, and just as Catherine commits Thomas Moss's 'The Beggar's Petition' to memory, after three months, so Jane would have done, though probably in a somewhat shorter time. Like Catherine, she would have been taught to read French by her mother and writing by her father, it being usual at that time for reading and writing to be taught separately. Her brothers too would no doubt have had a hand in her reading, in the same way that Edmund Bertram does with Fanny, as we have seen: like him, they would have 'recommended the books which charmed her leisure hours . . . encouraged her taste . . . corrected her judgment' and 'made reading useful by talking to her of what she read, and heightened its attraction by judicious praise';[47] certainly these phrases are echoed by James

Edward Austen-Leigh in his *Memoir*, where he claims that his father, James, had 'a large share in directing her reading and forming her taste'.[48] They also made her presents of books. Edward gave her a copy of Thomas Percival's didactic *A Father's Instructions; consisting of Moral Tales, Fables, and Reflections, designed to promote the Love of Virtue*, as she recalled in a letter to Cassandra when Percival's son arrived in Southampton in 1808: 'We have got a new Physician,' she wrote, 'a Dr Percival, the son of a famous Dr Percival of Manchester, who wrote Moral Tales for Edward to give to me'.[49] Thomas Percival was a student at the famous Dissenting Academy at Warrington, where Mrs Barbauld's father, John Aikin, was tutor first in Classics, then in Divinity; his book combined science and morality in an essentially secular way, following the ideas of Locke, by which the Academy was strongly influenced. A book of a very different kind was given to Jane for her confirmation: this was *A Companion to the altar* by William Vickers, a manual frequently given to confirmation candidates; according to a descendant of the family, it was a book of devotions that she 'always used'.[50]

Jane herself later also made presents of books to her young nephews and nieces. To Fanny Austen she gave a copy of the works of one of her own favourite poets, Cowper, and to James Edward a volume called *The British navigator, or A collection of voyages made in different parts of the world*.[51] Anna received a copy of *Elegant Extracts* and also Ann Murry's *Mentoria: or, The young ladies instructor*, in which information is conveyed by the means of stilted conversations between Mentoria and her two pupils, who perpetually congratulate themselves on their own knowledge, while smugly expressing surprise at the ignorance of their friend Miss Simple, thus, as Irene Collins has pointed out, providing the pattern for the dialogue between Maria and Julia and their Aunt Norris about cousin Fanny's educational failings.[52]

A child's reading necessarily exercises a considerable influence over its writing, since it will begin by imitating favourite books in juvenile efforts of its own. In Jane Austen's case, her creative response to literature was, at least to judge from the surviving *Juvenilia*, essentially parodic. She delighted in prefacing tiny stories with mock-pompous dedications to members of the family; 'The Memoirs of Mr Clifford', for example, is inscribed 'To Charles John Austen Esqre' and reads:

Sir,
Your generous patronage of the unfinished tale, I have already taken the Liberty of dedicating to you, encourages me to dedicate to you a second, as unfinished as the first. I am Sir with every expression
    of regard for you & yr noble
        Family, your most obed^t
           &c. &c . . . .
             The Author[53]

In another piece, 'Jack & Alice', she satirizes a well-worn structural feature of eighteenth-century fiction that must have struck her as inherently tedious, narrative autobiography. Not once but twice the heroine is regaled with the account of the vicissitudes of a character's life, and the joke is that on both occasions she actually asks for it. First she asks her friend Lady Williams to favour her with her 'Life & Adventures', to which she receives the reply, 'Willingly my Love'.[54] Two short chapters later, she is out walking with Lady Williams when she comes upon 'a lovely young Woman lying apparently in great pain beneath a Citron-tree'; disclosure is invited in exactly the same terms:

> 'You seem fair Nymph to be labouring under some misfortune which we shall be happy to releive if you will inform us what it is. Will you favour us with your Life and Adventures?'
> 'Willingly Ladies, if you will be so kind as to be seated.'[55]

By this time, Jane Austen was no longer reading only children's stories, as is clear from a reference in the same story to 'the great Sir Charles Grandison';[56] Richardson's novel was very much a favourite, and she read it first when she was quite young. Her writing also reflects her reading of adult histories. Although Newbery had published a children's *History of England* by Oliver Goldsmith in the form of 'a series of letters from a Nobleman to his Son', it was Goldsmith's later four-volume *The History of England from the Earliest Times to the Death of George II* that was used at Steventon rectory (the family copy has James's name in it) and which was annotated with marginal comments by Jane; and when she came to write her own comic 'History of England', the engraved portraits of monarchs in roundels inspired Cassandra's amusing drawings of kings and queens, some copied from figures in popular prints of the day (amusingly, as Deirdre Le Faye has pointed out, Henry VIII is the radical parliamentarian Charles James Fox).[57]

In the next generation, James's three children were also keen to write, and turned to Aunt Jane for advice. Anna was twenty-one when she sent sections of a novel that she was working on, eliciting in reply the frequently quoted comments that give an invaluable insight into Jane Austen's own approach to fiction.[58] Anna's younger half-sister Caroline discussed the books she was reading with her aunt; 'You seem to be quite my own Neice,' Jane told her at the age of ten, 'in your feelings towards M^{de} de Genlis. I do not think I could even now, at my sedate time of Life, read *Olimpe et Theophile* without being in a rage. It really is too bad! – Not allowing them to be happy together, when they *are* married. – Don't talk of it, pray.'[59]

Caroline also sent her melodramatic stories from an early age, and she responded in an appropriate tone:

> I wish I could finish Stories as fast as you can. – I am much obliged to you for the sight of Olivia, & think you have done for her very well; but the good for nothing Father, who was the real author of all her Faults & Sufferings, should not escape unpunished. – I hope *he* hung himself, or took the sur-name of *Bone* or underwent some direful penance or other.[60]

When her niece tried her hand at comedy, Jane was more amused: 'I have been very much entertained by your story of Carolina & her aged Father, it made me laugh heartily, & I am particularly glad to find you so much alive upon any topic of such absurdity, as the usual description of a Heroine's father. – You have done it full justice'; but there is a suggestion that she is laughing at the little girl, since she adds 'or if anything *be* wanting, it is the information of the venerable old Man's having married when only Twenty one, & being a father at Twenty two'.[61] On the whole, she seems to have thought that Caroline had less talent than her elder half-sister, and showed kindness rather than genuine appreciation for her writing: 'I look forward to the 4 new chapters with pleasure,' she told her. 'But how can you like Frederick better than Edgar? – You have some eccentric Tastes however I know, as to Heroes & Heroines.'[62] She took her efforts seriously enough to appraise them honestly, however: 'I am glad to hear of your proceedings & improvements in the Gentleman Quack,' she wrote in a later letter. 'There was a great deal of Spirit in the first part. Our objection to it You have heard, & I give your Authorship credit for bearing Criticism so well.'[63] 'Our objection' reveals that these youthful efforts were discussed by both her aunts, and no doubt her grandmother as well. The key to Jane's lack of warmth towards the story comes in another letter: 'I like Frederick & Caroline better than I did, but must still prefer Edgar & Julia. – Julia is a warm-hearted, ingenuous, natural Girl, which I like her for; – but I know the word *Natural* is no recommendation to you.'[64] It was truth to life that Caroline was not interested in; and writing lacking that quality could not possibly have pleased her aunt.

In later years, Caroline herself recalled discussions with her aunt about literature and her writing:

> As I grew older, she would talk to me more seriously of my reading, and of my amusements – I had taken early to writing verses and stories, and I am sorry to think *how* I troubled her with reading them. She was very kind about it, and always had some praise to bestow but at last she warned me against spending too much time upon them – She said – how well I recollect it! that she *knew* writing stories was a great amusement, and *she* thought a harmless one – tho' many people, she was aware, thought otherwise – but that at my age it would be bad for me to be much taken up with my own compositions – Later still – it was after she got to Winchester, she sent me a message to this effect – That if I would take her advice, I should cease writing till I was 16, and that she herself often wished she had *read* more, and written *less*, in the corresponding years of her own life.[65]

Besides acknowledging the debate between proponents of the practical and the imaginative in education, Jane Austen seemed to be admitting, perhaps rather surprisingly, to an inadequate literary preparation for her own youthful efforts.

In discussing the stories that her nieces and nephew were writing, it amused her to adopt the conspiratorial tone of co-authors. 'Edward is writing a Novel,' she wrote to Cassandra; 'we have all heard what he has written . . . Tell Caroline that I think it is hardly fair upon her & myself, to have him take up the Novel Line . . .'[66]

And with James Edward himself she shared a joke about Henry Austen, at that time acting as curate at Chawton: 'Uncle Henry writes very superior Sermons. – You & I must try to get hold of one or two, & put them into our Novels; – it would be a fine help to a volume; & we could make our Heroine read it aloud of a Sunday Evening . . . '[67] James Edward was eighteen and had been writing verses since he was a boy. Jane was impressed with the beginning of the novel: 'it is extremely clever; written with great ease & spirit; – if he can carry it on in the same way, it will be a firstrate work, & in a style, I think, to be popular'.[68] While acknowledging its differences from her own work, she clearly appreciated its quality; and when she heard from his mother that some of the manuscript had gone missing, beneath the characteristically self-deprecating humour of her response to him there was genuine admiration:

> two Chapters & a half to be missing is monstrous! It is well that *I* have not been at Steventon lately, & therefore cannot be suspected of purloining them; -- two strong twigs & a half towards a Nest of my own, would have been something. I do not think however that any theft of that sort would be really very useful to me. What should I do with your strong, manly, spirited Sketches, full of Variety & Glow? – How could I possibly join them on to the little bit (two Inches wide) of Ivory on which I work with so fine a Brush, as produces little effect after much labour?[69]

James Edward had already learnt an important lesson about style from his aunt, and her method of teaching, though playful, was emphatic. Having returned from Winchester College, he had written to her, heading his letter 'Steventon' and proceeding to tell her that he had arrived at home. She made much of this in her reply:

> I am glad you recollected to mention your being come home. My heart began to sink within me when I had got so far through your Letter without its being mentioned. I was dreadfully afraid that you might be detained at Winchester by severe illness, confined to your Bed perhaps & quite unable to hold a pen, & only dating from Steventon in order, with a mistaken sort of Tenderness, to deceive me. – But now, I am sure you would not say it so seriously unless it actually were so.[70]

Her very prolixity is a rebuke to his own. It was a lesson he did not forget, for when more than fifty years later he included her letter in the *Memoir*, he added a wry footnote: 'It seems that her young correspondent, after dating from home, had been so superfluous as to state in his letter that he was returned home, and thus to have drawn on himself this banter.'[71]

This lesson in economy of expression goes to the heart of Jane Austen's style. James Edward himself thought that it came from her mother. Referred to at the age of six by her uncle Theophilus Leigh, the Master of Balliol, as 'the Poet of the Family' after she had recited for him several 'Smart pieces promising a great Genius,'[72] Mrs Austen was adept at writing witty, succinct verses and riddles for the entertainment of her family and her husband's pupils in the rectory. 'In Mrs Austen', James Edward writes, 'was to be found the germ of much of the ability which was concentrated in Jane, but of which others of her children had a share. She united strong common sense with a lively imagination, and often expressed herself, both in writing and in conversation, with epigrammatic force and point.'[73] She had the art, which her daughter inherited, of knowing how few words were required to express what needed to be said. In Newbery's version of the Fox and Grapes, the most famous of all Aesop's fables is rendered in language which, though comparatively straightforward, is inflated by digression and unnecessary description:

REYNARD, by fraud and rapine fed,
The hen roosts and the lambkins dread;
Sated with slaughter, now grown nice,
A vine with clusters laden spies;
The fruit to warmest beams display'd,
In horizontal lines were laid.
Beauty has charms: but ah! in vain
We sigh for what we can't obtain.
Six feet above the ground and more,
The wall supports the purple store.
Beyond thy reach, ambitious creature,
Whose cunning far exceeds thy stature.
He longs, and thrice with utmost strain
Leaps at the Grapes, but leaps in vain.
Now tir'd, the disappointed thief,
Tho' sorely vex'd, thus hides his grief:
 'A plague, says he, d'ye call these ripe,
  'They'd kill one with the cholic:
 'I would not have them if I might,
  'I jump'd but for a frolic.'
   MORAL
Who have, by fortune malice crost,
Preferment or a mistress lost,
Wisely dissemble the miscarriage,
And what they cannot reach, disparage.[74]

While the Austens were living in Bath in 1804, Mrs Austen wrote her own version of this fable, possibly to be sent to Steventon to amuse the young James Edward:

Some fine ripe Grapes were hanging high,
A hungry Fox was passing by,
He lick'd his lips & long'd to eat 'em,
So Jump'd & Jump'd but could not get 'em;

> Convinced it was not in his power,
> I'm sure, said he, those Grapes are sour.[75]

It took Newbery's 'Abraham Æsop' twenty-four somewhat laboured lines to tell the story; Mrs Austen managed it in six.

8

Education

One morning in the autumn of 1813 the Revd James Austen set off from Steventon rectory with his son James Edward for Deane Gate, on their way to London. James intended to enter him for Eton, and they were going there to make the necessary arrangements. James Edward was nearly fifteen, and already a year above the usual age for boys to begin at the school; but in any case, as it turned out, it was not to be. Years later he recalled for his own children what had happened to alter his father's plan:

> We were riding down the lane which was to take us to the high road and the stage coach, when a stiff bramble hanging across the lane caught in my father's clothes and tore them so badly, that he said: 'Well, Edward, I cannot go on in this state, we must go back and make the journey another day.' We did so, but our second attempt was delayed for a few days, and before it could be made my father heard something or other about Eton which caused him to change his mind and resolve, instead, to send me to Winchester.[1]

What James Austen had heard was that even under the headmastership of John Keate, a notorious and energetic flogger, discipline at Eton was highly ineffectual; the school was rowdy, there was considerable unrest, and the very poor ratio of masters to boys meant that any kind of real control was virtually impossible.

This situation was not new; under Keate's more lenient predecessor, Goodall, there was persistent bullying among the pupils of a violent, even a dangerous kind; Shelley's life had been made a misery by the regular, sustained baiting to which he was subjected, and a contemporary of his, Edward Hawtrey, later to become headmaster himself, was nearly killed.[2] No doubt James was advised by his brother Edward, who had already sent four of his sons to Winchester and would subsequently send his other two there. In any case, the bramble proved a happy accident for James Edward, and he went to Winchester too – though that did not prevent him years later sending his own sons to Eton, where one of them returned to become a member of the staff; nor, for that matter, did it stop Jane Austen sending Edmund Bertram there.[3] James Austen turned his discovery into an amusing charade:

> My first can well finish a bottle of Wine
> But will never another begin

My second's large belly, if right I opine
Can a much larger portion take in,
They who live at my whole, though sent there to drink nought
But large draughts from Castalia's rill;
Are suspected to swallow more wine than they ought
    As their parents find out by their bill[4]

The solution is 'Eton'.

James might have been expected to educate his son at home, as the Revd George Austen had done with his boys, having provided them with a basic education and further prepared both James and his younger brother Henry for Oxford, alongside the other pupils he took into the rectory. But when James occupied Steventon rectory he seems not to have taken pupils; and, though he taught James Edward in his early years, when he reached the age of thirteen, perhaps because he felt that his son would benefit from the company of boys of his own age, he decided to send him away to school. The choice of Meyrick's School in Ramsbury, Wiltshire, may have been determined by the fact that James Edward's friend William Heathcote was already there. William's mother, one of Jane Austen's friends, the Biggs of Manydown Park, was the widow of the rector of Worting and sister-in-law of Sir Thomas Heathcote, the MP for Hampshire; in choosing Ramsbury she would have been influenced by its excellent reputation among the well-to-do and aristocratic families who sent their sons there. Set in an ancient agricultural village in the valley of the Kennet, the school had originally been housed in the vicarage but soon expanded into two other nearby buildings. When James Edward arrived in August 1812,[5] the Revd Edward Graves Meyrick had just succeeded his father, who had founded the school, both as schoolmaster and as vicar, though the day-to-day running of the place was undertaken by his brother Arthur.[6] Academically successful, Meyrick's provided a pleasant and relaxed atmosphere for its pupils, and there was a strong rapport between them and their masters. James Edward was undoubtedly happy there, and a poem he wrote in cipher during his first term, called 'The School-boys wish', was clearly meant to be taken in fun:

Me impsh it omp a toimsbud
A gobredy a hoimsbud.
A glomp me aump bibredy
A Pounup toob a sibredy
An aump a bib a funsbud
A Croismus oump a comesbud
Mub oump gaub a waysbud
Bub a maub oump staysbud
A Ramsburrudub mibredy
Nauba agaund oump sibredy[7]

['I wish it were time/To go home./Glad I would be/A Pound to see/And what a bit of fun/At Christmas would come/Misery would go away/Bright and merry I'd stay/And Ramsbury I/Never again would see']⁸

It was not only boys who were sent away to school. Girls' schools had proliferated during the eighteenth century, although it could hardly be said that most of them offered much more than the provision of the accomplishments that would equip young ladies for their entrance into the world and the finding of a husband – since the universities admitted only men, there would after all have been little point in giving girls a classical education. Furthermore, just as it was common for clergymen such as Mr Austen to take boys into the rectory as pupils, so there were women who did the same for girls. One such was Mrs Ann Cawley in Oxford, widow of a former principal of Brasenose College. She was the sister of Mrs Austen's brother-in-law, Dr Edward Cooper, who lived in Bath. Cassandra had been sent to stay with his family, and made friends with his daughter Jane; and it was agreed that both girls should go to Mrs Cawley for tutoring – and that Jane Austen should go too. It may seem slightly odd that both Austen girls should have been sent away from home, particularly since Jane, at seven, was, for that period, rather young to go to school.⁹ Cassandra, however, was ten, and it may well have been that Mr Austen felt that with his own hands full of the pupils who needed preparing for university, his elder daughter at least would benefit from some more systematic tuition than he was in a position to give; and it is probable that she would not have wanted to go without her sister, and indeed Jane is highly unlikely to have wanted to be separated from her. Besides, their eldest brother James was still resident at his college, St John's, so they would have a member of the family near at hand to keep an eye on them.

So in the spring of 1783 the girls went to Oxford and their father paid Mrs Cawley £15 for each of them for six months.¹⁰ The arrangement did not last, however – and indeed it nearly had disastrous consequences. In the summer Mrs Cawley took them, with their cousin Jane Cooper, to Southampton, presumably for a change of air; yet if the intention was to benefit their health, the effect was very different, since troops returning from Gibraltar had brought typhus to the town, and both sisters caught the disease.¹¹ Mrs Cawley did nothing to alert their parents, but Jane Cooper was sufficiently worried to write to her mother, as a result of which Mrs Cooper and Mrs Austen came down to fetch them. Jane Austen became seriously ill and nearly died; in time she recovered, but there was certainly no thought of returning either her or Cassandra to Mrs Cawley, who was paid a final cheque for £10 in September. The episode had a very sad outcome for the family nevertheless, since Mrs Cooper had herself caught the fever and by the end of October she was dead.

Dr Cooper was inconsolable. He left Bath and moved back to the area where he had grown up, becoming rector of Sonning. His son Edward was to go to Eton, but he needed to find a suitable school for his daughter, and the most convenient place was the Reading Ladies Boarding School (subsequently the Abbey House School).¹² Some months after Jane Cooper started there, the Austens again decided to send their daughters to school with her, though there were several places considerably nearer Steventon that they might have chosen. Nevertheless, on Monday 25 July 1785, Cassandra and Jane went off to begin the new term, and a month later Mr Austen paid a cheque for £37.19s for the fees for the half-year.[13] Cassandra was twelve years old, Jane nine.

Mrs La Tournelle's School, as it was often known, from the name of its principal, was situated in the gateway to the old abbey, the schoolhouse itself being a large building to the side of it. Its first principal, so far as is known, was a Miss Lydia Bell, who in 1755 took on her younger sister (or half-sister), Esther Hackett as an assistant; the obituary of the latter in the *Gentleman's Magazine* stated that 'having early in life, been engaged as a French teacher, her employers thought it right to introduce her into the school under a foreign name',[14] thus turning her into Mrs La Tournelle, the 'Mrs' being purely honorary. Under the two ladies the school thrived, and in 1781, on the death of Miss Bell (who had by then been for thirteen years Mrs William Spencer), Mrs La Tournelle took over. She did little of the teaching herself, except for the younger pupils; rather, she made herself responsible for running the domestic side of the school and looking after the girls' well-being. Stout and plain, she was remembered as being physically active, despite having an artificial leg, made of cork, the origins of which were obscure – though it must have fascinated her young charges.[15] The teaching of the older girls was in the hands of a Miss Pitts, who had originally, like Harriet Smith at Mrs Goddard's school, been sent as a parlour boarder, and who, unlike her, was accepted as a pupil teacher. Other teachers came and went, and a dancing master was of course always employed; and there was a close connection with the Reading School for boys nearby, under its ambitious and highly successful headmaster Dr Richard Valpy.

Such connections between boys' and girls' schools were obviously advantageous to the latter. An even closer arrangement existed in Winchester, where Mr Bennett's Academy in Southgate Street also housed his wife's school, at which, as her perennial advertisements in the *Hampshire Chronicle* proclaimed, young ladies were 'boarded and instructed in English, French, and Writing, at Sixteen Guineas per Annum. Entrance, £1. 1s. (no Entrance-money will be expected with those young Ladies who have been before at any Boarding School). Ornamental Needleworks, Music, Dancing, Drawing, Geography, and the Use of the Globes, taught separately, on moderate Terms.' Mrs Bennett could guarantee that her young ladies were properly taught, 'from her so near Alliance to Mr. Bennett, whose Abilities in several of those Branches are well known'. In parallel advertisements, Mr Bennett announced that at his Academy, 'Young Gentlemen' were 'boarded and instructed in English, Writing and Arithmetic at Eighteen Guineas per Annum'. Parents had to pay him two guineas more for educating their sons than they paid for their daughters; for that, however, the boys were provided with something that would not have been thought necessary for their sisters, since they were 'carefully instructed in the Classics'.

In later life Jane Austen described herself as 'the most unlearned, & uninformed

Female who ever dared to be an Authoress',[16] and though she was not being entirely serious, compared with the education that her brothers James and Henry received at Oxford, or her nephews at their public schools, there is no doubt that the knowledge she acquired at Mrs La Tournelle's school cannot have been very extensive. The great difference lay in the reading of classical literature. A boy's education placed stress on learning Latin and Greek, and on studying the major texts of Greek and Roman writers. Her comment was made in response to a suggestion by the Revd James Stanier Clarke, the Prince Regent's librarian, that she should write a book in which she depicted 'the Habits of Life and Character and enthusiasm of a Clergyman',[17] and the reasons she gave for feeling such a thing to be quite beyond her clearly indicate her consciousness of the wide gap between the education provided for boys and that (if any) allowed to girls. 'Such a Man's Conversation,' she wrote, 'must at times be on subjects of Science & Philosophy of which I know nothing – or at least be occasionally abundant in quotations & allusions which a Woman, who like me, knows only her own Mother-tongue & has read very little in that, would be totally without the power of giving. – A Classical Education, or at any rate, a very extensive acquaintance with English Literature, Ancient & Modern, appears to me quite Indispensable for the person who w^d do any justice to your Clergyman . . . '[18]

A classical education was what was offered at the great public schools, though lower down the social scale the more advanced grammar schools, catering for the sons of men in trade, increasingly began to teach modern subjects that would be of practical use to boys who would not be going to the universities: arithmetic, bookkeeping and various branches of commercial studies would equip them for the jobs they would do when they went out into the world to earn their own living.[19] This was no doubt the kind of education given in *Mansfield Park* to the young Prices, thanks to their uncle's generosity in paying for them to be sent to school. The pupils at Eton, Harrow, Westminster and the other public schools, however, were to be senators of the world, and a regime that consisted on the one hand of a traditional classical curriculum and on the other of a strict, indeed brutal, disciplinary rule in which they learned both to take and to mete out harsh punishment, was considered by their parents the best possible way of preparing them for their future responsibilities. Such were the boys that Jane Austen saw passing by in 'a countless number of Postchaises' on their way home from Winchester for the holidays, and whom she described as 'future Heroes, Legislators, Fools, & Villains' – many of them, no doubt, friends of James Edward, to whom she was writing at the time.[20]

William Cowper, in a poem that was well known to Jane Austen (and which she quotes in *Mansfield Park*), has a similar vision, when he imagines an ambitious man watching his little son playing:

The father, who designs his babe a priest,
Dreams him episcopally such at least;
And, while the playful jockey scowr's the room

Briskly, astride upon the parlour broom,
In fancy sees him more superbly ride
In coach with purple lined, and mitres on its side.
Events improbable and strange as these,
Which only a parental eye foresees,
A public school shall bring to pass with ease.[21]

Cowper attacks 'our public hives of puerile resort' on several grounds, not least for the unworthy motives for which boys were sent there. Parents combined ambition with a tendency to think that their sons' careers (he is thinking of the Church here) would prosper not as a result of the learning they acquired but through the influence of the aristocratic friends they would make:

Church-ladders are not always mounted best
By learned Clerks and Latinists profess'd.
Th' exalted prize demands an upward look,
Not to be found by poring on a book . . .
His wealth, fame, honors, all that I intend,
Subsist and center in one point – a friend.
A friend, whate'er he studies or neglects,
Shall give him consequence, heal all defects,
His intercourse with peers, and sons of peers –
There dawns the splendour of his future years . . . [22]

The young James Austen, in a paper that he wrote for his Oxford periodical *The Loiterer*, ironically expressed a similar view of the snobbery that the public schools gave rise to. It takes the form of a letter from one 'Luke Lickspittle', whose father, being 'the son of the half brother of the third cousin of an Irish peer' and having married 'the daughter of the wife of the steward to a great man', naturally expected his son to make his fortune 'by his alliance with the great':

The utility of good connexions, and the credit of fashionable acquaintance, were the first lessons I was taught. Servility and meanness were inculcated by precepts, enforced by example, and encouraged by rewards. I studied the arts of address, instead of learning my letters, and could flatter before I could spell. At the age of eight years I was sent to Eton, not because it was one of the best, but because it was one of the genteelest schools in the kingdom; where I exerted my insinuating talents with great success, and soon obtained a respectable acquaintance with the sons of our most illustrious nobility, and the heirs of immense possessions. I was their assistant in the exercises of the school, and their *fag* in the diversions out of it; often the confidant of their mischievous schemes, and sometimes the sufferer from their miscarriage: for all of which I was rewarded by frequent invitations to accompany them home, and had actually once the honour of spending my Christmas holidays in the house of a Duke.[23]

Another cause of disquiet about the public schools as far as Cowper was concerned was the undue weight that the teaching placed on classical mythology, which, he felt, led to a neglect of the Christian religion. Worse still, however, were the lax morals that were encouraged in the boys, partly from the influence of their fellow pupils and partly because of the freedom with which they were allowed out into the town, learning all too soon that 'pedantry is all that schools impart,/ But taverns teach the knowledge of the heart,/ There waiter Dick . . . His counsellor and bosom-friend shall prove,/ And some street-pacing harlot his first love'.[24] The older boys set the younger ones the very worst example:

> The stout tall Captain, whose superior size
> The minor heroes view with envious eyes,
> Becomes their pattern, upon whom they fix
> Their whole attention, and ape all his tricks.
> His pride, that scorns t'obey or to submit,
> With them is courage; his effront'ry wit.
> His wild excursions, window-breaking feats,
> Robb'ry of gardens, quarrels in the streets,
> His hair-breadth 'scapes, and all his daring schemes,
> Transport them, and are made their fav'rite themes.
> In little bosoms such achievements strike
> A kindred spark, they burn to do the like.[25]

One must allow for the fact that Cowper was bullied in his early years at school and detested Westminster, and that furthermore his poem was written for a clergyman who was tutoring his own sons at home; but even so, such criticism was by no means rare in the eighteenth century. The Scottish judge and philosophical writer Henry Home, Lord Kames, writing in the year before Jane Austen was born, deplored the absence of patriotism, or disinterest, from the ethos of the public schools, where young men were actively trained to be selfish: '*Keep what you get, and get what you can*, is a lesson that boys learn early at Westminster, Winchester, and Eaton; and it is the lesson that perhaps takes the fastest hold of them.' Not only were they in the habit of seeking gifts of money from complete strangers, but worse, the Eton scholars, he claimed, were at times 'sent to the highway to rob passengers'. Behaviour inside the schools was similarly lawless:

> The strong without control tyrannize over the weak, subjecting them to every servile office, wiping shoes not excepted. They are permitted to trick and deceive one another; and the finest fellow is he who is the most artful. Friendship indeed is cultivated, but such as we find among robbers: a boy would be run down, if he had no associate. I do not say, and am far from thinking, that such manners are inculcated by the masters; but I say, and am sorry to say, that nothing is done to prevent or correct them.[26]

It may not have been for financial reasons alone that the Revd George Austen, like Cowper's clergyman friend, educated his sons at home.

By the time James Austen sent his son to Winchester, the College, under its kindly headmaster Dr Henry Gabell, was very different from the type of public school that Cowper and Lord Kames so deplored. Certainly James Edward was very happy there, and he retained a lifelong interest in the school; most importantly, as his daughter wrote years later, he profited from Dr Gabell's determination to make his pupils express themselves in 'good and clear English'.[27] Verses written during the two years that he spent there show that he had a wide vocabulary and a command of style such that he could adroitly adapt his tone to the particular requirements of the occasion. Whether he was writing a sentimental poem to his elder sister Anna reflecting their common love of nature, or a verse in simpler language to his younger sister Caroline on her ninth birthday, or something concerned with more public matters such as the heroes commemorated in Westminster Abbey or the defeat of Napoleon at Waterloo, he had no difficulty in adopting the appropriate manner – moreover, in the case of the latter two subjects, Lord Kames could have found no fault with his spirit of patriotism.[28] Nor was he daunted by a religious subject: one winter's day he settled down in Commoners, the large hall for those who, like him, were not scholars of the College, and wrote a highly dramatic account in heroic couplets of Moses rebuking the Israelites for their complaints against him by striking water from the rock.[29] Classical languages were still predominant in the College curriculum, however; in a letter to Mrs Heathcote, reporting on William's progress, Dr Gabell expressed himself 'in high terms of commendation for his good temper, good conduct, & attention to business', but urged her 'to advise him to begin learning his standing-up very early' – standing up being the recitation from memory of a large number of lines of Latin or Greek verse.[30]

Winchester was not altogether exempt from the troubles from which Eton had suffered. A little over a year after James Edward left, there was a rebellion among the prefects in which one of his cousins, Charles Knight, seems to have been involved. Their uncle Henry Austen had been to the College, as James Edward heard from his father, and only 'with some difficulty' had he convinced the boy 'of the folly and impropriety of his behaviour'.[31] Henry described the whole business as 'most disgraceful' and called the behaviour of the prefects 'scandalous'. In fact it was a sufficiently serious disturbance for the military to be called in to restore order. The unrest must have been brewing for some years – since before James Edward went there – as Henry blamed Dr Gabell's predecessor for its origins. 'It is his opinion (upon what founded I know not),' wrote James Austen, 'that Dr. Goddard laid the train of the Rebellion and Dr. Gabell produced the explosion by injudicious and irregular attempts to curb the overgrown power of the Praefects!' The outcome was severe and effective: 'All the Commoner Praefects are expelled and five of those of the College ... Henry adds, "I now conceive discipline to be firmly re-established."' Caroline Austen, who was herself at a school in Winchester at the time, obviously knew from other girls, and perhaps even from the boys of the College, about the atmosphere there. She told her parents that the riot had not broken out earlier only because of the influence of William Heathcote; by the time it did, he was at Oxford.

If Dr Goddard had sown the whirlwind that the unfortunate Dr Gabell had reaped, it might not have altogether surprised Jane Austen, had she still been living, for she had crisply disposed of him ten years before. He was still head-master when Edward's eldest son started there, and on one occasion permission was sought for the boy to leave before the end of term to join a family party in Southampton. 'His Father writes to Dr Goddard to ask leave,' Jane told Cassandra, '& we have the Pupil's authority for thinking it will be granted.'[32] When the reply came, however, they were disappointed: the headmaster refused to give his consent. 'Being once fool enough to make a rule of never letting a Boy go away an hour before the Breaking up Hour,' Jane commented, 'he is now fool enough to keep it.'[33]

The passage from a public school to one of the universities was usual for the sons of families wealthy enough to be able to afford them. Thus in *Mansfield Park* Edmund Bertram goes from Eton to Oxford and Henry Crawford from Westminster to Cambridge, and Jane Austen, with no need to comment on the education provided by these institutions, other than allowing Edmund and Crawford to criticize the neglect of reading aloud, something which she herself considered to be an important accomplishment,[34] makes instead a moral point about each of the young men. In the case of Edmund, 'his leaving Eton for Oxford made no change in his kind dispositions [towards Fanny], and only afforded more frequent opportunities of proving them'.[35] Crawford, meanwhile, by his own admission, appears to have spent his time thinking less about what he was supposed to be learning than about the improvements he was going to make to his estate: 'I had not been of age three months,' he tells Julia Bertram, 'before Everingham was all that it is now. My plan was laid at Westminster – a little altered perhaps at Cambridge, and at one and twenty executed'.[36]

In a more sustained passage in *Sense and Sensibility*, the effects of a public school education are used to draw a comparable contrast in character between Edward Ferrars and his brother Robert. Edward was prepared for Oxford at Mr Pratt's in Devonshire – an essential element of the plot, since it is there that he met Lucy Steele – and it is to 'the misfortune' of this private education that his brother attributes 'the extreme *gaucherie*' that he believes keeps him from 'mix-ing in proper society'.[37] He himself, he maintains, 'though probably without any particular, any material superiority by nature, merely from the advantage of a public school, was as well fitted to mix in the world as any other man'.

"'My dear Madam,"' [he always tells his mother], "the evil is now irremediable, and it has been entirely your own doing. Why would you be persuaded by my uncle, Sir Robert, against your own judgment, to place Edward under private tuition, at the most critical time of his life? If you had only sent him to Westminster School as well as myself, instead of sending him to Mr. Pratt's, all this would have been prevented." This is the way in which I always consider the matter, and my mother is perfectly convinced of her error.'

Elinor would not oppose his opinion, because whatever might be her general estimation of the advantage of a public school, she could not think of Edward's abode in Mr. Pratt's family with any satisfaction.[38]

More than Edward's awkward social manners would have been prevented had he not been sent to Mr Pratt's, as Elinor knows, though Robert and his mother do not; but of course the irony here is that whatever manners were to be acquired at a public school, Robert, vain and affected as he is, is hardly a recommendation for them.

Elinor, it seems, does not value public schools particularly highly, and if she feels that Edward has acquired more pleasing manners from Mr Pratt than his brother has at Westminster, it is perhaps understandable that Jane Austen should have expressed through her sensible heroine a preference for the kind of private education that she had known at first hand from her father at Steventon rectory. Like many clergymen of his day, Mr Austen supplemented his income by taking boarding pupils. Some were the sons of friends or the neighbouring clergy or squirearchy; one was the son of the Bishop of Exeter. Most of them would have been able children, but in a letter to her sister-in-law in June 1773, Mrs Austen described one boy who had recently arrived, and who was about the same age as her own son Edward: 'Jemmy and Neddy,' she wrote, 'are very happy in a new play-fellow, Lord Lymington, whom Mr. Austen has lately taken the charge of; he is between five and six years old, very backward of his age, but good tempered and orderly: he is the eldest son of Lord Portsmouth who lives about ten miles from hence'.[39] He had a bad stammer, and by the end of the year he had been removed by his mother, who hoped that a doctor in London might cure him; in fact, however, his difficulties were more deep-seated, and when he grew older trustees had to be appointed to look after him.

Mr Austen's pupils were given a solid grounding in the classical languages and literature, particularly Latin, which were required for entrance to Oxford and Cambridge, while the genial Mrs Austen presided over their domestic lives, giving them encouragement and wholesome food, and from time to time writing light-hearted poems for them. Something of the happy atmosphere at the rectory can be caught from a verse that she wrote when Richard Buller, the Bishop's son, and one of his friends said that they couldn't possibly be expected to get on with their lessons when they had no sleep at night because of the noise made by the weathercock in the rectory garden as it revolved in the wind (a 'scrooping' sound, Anna Lefroy was to remember it as, years later);[40] she turned their cheeky complaint into a 'humble petition' to be presented to their tutor:

Dear sir, We beseech & intreat & request
You'd remove a sad nuisance that breaks our night's rest
That creaking old weathercock over our heads
Will scarcely permit us to sleep in our beds.

It whines & it groans & makes such a noise
That it greatly disturbs two unfortunate boys
Who hope you will not be displeased when they say
If they don't sleep by night they can't study by day.
But if you will kindly grant this their petition
And they sleep all night long without intermission
They promise to study hard every day
And moreover as bounden in duty will pray etc., etc.[41]

The boys were treated as part of the family, and several of them made friendships with the Austen children that lasted throughout their lives. It was a regime that Cowper would have wholeheartedly approved.

It was not, however, one from which Mr Austen himself had benefited when he was a boy. Orphaned at an early age, and with a stepmother who had no legal obligation to bring up the children of her late husband, and apparently no wish to do so, he was sent to live with an aunt in Tonbridge, and from the age of ten attended Tonbridge School, his education being paid for by another relation, his uncle Francis Austen, who was a wealthy attorney in Sevenoaks. Tonbridge was not then a public school but a grammar school, and it had been founded in 1553, for the education of boys from the town and the surrounding Kent countryside.[42] By the time George Austen went there in 1741, only a small proportion of the pupils were, like him, town boys, or 'Foundationers', the rest being boarders, many of them from well-to-do families in West Kent and East Sussex, some from London and a few from the West Indian plantations. The nine classes were taught together in the long Tudor schoolroom, with the Master and the Usher (or undermaster) giving instruction simultaneously as the boys sat on benches arranged facing each other down either side of the room. It was a school with a high reputation, at least until a new young headmaster, the Revd James Cawthorn, arrived in George's third year, and fears of his inexperience led to an abrupt fall in the school roll. Nevertheless, a rigorous academic standard was maintained. Pupils were required to be able to write competently in English and Latin before they were accepted and were ranked on entry (George was forty-second of the then fifty-three pupils). They progressively studied all the Latin authors, and were also taught rhetoric, having to argue persuasively in Latin according to set rules. The day was long, starting with prayers at 7 o'clock in the morning and not finishing until 5 or 6 o'clock in the evening, with a break of two hours in the middle of the day. Extras – writing, arithmetic, French, dancing – were available, but it was the classical curriculum that was at the centre of the boys' learning, and it was his success in this that enabled George Austen eventually to go up to St John's College, Oxford, with a Sir Thomas White Fellowship reserved for a scholar from Tonbridge. Some years later he returned to the school as Usher.

Jane Austen probably had less knowledge of life in such schools, other than what she may have heard of her father's schooldays, than of the ways of public schools, details of which she must have been regaled with by the various nephews who came to stay on their way to and from Winchester. In her fiction she rarely mentions grammar schools, though we know that John Thorpe's brother is at Merchant-Taylors', and in 'Catharine' Miss Stanley says with charming vagueness of the son of a deceased clergyman that she has a notion that 'somebody puts him to School somewhere in Wales'.[43] On the whole she seems to have approved of schooling for boys and thought that it developed their character. When her cousin the Revd Edward Cooper, rector of Hamstall Ridware, himself an old Etonian, sent his son to Rugby School, she noted that the boy was 'very happy in the idea of it'. 'I wish his happiness may last,' she added, reporting the news to Cassandra, 'but it will be a great change, to become a raw school boy from being a pompous Sermon-Writer, & a domineering Brother. – It will do him good I dare say.'[44]

Jane Austen's own days at the Reading school, like those of any girl in the eighteenth century, would have been far less demanding than her father's at Tonbridge, and her ability to express herself in 'good and clear English' was probably the result of her own reading, rather than having it rigorously taught to her as it would later be to her nephew James Edward by Dr Gabell. She did, however, like Mrs Bennett's young ladies in Winchester, have lessons in writing, French, drawing, needlework, music and dancing; and from the list of 'globes, armillary sphere, magic lanthorn with historical plates, thermometer, excellent charts and maps, amusing and instructive' offered for sale when the school was sold up in 1794, it is clear that rudiments of history and geography were also taught.[45] The Reading school could rightly claim, as it did in the notice of the sale, to have united 'every improved system of private tuition or public education'.

How enjoyable all this was for the girls it is hard to say; Jane Austen never referred to her schooldays in any of her surviving letters, except on one occasion to comment on a humorous letter from Cassandra, 'I could die of laughter at it, as they used to say at school' (even as a child she obviously had an alert ear for a silly catchphrase).[46] She certainly did not feel that there was anything very agreeable or fulfilling about the life led by teachers; in *The Watsons*, the heroine says 'I would rather be Teacher at a school (and I can think of nothing worse) than marry a Man I did not like', to which her sister replies 'I would rather do any thing than be Teacher at a school . . . *I* have been at school, Emma, & know what a Life they lead; *you* never have.'[47] In a letter to Cassandra dating from the period when she was writing *The Watsons*, Jane made a remark concerning the keeper of a school in Lansdown Crescent, Bath, who came to consult her about a servant, which does not suggest that she had a very high opinion of teachers in general: 'I hope I have acquitted myself pretty well,' she wrote; 'but having a very reasonable Lady to deal with, one who only required a *tolerable* temper, my office was not difficult. – Were I going to send a girl to school I would send her to this person; to be rational in anything is great praise, especially in the ignorant class of school mistresses.'[48]

This view might have been borne out by the experience of her contemporary Elizabeth Ham, who was sent to a boarding school in Tiverton, Devon, kept by the two Miss Wests:

Our studies were not extensive, nor very edifying. We learnt by rote either from the Dictionary, the Grammar, or Geography. Wrote no exercises, nor were we asked any questions about our lessons. We read from the Bible in the morning, and the History of England or Rome in the afternoon. A Master came to teach us writing and ciphering from eleven to twelve, and a Dancing Master twice a week.[49]

Devon was at that time well known for its cheap schools, but that run by the Miss Wests, she points out, was not one of the cheapest. Even so, the food served to the girls was hardly lavish. For breakfast they had tea with a drop of milk and a hot halfpenny roll 'with a little round hole cut in the top in which was inserted the smallest modicum of butter'; it was good, but not nearly enough to be satisfying, and Elizabeth often felt more hungry after breakfast than before.[50] For dinner the staples were mutton squab pie, potato pie and suet pudding, but there were only ever two small helpings. In a scene that seems to anticipate *Oliver Twist*, the girls determined one day to ask for a third helping:

Of course, the elder girl was to make the beginning. We were all breathless with anxiety and expectation watching the event.

'Would you like any more, Miss Smith?' asked Miss Mary West. 'If you please, Ma'am,' faltered out Miss Smith. A very small bit was put on Miss Smith's plate. No one else was asked. She was left alone in her glory to eat her morsel, which, little as it was, seemed likely to choke her. We were never asked again. Miss Smith was looked upon by us all as a disgraced person. Had the thing succeeded, she would have been a heroine.[51]

The Miss Smith at school in Highbury is more fortunate, since Mrs Goddard gives her girls 'plenty of wholesome food',[52] perhaps not dissimilar to the weekly fare served at Belvedere House in Bath, kept by the novelist Sophia Lee and her sisters, where Susan Sibbald was a pupil between 1797 and 1800. Summoned into dinner at one o'clock by Miss Mangle, with the admonition 'Gently, gently ladies', they could reliably expect to have roast beef on Monday, roast shoulder of mutton on Tuesday, a 'round of beef' on Wednesday, boiled leg of mutton on Thursday, roast shoulder of mutton again on Friday and on Saturday 'stewed beef with pickled walnuts . . . which was much liked'. 'Then two days in the week,' Mrs Sibbald remembered, 'we had "choke dogs" dumplings with currants in them, other days rice or other puddings, but after the meat not before, as was the case in some Schools.'[53]

As the only institutions, other than the Church, of which Jane Austen had first-hand knowledge, schools might have served her as a useful subject for irony. Of her heroines, however, only Anne Elliot has attended a school; the others have been educated at home (it is interesting to note in passing that in *Persuasion* most of the children are sent to school – not only Anne and Mary in their girlhoods, but all the various young Musgroves). In 'Lady Susan' an educational establishment does figure, albeit offstage and rather briefly. Lady Susan, having been prevented, she claims, by her husband's long illness from paying her daughter Frederica 'that attention which Duty & affection equally dictated', upon his death, instead of making up for lost time by looking after her herself, promptly dispatches her to 'one of the best Private Schools in Town';[54] for having previously neglected to provide her with a governess who was adequate to her charge, she now despises her as a child 'without Talent or Education'.[55] Despite the selfishness and hypocrisy that she displays in this, the action itself is not necessarily wrong; Frederica's aunt Catherine, who is not taken in by her corrupt and worldly sister-in-law, expresses her approval for various reasons: 'Miss Vernon', she informs her mother,

> is to be placed at a school in Town before [Lady Susan] comes to us, which I am glad of, for her sake and my own. It must be to her advantage to be separated from her Mother; & a girl of sixteen who has received so wretched an education would not be a very desirable companion here.[56]

In general the story lays emphasis on the importance of education in the development of moral character. Reginald De Courcy, captivated almost in spite of himself by Lady Susan's allure, defends her by imputing whatever errors she may have committed to 'her neglected Education & early Marriage'[57] (Mr Parker in Sanditon similarly attributes Lady Denham's faults to her lack of education). It is possible that Lady Susan's frustration at her daughter's ignorance arises partly from an awareness of her own; certainly Reginald is very ready to see 'solid affection for her Child' in her placing Frederica 'in hands, where her Education will be properly attended to'.[58]

The hands are those of Miss Summers, and Lady Susan intends Frederica to remain at her academy in Wigmore Street 'till she becomes a little more reasonable'.[59] It is not clear that her motives are entirely educational; for one thing, she does not want her daughter on her own hands, and for another she is thinking of social advantage, since she 'will make good connections there, as the Girls are all of the best Families'. Such places were not cheap, however: 'The price is immense', she comments, '& much beyond what I can ever attempt to pay'. As it turns out, she does not have to for long. Knowing that her mother intends to force her to marry a man she does not love, the desperate girl attempts to run away, and Miss Summers requests that she should be removed immediately. Lady Susan hopes that another school will be found for her, unless she can get her married at once. The sympathetic aunt Catherine, who does not know of Lady Susan's intentions, nevertheless suspects that Frederica had some reason to try to leave, other than, as her mother tries to persuade her, 'an impatience of restraint, & a desire of escaping from the tuition of Masters'.[60] All the same, she feels that if education is neglected early in life, it may well be difficult to begin it later on. When Frederica comes to stay, she has a piano available to her, but her aunt seldom hears her playing it; similarly, there are plenty of books in her room, 'but', she reflects, 'it is not every girl who has been running wild the first fifteen years of her life, that can or will read'. This may be so, of course, and Jane

Austen may well have believed it; however, she is not really concerned with theories of education here, but with exposing the cruelty and deceitfulness of Lady Susan's character. When Lady Susan tells her sister-in-law that she intends marrying Frederica to Sir James quite soon because 'she is too old ever to submit to school confinement', she is not of course concerned that she is both being dishonest about her own motive and failing to do justice to her daughter. A fairer and more kindly appraisal is made by Catherine Vernon herself; Frederica, she observes, 'tho' totally without accomplishment . . . is by no means so ignorant as one might expect to find her, being fond of books & spending the cheif of her time in reading'.[61]

The academy run by Miss Summers might well have been similar to the one at which Jane Austen visited the young Charlotte Craven, a cousin of the Lloyds, while she was staying in London in May 1813. She found Charlotte looking very well, her hair done up 'with an elegance to do credit to any Education'.[62] She was shown upstairs into a drawing-room, over which she cast a satirical eye. 'The appearance of the room,' she told Cassandra, 'so totally un-school-like, amused me very much. It was full of all the modern Elegancies – & if it had not been for some naked Cupids over the Mantlepiece, which must be a fine study for Girls, one should never have smelt Instruction.' She may also have been thinking of Charlotte Craven's school when she described the 'most respectable Girls Boarding School, or Academy, from Camberwell', whose proprietress, Mrs Griffiths, brings three of her charges to Sanditon.[63] Mrs Griffiths 'was a very well-behaved, genteel kind of Woman, who supported herself by receiving such great girls & young Ladies, as wanted either Masters for finishing their Education, or a home for beginning their Displays'.[64] About Mrs Griffiths's priorities and the girls' expectations from their place of learning Jane Austen is very clear: of all the young ladies

> Miss Lambe was beyond comparison the most important & precious, as she paid in proportion to her fortune. – She was about 17, half Mulatto, chilly & tender, had a maid of her own, was to have the best room in the Lodgings [in Sanditon], & was always of the first consequence in every plan of M[rs] G. – The other Girls, two Miss Beauforts were just such young Ladies as may be met with, in at least one family out of three, throughout the Kingdom; they had tolerable complexions, shewey figures, an upright decided carriage & an assured Look; they were very accomplished & very Ignorant, their time being divided between such pursuits as might attract admiration, & those Labours & Expedients of dexterous Ingenuity, by which they could dress in a stile much beyond what they *ought* to have afforded; they were some of the first in every change of fashion – & the object of all, was to captivate some Man of much better fortune than their own.[65]

This sounds very like the kind of place to which Mrs Goddard's school in *Emma* is so favourably compared, on the surface at least. For Mrs Goddard, it is stressed, is the mistress 'not of a seminary, or an establishment, or any thing which professed, in long sentences of refined nonsense, to combine liberal acquirements with elegant morality upon new principles and new systems – and where young ladies for enormous pay might be screwed out of health and into vanity'.[66] The tone is of course ironic, and the irony is only slightly abated in the subsequent account of what Mrs Goddard's school is actually like. Initially there is unambiguous authorial endorsement: it is 'a real, honest, old-fashioned Boarding-school'. While those three adjectives, solid as the puddings with which no doubt the growing girls are nourished, may carry a hint of gentle mockery, they are irreproachably respectable and, in a novel in which traditional ways of doing things are always preferred to new and brash social habits, such a description of the school is very much to its credit. Then, legitimately enough, Mrs Goddard sells 'a reasonable quantity of accomplishments at a reasonable price'; again, modesty and economy are valued above display and excess. But when it comes to the teaching, doubts begin to set in. Girls like Harriet Smith are sent there 'to be out of the way and scramble themselves into a little education, without any danger of coming back prodigies'; and the 'high repute' of the school seems to depend largely on its healthy location and the fancy needlework hung round the parlour walls like that round Mrs La Tournelle's, or for that matter the landscape in coloured silks hung above the mantelpiece at Mrs Jennings's house in proof of her daughter Charlotte's 'having spent seven years at a great school in town to some effect'.[67]

Yet in the Austen family, a girl's education was highly valued. When a reduction in James's income from his aunt Mrs Leigh Perrot meant that he was obliged to consider withdrawing Caroline from the school kept by the Miss Burneys in Winchester, James Edward wrote urgently to his father begging him not to do so, and offering to give up hunting for a couple of years to make economies:

> I am sure it is highly improper that I sho^d. be *indulging myself*, with my own horse in Sports, while you cannot afford to give my sister the *necessary* Education of a gentlewoman. Only let me beseech you to reflect, (that if one must be given up) how disproportionate is what I should lose, compared with what Caroline's Loss will be. I shall only lose a doubtful good, & the very Cessation will make the return to it, whenever I do return, with double pleasure; she will forgo a certain, & an inestimable advantage; she will be prevented from gaining that information & those accomplishments now, which it is now only that she can acquire; she may repent it all her life; for the Effects must remain through all her life; you must know, from experience, (if any body in this world ever did,) how much human happiness is increased in proportion as knowledge is extended; & if we sow not at the proper time its useless to sow afterwards. The same causes which would prevent her remaining at Winchester must equally prevent the possibility of travelling Masters; & do you think I w^d. sit easy on my horse if by giving him up I could secure to Caroline a continuance of instruction?[68]

There is no doubt that James Edward regarded the intellectual advantages of a good education as being just as important for a girl as for a boy.

Harriet Smith, at seventeen, has been raised 'from the condition of scholar to that of parlour-boarder';[69] that is to say, she now lives with Mrs Goddard as a member of the family – at higher cost. Her status, and by extension that of the school itself, becomes a matter of dispute between Mr Knightley and Emma. Mr Knightley, provoked by Emma's setting Harriet above Mr Martin, says dismissively that Harriet 'is known only as a parlour-boarder at a common school', where she 'has been taught nothing useful'. After receiving 'a very indifferent education she is left in Mrs. Goddard's hands to shift as she can'; she moves 'in Mrs. Goddard's line' among her acquaintance, and was perfectly happy in that set, he says, until Emma 'chose to turn her into a friend'.[70] Emma's view is a little more ambivalent, as it has to be, since on the one hand she wishes to promote Harriet as worthy of being her friend, but on the other, Mr Martin's sisters also attended the school; they, she tells Harriet, 'from a superior education, are not to be altogether objected to'.[71] Mr Knightley, recognizing that Emma has improved Harriet's manner – at least, she has cured her of her 'school-girl's giggle'[72] – nevertheless warns her that if she encourages her to expect that she can marry above her station, 'she may be a parlour-boarder at Mrs. Goddard's all the rest of her life – or, at least . . . till she grow desperate, and is glad to catch at the old writing master's son'.[73]

Mrs Goddard, like Mrs La Tournelle, is the proprietress rather than the principal teacher; and while 'the old writing master' would have been brought in like a dancing master or a drawing master to supplement the normal daily lessons, the work of the school is carried out by the three mistresses, Miss Nash, Miss Prince and Miss Richardson. With the gradations of foreground, middle and background with which Jane Austen so carefully depicts the inhabitants of Highbury, we are shown little of the latter two; but of Miss Nash, the head-teacher, we do learn something. Academically her aspirations are somewhat limited. When Harriet embarks on 'the only literary pursuit' that she engages with, the 'only mental provision' she makes for 'the evening of life', which is 'the collecting and transcribing all the riddles of every sort that she could meet with, into a thin quarto of hot-pressed paper . . . ornamented with cyphers and trophies', the inspiration has come from Miss Nash, who has made a similar collection herself and 'written out at least three hundred'; and Harriet's urge to scholarly improvement is limited to the hope that, with Miss Woodhouse's help, she will 'get a great many more'.[74] Miss Nash has also copied down all the texts Mr Elton has preached on since he came to Highbury: she is clearly in love with him. She follows his movements and watches him as he passes by the window and she delights in talking about him and repeating his name; for as she confides to Harriet, 'any woman whom Mr. Elton could prefer, she should think the luckiest woman in the world; for, beyond a doubt, Mr. Elton had not his equal for beauty or agreeableness'.[75]

Poor Miss Nash – for so we feel she will remain, unless like Mrs La Tournelle's assistant, Miss Pitts, she can become a partner in the school, when her marriage prospects might possibly improve. But this seems unlikely. Headmasters in boys' schools, especially if they were scholars like Dr Gabell at Winchester or James Cawthorn at Tonbridge, were accorded a respectable place in society and were able to live as men of a certain distinction. When George III passed through Winchester in 1804, he stopped and talked to Gabell's predecessor, Dr Goddard, and 'desired the boys might have 2 or 3 weeks added to their holidays at Christmas'.[76] Such a compliment would hardly have been paid to Miss Nash; a teacher in a small girls' school which she did not own belonged to a lower class altogether. Mrs Goddard, whose name, playing on that of the former Winchester headmaster, Jane Austen may well have intended as a family joke, is frequently asked to keep Mr Woodhouse company when Emma goes out for the evening; but her staff would never be invited to Hartfield: they would not have been ranked, at least by Emma, even with the Coles and the Perrys. They were fairly low in the social scale, and were all too well aware of the fact. 'Miss Nash thinks her own sister very well married,' Harriet tells Emma, 'and it is only a linen-draper.'[77]

'One should be sorry to see greater pride or refinement in the teacher of a school,' comes the swift reply.

9

Maturity

'One does not care for girls till they are grown up,' remarked Jane Austen.[1] She was not talking about real life, of course; we have seen ample evidence of the great interest she took in her nieces (and nephews) from the earliest age, and of the very real affection she had for them. They undoubtedly amused her, even if at times their behaviour caused her to be critical – generally of their parents if she needed to find fault with some aspect of the way in which they were being brought up. The statement concerned literature and was made in one of the letters to Anna Lefroy in which she gave her niece advice about the novel she was writing. 'You are but *now* coming to the heart & beauty of your book; till the heroine grows up, the fun must be imperfect.'[2]

In her own novels the heroines are grown up, and their characters firmly established, when the mechanism of the main plot is set in motion. In *Sense and Sensibility* and *Pride and Prejudice* hardly anything is said about the childhood of the Dashwood or the Bennet sisters; understanding of their characters is revealed through the contrast between them, and there is no need for us to know about how they have developed from children into what they are now: our interest is in the way they react to the experiences which we see them undergoing. The same is not quite true of Emma, since it is the loss of her mother in infancy and the indulgent upbringing that she received at the hands of her father and, more importantly, Miss Taylor that have contributed to the defects in her character which the events of the novel must correct; it is significant – and endearing – that when talking about the prospect of Jane Fairfax's becoming a governess, Emma should refer unflatteringly to what she remembers herself to have been as a child.[3] Anne Elliot, from whose childhood we are doubly distanced by the period of seven years that separates the present from her original meeting with Wentworth, is the most mature of all the heroines; yet the picture of her as she was when she had first known Miss Hamilton, later Mrs Smith, brings the vulnerability of her young self vividly before us: as we have seen, she 'had gone unhappy to school, grieving for the loss of a mother whom she had dearly loved, feeling her separation from home, and suffering as a girl of fourteen, of strong sensibility and not high spirits, must suffer at such a time.'[4] Only two of the heroines are presented to us at first as children, and their passage into adulthood is dealt with briefly – in Catherine Morland's case ironically, in Fanny Price's seriously.

The period in a young lady's life when, her education complete, she was deemed ready to leave the schoolroom and take her place in the social world as an independent person was vested with considerable significance. At the highest level of society, it was marked by the elaborate ritual of being presented at one of the court drawing-rooms. For these all-important occasions there were strict rules as to what should be worn, and they were rigorously enforced. Throughout the reign of George III, young ladies being presented to Queen Charlotte had to wear an ornate hoop-skirted court dress, even when, by Jane Austen's time, simple, high-waisted dresses were the normal style; the headdress included a veil, and one tall ostrich feather was attached, sometimes more (by the end of Queen Victoria's reign, there would always be three). A deep court curtsy was performed, after which the nervous young lady had to walk away backwards from the royal presence, managing her dress as best she could. Each débutante was accompanied by a sponsor, usually her mother. An ambassador to George III's court noted:

> The Queen stood on the Royal dais while the ladies brought their daughters forward to be presented . . . I learned that young ladies are not presented to the Queen before the age of seventeen, and that, until they have had that honour, they do not go out in society or attend dinner parties and receptions. No member of a family touched by scandal is received at court.[5]

One débutante recorded the experience in her diary on 13 February 1800; she was originally to have been presented by Lady Banks, but she died just before the occasion, and it was her mother who presented her to Queen Charlotte:

> I was presented by Mama . . . I was dressed in white with a festoon of roses, three yellow feathers and a gold chain in my hair, a set of topaz earings [sic], clasp and locket, all kind presents . . . The Queen was very gracious and good humoured . . . Mama was in purple velvet.[6]

Lady Mary Strangways was very nervous when she was presented in 1793, though it was reported that she 'looked vastly well, was dressed vastly well and held [herself] vastly well'.[7] Her sister, Lady Harriot was presented four years later, in April 1797. The event was described by her governess, Agnes Porter, in her diary; she does not record what the young lady's feelings were, but she gives a very full account of what everybody was wearing:

> Lady Harriot Strangways, my third dear pupil, was presented at Court. Lady Ilchester, Lady Elizabeth Talbot, and Miss Lily Digby (the Colonel's daughter) accompanied her, They were all most elegantly dressed and looked extremely well indeed. Lady Harriot's dress was a crape white petticoat trimmed with silver flowers, a wreath of pearls in her hair, large pearl earrings, and a laylock [lilac] gown; Lady Elizabeth's was simple: elegant white and silver. Lady Ilchester, a pale yellow gown with a white petticoat, large emerald earrings set in diamond; a diamond; a diamond feather in her hair of remarkable lustre. They had all feathers. Miss Digby's dress was laylock and white with bugles [tube-shaped beads] – she looked perfectly delicate and neat, but was eclipsed by the blooming Harriot,

the elegant Eliza and the tall and (in full dress) the graceful-looking Lady Ilchester. Lord Ilchester was in purple and silver . . . Lady Harriot Acland and Lady Mary Talbot came to see them dressed.[8]

Lady Harriot marked the occasion by making Miss Porter a present of 'a very pretty pair of bracelets – cornelians set in gold and intermixed with golden links – very pretty indeed'.

This of course was far removed from the world of both Jane Austen and the characters in her novels, though her cousin (and later sister-in-law) Eliza de Feuillide attended a drawing-room in 1787, standing for two hours, 'loaded with a great Hoop of no inconsiderable Weight';[9] she was not a débutante, however, being already married and a mother at the time.

In less exalted circles there was nevertheless a definite moment at the age of seventeen or eighteen, possibly sometimes earlier, when a mother would decide that it was time to allow her daughter to put her hair up, accompany her on morning visits and attend balls and assemblies. Until then, she was restricted more or less to family activities, and if there were guests she was generally expected to take a back seat, not pushing herself forward and speaking only when spoken to. It cannot be said exactly when Jane Austen passed through this stage, presumably about 1792 or shortly after; but by the time Mrs Mitford, formerly a childhood neighbour of the Austens, saw her ('the prettiest, silliest, most affected, husband-hunting butterfly she ever remembered',[10] as she described her years later to her daughter, the writer Mary Russell Mitford) Jane was dancing at public assemblies.

The etiquette surrounding these matters was in some ways quite strict. Lady Catherine de Bourgh is astonished to find that all Elizabeth's sisters are out:

'All! – What, all five out at once? Very odd! – And you only the second. – The younger ones out before the elder are married! – Your younger sisters must be very young?'

'Yes, my youngest is not yet sixteen. Perhaps *she* is full young to be much in company. But really, Ma'am, I think it would be very hard upon younger sisters, that they should not have their share of society and amusement because the elder may not have the means or inclination to marry early. – The last born has as good a right to the pleasures of youth, as the first. And to be kept back on *such* a motive! – I think it would not be very likely to promote sisterly affection or delicacy of mind.'[11]

Elizabeth's defence of a decidedly unorthodox way of doing things is spirited and fair-minded, and she is no doubt stung into being more outspoken than she might have been by Lady Catherine's inquisitiveness. But all the same, this is another way in which the Bennets have failed to exercise due control of their daughters, and the reservation that Elizabeth expresses with regard to Lydia is of course eventually proved to be only too justified.

An account of the whole process of coming out occurs in one of the pieces contained in *Volume the Second* of the *Juvenilia*, 'A Collection of Letters'. This is chiefly of interest, perhaps, for 'Letter the second: From a Young lady crossed in Love to her freind', which anticipates *Sense and Sensibility* – or was perhaps plundered for it – since it concerns a young lady who has been jilted by a man named Willoughby, and is consoled by hearing the life story of 'Miss Jane', widow of the late Henry Dashwood.[12] 'Letter the first', however, is written by a mother informing her friend about the entry into the world of her two daughters, and it shows that Jane Austen was familiar with the way in which things were managed. Since it was written as a joke, some of the details may not be altogether accurate; nevertheless, it is worth quoting in full:

My Children begin now to claim all my attention in a different Manner from that in which they have been used to receive it, as they are now arrived at that age when it is necessary for them in some measure to become conversant with the World. My Augusta is 17 & her Sister scarcely a twelve-month younger. I flatter myself that their education has been such as will not disgrace their appearance in the World, & that *they* will not disgrace their Education I have every reason to beleive. Indeed they are sweet Girls –. Sensible yet unaffected – Accomplished yet Easy –. Lively yet Gentle –. As their progress in every thing they have learnt has been always the same, I am willing to forget the difference of age, and to introduce them together into Public. This very Evening is fixed on as their first entrée into life, as we are to drink tea with Mrs Cope & her Daughter. I am glad that we are to meet no one for my Girls sake, as it would be awkward for them to enter too wide a Circle on the very first day. But we shall proceed by degrees –. Tomorrow Mr Stanly's family will drink tea with us, and perhaps the Miss Phillips will meet them. On Tuesday we shall pay Morning-Visits – On Wednesday we are to dine at Westbrook. On Thursday we have Company at home. On Friday we are to be at a private concert at Sir John Wynne's – & on Saturday we expect Miss Dawson to call in the morning, – which will complete my Daughters Introduction into Life. How they will bear so much dissipation I cannot imagine; of their Spirits I have no fear, I only dread their health.

———

This mighty affair is now happily over, & my Girls *are out*. As the moment approached for our departure, you can have no idea how the sweet Creatures trembled with fear & expectation. Before the Carriage drove to the door, I called them into my dressing-room, & as soon as they were seated thus addressed them. 'My dear Girls the moment is now arrived when I am to reap the rewards of all my Anxieties and Labours towards you during your Education. You are this Evening to enter a World in which you will meet with many wonderfull Things; Yet let me warn you against suffering yourselves to be meanly swayed by the Follies & Vices of others, for beleive me my beloved Children that if you do – I shall be very sorry for it.' They both assured me that they would ever remember my advice with Gratitude, & follow it with Attention; That they were prepared to find a World full of things to amaze & shock them: but that they trusted their behaviour would never give me reason to repent the Watchful Care with which I had presided over their infancy & formed their Minds –. 'With such expectations & such intentions (cried I) I can have nothing to fear from you – & can chearfully conduct you to Mrs Cope's without a fear of your being seduced by her Example or contaminated by her Follies. Come, then my Children (added I) the Carriage is driving to the door, & I will not a moment delay

the happiness you are so impatient to enjoy.' When we arrived at Warleigh, poor Augusta
could hardly breathe, while Margaret was all Life & Rapture. 'The long-expected Moment
is now arrived (said she) and we shall soon be in the World.' – In a few moments we were
in Mrs Cope's parlour –, where with her daughter she sat ready to receive us. I observed
with delight the impression my Children made on them –. They were indeed two sweet,
elegant-looking Girls, & tho' somewhat abashed from the peculiarity of their Situation,
Yet there was an ease in their Manners & Address which could not fail of pleasing –.
Imagine my dear Madam how delighted I must have been in beholding as I did, how
attentively they observed every object they saw, how disgusted with some Things, how
enchanted with others, how astonished at all! On the whole however they returned in
raptures with the World, its Inhabitants, & Manners. Yrs Ever – A-F –.[13]

The exaggeration and absurdity so characteristic of the *Juvenilia* cannot quite
conceal the reality of the experience that so many girls of seventeen went through.
Their trembling 'with fear & expectation' exactly captures the combination of
trepidation and excitement experienced in the anticipation of crossing from
the entirely private world that had hitherto protected them into the very public
and open life required of them once they entered into society. And the passage
is convincing, too, about the worries that any mother had both as to how her
daughters would comport themselves and about the dangers to which they
might be exposed. While it is highly unlikely that girls would show quite so
much rapture about 'the World, its Inhabitants, & Manners' after meeting one of
their mother's acquaintances, or indeed that they would run much risk of being
'seduced by her Example or contaminated by her Follies' over a mere cup of tea,
the anxiety with which the mother watches their behaviour, and the pleasure
with which she observes the 'ease in their Manners & Address', are convincing
enough. Most mothers taking their daughters with them on a visit for the first
time must have had such feelings.

This stage in a young lady's development was absolutely crucial, since it prepared her for the principal business of the next few years, which was to make a
good marriage. Outward appearance, the way she carried herself, was of course
important, since, as a guide to etiquette of the period put it, 'an elegant and
appropriate air' was an 'indispensable assistant-grace of beauty'.[14] The author
of this book, 'a Lady of Distinction', made unfavourable comparisons between
the deportment of English girls and that of those who had been brought up
abroad, she herself having 'studied the graces at more than one of the courts of
the Bourbons'; not that she wished to deny their natural attractions – she merely
regretted the lack of style:

There is scarcely an observer of manners and their effects who will not maintain that
the most beautiful and well-dressed woman will soon cease to please unless her charms
are accompanied with the ineffable enchantment of a graceful demeanour. A pretty face
may be seen every day, but grace and elegance, being generally the offspring of a polished
mind, are more rare; and are consequently more distinguished. While we exult in the

preeminent beauty of our fair countrywomen; while we talk of their lilies and roses, and downy skins; we cannot but shrink from comparison when we bring their manners in parallel with the females of other nations who have not half their corporeal advantages.

How, practically, should these manners be achieved? Well, it depends on the young lady's figure, since although 'no demeanour, whether in a princess or a country-girl, can be becoming that is not grounded in *feminine delicacy* . . . a different deportment is expected from different persons'.[15] While 'the moderated majestic mien' belongs to 'a greater *embonpoint*', the 'easy, graceful air . . . belongs exclusively to the slender beauty'.[16] So 'the woman of delicate proportions . . . must enter a room with the buoyant step of a young nymph . . . Her mode of salutation should be rather a bow than a courtesy; and when she sits, she should model her easy attitude rather by the ideas of the painter, when he would portray a reclining nymph, than according to the lessons of a grace-destroying governess, who would marshal her pupils on their chairs like a rank of drilled recruits'.[17]

But manners and deportment alone will not do; they are, as the Lady of Distinction is at pains to point out, only the adornment of the moral character which must be inculcated in any young lady:

> Let girls, advancing to womanhood, be told the true state of the world with which they are to mingle. Let them know its real opinions on the subjects connected with themselves as women, companions, friends, relatives. – Hide not from them what society thinks and expects on all these matters; but fail not to show them, at the same time, where the fashions of the day would lead them wrong; where the laws of heaven and man's approving (though not always submitting) reason would keep them aright.
>
> Let religion and morality be the foundation of the female character. The artist may then adorn the structure without any danger to its safety. When a girl is instructed on the great purposes of her existence; that she is an immortal being, as well as a mortal woman; you may, without fearing ill impressions, show her, that as we admire the beauty of the rose, as well as esteem its medicinal power, so her personal charms will be dear in the eyes of him whose heart is occupied by the graces of her, yet more estimable, mind. We may safely teach a well-educated girl that virtue ought to wear an inviting aspect; that it is due to her excellence to decorate her comely apparel. – But we must never cease to remember that it is VIRTUE we seek to adorn . . . We must impress upon the yet ingenuous maid, that while beauty attracts, its influence is transient, unless it presents itself as the harbinger of that good-sense and principle which can alone secure the affection of a husband, the esteem of friends, and the respect of the world. Show her that regularity of features and symmetry of form are not essentials in the composition of the woman whom the wise man would select as the partner of his life.[18]

The stress laid here not just on the physical attractions, important as they are, but also on moral ones, reflects in a more serious way the mother's anxious advice to her daughters with which Jane Austen had such fun. According to Mary Wollstonecraft, however, such admonition would go against the grain of girls exposed for the first time to the excitement of direct contact with the opposite sex – something which would be avoided if schools, instead of ensuring that young people were brought up separately, were co-educational:

> what can be more indelicate than a girl's *coming out* in the fashionable world? Which, in other words, is to bring to market a marriageable miss, whose person is taken from one public place to another, richly caparisoned. Yet, mixing in the giddy circle under restraint, these butterflies long to flutter at large, for the first affection of their souls is their own persons, to which their attention has been called with the most sedulous care whilst they were preparing for the period that decides their fate for life.[19]

Jane Austen might well have endorsed this view, to judge by a comment in one of her letters to Anna on a character in the novel that her niece has been writing: 'I have not yet noticed St Julian's serious conversation with Cecilia, but I liked it exceedingly; – what he says about the madness of otherwise sensible Women, on the subject of their Daughters coming out, is worth its' weight in gold.'[20]

The fact that the five Bennet sisters, ranging in age from fifteen to twenty-two, are all out at once reflects the debate about the age at which a young lady might first appear in public. Fanny Burney's Evelina is, like the elder of the two girls in 'A Collection of Letters', seventeen when she makes 'her entrance into the world'. But girls could become impatient with the restraints of the schoolroom and look for opportunities to put their hair up and taste the pleasures of society as soon as possible; thus when Charlotte Lucas marries Mr Collins, her younger sisters see the possibility of advancing by a couple of years and form hopes 'of *coming out* a year or two sooner than they might otherwise have done'.[21] In the middle of the century, Mary Delany had suggested that from as early as thirteen years of age a girl ought to have some exposure to society, so that she could develop that 'grace and manner which cannot be attained without conversing with a variety of well bred people'; though for 'all public places, till after fifteen (except a play or oratorio) she should not know what they are, and then very rarely'.[22] Despite the notoriety of spas and other places where people gathered in temporary association, Hester Thrale took her daughter to Bath when she was only eleven; then at Brighton she allowed her to dance at balls, before taking her to London for the theatre, opera and other forms of amusement. Girls as young as thirteen might be seen at Ranelagh, though the dangers of the great pleasure gardens would be known to anyone who had read *Evelina*, in which the heroine only just escapes being ravished when she becomes separated from her friends during an evening visit to Vauxhall.[23]

Jane Austen does not expose her young heroines to such threats. Catherine Morland is seventeen when she is taken from her home at Fullerton to Bath under the care of Mr and Mrs Allen. *Northanger Abbey* might, like *Evelina*, justly be subtitled 'A Young Lady's Entrance into the World'; and in so far as the purpose of a girl's coming out was eventually to find a husband, Catherine's is entirely, and really very rapidly, successful. Though in real life there must undoubtedly have been risks in the encounters made at the Pump Room or the Assembly Rooms similar to those to which Evelina is exposed, Jane Austen is not concerned with episodes that would have struck her as melodramatic; indeed she specifically repudiates such adventures when, in seeing Captain Tilney for the first time and immediately relating him to the anti-heroes beloved of Catherine's Gothic novelists, she insists that, since he not only protests 'against every thought of dancing himself' but laughs openly at Henry 'for finding it possible',

> it may be presumed that, whatever might be our heroine's opinion of him, his admiration of her was not of a very dangerous kind; not likely to produce animosities between the brothers, nor persecutions to the lady. *He* cannot be the instigator of the three villains in horsemen's great coats, by whom she will heareafter be forced into a travelling-chaise and four, which will drive off with considerable speed.[24]

Captain Tilney of course *is* a villain, of a limited and entirely everyday kind, since his flirting with Isabella causes James Morland to break off his engagement to her; but since this is an entirely desirable outcome, the reader judges his conduct less for its own sake than for what it reveals of Isabella's insincerity. John Thorpe, too, can hardly be said to represent any very great threat to Catherine's safety, except perhaps in his driving; for in being whisked away in his gig she runs no danger other than that of doing the wrong thing by not keeping her appointment with the Tilneys.

Other heroines in Jane Austen's novels must at some stage have come out, though since they live, as she did, in country houses, their entrance into the world, which in all but one case took place before the novels begin, probably consisted of nothing more than putting up their hair, beginning to pay morning calls and attending balls in the houses of friends or at the assembly rooms in the local town. It would all have been very much more informal than it was for the young ladies of higher rank who were presented at court. It is hard to imagine that Sir Walter Elliot took much trouble for either of his younger daughters, though presumably at some stage after returning from school, Anne, doubtless under the patronage of Lady Russell, began to attend such evening parties as were held in the locality of Kellynch, and thus became acquainted with the brother of Mr Wentworth, the curate of Monkford. Mr Woodhouse's daughters must also have had a somewhat restricted entrance into society, since Miss Taylor would have been unable to introduce them much beyond the 'little circle' round Hartfield itself, as is borne out by Isabella having married the brother of one of her father's limited number of friends. It is hard to tell when exactly Emma would have started mixing in adult company, but given that, as Mr Knightley points out, 'ever since she was twelve' she 'has been the mistress of the house and of you all',[25] it was probably at an early age, and just when she wanted to.

In some ways, of course, Emma seems hardly to have come out at all. Devoted to her father, determined always to look after him and declaring that she will never marry, she has something oddly immature about her, despite her intelligence and powers of social command; she has apparently never ventured far outside Highbury, and knows no one other than the handful of local families with whom she consents to mix. At almost twenty-one she seems naive in her enthusiastic taking up of Harriet Smith as a substitute for Miss Taylor; in fact their friendship is reminiscent of that of the much younger Catherine Morland and Isabella Thorpe. And when, in default of her making an entrance into the world, the long-awaited Frank Churchill enters her world, her inexperience is revealed not just in her excitement but in all her behaviour with him. Presumably we see her eventual marriage to Mr Knightley as either the consequence of her never having entered any society beyond Highbury or, in terms of the narrative purposes of the novel, the reason for it.

The one heroine for whom the question of coming out formally is seriously addressed is Fanny Price. She will not of course be presented at court; and neither, for that matter, will her cousins. As children Maria and Julia know that they are to keep their governess and continue in the schoolroom until they are seventeen, the time at which they will enter society;[26] and as the daughters of a baronet and an MP, they might expect to do so in London and indeed to be presented. But at the time of Fanny's going to live at Mansfield, Lady Bertram, 'in consequence of a little ill-health, and a great deal of indolence, gave up the house in town, which she had been used to occupy every spring';[27] and she and her daughters remain in the country, leaving Sir Thomas to go up to Parliament on his own, 'with whatever increase or diminution of comfort might arise from her absence'. The girls develop into young ladies, then, at home; it is in the country, rather than in the more sophisticated atmosphere familiar to the Crawfords, that 'the Miss Bertrams continued to exercise their memories, practise their duets, and grow tall and womanly', and where their father sees them becoming 'in person, manner, and accomplishments, every thing that could satisfy his anxiety'. A sheltered upbringing, far removed from the temptations and dangers of London, might appear to their father to be a safeguard for his daughters; certainly he feels that 'while they retained the name of Bertram' they 'must be giving it new grace, and in quitting it he trusted [they] would extend its respectable alliances'.[28] The irony, appreciable only by the end of the novel, is considerable, since one of them commits adultery and the other elopes. But perhaps it is the very fact that they have not experienced a wider society than that of their own home that makes them a prey to people who encroach on it from the outside world; Emma is subject to a similar danger, though of a less morally destructive kind.

It is in the winter of Sir Thomas's departure to Antigua that the novel is first concerned with Maria and Julia as fully developed young women enjoying the local entertainments of the season. Throughout *Mansfield Park*, apart from the Portsmouth scenes, Jane Austen severely restricts the action of the novel to the house and parsonage, with the exception of the visit to Sotherton; and the reader has little impression of the 'neighbourhood' among whose 'belles' the Miss Bertrams are now 'fully established',[29] and to which, after Maria's disgrace, Sir Thomas will not offer 'so great an insult' as 'to expect it to notice her';[30] but whoever it consists of (perhaps the families of the young men described by Tom as 'wild' to join their play), Maria and Julia possess 'its favour as well as its admiration'. It is Mrs Norris who superintends their activities, being only too willing to take the place of their mother:

> Lady Bertram did not go into public with her daughters. She was too indolent even to accept a mother's gratification in witnessing their success and enjoyment at the expense of any personal trouble, and the charge was made over to her sister, who desired nothing better than a post of such honourable representation, and very thoroughly relished the means it afforded her of mixing in society without having horses to hire.[31]

The besetting sins of Lady Bertram and Mrs Norris, lethargy and avarice, are neatly set out in this passage; they are both contributors to the moral deficiencies of Maria and Julia, whose vanity and essential weakness of character make them less able to withstand them than their cousin Fanny.

Fanny of course does not share in their engagements, being left behind to keep Lady Bertram company when they attend a ball or a party. Without any sense of resentment, or even apparently of minding very much, she loves 'to hear an account of them, especially the balls' and, significantly, 'whom Edmund had danced with'; but she thinks 'too lowly of her own situation to imagine she should ever be admitted to the same'.[32] There would of course be nothing to prevent her being included, were it not for Lady Bertram's dependence on her and Mrs Norris's spitefulness. When, after Maria's marriage, Mrs Grant invites her to dine at the parsonage, Mrs Norris is outraged:

> you ought to look upon it as something extraordinary: for I hope you are aware that there is no real occasion for your going into company in this sort of way, or ever dining out at all; and it is what you must not depend upon ever being repeated.[33]

Mrs Norris is resentful that anyone assumes that Fanny should take her place among any kind of society; indeed she seems to assign her to a role analogous to that of a paid companion, hardly part of the family at all.

It is perhaps this oddly anomalous position that leads Mary Crawford, on her coming to Mansfield, to admit that she does not understand Miss Price:

> Pray, is she out, or is she not? – I am puzzled. – She dined at the parsonage, with the rest of you, which seemed like being *out*; and yet she says so little, that I can hardly suppose she *is*.[34]

Fanny's natural modesty and shyness, reinforced by her sense of inferiority to her cousins, leads her to behave, even when dining out, as a young girl would who sits quietly at the table at home when there are guests. In the discussion that follows about being out, Mary is much more familiar with the conventions than Edmund, who replies that while he believes he knows what she means, he cannot undertake to answer the question: 'My cousin is grown up. She has the age and sense of a woman, but the outs and not outs are beyond me.' In a passage which shows Jane Austen herself to have formed a clear view of the development that a girl undergoes at this very precise stage in her life, Mary offers a perceptive analysis of one view of the differences in behaviour that coming out can bring:

> The distinction is so broad. Manners as well as appearance are, generally speaking, so totally different. Till now, I could not have supposed it possible to be mistaken as to a girl's being out or not. A girl not out, has always the same sort of dress; a close bonnet, for instance, looks very demure, and never says a word. You may smile – but it is so I assure you – and except that it is sometimes carried a little too far, it is all very proper. Girls should be quiet and modest. The most objectionable part is, that the alteration of manners on being introduced into company is frequently too sudden. They sometimes pass in such very little time from reserve to quite the opposite – to confidence! *That* is the faulty part of the present system. One does not like to see a girl of eighteen or nineteen so immediately up to every thing – and perhaps when one has seen her hardly able to speak the year before.

Being concerned with appearance, and by insisting on the importance of manner, Mary Crawford loses sight of the 'religion and morality' – the 'virtue' – on which the Lady of Distinction placed such stress; and the passage is very revealing of her own lack of moral strength.

Tom Bertram, who in his understanding of the business of coming out shows himself to belong much more to her world than Edmund does, illustrates her point with an account of an incident that had happened to him. A friend of his had first introduced him to his sister a couple of years before, when she was 'not *out*', and he could not get her to speak a word to him: 'I could hardly get a word or a look from the young lady – nothing like a civil answer – she screwed up her mouth, and turned from me with such an air!' A year later he met her again, by which time she had come out; but he did not remember her: 'She came up to me, claimed me as an acquaintance, stared me out of countenance, and talked and laughed till I did not know which way to look. I felt that I must be the jest of the room . . .' Mary comments that it is 'too common a fault. Mothers certainly have not yet got quite the right way of managing their daughters.' And she adds that, while she does not pretend to set people right, she does see that they are often wrong. Tom, paying a compliment to Mary, says that 'Those who are showing the world what female manners *should be* . . . are doing a great deal to set them right.' The 'less courteous Edmund' puts the matter more bluntly:

> The error is plain enough . . . such girls are ill brought up. They are given wrong notions from the beginning. They are always acting upon motives of vanity – and there is no more real modesty in their behaviour *before* they appear in public than afterwards.

Jane Austen here employs a vocabulary that sets out the two sides of the argument. Tom's emphasis on 'manners' and Edmund's sense of the importance of 'real modesty' give precise definitions of the opposed attitudes to the qualities that maturity should bring to a young lady. Furthermore, the terms also define an antithesis between the characters. Fanny is an embodiment of modesty in its simplest form; but in a more subtle way, the 'vanity' of Maria and Julia is 'in such good order' that they seem to be 'quite free from it'.[35] Mrs Norris also shares in this, later telling Sir Thomas that Fanny has been brought up 'with all the benefit of her cousins' manners before her'.[36] Thus the alignment of Maria, Julia, the Crawfords and Mrs Norris on the one hand, and Fanny on the other, is rooted in a fundamental opposition not only of disposition but of language; and when Edmund attempts to cross from one to the other, his interior struggle is between the emotions, which draw him towards Mary Crawford, and the intellect, which leads him back to Fanny through the *language* of his attempts to justify Mary's behaviour to her.

Mary, unwilling perhaps to admit of too much necessity for girls to be modest once they are in society, disputes Edmund's view, asserting that 'It is much worse to have girls *not out*, give themselves the same airs and take the same liberties as if they were'.[37] Tom's readiness with another story to illustrate her point (another sign of the moral connection between them) gives little time for reflection on the implication of her words for her own character, though 'give themselves . . . airs' and 'take . . . liberties' are revealing phrases. Tom's account of meeting the family of his friend Sneyd in Ramsgate, however, demonstrates what trouble a young man could get into if he was led into making a mistake as to whether or not a girl had come out:

> I made my bow in form, and as Mrs. Sneyd was surrounded by men, attached myself to one of her daughters, walked by her side all the way home, and made myself as agreeable as I could; the young lady perfectly easy in her manners, and as ready to talk as to listen. I had not a suspicion that I could be doing any thing wrong. They looked just the same; both well dressed, with veils and parasols like other girls; but I afterwards found that I had been giving all my attention to the youngest, who was not *out*, and had most excessively offended the eldest. Miss Augusta ought not to have been noticed for the next six months, and Miss Sneyd, I believe, has never forgiven me.[38]

The length of the anecdote, as well as the light-hearted tone in which it is recounted, suggest that Jane Austen perhaps regarded such conventions, with the opportunities they gave for needless offence, to have been rather unnecessary; on the other hand, it is the 'perfectly easy' manners of Lydia Bennet, out two years at least before her time, among the officers, that lead to her downfall. Mary Crawford is clear that in the case of Miss Sneyd 'it was entirely the mother's fault. Miss Augusta should have been with her governess. Such half and half doings never prosper.' And she is equally clear about Fanny; on being told by Edmund that she has never been to a ball, she pronounces definitively that 'Miss Price is *not* out'.

Mary tells Fanny that she supposes that she is 'now preparing for her *appearance* as of course she would come out when her cousin was married'.[39] But naturally Fanny is thinking of no such thing, and when Sir Thomas gives the ball for her, at which she is 'to make her first appearance', she has no idea of its significance; having not 'been brought up to the trade of *coming out* . . . had she known in what light this ball was, in general, considered respecting her, it would very much have lessened her comfort by increasing the fears she already had, of doing wrong and being looked at'.[40] When, 'attractive' and 'modest', she *is* looked at, with 'general favour', and Sir Thomas watches 'her progress down the dance with much complacency', he is proud of her; 'and without attributing all her personal beauty, as Mrs. Norris seemed to do, to her transplantation to Mansfield', he is 'pleased with himself for having supplied every thing else; – education and manners she owed to him'.[41] What he sees as he looks at her – 'young, pretty, and gentle', with 'no awkwardnesses that were not as good as graces' – must accord exactly with what the Lady of Distinction recommends for a young lady with Fanny's slight figure and graceful beauty:

> for a slender or thin woman to be stiff at any time, is, in the first case, to render of no effect the advantages of nature; and in the next, to increase her defect, by making it more conspicuous by a constrained and over-ridiculous carriage. Though we cannot unite the majestic air which declares command with this easy, nymph-like deportment, the dignity of modesty may be its inseparable companion. The timid, the retreating step, the down-cast eye, the varying complexion, 'blushing at the deep regard she draws!' all these belong to this class of females; and they are charms so truly feminine, so exquisitely lovely, that I cannot but place them with their counterpart, the ethereal form, as the perfection of female beauty.[42]

As it is in fact Fanny's coming out ball, she 'must be regarded as the Queen of the evening',[43] and is required to undertake the formalities expected of her. Before it starts, following Edmund's asking her to keep two dances for him, she has 'hardly ever been in a state so nearly approaching high spirits in her life';[44] but when the guests arrive, this gaiety of heart is 'much subdued' and 'the sight of so many strangers' throws her 'back into herself'. To be 'introduced here and there by her uncle, and forced to be spoken to, and to curtsey, and speak again' is 'a hard duty'; worse still is learning that she is 'to lead the way and open the ball; an idea that had never occurred to her before'. As the ball begins, it is 'rather honour than happiness' to her, 'for the first dance at least'; and she is 'a great deal too much frightened to have any enjoyment, till she could suppose herself no longer looked at'. Eventually, however, despite Henry Crawford's attentions, she has 'a good deal of enjoyment in the course of the evening'.

For most débutantes, the first ball would merely be the very beginning of their search for a husband, but Fanny's comes when she is already the subject of matrimonial schemes. When she tells her uncle that she is engaged for the first dance to Mr Crawford, it is 'exactly what he had intended to hear';[45] and at the end of the evening Crawford's ready acceptance of his invitation to join them at breakfast before he and William leave the next morning convinces Sir Thomas 'that the suspicions whence, he must confess to himself, this very ball had in great measure sprung' are well founded. Shortly afterwards, in advising a tired-looking Fanny, as Crawford looks on, 'to go immediately to bed', 'advise' being 'the advice of absolute power', he may well 'mean to recommend her as a wife by shewing her persuadableness'.[46]

'Society', wrote Sarah Ellis,[47] 'is to the daughters of a family, what business is to the man.' It was perhaps even more so to their mother. In *Pride and Prejudice* 'the business', we know, of Mrs Bennet's life is 'to get her daughters married';[48] and this was the business of most women between the time of their daughters' coming out and the eventual achievement of their marriage. It is of course precisely with this time of a young lady's life that the action of Jane Austen's novels – and those of countless other novelists of the eighteenth and nineteenth centuries – is concerned. With most of her heroines their coming out is rather taken for granted, as if she were not really interested in the process (which I have suggested she was not); and she deals with it at some length in the case of Fanny Price precisely because of the ways in which it is unusual – not the least of those being that it has been managed by a man. Finding a husband, however, is the plot on which everything else – everything that makes her novels distinctive, and great – hangs.

The degree to which the parents of a girl, in particular, can or ought to be involved in the choice of a husband for her is naturally a matter for consideration to an author who on the whole, at least for her heroines, favours marriage for love. In *Pride and Prejudice* the theme is treated comically, Mrs Bennet's instinct for grasping at any eligible young man who comes in her daughters' way being contrasted with her husband's more circumspect approach; there is high comedy over Mr Collins, but with Darcy, Mr Bennet's understandable reservations about his suitability for Elizabeth provide one of the few scenes in which for a moment he speaks without irony. He is genuinely concerned for her happiness, which with him, unlike with many fathers, weighs it far more heavily than the material advantages of the match. 'He is rich, to be sure', he says, 'and you may have more fine clothes and fine carriages than Jane. But will they make you happy?'[49] Speaking from his knowledge of her character, and from his own experience, he is only too much aware of the danger of her marrying a man she could not love:

> I know your disposition, Lizzy. I know that you could be neither happy nor respectable, unless you truly esteemed your husband; unless you looked up to him as a superior. Your lively talents would place you in the greatest danger in an unequal marriage. You could scarcely escape discredit and misery. My child, let me not have the grief of seeing *you* unable to respect your partner in life. You know not what you are about.

Elizabeth of course is able to reassure him, and the episode ends, inevitably, with an ironic remark, as Mr Bennet tells her, as she leaves his library, 'If any young men come for Mary or Kitty, send them in, for I am quite at leisure'.

The passage is written in dialogue, father and favourite daughter both speaking frankly and honestly. When in a parallel scene Sir Thomas Bertram, realizing that 'indifference' is 'the most favourable state' that Maria and Mr Rushworth can be in, seeks to express his concerns to his daughter, the discussion is relayed in reported speech; her evasions and his underlying reluctance to give up so prosperous a match (Mr Rushworth is the richest man in Jane Austen's novels) require a certain distance from the reader, as there is between them. He is genuinely anxious to know that she will be happy, and she is grateful for that; but the vocabulary through which the conversation is described is painfully awkward and formal, signifying the limited transactions between two people who have never learnt to be warm with each other:

> With solemn kindness Sir Thomas addressed her; told her his fears, inquired into her wishes, entreated her to be open and sincere, and assured her that every inconvenience should be braved, and the connection entirely given up, if she felt herself unhappy in the prospect of it. He would act for her and release her. Maria had a moment's struggle as she listened, and only a moment's: when her father ceased, she was able to give her answer immediately, decidedly, and with no apparent agitation. She thanked him for his great attention, his paternal kindness, but he was quite mistaken in supposing she had the smallest desire of breaking through her engagement, or was sensible of any change of opinion or inclination since her forming it. She had the highest esteem for Mr. Rushworth's character and disposition, and could not have a doubt of her happiness with him.[50]

Satisfied, Sir Thomas reasons that if she 'could now speak so securely of her happiness with him, speaking certainly without the prejudice, the blindness of love, she ought to be believed'; relieved that he will not have to undergo the 'embarrassing evils' of breaking off the engagement, and 'happy to secure a marriage which would bring him such an addition of respectability and influence', he is 'very happy to think any thing of his daughter's disposition that was most favourable for the purpose'. Maria, opting for wealth and perversely glad to be 'safe from the possibility of giving Crawford the triumph of governing her actions, and destroying her prospects', ends the interview 'determined only to behave more cautiously to Mr. Rushworth in future, that her father might not again be suspecting her'.

Jane Austen reserves her dialogue for the passage later in the novel when Sir Thomas discusses the marriage he very much wants to take place between Fanny and Henry Crawford. It is a very good match for a niece who has no fortune and for whom he will not be able to provide much of a one; and where in the case of Maria he could readily see Mr Rushworth's limitations, he, like everybody except Fanny herself, can see none whatever in Mr Crawford. That she 'cannot like him . . . well enough to marry him' is something which her uncle's 'comprehension does not reach'. As far as he can see, he is a young man with every thing to recommend him; not merely situation in life, fortune, and character, but with more than common agreeableness, with address and conversation pleasing to every body. And he is not an acquaintance of to-day, you have now known him some time. His sister, moreover, is your intimate friend, which I should suppose would have been almost sufficient recommendation to you, had there been no other. It is very uncertain where my interest might have got William on. He has done it already.[51]

The tone of 'calm displeasure' in which Sir Thomas speaks draws from Fanny a simple 'Yes' in 'a faint voice', and a sense of feeling 'almost ashamed . . . for not liking Mr. Crawford'. Where the earlier conversation with Maria was awkward and formal, this, direct, rational and in every way but one unanswerable, opposes two irreconcilable views of marriage: one masculine, logical and drawing on evidence strongly connected with the exterior advantages of position, wealth, pleasing manners and that all-important eighteenth-century consideration of interest; the other feminine, emotional, abashed and yet quietly insistent, derived from a profound knowledge of one's own heart. Of Fanny's heart Sir Thomas does have a momentary suspicion, in searching for an explanation of what seems to him to be otherwise inexplicable:

> 'Young as you are, and having seen scarcely any one, it is hardly possible that your affections –'
> He paused and eyed her fixedly. He saw her lips formed into a *no*, though the sound was inarticulate, but her face was like scarlet. That, however, in so modest a girl might be very compatible with innocence; and chusing at least to appear satisfied, he quickly added, 'No, no, I know *that* is quite out of the question – quite impossible. Well, there is nothing more to be said.'

With little experience, perhaps, of reading beyond the superficial into the human heart, Sir Thomas is nevertheless not quite satisfied, even if he does choose to appear so. A moment later he leads in a roundabout way to a more direct question:

> 'Edmund I consider from his disposition and habits as much more likely to marry early than his brother. *He*, indeed, I have lately thought has seen the woman he could love, which, I am convinced, my eldest son has not. Am I right? Do you agree with me, my dear?'
> 'Yes, Sir.'
> It was gently, but it was calmly said, and Sir Thomas was easy on the score of the cousins.

As Fanny's 'unaccountableness' is confirmed, her uncle's 'displeasure' increases; he asks her if she has any reason 'to think ill of Mr. Crawford's temper?' (essentially the doubt that Mr Bennet has on Elizabeth's behalf about Darcy). She says no but longs to add 'but of his principles I have'; and herein lies her difficulty:

Her ill opinion of him was founded chiefly on observations, which, for her cousins' sake, she could scarcely dare mention to their father. Maria and Julia – especially Maria, were so closely implicated in Mr. Crawford's misconduct, that she could not give his character, such as she believed it, without betraying them.

In truth Sir Thomas understands neither Crawford's character nor his daughters'. He had, however, begun to understand Fanny's, but now, crucially, allows her refusal to cloud his view of her:

> you have disappointed every expectation I had formed, and proved yourself of a character the very reverse of what I had supposed. For I *had*, Fanny, as I think my behaviour must have shewn, formed a very favourable opinion of you from the period of my return to England. I had thought you peculiarly free from wilfulness of temper, self-conceit, and every tendency to that independence of spirit, which prevails so much in modern days, even in young women, and which in young women is offensive and disgusting beyond all common offence. But you have now shewn me that you can be wilful and perverse, that you can and will decide for yourself, without any consideration of deference for those who have surely some right to guide you – without even asking their advice.[52]

Again he cites the essentially masculine reasoning of the material advantages of the marriage (though of course it is precisely the same reasoning that has led Maria to marry Mr Rushworth – she is her father's daughter in that respect):

> The advantage or disadvantage of your family – of your parents – your brothers and sisters – never seems to have had a moment's share in your thoughts on this occasion. How *they* might have benefited, how *they* must rejoice in such an establishment for you – is nothing to *you*. You think only of yourself; and because you do not feel for Mr. Crawford exactly what a young, heated fancy imagines to be necessary for happiness, you resolve to refuse him at once, without wishing even for a little time to consider of it – a little more time for cool consideration, and for really examining your own inclinations – and are, in a wild fit of folly, throwing away from you such an opportunity of being settled in life, eligibly, honourably, nobly settled, as will, probably, never occur to you again.

He stresses again Mr Crawford's virtues – and his wealth – and adds with considerable irony for the reader, who knows so much more about Maria and Julia than he does:

> 'Gladly would I have bestowed either of my own daughters on him. Maria is nobly married – but had Mr. Crawford sought Julia's hand, I should have given it to him with superior and more heartfelt satisfaction than I gave Maria's to Mr. Rushworth.' After a moment's pause – 'And I should have been very much surprised had either of my daughters, on receiving a proposal of marriage at any time, which might carry with it only *half* the eligibility of *this*, immediately and peremptorily, and without paying my opinion or my regard the compliment of any consultation, put a decided negative on

it. I should have been much surprised, and much hurt, by such a proceeding. I should have thought it a gross violation of duty and respect. *You* are not to be judged by the same rule. You do not owe me the duty of a child. But, Fanny, if your heart can acquit you of *ingratitude –*'

The nexus of misconceptions meeting in Sir Thomas – his ignorance of the characters of his own daughters; his inability to discern the dependability of his niece's feelings, not least towards himself; his blindness to the palpable rightness of a marriage between her and his son, should it come about – make his situation the most complex and fascinating of any parent, or surrogate parent, in Jane Austen. Yet it is also a situation that is essential to the structure of the novel, since it is only by means of the catastrophe to which Sir Thomas's incomprehension leads that Edmund can be brought to see the truth of things, and that Fanny can be released from the enormous pressure exerted on her by her secret love and attain final emotional maturity, resolving incidentally thereby the division in her heart between her cousin and her brother.

The conflict in what might be termed the marriage debate in *Mansfield Park* between the worldly demands of wealth, position and, to do Sir Thomas justice, security and the emotional pull of love is played out not only in Fanny but in a lesser way in Maria, too. Wilful, ambitious and selfish, on Crawford's departure she settles for material luxury, only to throw it all away as soon as in his vanity he awakens her feelings for him again. Though outwardly so much more assured than her cousin, she proves to have the weaker character, and in the final hellish existence to which she is consigned with Mrs Norris, 'where, shut up together with little society, on one side no affection, on the other, no judgment, it may reasonably be supposed that their tempers became their mutual punishment',[53] no growth towards emotional maturity will be possible.

Fanny's suffering through much of the novel is what she has to pay for ultimately marrying for love, and it can be seen as tempering her quite as much as her visit to her disordered, noisy family home at Portsmouth. It is surprising, perhaps, that she is the only one of Jane Austen's heroines, or indeed of her young women in general, to be subject to pressure to marry a man whom she does not love (we can discount Mrs Bennet's attempt to make Elizabeth marry Mr Collins, since it is treated entirely comically and in any case is utterly undermined by her husband). This reflects the change that had taken place in the choosing of marriage partners by the end of the eighteenth century. In earlier times, at least for people with property, it had been the norm for families to arrange advantageous marriages for their children with members of comparable families, from which wealth and property would come. This was probably not seen by the children themselves as authoritarian since in general they would have acquiesced in their parents' view of the desirability of making a good match. Poets and playwrights might have asserted the supremacy of love, but in the cold pragmatism of the sixteenth century such sentiments were confined to the stage or the sonnet. Later, other considerations might apply, among them the assurance that a woman was a good breeder, some men choosing wives much as they would select mares for their stallions.[54]

By the end of the seventeenth century, however, it was clear that if marriage was to succeed there should be some degree of freedom in choosing a partner and that there were other criteria to be taken into account than those of wealth or status. Arranged marriages were the butt of the Restoration playwrights; and later it was conceded, for example in Fielding's *Tom Jones*, that the most a girl should be expected to tolerate was a parental right of veto, promising not to marry without her father's consent. Sarah Pennington, writing in 1761, expressed herself frankly and forcefully on the subject to her daughters. So unhappy was her married life that she almost hoped they would not marry at all; but since she assumed that in the natural course of things they probably would, she urged them 'to proceed with the utmost care and with deliberate circumspection':

> In fortune and family it is the sole province of your father to direct: he certainly has always an undoubted right to a negative voice, tho' not to a compulsive one: as a child is very justifiable in the refusal of her hand, even to the absolute command of a father, where her heart cannot go with it, so is she extremely culpable, in giving it contrary to his approbation. Here, I must take shame to myself! And, for this unpardonable fault, I justly acknowledge that the subsequent ill consequences of a most unhappy marriage were the proper punishment.[55]

Romantic love and physical attraction were still regarded as perilously insubstantial bases for choosing a marriage partner, however much the novels that young ladies obtained from circulating libraries might encourage them to think that the first requirement in a prospective husband was that they should be in love with him. Even while permitting the young to find their own partners, parents hoped that they would choose sensibly; and for girls in particular there was always a danger that they would mistake the attentions of young men for love when in fact they stemmed from nothing more than lust. 'The effects of love among men are diversified by their different tempers,' Dr John Gregory warned his young daughters in the year before Jane Austen was born:

> An artful man may counterfeit every one of them so as easily to impose on a young girl of an open, generous, and feeling heart, if she be not extremely on her guard. The finest parts in such a girl may not always prove sufficient for her security. The dark and crooked paths of cunning are unsearchable and inconceivable to an honourable and elevated mind.[56]

How then can a woman know if a man is paying his attentions to her honestly? Gregory suggested the different ways in which genuine love manifests itself:

> True love, in all it's stages, seeks concealment, and never expects success. It renders a man not only respectful, but timid to the highest degree in his behaviour to the woman he loves . . . He magnifies all her real perfections in his imagination, and is either blind

to her failings, or converts them into beauties. Like a person conscious of guilt, he is jealous that every eye observes him; and to avoid this, he shuns all the little observances of common gallantry. His heart and his character will be improved in every respect by his attachment. His manners will become more gentle, and his conversation more agreeable; but diffidence and embarrassment will always make him appear to disadvantage in the company of his mistress. If the fascination continue long it will totally depress his spirit, and extinguish every active, vigorous, and manly principle of his mind.

If she sees 'evident proofs of a gentleman's attachment', Dr Gregory is insistent that a woman should let him know at once if she does not love him in return; she must not 'let him linger in a miserable suspense'. Naturally, in a period when a woman could not speak to a man of her feelings until he had spoken to her of his, she had to convey the fact that she was not attached to him in indirect ways, and Gregory suggests a number of them. A 'certain species of easy familiarity' in her behaviour 'may satisfy him, if he have any discernment left, that he has nothing to hope for'; if, however, her 'particular temper may not admit of this', she will have to try other methods. She can of course easily show him that she wants to avoid his company, but if she wishes to preserve his friendship, that will not do. She could 'get a common friend to explain matters to him', or make use of some other device. At the very least, she must not 'shun opportunities of letting him explain himself'; and if he brings her to an explanation, she should give him 'a polite, but resolute and decisive answer' (just as Elizabeth Bennet endeavours to do to Mr Collins).[57]

If, on the other hand, she wishes to accept him, she must be sure that she is not giving way to 'a sudden sally of passion', since 'genuine love is not founded on caprice' but 'in nature, on honourable views, on virtue, on similarity of tastes and sympathy of souls'.[58] It 'is very seldom produced at first sight' but is 'founded on esteem, in a correspondence of tastes and sentiments, and steals on the heart imperceptibly'.[59] The 'tumult of passion will necessarily subside; but it will be succeeded by an endearment, which affects the heart in a more equal, more sensible, and tender manner'.[60]

Mary Wollstonecraft too warned against the chimera of passion in determining whom to marry. 'In the choice of a husband', she wrote, women 'should not be led astray by the qualities of a lover – for a lover the husband, even supposing him to be wise and virtuous, cannot long remain.'[61] In her aspiration for women to be considered rational, she took a clear-eyed view about how they should enter into marriage:

> To speak disrespectfully of love is, I know, high treason against sentiment and fine feelings; but I wish to speak the simple language of truth, and rather to address the head than the heart . . . Youth is the season for love in both sexes; but in those days of thoughtless enjoyment provision should be made for the more important years of life, when reflection takes place of sensation. But Rousseau, and most of the male writers who have followed his steps, have warmly inculcated that the whole tendency of female

education ought to be directed to one point; – to render them pleasing. Let me reason with the supporters of this opinion who have any knowledge of human nature, do they imagine that marriage can eradicate the habitude of life? The woman who has only been taught to please will soon find that her charms are oblique sunbeams, and that they cannot have much effect on her husband's heart when they are seen every day, when the summer is passed and gone.[62]

It is precisely because Mr Bennet, 'in his days of thoughtless enjoyment' made no provision 'for the more important years of life, when reflection takes place of sensation' that his marriage is unsatisfactory; he may have 'very often wished . . . that, instead of spending his whole income, he had laid by an annual sum, for the better provision of his children, and of his wife,'[63] but a far better provision would have been to marry a more sensible woman.

Sense was also something a girl should look for in a husband. 'Good sense and good nature are almost equally requisite,' Mrs Pennington told her daughters; for 'if the former be wanting, it will be next to impossible for you to esteem the person of whose behaviour you may have cause to be ashamed, and mutual esteem is as necessary to happiness in the married state, as mutual affection.'[64] The presence of good sense in a young man is easy enough to detect (Mr Rushworth's deficiency in this respect is after all readily apparent to both Maria and her father); but it is more difficult to be sure whether or not he is possessed of genuine good nature, since it may easily be confused with the more superficial quality of mere good humour. By good nature, Mrs Pennington says, she means

> that true benevolence which shares in the felicity of all mankind, which promotes the satisfaction of every individual within the reach of it's ability, which relieves the distressed, comforts the afflicted, diffuses blessings, and communicates happiness, as far as it's sphere of action can extend; and which, in the private scenes of life, will shine conspicuous in the dutiful son, in the affectionate husband, the indulgent father, the faithful friend, and in the compassionate master, both to man and beast . . .

The possession of this 'amiable virtue' cannot be judged by the opinion of people in general, since they will know only if a young man is good-humoured; to avoid deception, therefore, it is best

> to lay no stress on outward appearances, which are too often fallacious, but to take the rule of judging from the simple unpolished sentiments of those, whose dependent connections give them an undeniable certainty: who not only see, but hourly feel, the good or bad effects of that disposition, to which they are subjected.[65]

More specifically, she says, a man's true character is known best to his servants and tenants – just as Elizabeth Bennet finds to be the case with Mr Darcy at Pemberley:

if a man is equally respected, esteemed, and beloved by his tenants, by his dependents and domestics, from the substantial farmer to the laborious peasant, from the proud steward to the submissive wretch, who, thankful for employment, humbly obeys the menial tribe, you may justly conclude, he has that true good nature, that real benevolence, which delights in communicating felicity, and enjoys the satisfaction it diffuses; but if, by these, he is despised and hated, served merely from a principle of fear, devoid of affection, which is ever easily discoverable, whatever may be his public character, however favourable the general opinion, be assured, that his disposition is such as can never be productive of domestic happiness.

Elizabeth's problem is not of course to distinguish 'good humour' from 'true good nature' in Darcy; but the housekeeper's opinion of him, and Elizabeth's reflections on it, are so strongly reminiscent of this passage as to suggest the possibility that Jane Austen knew it, and had it in her mind. Mrs Reynolds pays generous testimony to Darcy's character:

He is the best landlord, and the best master . . . that ever lived. Not like the wild young men now-a-days, who think of nothing but themselves. There is not one of his tenants or servants but what will give him a good name.[66]

And going into the room fitted up for Miss Darcy, she adds

And this is always the way with him . . . Whatever can give his sister any pleasure, is sure to be done in a moment. There is nothing he would not do for her.

Elizabeth's thoughts seem to echo Mrs Pennington's ideas almost systematically:

What praise is more valuable than the praise of an intelligent servant? As a brother, a landlord, a master, she considered how many people's happiness were in his guardianship! – How much of pleasure or pain it was in his power to bestow! – How much of good or evil must be done by him! Every idea that had been brought forward by the housekeeper was favourable to his character . . .[67]

In the marriage of Elizabeth and Darcy, Jane Austen demonstrates the changes that had come about during the century in the way that even very rich men might choose their wives. It was intended, if Lady Catherine is to be believed, that he should marry his cousin, Miss de Bourgh. 'From their infancy,' it will be remembered Lady Catherine informs Elizabeth, 'they have been intended for each other. It was the favourite wish of *his* mother, as well as of her's. While in their cradles, we planned the union . . .'[68] This is a very old-fashioned arrangement indeed, harking back to infant betrothals in noble families in the Middle Ages. But times have changed: Darcy's parents are dead, and Lady Catherine, in endeavouring to exert an outdated authority over both her nephew and Elizabeth, unwittingly acts as the catalyst to the very marriage she is seeking to prevent. Darcy marries for love, certainly; but that love is founded on a knowledge of Elizabeth's character, tastes and worth that might assure him that he will avoid the risks that Mary Wollstonecraft warns against.

The wise Dr Gregory, like Mrs Pennington, urged his daughters to find out as much as they could from reliable sources about any man who they thought might pay them his addresses, before they allowed their 'affections to become engaged'; they should, he said,

> in the most prudent and secret manner . . . procure from your friends every necessary piece of information concerning him; such as his character for sense, his morals, his temper, fortune, and family; whether it be distinguished for parts and worth, or for folly, knavery, and loathsome hereditary diseases. When your friends have informed you of these; they have fulfilled their duty.[69]

While Dr Gregory had no wish to influence their choice of husbands, he offered them very specific suggestions about the sort of men they should avoid:

> From what I have said, you will easily see that I could never pretend to advise whom you should marry; but I can with great confidence advise whom you should not marry. Avoid a companion who may entail any hereditary disease on your posterity, particularly (that most dreadful of all human calamities) madness . . . Do not marry a fool; he is the most intractable of all animals; he is fed by his passions and caprices, and is incapable of hearing the voice of reason . . . A rake is always a suspicious husband, because he has only known the most worthless of your sex. He likewise entails the worst diseases on his wife and children, if he have the misfortune to have any. If you have a sense of religion yourselves, do not think of husbands who have none.[70]

'As I look on your choice of a husband to be of the greatest consequence to your happiness,' he concluded, 'I hope you will make it with the greatest circumspection.' There is no hint that he would intervene to prevent them making an unsuitable marriage; in fact he made it perfectly clear that, once they were grown up he would not interfere in their lives at all:

> If I live till you arrive at that age when you shall be capable of judging for yourselves, and do not strangely alter my sentiments, I shall act towards you in a very different manner from what most parents do. My opinion has always been, that, when that period arrives, the parental authority ceases. I hope I shall always treat you with that affection and easy confidence which may dispose you to look on me as your friend. In that capacity alone I shall think myself intitled to give you my opinion; in the doing of which, I should think myself highly criminal, if I did not to the utmost of my power endeavour to divest myself of all personal vanity, and all prejudices in favour of my particular taste. If you did not chuse to follow my advice, I should not on that account cease to love you as my children. Tho' my right to your obedience was expired, yet I should think nothing could release me from the ties of nature and humanity.[71]

Dr Gregory's tone anticipates that of the wiser parental figures in Jane Austen. The act of veto is represented by her as something arbitrary and unreasonable, and those who seek to exercise it – Lady Catherine, Mrs Ferrars, General Tilney – find that it is no longer in their power to do so. In *Persuasion* Lady Russell, combining as she does an outmoded deference to rank with a genuine and generous love for her god-daughter, comes to recognize that the well-meant influence she exerted on Anne eight years previously must give way to the right of a young woman to follow the dictates of her own feelings.

Jane Austen is in no doubt that people can make mistakes. Sometimes these can be rectified in time, sometimes the recognition of them comes too late. James Morland's infatuation with Isabella Thorpe and her subsequent flirtation with Captain Tilney teach him a useful lesson, as his mother sensibly acknowledges:

> We are sorry for him . . . but otherwise there is no harm done in the match going off; for it could not be a desirable thing to have him engaged to a girl whom we had not the smallest acquaintance with, and who was so entirely without fortune; and now, after such behaviour, we cannot think at all well of her. Just at present it comes hard to poor James; but that will not last for ever; and I dare say he will be a discreeter man all his life, for the foolishness of his first choice.[72]

In *Persuasion* the Musgroves, who allow Henrietta and Louisa a free rein in the choice of husbands, 'either from seeing very little, or from an entire confidence in the discretion of both their daughters, and of all the young men who came near them',[73] presumably allowed Charles the same freedom; and it is clear that in retrospect the whole family sometimes wish that he had chosen Anne (as indeed he first did) instead of the rather difficult Mary.[74] A sense of the residual influence left in the hands of parents is delightfully caught at the beginning of the scene in the White Hart in Bath when Mrs Musgrove gives Mrs Croft details of the engagement between Henrietta and her cousin, the curate Charles Hayter; though the Musgroves had always thought 'it would not be a great match for her', Charles's attentions to her 'had been observed by her father and mother without any disapprobation',[75] and now Anne cannot help overhearing

> how Mr. Musgrove and my brother Hayter had met again and again to talk it over; what my brother Hayter had said one day, and what Mr. Musgrove had proposed the next, and what had occurred to my sister Hayter, and what the young people had wished, and what I said at first I never could consent to, but was afterwards persuaded to think might do very well . . .[76]

Eventually the comedy of free indirect speech gives way to a firmer expression of the kindly, pragmatic, commonsensical view of the promotion of children's happiness that seems to reflect exactly the attitude of most sensible parents by the beginning of the nineteenth century:

'And so, ma'am, all these things considered,' said Mrs. Musgrove in her powerful whisper, 'though we could have wished it different, yet altogether we did not think it fair to stand out any longer; for Charles Hayter was quite wild about it, and Henrietta was pretty near as bad; and so we thought they had better marry at once, and make the best of it, as many others have done before them. At any rate, said I, it will be better than a long engagement.'

'That is precisely what I was going to observe,' cried Mrs. Croft. 'I would rather have young people settle on a small income at once, and have to struggle with a few difficulties together, than be involved in a long engagement. I always think that no mutual –'

'Oh! dear Mrs. Croft,' cried Mrs. Musgrove, unable to let her finish her speech, 'there is nothing I so abominate for young people as a long engagement. It is what I always protested against for my children. It is all very well, I used to say, for young people to be engaged, if there is a certainty of their being able to marry in six months, or even in twelve, but a long engagement!'

'Yes, dear ma'am,' said Mrs. Croft, 'or an uncertain engagement; an engagement which may be long. To begin without knowing that at such a time there will be the means of marrying, I hold to be very unsafe and unwise, andwhat, I think, all parents should prevent as far as they can.'

The conversation applies to Anne, and Jane Austen uses it to move the scene forward towards Captain Wentworth's eventual proposal; but in itself it offers a sensible, tolerant view, even where, as in Charles Hayter's case, there is no immediate prospect of any very substantial income as a basis for marriage.

The easy-going Musgroves are very different from unreasonable autocrats such as Mrs Ferrars in *Sense and Sensibility*. Having wanted Edward 'to make a fine figure in the world in some manner or other' and 'wished to interest him in political concerns, to get him into parliament, or to see him connected with some of the great men of the day',[77] she likewise intends him to make a rich marriage, and is willing to settle £1,000 a year on him if it takes place, as John Dashwood informs Elinor:

The lady is the Hon. Miss Morton, only daughter of the late Lord Morton, with thirty thousand pounds. A very desirable connection on both sides, and I have not a doubt of its taking place in time. A thousand a-year is a great deal for a mother to give away, to make over for ever; but Mrs. Ferrars has a noble spirit.[78]

Her noble spirit cannot quite rise to the occasion, however, when she finds out that he intends marrying Lucy Steele:

His own two thousand pounds she protested should be his all; she would never see him again; and so far would she be from affording him the smallest assistance, that if he were to enter into any profession with a view of better support, she would do all in her power to prevent his advancing in it.[79]

Despite feeling then that his marrying Elinor 'would not have given her half
the vexation' and would have been 'beyond comparison . . . the least evil of the
two, and she would be glad to compound *now* for nothing worse', when Lucy
jilts him for Robert, in whose favour he has been disinherited, her relief hardly
manifests itself in any very material way. The collapse of Mrs Ferrars's regressive
attempts at controlling her sons' marriages is treated with rich irony in a letter to
Elinor from John Dashwood – no doubt preserved more or less intact from Jane
Austen's original epistolary 'Elinor and Marianne', the opening only translated
into reported speech, to heighten the comedy:

> Mrs. Ferrars was the most unfortunate of women – poor Fanny had suffered agonies of
> sensibility – and he considered the existence of each, under such a blow, with grateful
> wonder. Robert's offence was unpardonable, but Lucy's was infinitely worse. Neither of
> them was ever again to be mentioned to Mrs. Ferrars; and even, if she might hereafter be
> induced to forgive her son, his wife should never be acknowledged as her daughter, nor be
> admitted to appear in her presence . . . he called on Elinor to join with him in regretting
> that Lucy's engagement with Edward had not rather been fulfilled, than that she should
> thus be the means of spreading misery farther in the family. – He thus continued: 'Mrs.
> Ferrars has never yet mentioned Edward's name, which does not surprise us; but to our
> great astonishment, not a line has been received from him on the occasion . . . his sister
> and I both think a letter of proper submission from him, addressed perhaps to Fanny, and
> by her shewn to her mother, might not be taken amiss; for we all know the tenderness
> of Mrs. Ferrars's heart, and that she wishes for nothing so much as to be on good terms
> with her children.'[80]

While refusing to write any such 'letter of proper submission', Edward does
agree to ask John and Fanny to intercede for him, and after 'a proper resistance
. . . just so violent and so steady as to preserve her from that reproach which
she always seemed fearful of incurring, the reproach of being too amiable', his
mother admits him to her presence and pronounces him 'to be again her son'.[81]
Eventually she even issues 'her decree of consent' to his marrying Elinor, 'after
such an ungracious delay as she owed to her own dignity, and as served to prevent
every suspicion of good-will'. Nevertheless, it is Robert whom she allows £1,000
a year, leaving Edward with the £250 from the living to which Colonel Brandon
has presented him and promising him nothing 'either for the present or in
future, beyond the ten thousand pounds, which had been given with Fanny'.[82]
This enables Jane Austen to make a final crisp comment on financial dealings
within families:

> What Edward had done to forfeit the right of eldest son, might have puzzled many
> people to find out; and what Robert had done to succeed to it, might have puzzled them
> still more. It was an arrangement, however, justified in its effects, if not in its cause; for
> nothing ever appeared in Robert's style of living or of talking, to give a suspicion of his
> regretting the extent of his income, as either leaving his brother too little, or bringing

himself too much; – and if Edward might be judged from the ready discharge of his duties in every particular, and from an increasing attachment to his wife and his home, and from the regular cheerfulness of his spirits, he might be supposed no less contented with his lot, no less free from every wish of an exchange.[83]

While Robert, 'proud of his conquest, proud of tricking Edward, and very proud of marrying without his mother's consent', has the material advantage, he has 'frequent domestic disagreements' with Lucy; and a novel that begins with the whittling down of a dead father's financial provision for his wife and children ends with the assertion of the supremacy of love over money in a happy marriage.

When Jane Austen was only thirteen, her brother James had come to the same conclusion in *The Loiterer*, though he expressed it with sustained irony in a paper on 'The Absurdity of marrying from Affection'.[84] The young, he wrote, 'have taken it into their heads to imagine that Youth and Beauty, Good Temper and Good Sense, are the best recommendations in a Wife; that on this occasion similarity of dispositions should be consulted rather than equality of fortunes, and that mutual Affection is a surer basis of Conjugal Happiness than a Hundred Thousand Pounds'. The old, on the other hand, think that 'it is no matter how wide the tempers are separated, provided that the estates join' and that 'in order to get possession of a rotten Borough' they would 'gladly exchange all the beauties of the person, and all the graces of the mind; and (rather than stand upon trifles) give the four Cardinal Virtues into the bargain'. Although in other respects he 'may lean to the side of the young, (well knowing that their experience and cool-ness must nine times out of ten give them the advantage over the Adversaries)', in this matter he agrees with the old. Marrying for affection is harmful to individual happiness and 'detrimental to the interests of the Community'.

Married couples who love each other suffer many 'sorrows, cares, and vexa-tions' from which those who do not are entirely free. 'If the Lady looks too pale or too red, too thin or too plump, the Husband is immediately under the most cruel alarm for her health. He has a whole list of Disorders which he thinks she may have, and what is worse, a whole list of Remedies to cure them. While on the other side, the Lady . . . is in continual apprehension from the falling of Horses, and the bursting of Guns.' Furthermore, among those who make 'prudential marriages', rather than marrying from affection, especially in 'the higher ranks of life', there is nothing more common than 'to see Husbands losing their fortunes, and Wives their reputations, without causing any alteration in the behaviour, or any diminution in the Affection of the other'.

Matches of affection also 'materially affect the Interests of the Community', since they result in large families 'in a Country which cannot already support half its inhabitants', and he cannot approve of bringing into the world 'a set of beings, who when they come to years of discretion, may perhaps have no alternative than either to starve or to be hanged'. Worse still, 'if once people take it into their heads to marry for love, there is no knowing whether they may not continue to love all their lives' – and then what will happen to the divorce lawyers and the scandal-mongering newspaper writers? There is therefore only one possible conclusion:

> Beauty and Elegance are very fleeting commodities, Wit and Good Temper very uncertain ones, and a Woman may sometimes chance to outlive them all. Whereas, Farms, and Woods, India Bonds, and Annuities, are very solid and substantial goods; will, with a little management, last during (what the law terms) a Man's natural life; that is, till his Spirits and Constitution are ruined; and are to be obtained at the very trifling Sacrifice of social happiness and domestic comfort.

When in 1796 James married Mary Lloyd as his second wife, his mother wrote her a letter that shows clearly how ready the Austens were to support their children in their choice of marriage partners. Of course, James was by then no longer a boy but a widower of thirty, with a daughter and an independent living; even so, the particular warmth of Mrs Austen's tone says much for the readiness of the family to welcome new members into it:

> Mr Austen & Myself desire you will accept our best Love, and that you will believe us truly sincere when we assure you that we feel the most heartfelt satisfaction at the prospect we have of adding you to the Number of our very good Children. Had the election been mine, you, my dear Mary, are the person I should have chosen for *James's Wife, Anna's Mother*, and *my Daughter*; being as certain, as I can be of anything in this uncertain World, that you will greatly increase & promote the happiness of each of the three. Pray give our Love to Mrs Lloyd & Martha, & say, we hope they are as well pleas'd with, and as much approve of, their future Son & Brother, as we with, & of, our Daughter. I look forward to you as a real comfort to me in my old age . . .[85]

As it turned out, Mary may not perhaps have greatly promoted the happiness of her stepdaughter; but she kept Mrs Austen's letter all her life.

That same stepdaughter, Anna, was sometimes a cause of concern to both Mary and James. At the age of seventeen she greatly alarmed them by falling in love with a man twice her age, the thirty-five year-old Michael Terry, of nearby Dummer House.[86] She expressed her sentiments on receiving a letter from him in a sentimental poem:

> With what delight I view each line
> Trac'd by the hand I love
> Where warm esteem & Grace combine
> A feeling heart to move
>
> Then come sweet letter to my breast
> Thou'lt find no coldness there
> Close to my heart for ever rest
> It's warmth for ever share –[87]

After much persuasion, her father gave Mr Terry permission to address Anna, only to find that she subsequently caused even more offence by deciding to break off the engagement. Writing to Cassandra from Chawton, where Anna was staying, Jane mentioned an evening party at which some of the Terrys were present, and to which Anna, though invited, had not been free to go; 'I think it always safer to keep her away from the family,' she commented, 'lest she sh^d be doing too little or too much'.[88] Three years later Anna again surprised her family by engaging herself to Ben Lefroy, whose mother had been Jane's great friend Madam Lefroy, wife of the rector of the neighbouring parish of Ashe. At the time it did not seem perhaps an ideal match, though, as Jane told her brother Francis, it was one that was as likely to succeed as any other that the rather wayward Anna might make:

> I take it for granted that Mary has told you of Anna's engagement to Ben Lefroy. It came upon us without much preparation; – at the same time, there was *that* about her which kept us in a constant preparation for something. – We are anxious to have it go on well, there being quite as much in his favour as the Chances are likely to give her in any Matrimonial connection. I beleive he is sensible, certainly very religious, well connected & with some Independance. – There is an unfortunate dissimilarity of Taste between them in one respect which gives us some apprehensions, he hates company & she is very fond of it; – This, with some queerness of Temper on his side & much unsteadiness on hers, is untoward.[89]

One of the worries that Anna's family had was how the young people were going to live. Unwilling to take orders before he felt the time was right, Ben turned down a valuable curacy, much to James Austen's dismay; Jane told Cassandra that Ben's view was that 'if her Father makes a point of it, he must give Anna up rather than do what he does not approve'.[90] Jane added 'He must be maddish', a theme she took up a little later when telling Cassandra that she was to meet Ben's aunt, Mrs Harrison, and that she would talk to her about Ben and Anna:

> 'My dear Mrs Harrison, I shall say, I am afraid the young Man has some of your Family Madness – & though there often appears to be something of Madness in Anna too, I think she inherits more of it from her Mother's family than from ours –' That is what I shall say – & I think she will find it difficult to answer me.[91]

Eventually, in spite of these drawbacks, it was to prove a very happy marriage.

Jane's other favourite niece, Fanny, also got herself into difficulties; she could not decide whether or not to marry John Plumptre, the son of a wealthy neighbouring family, and, having no mother to advise her, sought help from her aunt. Their discussion was kept entirely between themselves, neither Fanny's father nor Cassandra being told about it; in fact, Fanny resorted to the subterfuge of sending a parcel of music so that neither of them would realize that her aunt had received a letter.

Jane Austen knew that to give advice on so important a matter was a great responsibility. Anne Elliot reflects on this, when thinking of Lady Russell's advice to her not to marry Frederick Wentworth:

> She did not blame Lady Russell, she did not blame herself for having been guided by her; but she felt that were any young person, in similar circumstances, to apply to her for counsel, they would never receive any of such certain immediate wretchedness, such uncertain future good. . . .
>
> How eloquent Anne Elliot could have been – how eloquent, at least, were her wishes on the side of early warm attachment, and a cheerful confidence in futurity, against that over-anxious caution which seems to insult exertion and distrust Providence![92]

The difficulty that Jane faced, however, was not whether Mr Plumptre offered Fanny a secure married life – he certainly did, since he was well off and of a very serious disposition – but whether Fanny really loved him enough, since she had come to find certain aspects of his manner off-putting; and in the letters that Jane wrote at the time, we can see the woman who as a novelist could dispose of her characters and their futures as she wished wrestling with the far less malleable problem of a niece whose feelings she had to weigh up as best she could from the conflicting evidence she was presented with.

In the first letter,[93] she acknowledges that she has 'no hope of writing anything to the purpose' and that she will 'do very little more . . . than say over again' what Fanny has said before:

> I was certainly a good deal surprised *at first* – as I had no suspicion of any change in your feelings, and I have no scruple in saying that you cannot be in Love. My dear Fanny, I am ready to laugh at the idea – and yet it is no laughing matter to have had you so mistaken as to your own feelings – And with all my heart I wish I had cautioned you on that point when first you spoke to me; – but tho' I did not think you then so *much* in love as you thought yourself, I did consider you as being attached in a degree – quite sufficiently for happiness, as I had no doubt it would increase with opportunity. – And from the time of our being in London together, I thought you really very much in love. – But you certainly are not at all – there is no concealing it. – What strange creatures we are! – It seems as if your being secure of him (as you say yourself) had made you Indifferent.

Jane Austen, who deals so perceptively and sensitively with the human heart in her fiction, is completely at a loss.

> My dearest Fanny, I am writing what will not be of the smallest use to you. I am feeling differently every moment, & shall not be able to suggest a single thing that can assist your Mind. – I could lament in one sentence & laugh in the next, but as to Opinion or Counsel I am sure none will [be] extracted worth having from this Letter.

And yet she does see what has brought these complex and contradictory feelings about:

Oh! dear Fanny, Your mistake has been one that thousands of women fall into. He was the *first* young Man who attached himself to you. That was the charm, & most powerful it is.

It is of course the same powerful charm that so devastatingly attracts Marianne to Willoughby. But John Plumptre has many real advantages as a husband for Fanny:

His situation in life, family, friends, & above all his Character – his uncommonly amiable mind, strict principles, just notions, good habits – *all* that *you* know so well how to value, *All* that really is of the first importance – everything of this nature pleads his cause most strongly. – You have no doubt of his having superior Abilities – he has proved it at the University – he is I dare say such a Scholar as Your agreable, idle Brothers would ill bear a comparison with. – Oh! my dear Fanny, the more I write about him, the warmer my feelings become, the more strongly I feel the sterling worth of such a young Man & the desirableness of your growing in love with him again. I recommend this most thoroughly.

Is it practicable, in real life as opposed to fiction, to wait for the perfect husband?

There *are* such beings in the World perhaps, one in a Thousand, as the Creature You & I should think perfection, where Grace & Spirit are united to Worth, where the Manners are equal to the Heart & Understanding, but such a person may not come in your way, or if he does, he may not be the eldest son of a Man of Fortune, the Brother of your particular friend, & belonging to your own County. Think of all this, Fanny. Mr J.P.- has advantages which do not often meet in one person.

Having almost come to the conclusion that Fanny should marry him, she abruptly draws back and gives the contrary opinion:

And now, my dear Fanny, having written so much on one side of the question, I shall turn round & entreat you not to commit yourself farther, & not to think of accepting him unless you really do like him. Anything is to be preferred or endured rather than marrying without Affection; and if his deficiencies of Manner &c &c strike you more than all his good qualities, if you continue to think strongly of them, give him up at once.

Ten days later, in response to another letter from Fanny, Jane wrote in some alarm, since her niece had clearly suggested that she would be guided by her aunt's advice:

You frighten me out of my Wits by your reference. Your affection gives me the Highest pleasure, but indeed you must not let anything depend on my opinion. Your own feelings & none but your own, should determine such an important point.[94]

By now Jane is fairly sure that Fanny should turn him down, and she comes back to the inexperience of the twenty-one-year-old:

When I consider how few young Men you have yet seen much of – how capable you are (yes, I do think you *very* capable) of being really in love – and how full of temptation the next 6 or 7 years of your life will probably be – (it is the very period of Life for the *strongest* attachments to be formed) – I cannot wish you with your present very cool feelings to devote yourself in honour to him.

It seems that Fanny had more or less decided to take her aunt's advice early in the former letter to marry him, since she might never meet anyone else so worthy who would offer. But again Jane Austen expresses strong reservations:

It is very true that you may never attach another Man, his equal altogether, but if that other Man has the power of attaching you *more*, he will be in your eyes the most perfect. – I shall be glad if you *can* revive past feelings, & from your unbiassed self resolve to go on as you have done, but this I do not expect, and without it I cannot wish you to be fettered.

Finally, she reiterates her conviction that 'nothing can be compared to the misery of being bound *without* Love, bound to one, & preferring another'. That, she says, is a punishment which Fanny does not deserve.

Fanny Knight turned down Mr Plumptre. Six years later she married a widower baronet, Sir Edward Knatchbull, of Mersham Hatch, Kent, who was twelve years her senior; by his first wife he had six children, and Fanny gave him nine more.

Jane had told her niece that the next six or seven years of her life – the early and mid-twenties – was the period in which the strongest attachments are made, yet of the heroines in her novels Anne Elliot is the only one not to be married by the time she is in her early twenties, and she marries the man whom she originally fell in love with when she was nineteen. Catherine Morland, who, apart from Fanny Price, is the one heroine whom we actually see, as it were, coming out, makes the transition from girl to married woman in under a year, meeting Henry Tilney after only a few days in Bath; in fact, Jane Austen seems intent on condensing into the short period of eleven weeks covered by the action of *Northanger Abbey* the whole process of coming out, the first (and in Catherine's case only) season and the social and financial complications of becoming engaged. In responding to Fanny Burney's *Evelina* (where the heroine is allowed seven months in London to undergo the same stages of her life), Jane Austen places Catherine in one of the two national marriage markets; her other heroines, like her two nieces, marry young men they meet in their own neighbourhood, local assembly rooms or the ballrooms of inns being the places provided to enable the children of families such as the Bennets or the Austens to encounter safe and respectable prospective partners.

Catherine's sad return to Fullerton, after General Tilney's abrupt dismissal of her from Northanger, is marked by the clearest delineation of the end of childhood that Jane Austen depicted. As she goes with her mother to visit the Allens, she thinks of herself as she was when she last walked on the path to their house, before the momentous events that had subsequently changed her view of the world for ever:

> It was not three months ago since, wild with joyful expectation, she had there run backwards and forwards some ten times a-day, with an heart light, gay, and independent; looking forward to pleasures untested and unalloyed, and free from the apprehension of evil as from the knowledge of it. Three months ago had seen her all this; and now, how altered a being did she return![95]

Yet, by a masterstroke, we see that girls do not grow up completely in three short months, even if during that time they have made their entrance into the world and fallen in love. Moping at home, with the thought that she may never see Henry again, or that if they do meet at some time in the future he may have forgotten her, she exhibits all the characteristics of adolescent lassitude:

> She could neither sit still, nor employ herself for ten minutes together, walking round the garden and orchard again and again, as if nothing but motion was voluntary; and it seemed as if she could even walk about the house rather than remain fixed for any time in the parlour. Her loss of spirits was a yet greater alteration. In her rambling and her idleness she might only be a caricature of herself; but in her silence and sadness she was the very reverse of all that she had been before.[96]

Her mother assumes that she misses the social life that she was so recently enjoying and tells her 'Your head runs too much upon Bath; but there is a time for every thing – a time for balls and plays, and a time for work. You have had a long run of amusement, and now you must try to be useful.' Catherine says 'in a dejected voice, that "her head did not run upon Bath – much."' Her gloom increases when her mother suggests that the grandeur of life at Northanger has made her dissatisfied with her home; 'I did not quite like, at breakfast,' she tells her, 'to hear you talk so much about the French-bread at Northanger', to which Catherine replies 'I am sure I do not care about the bread. It is all the same to me what I eat.' Henry's arrival puts everything right, however; Catherine's more mature demeanour is restored and, by way of contrast, when, wishing to have her to himself, he asks her to show him the way to the Allens' so that he can pay his compliments, there is an amusing little vignette of a younger sister, Sarah, helpfully pointing out to him 'You may see the house from this window, sir', which produces only 'a bow of acknowledgment' from him and 'a silencing nod' from Mrs Morland.[97]

The Morlands, though they are surprised at Henry's asking for Catherine's hand, rationalize that 'nothing, after all, could be more natural than Catherine's being beloved', and for their own part have no objection; her mother thinks that she will 'make a sad, heedless young housekeeper', but 'quick was the consolation of there being nothing like practice'.[98] Fond and sensible parents as they are, however, they will not sanction the engagement while the General is opposed to it. Although they do not stipulate that he 'should come forward to solicit the alliance, or that he should even very heartily approve it', they do insist that 'the decent appearance of consent must be yielded'. Their conscientious, kindly and essentially pragmatic stance is characteristic of that of most families by the end of the eighteenth century; and the reaction of the young people themselves is equally rational: they 'could not be surprised at a decision like this. They felt and they deplored – but they could not resent it'. The General's consent finally obtained, their marriage takes place 'within a twelvemonth from the first day of their meeting', and the author wisely comments that 'to begin perfect happiness at the respective ages of twenty-six and eighteen, is to do pretty well' and that the delay, 'so far from being really injurious to their felicity, was perhaps rather conducive to it, by improving their knowledge of each other, and adding strength to their attachment'.[99]

Jane Austen is not generally so precise in giving the period that elapses between the heroine's becoming engaged and the marriage itself, since she has brought the action of the novel to a climax with the proposal, and the tidying up that is necessary to allow the wedding to take place is rather summarily described. At the end of *Mansfield Park* in particular she is altogether reluctant to commit herself to dates and times and the reader is drawn into the writing of the novel by being invited to supply the appropriate period for 'unconquerable passions' to be cured and 'unchanging attachments' transferred, since such things must 'vary much as to time in different people'.[100] The implication, however, is that the period is not a very long one. Similarly, we are not to know exactly when the death of Dr Grant frees the living of Mansfield for Edmund to take it up.

There is, incidentally, an interesting riddle here. When Dr Grant succeeds to his stall in Westminster, 'affording', as we are told, 'an occasion for leaving Mansfield' and 'an excuse for residence in London',[101] who takes the services? And who, for that matter, moves into the parsonage? Dr Grant is of course still the rector, holding the living now in plurality; but in his absence he would have been expected to put in a curate, whom he would have paid himself. Reference is made to 'an increase of income to answer the expenses of the change', but nothing is said about whether the stipend of a curate made part of such expenses. The obvious person to have been installed is Edmund, since he is going to be the next rector. This is what Henrietta Musgrove is anxious to happen to Charles Hayter in *Persuasion*, if only the good Dr Shirley can be persuaded to take his well-earned retirement;[102] and it is also of course what happened when Jane Austen's father retired to Bath in 1801 and put his son James as curate into Steventon rectory. But it does not happen here: Edmund is still at Thornton Lacey, where he remains until Dr Grant dies and the living becomes vacant, when of course his father presents him to it. There is a rather surprising looseness here, which is perhaps best explained by the fact that it is necessary to keep Edmund and Fanny away from Mansfield a little longer than the preferment of Dr Grant makes probable, and the question is passed over with the assumption that the reader will not think of raising it.

The Grants' stay in Bath, begun while Fanny was at Portsmouth, is 'purposely lengthened' 'for some months', before it is ended by their 'permanent removal' to Westminster, when Mary Crawford goes to live with them. Three words, 'They lived together', and a semicolon are all that delays the self-indulgent canon from hastening towards his end; and he is finally disposed of in a brisk sub-clause: 'and when Dr. Grant had brought on apoplexy and death, by three great institutionary dinners in one week, they still lived together'. Seen from Edmund and Fanny's point of view, living in the parsonage at Thornton Lacey, this event occurs 'just after they had been married long enough to begin to want an increase of income, and feel their distance from the paternal abode an inconvenience'; in other words, when a child, or perhaps a second child, had arrived. And yet, in apparent contradiction of that rather short time-span, we are told that when they go to Mansfield the parsonage, which under the Norrises and the Grants had always caused Fanny 'some painful sensation of restraint or alarm', soon grows as dear to her heart 'and as thoroughly perfect in her eyes, as everything else, within the view and patronage of Mansfield Park, had long been'.[103] Are we to think that whereas for years Fanny had been disturbed by occurrences at the parsonage, first under Mrs Norris and subsequently with the arrival of the Crawfords, everything that happened at the Park had caused her unmitigated pleasure? Clearly not. On the other hand, if we are to assume that a distinction is being drawn between how Fanny regarded the two places after her marriage, we need to know whether Dr Grant put in a curate after his removal to Westminster, which, as we have seen, does not seem to have been the case – anyway no mention is made of any 'owner' other than Mr Norris and Dr Grant; but then the word 'long' ('as everything else, within the view and patronage of Mansfield Park had *long* been') is troubling, since, not only is it improbable that the parsonage would have been left uninhabited for a very long period, but, as we have seen, the implication is that Dr Grant's period of enjoying institutionary dinners in London was probably a short, if a merry, one.

With the exception of *Mansfield Park*, and the implied reason that Edmund and Fanny have for welcoming the change to a larger house, Jane Austen does not pursue her heroes and heroines far enough into their married lives to envisage them with children of their own. Yet in the course of the novels she supplies us with sufficient clues for us to be able to speculate on what sort of parents they will be. Henry Tilney will teach his children to appreciate art and read history, and they will be brought up to express themselves in good, clear English, their young mother no doubt learning alongside them as they go on.

We already know from *Sense and Sensibility* that before he is disinherited and takes orders, Edward Ferrars suffers from being in the position of the elder son and having no work to do; he is emphatic that he will not allow this to happen to any boys he may have. Mrs Dashwood supposes that 'since leisure has not promoted' his own happiness, they 'will be brought up to as many pursuits, employments, professions, and trades as Columella's'.[104] Her reference is to the eponymous character in a novel who finds various occupations for his sons, apprenticing one of them to a man 'who had united in his own person the several professions of apothecary, surgeon, man-midwife, bone-setter, tooth-drawer, hop-dealer, and brandy-merchant', hoping that they would 'be secured from that tedium and disgust of life which *he* experienced, and which he had brought upon himself by a life of indolence and inactivity'.[105] Edward answers, 'in a serious accent', that they will be brought up to be as unlike himself as possible, 'in feeling, in action, in condition, in every thing'.

The little Darcys and the little Bingleys, like the little Ferrarses and the little Brandons, will benefit from the closeness of their mothers and the mutual respect and affection of their fathers (and from the nearness of their homes) to grow up together as cousins. Bingley will perhaps be the more easy-going father, but sound advice will never be lacking from his brother-in-law at Pemberley.

Mr Knightley will treat his own boys as he has always done his nephews, tossing them up in the air, to the horror of their grandfather; he will also no doubt guide their reading more closely than their mother is inclined to. It is quite possible that one of them will grow up to marry Miss Weston of Randalls, after Isabella has inherited Hartfield.

When Anne and Captain Wentworth have children they will share the precarious existence foreseen at the end of *Persuasion*; like the children of Jane Austen's sailor brothers, they may well be left from time to time while their father is at sea, possibly with Lady Russell or the kindly Musgroves, possibly with the Crofts at Kellynch or, if there is room, the Harvilles at Lyme. They are unlikely to receive much attention from their grandfather and his other two daughters.

Of all Jane Austen's heroes and heroines, however, it may be that Edmund and Fanny are the ones who will make the best parents. Wise, sensitive and gentle, Fanny will remember the fears and uncertainties of her own childhood, and will know when to reassure and encourage, and above all when to give comfort. We have already seen that she realizes what can be done for children, given patience and imagination, in dealing with her younger brothers and sisters, particularly Susan, when she goes back to Portsmouth. She will be a very different kind of mother from Mrs Price, just as Edmund, who as a boy had such tenderness for her when she was alone and frightened, and who helped and guided her with kindness and intelligence, will be a very different father from Sir Thomas. No doubt Mansfield Parsonage will much resemble Steventon rectory when Jane Austen was a girl – full of books, learning, intelligent conversation, witty word-games, perhaps even the occasional play-reading (though not of anything as risqué as *Lovers' Vows*). If Fanny will never perhaps quite be able to promote fun in the way that Mrs Austen did, she will encourage her children to exercise their minds and extend their knowledge of life by overseeing their reading. Edmund will be in every way the conscientious and scholarly clergyman, preparing some of his sons for university as Mr Austen prepared two of his, and energetically finding careers for the others;

like Jane and Cassandra, his daughters will profit from their brothers' lessons. Life at Mansfield, as at Steventon, will be founded on kindness and tolerance, on moral goodness and on sound Christian principles. It will be an admirable home in which to bring up children.

Notes

References to Jane Austen's novels, letters and verses are as follows:
The Novels of Jane Austen, ed. R. W. Chapman, 5 vols, 3rd edn (Oxford, 1932–4):

E   Emma
MP   *Mansfield Park*
NA   *Northanger Abbey*
P   *Persuasion*
P&P   *Pride and Prejudice*
S&S   *Sense and Sensibility*
MW   *The Works of Jane Austen*, vi, *Minor Works*, ed. R. W. Chapman, rev. B. C. Southam (Oxford, 1969).
L   *Jane Austen's Letters*, ed. Deirdre Le Faye, 3rd edn (Oxford, 1995).
Jane Austen Collected Poems
Jane Austen Collected Poems and Verse of the Austen Family, ed. David Selwyn (Manchester, 1996).
Collected Reports
Collected Reports of the Jane Austen Society, 6 vols (1949–2005).

Notes to Introduction

1   See Roy Porter, *English Society in the Eighteenth Century*, pp. 266–8.
2   See Andrew O'Malley, *The Making of the Modern Child: Children's Literature and Childhood in the Late Eighteenth Century*, p. 41.
3   See Porter, *English Society in the Eighteenth Century*, p. 325.
4   See Helen Lefroy, 'Silkmaking and Papermaking in Hampshire', Jane Austen Society *Report for 2007*, pp. 90–3.
5   *E*, p. 292.
6   *E*, p. 293.
7   *E*, p. 296.
8   *E*, p. 312.

Notes to Chapter 1: Confinement

1   *E*, p. 449.
2   See *E*, p. 224.
3   William Shakespeare, *Much Ado About Nothing*, II. iii. 262.
4   *S&S*, p. 379.
5   *L*, p. 16.

6   *L*, p. 20.

7   See Hazel Jones, *Jane Austen and Marriage*, p. 160.

8   *L*, p. 21.

9   *L*, p. 24.

10   *L*, p. 140.

11   *L*, p. 223.

12   *L*, p. 320.

13   *L*, p. 337.

14   *L*, p. 330.

15   *L*, p. 332.

16   *L*, p. 336.

17   *L*, p. 332.

18   Mary Wollstonecraft, *The Vindications: The Rights of Men, The Rights of Woman*, ed. D. L. Macdonald and Kathleen Scherf, p. 339.

19   *The Wrongs of Woman* (unfinished), *The Young Philosopher* (1798) and *Adeline Mowbray* (1805) respectively.

20   For a discussion of the treatment of pregnancy in these three novels, see Clare Hanson, *A Cultural History of Pregnancy: Pregnancy, Medicine and Culture, 1750–2000*, pp. 29–35.

21   Ibid., p. 24.

22   William Shakespeare, *King Lear*, II. iv. ll. 56–8.

23   See *E*, p. 392.

24   Dr William Buchan, *Domestic Medicine, or, The Family Physician*, pp. 567–8.

25   Quoted in Amanda Vickery, *The Gentleman's Daughter: Women's Lives in Georgian England*, p. 100.

26   R. A. Austen-Leigh, *Austen Papers*, p. 28.

27   Ibid., pp. 31–2.

28   *L*, p. 61.

29   *S&S*, p. 107.

30   *S&S*, p. 163.

31   *S&S*, p. 164.

32   See *S&S*, p. 175.

33   *S&S*, p. 238.

34   Hanson, *A Cultural History of Pregnancy*, p. 36.

35   *S&S*, p. 208.

36   See *S&S*, p. 66.

37   *S&S*, p. 211.

38   See Belinda Meteyard, 'Illegitimacy and marriage in eighteenth-century England', *Journal of Interdisciplinary History*, 10/3 (1980), 479–89.

39   *L*, p. 118.

40   *S&S*, p. 207.

41   See *P&P*, pp. 201–2.

42   *E*, p. 22.

43   *E*, p. 62.

44   *E*, pp. 481–2.

Notes to Chapter 2: Birth

1   R. A. Austen-Leigh, *Austen Papers*, pp. 32–3.
2   *P&P*, p. 308.
3   Quoted in Richard Holmes, *Marlborough: England's Fragile Genius*, p. 236.
4   Lady Charlotte Finch, quoted in Flora Fraser, *Princesses: The Six Daughters of George III*, p. 72.
5   See Christopher Hibbert, *George III: A Personal History*, p. 242.
6   Ibid., p. 99.
7   Michael Underwood, *Disorders of Children* (1797 and 1805 edns).
8   See Susan Sibbald, *Memoirs of Susan Sibbald, 1783–1812*, ed. Francis Paget Hett, pp. 212–15.
9   Anne Lefroy, *The Letters of Mrs Lefroy: Jane Austen's Beloved Friend*, ed. Helen Lefroy and Gavin Turner, pp. 58–9.
10 *L*, p. 265.
11 *L*, p. 17.
12 Dr William Buchan, *Domestic Medicine, or, The Family Physician*, p. 568.
13 Her husband's detailed account of the horrifying procedure is quoted in full by Amanda Vickery in *The Gentleman's Daughter: Women's Lives in Georgian England*, pp. 103–4.
14 Quoted in Joanna Martin, *Wives and Daughters: Women and Children in the Georgian Country House*, p. 180.
15 *L*, p. 139.
16 *L*, p. 341.
17 William Moss, *An Essay on the Management & Nursing of Children*, pp. 37–9.
18 Quoted in Ian Carr's very useful online essay, 'Dying to have a baby – the history of childbirth' (www.umanitoba.ca/outreach/manitoba_womens_health/hist1.htm).
19 Vickery, *The Gentleman's Daughter*, p. 315 n. 69.
20 Lawrence Stone, *The Family, Sex and Marriage in England 1500–1800*, p. 64.
21 See Martin, *Wives and Daughters*, p. 181.
22 *L*, p. 27.
23 See Deirdre Le Faye, *Jane Austen: A Family Record*, p. 24.
24 J. E. Austen-Leigh, *A Memoir of Jane Austen and Other Family Recollections,* ed. Kathryn Sutherland, p. 14.
25 R. A. Austen-Leigh, *Austen Papers*, pp. 22–3.
26 Ibid., p. 24.
27 Quoted in Le Faye, *A Family Record*, p. 24.
28 R. A. Austen-Leigh, *Austen Papers*, p. 28.
29 *S&S*, p. 246.
30 *S&S*, p. 257.
31 Alexander Hamilton, *A Treatise of Midwifery*, p. 403.
32 *S&S*, p. 248.
33 See Maggie Lane, *Jane Austen and Names*, p. 29.
34 *E*, p. 422.
35 *E*, p. 468.
36 *E*, p. 461.
37 *E*, p. 479.
38 *E*, p. 480.

Notes to Chapter 3: Infancy

1   Mary Wollstonecraft, *The Vindications: The Rights of Men, The Rights of Woman*, ed. D. L. Macdonald and Kathleen Scherf, p. 192.
2   Ibid., p. 339.
3   In his 'Essay upon Nursing and the Management of Children'; see Lawrence Stone, *The Family, Sex and Marriage in England 1500–1800*, p. 272.
4   Samuel Richardson, *Sir Charles Grandison*, vol. 7, Letter XLIII.
5   Wollstonecraft, *The Vindications*, p. 279.
6   Quoted in Stone, *The Family, Sex and Marriage in England 1500–1800*, p. 272.
7   Bessy Ramsden, writing in 1768, quoted in Amanda Vickery, *The Gentleman's Daughter: Women's Lives in Georgian England*, p. 109.
8   *L*, p. 122.
9   Dr William Buchan, *Domestic Medicine, or, The Family Physician*, pp. 21–2.
10 See William Moss, *An Essay on the Management & Nursing of Children*, p. 122.
11 Ibid., pp. 266–69.
12 R. A. Austen-Leigh, *Austen Papers*, p. 237.
13 R. A. Austen-Leigh, *Austen Papers*, p. 29.
14 J. E. Austen-Leigh, *A Memoir of Jane Austen and Other Family Recollections*, ed. Kathryn Sutherland, p. 39.
15 See Irene Collins, *Jane Austen: The Parson's Daughter*, p. 18; Claire Tomalin, *Jane Austen: A Life*, pp. 6–7.
16 Kathryn Sutherland, for example, expresses this view in her edition of the *Memoir*, p. 217.
17 See Susan Sibbald, *Memoirs of Susan Sibbald, 1783–1812*, ed. Francis Paget Hett, p. 21.
18 See Deirdre Le Faye, 'The Austens and the Littleworths', *Collected Reports*, vol. 4, pp. 64–70.
19 See Stone, *The Family, Sex and Marriage in England 1500–1800*, pp. 267–9.
20 Buchan, *Domestic Medicine, or, The Family Physician*, p. 14.
21 See Michael Underwood, *Disorders of Children* (1797 edn), vol. 3, pp. 36–9.
22 I am very grateful to Deirdre Le Faye for this interesting fact, as I am for much of the information on paediatric medicine in this chapter, and in particular for access to her work on Buchan, Moss and Underwood.
23 Moss, *An Essay on the Management & Nursing of Children*, p. 41.
24 See *MP*, p. 71.
25 *L*, p. 17.
26 They are printed in full by Deirdre Le Faye in 'The business of mothering: two Austenian dialogues', *The Book Collector*, Autumn 1983, pp. 296–314.
27 *L*, p. 242.
28 R. A. Austen-Leigh, *Austen Papers*, p. 31.
29 *L*, p. 8.
30 *L*, p. 76.
31 R. A. Austen-Leigh, *Austen Papers*, p. 31.
32 *L*, p. 327.
33 *L*, p. 15.
34 *L*, p. 17.
35 *L*, p. 26.
36 *L*, p. 34.
37 *L*, p. 71.
38 *L*, p. 126.

39   See *L*, p. 127.
40   *L*, p. 132.
41   *L*, p. 128.
42   *L*, p. 132.
43   *L*, p. 137.
44   Caroline Mary Craven Austin, *Reminiscences of Caroline Austen*, p. 20.
45   *L*, p. 129.
46   *L*, p. 238.
47   *L*, p. 240.
48   *MP*, p. 377.
49   *MP*, p. 382.
50   *MP*, p. 387.
51   *MP*, p. 407.
52   *MP*, p. 391.
53   *MP*, p. 440.
54   *MP*, p. 389.
55   *MP*, p. 396.
56   Maria and Richard Lovell Edgeworth, *Practical Education*, p. 125.
57   Ibid, pp. 131–2.
58   Ibid., pp. 127 –8.
59   *MP*, p. 389.
60   *MP*, p. 386.
61   Michael Tatham, 'Without Education, Fortune or Connections . . . ', *Collected Reports*, vol. 5, p. 351.
62   *MP*, p. 397.
63   See *L*, pp. 160–1.
64   R. A. Austen-Leigh, *Austen Papers*, p. 23.
65   R. A. Austen-Leigh, *Austen Papers*, p. 27.
66   *L*, p. 131.
67   *L*, p. 137.
68   *E*, p. 83; p. 86.
69   *E*, p. 333; p 233.
70   *E*, p. 39.
71   *E*, p. 6.
72   *E*, p. 104.
73   See Underwood, *Disorders of Children* (1797 edn), vol. 1, pp. 60–70.
74   Ibid., p. 155.
75   Ibid., pp. 134–54.
76   See Buchan, *Domestic Medicine*, pp. 438–41.
77   Underwood, *Disorders of Children* (1805 edn), vol. 1, p. 135.
78   Ibid. (1797 edn), pp. 349–54.
79   Ibid., p. 181; pp. 226–39.
80   See Buchan, *Domestic Medicine*, pp. 592–3.
81   *E*, p. 101.
82   *E*, pp. 105–6.
83   See Moss, *An Essay on the Management & Nursing of Children*, pp. 51–2; 123.
84   *P*, p. 241.
85   Buchan, *Domestic Medicine*, p. 42.

86   From *First Impressions or Sketches from Art and Nature Animate & Inanimate*, quoted in Timothy Mowl, *To Build the Second City: Architects and Craftsmen of Georgian Bristol*, p. 119.

87   *E*, p. 183.

88   Maria Edgeworth, *The Parent's Assistant, or Stories for Children*, 'The Mimic', ch. 1.

89   *MW*, p. 114.

90   Joanna Martin, ed., *A Governess in the Age of Jane Austen: The Journals and Letters of Agnes Porter*, p. 288.

91   See Joanna Martin, *Wives and Daughters: Women and Children in the Georgian Country House*, pp. 173–4.

92   Quoted in ibid.

93   Martin, *A Governess in the Age of Jane Austen*, p. 302.

94   *S&S*, p. 307.

95   *MW*, p. 383.

96   Martin, *A Governess in the Age of Jane Austen*, p. 300.

97   Ibid., p. 301.

98   Deirdre Le Faye, 'The business of mothering: two Austenian dialogues', *The Book Collector*, p. 302.

99   Ibid., pp. 305–6.

100   Elizabeth Ham, *Elizabeth Ham: By Herself 1783–1820*, ed. Eric Gillett, p. 14.

101   Quoted in Martin, *Wives and Daughters*, p. 171.

102   *L*, p. 220.

103   *L*, p. 223.

104   *P*, p. 53.

105   *P*, p. 54.

106   *P*, pp. 58–9.

107   *P*, p. 63.

108   *P*, p. 77.

109   *P*, p. 79.

110   *E*, p. 98.

111   *P*, p. 80.

Notes to Chapter 4: Childhood

1   J. E. Austen-Leigh, *A Memoir of Jane Austen and Other Family Recollections*, ed. Kathryn Sutherland, pp. 25–6.

2   R. A. Austen-Leigh, *Austen Papers*, p. 131.

3   Ibid., p. 142.

4   Ibid., p. 144.

5   Ibid., p. 148.

6   *NA*, pp. 13–15.

7   Quoted in Deirdre Le Faye, *Jane Austen: A Family Record*, p. 50.

8   James Austen, *The Complete Poems of James Austen*, ed. David Selwyn, 'The Rash Resolution', p. 11.

9   *Jane Austen Collected Poems*, p. 11.

10   *L*, p. 284.

11   *L*, p. 320.

12   *Jane Austen Collected Poems*, p. 12.
13   *L*, p. 332.
14   *L*, p. 290.
15   *L*, p. 315.
16   *L*, pp. 119–20.
17   *E*, p. 382.
18   *L*, p. 294.
19   *L*, p. 326.
20   *L*, p. 335.
21   *L*, p. 272.
22   *L*, p. 324.
23   Quoted in Deirdre Le Faye, *Fanny Knight's Diaries: Jane Austen through her niece's eyes*, p. 7.
24   Fanny Knight's diary, quoted in Margaret Wilson, *Almost Another Sister: The Story of Fanny Knight, Jane Austen's Favourite Niece*, p. 25.
25   Caroline Mary Craven Austen, *My Aunt Jane Austen: A Memoir*, p. 10.
26   See *P&P*, p. 18.
27   J. E. Austen-Leigh, *Memoir*, p. 77.
28   Mrs George Austen, letter to Mary Lloyd (Mrs James Austen), Hampshire Record Office, Austen-Leigh archive, 23M93/62/2.
29   *L*, p. 107.
30   *MW*, p. 37.
31   *S&S*, p. 119.
32   An example of 'The New Game of Human Life' may be seen at the Bethnal Green Museum of Childhood, London.
33   *MW*, p. 13.
34   See *MP*, p. 18.
35   Quoted in Pauline Flick, *Old Toys*, p. 8.
36   *MP*, p. 17.
37   *E*, p. 347.
38   Joanna Martin, ed., *A Governess in the Age of Jane Austen: The Journals and Letters of Agnes Porter*, p. 115.
39   *L*, p. 107. This was the four-handed version of the game, played with partners.
40   *L*, p. 152.
41   *L*, p. 162.
42   *L*, pp. 163–64.
43   *L*, p. 167.
44   *NA*, p. 15.
45   *NA*, p. 13.
46   See Michael Davis, 'Jane Austen and Cricket', *Collected Reports*, vol. V, pp. 307–11.
47   The painting, which hangs *in situ* in Royal Fort House, is in the possession of the University of Bristol.
48   John Newbery, *A Little Pretty Pocket-Book* (1787 edn.), p. 43.
49   HRO 63M84/234.
50   Maria and Richard Lovell Edgeworth, *Practical Education*, p. 1.
51   Ibid., pp. 3–4.
52   Ibid., p. 17.
53   *L*, p. 314.
54   *L*, p. 165.

55   *L*, p. 148.

56   24–25 October, 1808, *L*, pp. 149–52.

57   *P*, p. 134.

58   *E*, p. 336.

59   *NA*, p. 14.

60   *MP*, p. 391.

61   Martin, *A Governess in the Age of Jane Austen*, p. 121.

62   Elizabeth Ham, *Elizabeth Ham: By Herself 1783–1820,* ed. Eric Gillett, p. 223.

63   Ibid., p. 225.

64   See Ruth Brandon, *Other People's Daughters: The Life and Times of the Governess*, p. 160.

65   See Martin, *A Governess in the Age of Jane Austen*, p. 39.

66   Mary Wollstonecraft, *The Vindications: The Rights of Men, The Rights of Woman*, ed. D. L. Macdonald and Kathleen Scherf, p. 331.

67   Quoted in Flora Fraser, *Princesses: The Six Daughters of George III*, p. 51.

68   Quoted in Brandon, *Other People's Daughters*, p. 167.

69   Ham, *Elizabeth Ham: By Herself*, pp. 223–4.

70   Quoted in Margaret Elton, *Annals of the Elton Family, Bristol Merchants and Somerset Landowners*, p. 146.

71   *The Travellers' Breakfast* by E. P. Rippingille is the property of the National Trust and hangs in Clevedon Court.

72   Ham, *Elizabeth Ham: By Herself*, p. 226.

73   Ibid., p. 223.

74   Quoted in Brandon, *Other People's Daughters*, p. 16.

75   Martin, *A Governess in the Age of Jane Austen*, p. 297.

76   Miss Eyre, governess to the daughters of the Congreve family in Staffordshire, was required by their mother to call the eldest daughter, who was fifteen when she was appointed in 1817, not Mary Anne but Miss Congreve (see Anthony Fletcher, *Growing Up in England: The Experience of Childhood 1600–1914*, p. 226).

77   Quoted in ibid., p. 235.

78   Margaret Wilson in *Almost Another Sister* and Deirdre Le Faye in *Fanny Knight's Diaries* both draw on them extensively.

79   Quoted in Le Faye, *Fanny Knight's Diaries*, p. 6.

80   *L*, p. 573.

81   *L*, p. 321.

82   *MW*, p. 434.

83   *MW*, p. 436.

84   *L*, p. 250.

85   See *L*, pp. 340–1.

86   *L*, p. 346.

87   Quoted in Wilson, *Almost Another Sister*, p. 21.

88   Quoted in Le Faye, *Fanny Knight's Diaries*, p. 21.

89   *L*, p. 186.

90   Fanny, quoted in Le Faye, *Fanny Knight's Diaries*, p. 25.

91   Quoted in Wilson, *Almost Another Sister*, p. 63.

92   *L*, p. 205.

93   *L*, p. 227.

94   *L*, p. 242.

95   *MW*, p. 432.

96 *L*, p. 333.
97 *MW*, p. 17.
98 *S&S*, p. 155.
99 *P&P*, p. 164.
100 For an account of him, see H. Neville Davies, 'More Light on Mr Chard', *Collected Reports*, vol. 4, pp. 140–2. Jane Austen continued to have lessons with Mr Chard into her twenties (see *L*, p. 7), though when years later she engaged a tutor, the harpist Philip Meyer, to give Fanny lessons three times a week while they were staying in London, she commented 'I have not Fanny's fondness for Masters, & Mr Meyers does not give me any Longing after them. The truth is I think, that they are all, at least Music Masters, made of too much consequence & allowed to take too many Liberties with their Scholar's time' (*L*, p. 303).
101 *P&P*, p. 163.
102 *P&P*, p. 166.
103 *P&P*, p. 67.
104 *MP*, p. 19.
105 *MP*, p. 91.
106 *MP*, p. 10.
107 *MP*, pp. 9–10.
108 *MP*, pp. 18–19.
109 *MP*, p. 14.
110 *MP*, p. 22.
111 Susan Sibbald, *Memoirs of Susan Sibbald, 1783–1812*, ed. Francis Paget Hett, p. 213.
112 *E*, p. 5.
113 *E*, p. 6.
114 See *E*, p. 224.
115 *E*, p. 192.
116 *E*, p. 37.
117 *MP*, p. 6.
118 Wollstonecraft, *The Vindications*, p. 179; p. 142.
119 Ibid., p. 140.
120 *P&P*, p. 239.
121 *E*, p. 16.
122 See Brandon, *Other People's Daughters*, pp. 169–76.
123 See Wilson, *Almost Another Sister*, p. 92.
124 *L*, p. 265.
125 *E*, p. 164.
126 *E*, p. 165.
127 *E*, p. 167.
128 *E*, p. 201.
129 *E*, p. 284.
130 *E*, p. 299–300.
131 *E*, p. 382.
132 Wollstonecraft, *The Vindications*, pp. 286–7.
133 See *MP*, pp. 126–7.
134 *MW*, p. 363.
135 *MW*, p. 330.
136 *MP*, p. 169.

137   James Austen, *The Complete Poems of James Austen*, 'To Edward On the death of his first Pony', p. 35.
138   *MW*, pp. 330-1.
139   *MW*, p. 332.

Notes to Chapter 5: Parents

1   *E*, p. 37.
2   *P*, p. 152.
3   *NA*, p. 180.
4   J. E. Austen-Leigh, *Fugitive Pieces, Trifles Light as Air: The Poems of James Edward Austen-Leigh*, ed. David Selwyn, p. 7.
5   Ibid., p. 9.
6   James Nelson, quoted in Lawrence Stone, *The Family, Sex and Marriage in England 1500-1800*, p. 274.
7   *Rambler*, 148.
8   Ibid.
9   *NA*, p. 162.
10   *NA*, p. 165.
11   *NA*, p. 210.
12   *NA*, p. 252.
13   Fanny Caroline Lefroy, 'Family History' MS, HRO 23M93/85.
14   *S&S*, pp. 376-7.
15   *MP*, p. 448.
16   *L*, p. 121.
17   Quoted in Deirdre Le Faye, *Jane Austen: A Family Record*, p. 111.
18   *L*, p. 289.
19   *L*, p. 216.
20   *L*, p. 326.
21   *P&P*, p. 231.
22   *S&S*, p. 32.
23   *S&S*, p. 120.
24   Charles Dickens, *A Christmas Carol* (1843), Stave Two.
25   *S&S*, pp. 121-2.
26   *S&S*, p. 144.
27   Mary Wollstonecraft, *The Vindications: The Rights of Men, The Rights of Woman*, ed. D. L. Macdonald and Kathleen Scherf, p. 290.
28   Ibid., ch. 11.
29   *P&P*, p. 152.
30   *P&P*, p. 286.
31   *L*, p. 100.
32   See Maggie Lane, 'Richard Buller', *Collected Reports*, vol. 6, pp. 17-20.
33   *P*, p. 69.
34   *P*, p. 113.
35   *L*, p. 256.
36   *L*, p. 262.
37   *P*, p. 6.

38 *E*, p.37.
39 *E*, p. 93.
40 *E*, pp. 10–11.
41 See Richard Jenkyns, *A Fine Brush on Ivory: An Appreciation of Jane Austen*, ch. 5, 'The Prisoner of Hartfield'.
42 *E*, p. 92.
43 *E*, p. 93.
44 *E*, p. 109.
45 *E*, p. 100.
46 *E*, p. 113.
47 *E*, p. 92.
48 *E*, P. 311.
49 *P*, p. 53.
50 *P*, p. 56.
51 *P*, p. 114.
52 *P*, p. 163.
53 *P*, p. 44.
54 *P*, p. 38.
55 *P*, p. 43.
56 *MP*, p. 377.
57 Elizabeth Ham, *Elizabeth Ham: By Herself 1783–1820*, ed. Eric Gillett, p. 21.
58 Quoted in Rupert Willoughby, *Sherborne St John & The Vyne in the Time of Jane Austen*, p. 22.
59 *L*, p. 331.
60 *MW*, pp. 33–4.
61 *L*, pp. 105–6.
62 *L*, p. 26.
63 *MP*, p. 387.

Notes to Chapter 6: *The child in the family*

1 *E*, p. 174.
2 *A Goodly Heritage: A History of Jane Austen's Family*, by George Holbert Tucker.
3 Quoted in Deirdre Le Faye, *Jane Austen's 'Outlandish Cousin': The Life and Letters of Eliza de Feuillide*, p. 116.
4 Ibid., pp. 86–7.
5 Caroline Mary Craven Austen, *My Aunt Jane Austen: A Memoir*, p. 6.
6 Fanny Caroline Lefroy, 'Family History' MS, HRO 23M93/85.
7 Ibid.
8 J. E. Austen-Leigh, *A Memoir of Jane Austen and Other Family Recollections*, ed. Kathryn Sutherland, p. 158.
9 *Jane Austen Collected Poems*, p. 23.
10 *L*, p. 294.
11 Caroline Mary Craven Austen, *My Aunt Jane Austen: A Memoir*, pp. 5–6.
12 Ibid., p. 6.
13 Quoted in Austen-Leigh, *A Memoir of Jane Austen and Other Family Recollections*, pp. 157–8.

14   Ibid., pp. 158–9.
15   *L*, p. 144.
16   Quoted in Le Faye, *Jane Austen's 'Outlandish Cousin'*, p. 134.
17   *L*, p. 116.
18   Caroline Austen, *My Aunt Jane Austen*, p. 15; p. 17.
19   *MP*, p. 235.
20   *L*, p. 38.
21   *L*, p. 177.
22   *MP*, p. 235.
23   *MP*, p. 21.
24   *MP*, pp. 21–2.
25   *MP*, p. 22.
26   *MP*, p. 234.
27   *MP*, p. 244.
28   *MP*, p. 26.
29   *MP*, p. 222.
30   J. E. Austen-Leigh, *Fugitive Pieces, Trifles Light as Air: The Poems of James Edward Austen-Leigh*, ed. David Selwyn, p. 22.
31   *MP*, p. 6.
32   *MP*, pp. 6–7.
33   Quoted in Le Faye, *Jane Austen's 'Outlandish Cousin'*, p. 132.
34   *MP*, p. 269.
35   *MP*, pp. 92–3.
36   *MP*, p. 234.
37   *MP*, p. 229.
38   *MP*, p. 231.
39   *L*, p. 229.
40   Ibid.
41   *NA*, p. 48.
42   *NA*, p. 107–8.
43   *P*, p. 122.
44   *P*, p. 133.
45   *MW*, p. 31.
46   *MW*, pp. 32–3.
47   *L*, pp. 88–9.
48   *P*, p. 223.
49   *P*, p. 88.
50   *MW*, pp. 318–19.
51   *P*, p. 3.
52   *P*, p. 5.
53   See Maggie Lane, *Jane Austen and Names*, p. 23.
54   *P*, p. 143.
55   *MP*, pp. 10–11.
56   *MP*, p. 17.
57   *MP*, p. 21.
58   *MP*, p. 24.
59   See Deirdre Le Faye, *Jane Austen: A Family Record*, p. 11; p. 17.
60   Ibid., p. 20.

61   Ibid., p. 25.
62   Ibid., pp. 72–3.
63   *S&S*, p. 284.
64   *MP*, p. 381.
65   *P&P*, p. 385.
66   *E*, p. 92.
67   Quoted in Le Faye, *Jane Austen's 'Outlandish Cousin'*, p. 75.
68   *MW*, p. 76.
69   See James Austen, *The Complete Poems of James Austen*, ed. David Selwyn, pp. 27–9.
70   *Jane Austen Collected Poems*, pp. 57–8.
71   *P&P*, p. 355,
72   *MW*, p. 4.
73   *S&S*, p. 118.
74   *S&S*, p. 272.
75   *P*, p. 152.
76   James Austen, *The Complete Poems of James Austen*, p. 1.
77   *MW*, p. 439.

Notes to Chapter 7: Reading and writing

1   For a description of the book, see David Gilson, *A Bibliography of Jane Austen*, p. 442.
2   Quoted by Humphrey Carpenter and Mari Prichard in *The Oxford Companion to Children's Literature*, p. 214.
3   *The History of Little Goody Two-Shoes; Otherwise called Mrs. Margery Two-Shoes*, 2nd edn, p. 14.
4   Ibid., p. 34.
5   Ibid., p. 69.
6   J. H. Plumb, 'The new world of children in eighteenth-century England', in *The Birth of a Consumer Society: The Commercialization of Eighteenth-Century England*, ed. N. McKendrick, J. Brewer and J. H. Plumb, p. 290.
7   *The History of Little Goody Two-Shoes*, 2nd edn, p. 16.
8   See *E*, pp. 347–8.
9   *The History of Little Goody Two-Shoes*, 2nd edn, p. 6.
10   Ibid., p. 8.
11   Ibid., p. 31.
12   Maria and Richard Lovell Edgeworth, *Practical Education*, p. 335.
13   Ibid., p. 326.
14   Ibid., p. 327.
15   *NA*, p. 200.
16   See Gilson, *Bibliography*, pp. 440–1.
17   Quoted in Andrew O'Malley, *The Making of the Modern Child: Children's Literature and Childhood in the Late Eighteenth Century*, p. 51.
18   *NA*, p. 14.
19   John Gay, 'The Hare and Many Friends', ll. 35–44.
20   See *E*, p. 68.
21   *E*, p. 454.
22   Thomas Mozeen, *Fables in Verse*, Dedication.

23 See *NA*, p. 109; Gilson, *Bibliography*, pp. 442–3.
24 Sarah Trimmer, *A Description of a Set of Prints of English History; Contained in a Set of Easy Lessons*, p. 28.
25 Ibid., pp. 31–2.
26 Anna Laetitia Barbauld, *Lessons for Children, From Two to Three Years Old*, p. 4.
27 Ibid., pp. 5–6.
28 *The History of Little Goody Two-Shoes*, 2nd edn, p. 39.
29 Barbauld, *Lessons for Children, from Two to Three Years Old*, p. 7.
30 Ibid., pp. 25–26.
31 Barbauld, *Lessons for Children of Three Years Old*, Part I, pp. 78–83.
32 Ibid., pp. 53–54.
33 Barbauld, *Lessons for Children from Three to Four Years Old*, p. 4.
34 Ibid., p. 19.
35 Ibid., p. 30–1.
36 Letter from Charles Lamb to Samuel Taylor Coleridge, 4 November 1802.
37 Edgeworths, *Practical Education*, p. 317.
38 Ibid., pp. 317–18.
39 Ibid., p. 320.
40 Ibid., p. 325.
41 See Gilson, *Bibliography*, pp. 438–9.
42 Edgeworths, *Practical Education*, p. 325.
43 Ibid., p. 332.
44 Ibid., p. 336.
45 Ibid., p. 550.
46 *NA*, pp. 109–10.
47 *MP*, p. 22.
48 J. E. Austen-Leigh, *A Memoir of Jane Austen and Other Family Recollections*, ed. Kathryn Sutherland, p. 16.
49 *L*, p. 145.
50 See Gilson, *Bibliography*, p. 445.
51 Ibid., pp. 433–4.
52 See Irene Collins, *Jane Austen: The Parson's Daughter*, pp. 69–70.
53 *MW*, p. 42.
54 *MW*, p. 16.
55 *MW*, p. 20.
56 *MW*, p. 15.
57 See *The History of England by Jane Austen: A Facsimile*; Deirdre Le Faye, *Jane Austen: A Chronology of Jane Austen and her Family*, p. 138; Adrienne Bradney-Smith, 'Art and the Austen Family', Jane Austen Society *Report for 2008*, p. 130.
58 See Le Faye, *Jane Austen: A Family Record*, pp. 213–15.
59 *L*, p. 310.
60 *L*, p. 288.
61 *L*, p. 317.
62 *L*, p. 331.
63 *L*, p. 334.
64 *L*, p. 338.
65 Caroline Mary Craven Austen, *My Aunt Jane Austen*, p. 10.
66 *L*, p. 319.

67   *L*, p. 323.
68   *L*, p. 319.
69   *L*, p. 323.
70   *L*, p. 316.
71   J. E. Austen-Leigh, *Memoir*, p. 121.
72   *Family Record*, p. 10
73   J. E. Austen-Leigh, *Memoir*, p. 15.
74   Abraham Æsop, Esq., *Fables in Verse, For the Improvement of the Young and the Old*, pp. 122–3.
75   *Jane Austen Collected Poems*, p. 31.

Notes to Chapter 8: Education

1   Mary Augusta Austen-Leigh, *James Edward Austen Leigh: A Memoir by His Daughter*, pp. 2–3.
2   Ian Gilmour, *The Making of the Poets: Byron and Shelley in Their Time*, p. 96.
3   *MP*, p. 19
4   James Austen, *The Complete Poems of James Austen*, ed. David Selwyn, p. 126.
5   Chris Viveash, 'Placed at School', in Jane Austen Society, *Collected Reports*, vol. 5, pp. 250–2.
6   For details of the Meyrick School, see Barbara Croucher, *The Village in the Valley: A History of Ramsbury*, pp. 184–94.
7   J. E. Austen-Leigh, *Fugitive Pieces, Trifles Light as Air: The Poems of James Edward Austen-Leigh*, ed. David Selwyn, p. 20.
8   Based on a transcription by Janet Clarke in J. E. Austen-Leigh, *Fugitive Pieces*, p. 106.
9   Irene Collins, *Jane Austen: The Parson's Daughter*, p. 33.
10   Deirdre Le Faye, *Jane Austen: A Family Record*, p. 292, n. 39.
11   Ibid., pp. 48–9.
12   For details of the Reading School, see T. A. B. Corley, 'Jane Austen's School Days', in Jane Austen Society, *Collected Reports*, vol. 5, pp. 14–24.
13   Ibid., p. 15.
14   Ibid., p. 17.
15   Memories of the Reading School in the period just after Jane and Cassandra attended it are to be found in the reminiscences of Mrs Sherwood, a prolific author who, as Martha Butt, was a parlour boarder there (see Bibliography).
16   *L*, p. 306.
17   *L*, p. 296.
18   *L*, p. 306.
19   See Roy Porter, *English Society in the Eighteenth Century*, p. 160.
20   *L*, p. 306.
21   William Cowper, 'Tirocinium; or, A Review of Schools' (1784), ll. 364–71.
22   Ibid., ll. 381–4; 389–94.
23   Robert L. Mack, ed., *The Loiterer*, pp. 63–6.
24   Cowper, 'Tirocinium', ll. 212–14; 215–17.
25   Ibid., ll. 222–33.
26   Henry Home, Lord Kames, *Sketches of the History of Man*, vol. 2, pp. 336–7.
27   Mary Augusta Austen-Leigh, *James Edward Austen Leigh: A Memoir by His Daughter*, p. 3.
28   See J. E. Austen-Leigh, *Fugitive Pieces*, p. 23; p. 33; p. 40; p. 47.

29   J. E. Austen-Leigh, *Fugitive Pieces*, p. 54.

30   HRO 63M84/234.

31   R. A. Austen-Leigh, *Austen Papers*, pp. 260–1.

32   *L*, p. 133.

33   *L*, p. 138.

34   *MP*, p. 339.

35   *MP*, p. 21.

36   *MP*, p. 61.

37   *MP*, pp. 250–1.

38   *MP*, p. 251.

39   R. A. Austen-Leigh, *Austen Papers*, p. 29.

40   Lefroy MS, quoted in Le Faye, *Jane Austen: A Family Record*, p. 21.

41   Mrs Austen, 'The humble petition of R^{d}. Buller & W. Goodenough', in *Jane Austen Collected Poems*, p. 28.

42   For details of the school, see Margaret Wilson, *Jane Austen's Family and Tonbridge*, pp, 21–4 and Brian Southam, 'George Austen: Pupil, Usher and Proctor', in Jane Austen Society, *Collected Reports*, vol. 5, pp. 289–94.

43   *MW*, p. 203.

44   *L*, p. 172.

45   Corley, Jane Austen's School Days', p. 19.

46   *L*, p. 5.

47   *MW*, p. 318.

48   *L*, p. 101.

49   Elizabeth Ham, *Elizabeth Ham: By Herself 1783–1820*, ed. Eric Gillett, p. 40.

50   Ibid., p. 39.

51   Ibid.

52   *E.*, p. 22.

53   *Memoirs of Susan Sibbald, 1783–1812*, ed. Francis Paget Hett, p. 38.

54   *MW*, p. 244.

55   *MW*, p. 282.

56   *MW*, p. 247.

57   *MW*, p. 256.

58   *MW*, p. 265.

59   *MW*, p. 256.

60   *MW*, p. 271.

61   *MW*, p. 273.

62   *L*, p. 211.

63   *MW*, p. 387.

64   *MW*, p. 420–1.

65   *MW*, p. 421.

66   *E*, p. 21.

67   *S&S*, p. 160.

68   HRO 23M93/60/2/6.

69   *E*, p. 23.

70   *E*, pp. 61–3.

71   *E*, p. 30.

72   *E*, p. 58.

73   *E*, pp. 64–5.

74 *E*, pp. 69–70.

75 *E*, p. 68.

76 Letter from Mrs Lefroy of 9 November 1804, see Anne Lefroy, *The Letters of Mrs Lefroy: Jane Austen's Beloved Friend*, ed. Helen Lefroy and Gavin Turner, p. 177.

77 *E*, p. 56.

Notes to Chapter 9: Maturity

1 *L*, p. 276.

2 *L*, p. 275.

3 See *E*, p. 382.

4 *P*, p. 152.

5 Mirza Abul Hassan Khan, the Persian Ambassador, from Margaret Cloake, trans. and ed., *A Persian at the Court of King George 1809-1810*, quoted in Christopher Hibbert, *George III: A Personal History*, p. 83.

6 Sophia Baker, quoted in Anthony Fletcher, *Growing Up in England: The Experience of Childhood 1600-1914*, p. 360.

7 Quoted in Joanna Martin, *Wives and Daughters: Women and Children in the Georgian Country House*, p. 101.

8 Joannna Martin, ed., *A Governess in the Age of Jane Austen: The Journals and Letters of Agnes Porter*, pp. 177–8.

9 Deirdre Le Faye, *Jane Austen's 'Outlandish Cousin': The Life and Letters of Eliza de Feuillide*, p. 76.

10 Quoted in Deirdre Le Faye, *Jane Austen: A Family Record*, p. 81. See also E. E. Duncan-Jones, 'Miss Mitford's Jane Austen', in Jane Austen Society, *Collected Reports* vol. 4, pp. 180–1.

11 *P&P*, p. 165.

12 See *MW*, pp. 152–5.

13 *MW*, pp. 150–2.

14 *Regency Etiquette: The Mirror of Graces (1811) by a Lady of Distinction*, p. 138.

15 Ibid., p. 153.

16 Ibid., p. 158.

17 Ibid., pp. 155–6.

18 Ibid., pp. 14–16.

19 Mary Wollstonecraft, *The Vindications: The Rights of Men, The Rights of Woman*, ed. D. L. Macdonald and Kathleen Scherf, p. 313.

20 *L*, p.269.

21 *P&P*, p. 122.

22 Quoted in Fletcher, *Growing Up in England*, p. 271.

23 See Fanny Burney, *Evelina*, vol. 2, Letter XV.

24 *NA*, p. 131.

25 *E*, p. 37.

26 *MP*, p. 19.

27 *MP*, p. 20.

28 Ibid.

29 *MP*, p. 34.

30 *MP*, p. 465.

31 *MP*, p. 35.
32 Ibid.
33 *MP*, p. 220.
34 *MP*, p. 48.
35 *MP*, p. 35.
36 *MP*, p. 272.
37 *MP*, p. 50.
38 *MP*, p. 51.
39 *MP*, p. 147.
40 *MP*, pp. 266–7.
41 *MP*, p. 276.
42 *The Mirror of Graces*, p. 156.
43 *MP*, p. 267.
44 *MP*, p. 272.
45 *MP*, p. 275.
46 *MP*, p. 281.
47 In *Daughters of England* (1842), quoted in Fletcher, *Growing Up in England*, p. 31.
48 *P&P*, p. 5.
49 *P&P*, p. 376.
50 *MP*, p. 200.
51 *MP*, pp. 315–16.
52 *MP*, p. 318.
53 *MP*, p. 465.
54 A point made deftly by Lawrence Stone; see *The Family, Sex and Marriage in England, 1500–1800*, p. 160.
55 Sarah Pennington, *An Unfortunate Mother's Advice to Her Absent Daughters, a Letter to Miss Pennington*, p. 32.
56 John Gregory, *A Father's Legacy to his Daughters*, pp. 24–5.
57 Ibid., p. 26.
58 Ibid., p. 38.
59 Ibid., p. 34.
60 Ibid., p. 39.
61 Wollstonecraft, *The Vindications*, p. 249.
62 Ibid., p. 136.
63 *P&P*, p. 309.
64 Pennington, *An Unfortunate Mother's Advice*, p. 33.
65 Ibid. p. 35.
66 *P&P*, p. 249.
67 *P&P*, pp. 250–1.
68 *P&P*, p. 355.
69 Gregory, *A Father's Legacy*, p. 34.
70 Ibid., p. 37.
71 Ibid., p. 33.
72 *NA*, pp. 236–7.
73 *P*, pp. 74–5.
74 See *P*, pp. 88–9.
75 *P*, p. 74.
76 *P*, p. 230.

77   *S&S*, pp. 15–16.
78   *S&S*, p. 224.
79   *S&S*, p. 267.
80   *S&S*, p. 371.
81   *S&S*, p. 373.
82   *S&S*, p. 374.
83   *S&S*, p. 377.
84   Robert L. Mack, ed., *The Loiterer*, pp. 159–63.
85   HRO 23M93/62/2, quoted in R. A. Austen-Leigh *Austen Papers*, and, more accurately, in Le Faye, *Jane Austen: A Family Record*, p. 99.
86   See Margaret Wilson, 'Anna Austen's Poems and Her Attachment to Mr Terry', Jane Austen Society, *Collected Reports*, vol. 4, pp. 70–3.
87   *Jane Austen Collected Poems*, p. 57.
88   *L*, p. 188.
89   *L*, pp. 231–2.
90   *L*, p. 246.
91   *L*, p. 249.
92   *P*, p. 30.
93   Of 18–20 November 1814, *L*, pp. 278–2.
94   *L*, p. 285.
95   *NA*, p. 237.
96   *NA*, p. 240.
97   *NA*, p. 243.
98   *NA*, p. 249.
99   *NA*, p. 252.
100 *MP*, p. 470.
101 *MP*, p. 469.
102 See *P*, pp. 102–3.
103 *MP*, p. 473.
104 *S&S*, p. 103.
105 Richard Graves, *Columella; or, The Distressed Anchoret*, vol. 2, ch. 28.

Bibliography

UNPUBLISHED SOURCES

Chawton (Jane Austen Memorial Trust), Austen, Mrs George, Letters; Jane Austen's House
Winchester, Hampshire Record Office, Austen-Leigh archive
Cologny-Genève, Fondation Martin Bodmer, Bodmer MS (facsimile in the British Library)
Maidstone, Centre for Kentish Studies, Knatchbull family papers
Winchester, Hampshire Record Office, Knight family papers
Cumbria, Isel Hall, MSS collections

PUBLISHED SOURCES

Æsop, Esq. Abraham, *Fables in Verse, For the Improvement of the Young and the Old;* (London, 1757; later edn, 1783).
Austen, Caroline Mary Craven, *My Aunt Jane Austen: A Memoir* (Chawton, 1952).
___, *Reminiscences of Caroline Austen*, ed. Deirdre Le Faye (Chawton, 1986).
Austen, James, *The Complete Poems of James Austen*, ed. David Selwyn (Chawton, 2003).
Austen, Jane, *The Novels of Jane Austen*, ed. R. W. Chapman, 5 vols, 3rd edn (Oxford, 1932–4).
___, *The Works of Jane Austen*, vol. 6: *Minor Works*, ed. R. W. Chapman, rev. B. C. Southam (Oxford, 1969).
___, *The History of England: A Facsimile of Her Manuscript*, Introduction by Deirdre Le Faye (London, 1993).
___, *Jane Austen's Letters*, ed. Deirdre Le Faye (Oxford, 1995).
___,*The Cambridge Edition of the Works of Jane Austen*, general editor Jan Todd, 9 vols (Cambridge, 2005–8).
Austen-Leigh, J. E., *A Memoir of Jane Austen and Other Family Recollections* (1871), ed. Kathryn Sutherland (Oxford, 2002).
___, *Fugitive Pieces, Trifles Light as Air: The Poems of James Edward Austen-Leigh*, ed. David Selwyn (Winchester, 2006).
Austen-Leigh, Mary Augusta [?], *Charades &c. Written a Hundred Years Ago by Jane Austen and Her Family* (London, 1895).
___, *James Edward Austen Leigh: A Memoir by His Daughter* (privately printed, 1911).
___, *Personal Aspects of Jane Austen* (London, 1920).

Austen-Leigh, R. A., *Austen Papers* (London, 1942).

[_____,] *Bouts-Rimés and Noun Verses* (Eton, n.d. [*c*.1905]).

Barbauld, Anna Laetitia, *Lessons for Children, From Two to Three Years Old* (London, 1787).

_____, *Lessons for Children of Three Years Old* (London, 1788).

_____, *Lessons for Children, From Three to Four Years Old* (London, 1788).

Black, Jeremy, and Porter, Roy, *A Dictionary of Eighteenth-Century World History* (Oxford, 1994).

Bowden, Jean K., *Jane Austen's House* (Chawton, 1994).

Brabourne, Edward, 1st Lord, ed., *Letters of Jane Austen* (London, 1884).

Brandon, Ruth, *Other People's Daughters: The Life and Times of the Governess* (London, 2008).

Brewer, John, *The Pleasures of the Imagination: English Culture in the Eighteenth Century* (London, 1997).

Buchan, William, *Domestic Medicine, or, The Family Physician* (Edinburgh, 1769).

Burney, Fanny, *Evelina or, a Young Lady's Entrance into the World* (London, 1778).

Burton, Anthony, *Bethnal Green Museum of Childhood* (London, 1986).

Cadogan, William, *An Essay upon Nursing and the Management of Children* (London, 1748).

Carpenter, Humphrey and Prichard, Mari, eds, *The Oxford Companion to Children's Literature* (Oxford, 1984).

Chapman, R.W., *Jane Austen's Letters to Her Sister Cassandra and Others*, 2 vols (Oxford, 1932).

_____, *Jane Austen: Facts and Problems* (Oxford, 1948).

Collins, Irene, *Jane Austen and the Clergy* (London, 1994).

_____, *Jane Austen: The Parson's Daughter* (London, 1998).

Copeland, Edward, and McMaster, Juliet, eds, *The Cambridge Companion to Jane Austen* (Cambridge, 1997).

Cowper, William, *The Poems of William Cowper*, ed. John D. Baird and Charles Ryskamp (Oxford, 1995).

Croucher, Barbara, *The Village in the Valley: A history of Ramsbury* (Ramsbury, 1986).

_____, *Hole Cross Church Ramsbury: A Guide, History and Meditation* (Ramsbury, 2005).

Darton, F. J. H., *The Life and Times of Mrs Sherwood* (London, 1910).

Day, Malcolm, *Voices from the World of Jane Austen* (Newton Abbot, 2006).

Denman, Thomas, *An Introduction to the Practice of Midwifery* (London, 1788).

Duckworth, Alistair M., *The Improvement of the Estate* (Baltimore, 1971).

Eagle, Dorothy and Carnell, Hilary, eds, *The Oxford Literary Guide to the British Isles* (Oxford, 1977).

Edgeworth, Maria, *The Parent's Assistant, or Stories for Children*, 6 vols (London, 1796–1800; selected edn, London, 1897).

_____, and Edgeworth, Richard Lovell, *Practical Education*, London, 1798).

Elton, Margaret, *Annals of the Elton Family, Bristol Merchants and Somerset Landowners* (Stroud, 1994).

Enigmas and Charades, Never Before Printed: With a Preface by the Author, Illustrative *of the Advantages Desirable, by the Mind of Youth, from Composition of*

Such Like Characters, Under Proper Regulation and Observance (London and Bath, 1823).

Erickson, Carolly, *Our Tempestuous Day: A History of Regency England* (London, 1996).

Fielding, Sarah, *The Governess, or Little Female Academy* (London, 1749).

Fletcher, Anthony, *Growing Up in England: The Experience of Childhood 1600–1914* (New Haven and London, 2008).

Flick, Pauline, *Old Toys* (Princes Risborough, 1995).

Foster, R. F., *Foster's Complete Hoyle: An Encyclopedia of Games* (London, n.d.).

Fraser, Flora, *Princesses: The Six Daughters of George III* (London, 2004).

Freeman, Jean, *Jane Austen in Bath* (Alton, 1969; rev. edn, Chawton, 2002).

Fremantle, Anne, ed., *The Wynne Diaries*, 3 vols (Oxford, 1935–40).

Fritzer, Penelope Joan, *Jane Austen and Eighteenth-Century Courtesy Books* (Westport, CT, and London, 1997).

Fyfe, Aileen, 'Reading children's books in late eighteenth-century dissenting families', *The Historical Journal*, 43/2 (2000), 453–73.

Gilmour, Ian, *The Making of the Poets: Byron and Shelley in Their Time* (London, 2002).

Gilson, David, *A Bibliography of Jane Austen*, 2nd edn (Winchester, 1997).

___, *Jane Austen: Collected Articles and Introductions* (privately printed, 1998).

Girouard, Mark, *Life in the English Country House* (New Haven and London, 1978).

Graves, Richard, *Columella; or, The Distressed Anchoret* (London, 1779).

Gregory, John, *A Father's Legacy to His Daughters* (1774; reprinted Ludlow, 1801[?]).

Grey, J. David, ed., *The Jane Austen Handbook* (London, 1986).

Ham, Elizabeth, *Elizabeth Ham: By Herself 1783–1820*, ed. Eric Gillett (London, 1945).

Hamilton, Alexander, *A Treatise of Midwifery* (London,1781).

Hanson, Clare, *A Cultural History of Pregnancy: Pregnancy, Medicine and Culture, 1750–2000* (Basingstoke, 2004).

Hibbert, Christopher, *George III: A Personal History* (London, 1998).

History of Little Goody Two-Shoes; Otherwise called Mrs. Margery Two-Shoes, The (London, 1765; 2nd edn, Wellington, Shropshire, after 1804).

Holmes, Richard, *Marlborough: England's Fragile Genius* (London, 2008).

Home, Henry, Lord Kames, *Sketches of the History of Man*, vol. 2 (Edinburgh 1778).

___, *Loose Hints upon Education: Chiefly Concerning the Culture of the Heart*, 2nd edn (Edinburgh, 1782; repr. London, 1993).

Honan, Park, *Jane Austen: Her Life* (New York, 1987; new edn, London, 2007).

Hubback, J. H., and Edith C., *Jane Austen's Sailor Brothers* (London, 1906).

Inglis, Fred, *The Promise of Happiness: Value and Meaning in Children's Fiction* (Cambridge, 1981).

Jane Austen Society, *Collected Reports*, 6 vols (1949–2005).

___, *Report for 2006*.

___, *Report for 2007*.

___, *Report for 2008*.

Jane Austen Society (Kent), *Austentations* (2001–).

Jane Austen Society (Midlands), *Transactions* (1990–).

Jane Austen Society of Australia (JASA), *Sensibilities* (1990–).

Jane Austen Society of North America (JASNA), *Persuasions* (1979–).

Jenkins, Elizabeth, *Jane Austen: A Biography* (London, 1938).

Jenkyns, Richard, *A Fine Brush on Ivory: An Appreciation of Jane Austen* (Oxford, 2004).

John-the-Giant-Killer, *Food for the Mind: or, a New Riddle-Book* (London, 1787).

Johnson, Samuel, *The History of Rasselas, Prince of Abissinia* (London, 1759).

___, *The Rambler* (London, 1750–2).

Jones, Hazel, *Jane Austen and Marriage* (London, 2009).

Kelly, S., ed., *The Life of Mrs Sherwood* (London, 1854).

Kirkham, Margaret, *Jane Austen, Feminism and Fiction*, 2nd edn (London, 1997).

Kuhlicke, F. W., and Emmison, F. G., eds, *English Local History Handlist* (Historical Association, 1969).

Lane, Maggie, *Jane Austen's Family through Five Generations* (London, 1984).

___, *Jane Austen's England* (London, 1986).

___, *Jane Austen's World* (Carlton, 1996).

___, *Jane Austen and Names* (Bristol, 2002).

Lascelles, Mary, *Jane Austen and Her Art* (Oxford, 1939; pbk edn, 1963).

Laski, Marghanita, *Jane Austen and Her World* (London, 1969).

Le Faye, Deirdre, 'The business of mothering: two Austenian dialogues', *The Book Collector*, Autumn 1983, pp. 296–314.

___, *Jane Austen* (London, 1998).

___, *Fanny Knight's Diaries: Jane Austen through Her Niece's Ryes* (Chawton, 2000).

___, *Jane Austen: The World of Her Novels* (London, 2002).

___, *Jane Austen's 'Outlandish Cousin': The Life and Letters of Eliza de Feuillide* (London, 2002).

___, *Jane Austen: A Family Record*, 2nd edn (Cambridge, 2004).

___, *A Chronology of Jane Austen and Her Family* (Cambridge, 2006).

___, *Jane Austen's Steventon* (Chawton, 2007).

___, ed., *Jane Austen's Letters* (Oxford, 1995).

Lefroy, Anne, *The Letters of Mrs Lefroy: Jane Austen's Beloved Friend*, ed. Helen Lefroy and Gavin Turner (Winchester, 2007).

Lefroy, Helen, *Jane Austen* (Stroud, 1997).

Little Pretty Pocket Book, A (London, 1744).

Locke, John, *Some Thoughts Concerning Education* (London, 1693).

Lucas, Victor, *Jane Austen* (Andover, 1996).

Lybbe Powys, Mrs Philip, *Passages from the Diaries of Mrs Philip Lybbe Powys*, ed. Emily J. Climenson (London, 1899).

MacDonagh, Oliver, *Jane Austen: Real and Imagined Worlds* (New Haven and London, 1991).

Mack, Robert L., ed., *The Loiterer (1789–90)* (Lampeter, 2006).

Malcolmson, Robert W., *Popular Recreations in English Society: 1700–1850* (Cambridge, 1973).

Martin, Joanna, ed., *A Governess in the Age of Jane Austen: The Journals and Letters of Agnes Porter* (London, 1998).

___, *Wives and Daughters: Women and Children in the Georgian Country House* (London, 2004).

McKendrick, N., Brewer, J., and Plumb, J. H., eds, *The Birth of a Consumer Society: The Commercialization of Eighteenth-Century England* (London, 1982).

McMaster, Juliet, ed., *Jane Austen's Achievement* (London, 1976).

Mears, Martha, *The Midwife's Candid Advice to the Fair Sex: Or the Pupil of Nature* (London, 1797).

Meek, Margaret, Warlow, Aidan and Barton, Griselda, eds, *The Cool Web: The Pattern of Children's Reading* (London, 1977).

Meteyard, Belinda, 'Illegitimacy and marriage in eighteenth-century England', *Journal of Interdisciplinary History*, 10/3 (1980), 479–89.

Miller, D. A., *Jane Austen, or The Secret of Style* (Princeton and Oxford, 2003).

Mitton, G. E., *Jane Austen and Her Times* (London, 1905).

Moss, William, *An Essay on the Management & Nursing of Children* (London, 1781).

Mowl, Timothy, *To Build the Second City: Artists and Craftsmen of Georgian Bristol* (Bristol, 1991).

Mozeen, Thomas, *Fables in Verse* (London, 1765).

Murray, Venetia, *High Society: A Social History of the Regency Period, 1788–1830* (London, 1998).

Newbery, John, *A Little Pretty Pocket-Book* (London, 1744; Worcester, Mass., 1787).

Newman, Gerald and Brown, Leslie Ellen, *Britain in the Hanoverian Age, 1714–1837: An Encyclopedia* (New York and London, 1997).

Nicolson, Nigel, *The World of Jane Austen* (London, 1991).

___, *Was Jane Austen Happy in Bath?* (Bath, 2003).

O'Malley, Andrew, *The Making of the Modern Child: Children's Literature and Childhood in the Late Eighteenth Century* (New York and London, 2003).

Outhwaite, R.B., 'Age at marriage in England from the late seventeenth to the nineteenth century', in *Transactions of the Royal Historical Society*, fifth series, 23 (1973), 55–70.

Pennington, Sarah, *An Unfortunate Mother's Advice to Her Absent Daughters, a Letter to Miss Pennington* (1761; reprinted Ludlow, 1803).

Piggott, Patrick, *The Innocent Diversion: A Study of Music in the Life and Writings of Jane Austen* (London, 1979).

Plumb, J. H., *England in the Eighteenth Century* (Harmondsworth, 1950).

___, *The Commercialisation of Leisure in Eighteenth-Century England* (Reading, 1973).

___, *Georgian Delights* (London, 1980).

Pollock, Linda, *Forgotten Children: Parent-Child Relations from 1500 to 1900* (Cambridge, 1983).

Pool, Daniel, *What Jane Austen Ate and Charles Dickens Knew: Fascinating Facts of Daily Life in the Nineteenth Century*, 2nd edn (London, 1998).

Porter, Roy, *English Society in the Eighteenth Century*, revised edn (London, 1990).

___, and Roberts, Mary Mulvey, eds, *Pleasure in the Eighteenth Century* (London, 1996).

Powell, Violet, *A Jane Austen Compendium* (London, 1993).

Radford, E. and M. A. Radford, *Encyclopaedia of Superstitions*, ed. Christina Hole, (London, 1961).

Regency Etiquette: The Mirror of Graces (1811) by a Lady of Distinction (Mendocino, 1997).

Richardson, Samuel, *Sir Charles Grandison* (London, 1753–54).

Sales, Roger, *Jane Austen and Representations of Regency England* (London, 1994).

Sambrook, Pamela A., *The Country House Servant* (Stroud, 1999).

Selwyn, David, *Jane Austen and Leisure* (London, 1999).

___, ed., *Jane Austen: Collected Poems and Verse of the Austen Family* (Manchester, 1996).

Sibbald, Susan, *Memoirs of Susan Sibbald, 1783–1812*, ed. Francis Paget Hett (London, 1926).

Simond, Louis, *An American in Regency England: The Journal of a Tour in 1810–1811*, ed. Christopher Hibbert (London, 1968).

Smellie, William, *A Treatise on the Theory and Practice of Midwifery* (London, 1752).

Smith, Robert A., *Late Georgian and Regency England, 1760–1837*, Conference on British Studies: Bibliographical Handbooks (Cambridge, 1984).

Southam, B.C., *Jane Austen's Literary Manuscripts* (Oxford, 1964).

___, *Jane Austen and the Navy* (London, 2000).

___, ed., *Jane Austen: The Critical Heritage*, 2 vols (London, 1968 and 1987).

___, ed., *Critical Essays on Jane Austen* (London, 1968).

___, ed., *Jane Austen's 'Sir Charles Grandison'* (Oxford, 1980).

Stokes, Myra, *The Language of Jane Austen* (London, 1991).

Stone, Lawrence, *The Family, Sex and Marriage in England 1500–1800*, revised edn (Harmondsworth, 1979).

Tomalin, Claire, *Jane Austen: A Life* (London, 1997).

Trimmer, Sarah, *A Description of a Set of Prints of English History; Contained in A Set of Easy Lessons* (London, n.d. [?1787]).

Tucker, George Holbert, *A Goodly Heritage: A History of Jane Austen's Family* (Manchester, 1983).

___, *Jane Austen the Woman: Some Biographical Insights* (London, 1994).

Underwood, Michael, *Disorders of Children* (London, 1784; further edns, 1797, 1805).

Vickery, Amanda, *The Gentleman's Daughter: Women's Lives in Georgian England* (New Haven and London, 1998).

Watkins, Susan, *Jane Austen's Town and Country Style* (London, 1990).

Watts, Ruth, 'Writing for children in the late eighteenth and early nineteenth centuries', Jane Austen Society (Midlands) *Transactions* 19 (2008), 9–20.

Weinreb, Ben, and Hibbert, Christopher, eds, *The London Encyclopaedia* (London, 1983).

Willoughby, Rupert, *Sherborne St John & The Vyne in the Time of Jane Austen* (Sherborne St John, 2002).

Wilson, Margaret, *Almost Another Sister: The Story of Fanny Knight, Jane Austen's Favourite Niece*, 2nd edn (Maidstone, 1998).

___, *Jane Austen's Family and Tonbridge* (Chawton, 2001).

Wollstonecraft, Mary, *A Vindication of the Rights of Woman*, 2nd edn (London, 1792).

___, *The Vindications: The Rights of Men, The Rights of Woman*, ed., D. L. Macdonald and Kathleen Scherf (Peterborough, Ontario, 1997).

Wrigley, E. A., 'Explaining the rise in marital fertility in England in the "long" eighteenth century', in *Economic History Review*, new series, 51/3 (1998), 435–64.

Index

Note: Literary works (*in italics*) are by Jane
  Austen unless otherwise stated

adoption 115, 116
adventure stories 155
Aesop 150, 161–2
affection, parental 108–9
age at marriage 7, 212
air, good, health advantages of 48, 49–50
Allen, Miss (governess) 80
alphabet games 66–7
animal fables 148–50
Augusta, Princess 76
Austen, Anna *see* Lefroy, Anna
Austen, Caroline (daughter of James Austen)
  40, 62–3, 64, 99, 119–20, 121–2, 158–9,
  170–1, 178
Austen, Cassandra (Mrs George Austen, née
  Leigh) 10–11, 15, 22–4, 34, 38, 137, 160–2,
  172–3, 208
Austen, Cassandra (sister of Jane Austen) 22,
  59, 60, 71, 91, 121, 122, 140–1, 165–6
Austen, Cassandra (daughter of Charles
  Austen) 41, 61–2, 101
Austen, Charles 40–1, 101
Austen, Edward (brother of Jane Austen) 115
Austen, Edward (son of Edward Austen) *see*
  Knight, Edward
Austen, Eliza (Mrs Henry Austen, née
  Hancock, widowed as de Feuillide) 59, 119,
  127–8, 137
Austen, Elizabeth (Mrs Edward Austen, née
  Bridges) 6, 15, 20, 22, 33, 71, 120–1
Austen, Fanny (Mrs Charles Austen, née
  Palmer) 15, 40–1

Austen, Fanny (daughter of Edward Austen)
  see Knight, Fanny
Austen, Francis 60–1, 101–2
Austen, Revd George 15, 23, 135, 164,
  172–3
Austen, George (brother of Jane Austen)
  44–5
Austen, George (son of Edward Austen) *see*
  Knight, George
Austen, Henry 37–8, 119, 127, 160, 170
Austen, Henry Edgar (son of Francis Austen)
  122
Austen, James 60, 92–3, 141–2, 157, 163–4,
  168, 207–8
Austen, Mary (Mrs Francis Austen, née
  Gibson) 7, 15, 33
Austen, Mary (Mrs James Austen, née Lloyd)
  5–7, 22, 36–7, 52–3, 100–1, 123, 140–1,
  208
Austen, William (son of Edward Austen) *see*
  Knight, William
Austen-Leigh, James Edward (son of James
  Austen) 22–3, 34, 35, 59, 64, 92–3, 96, 122,
  126, 156–7, 159–61, 163, 164–5, 170, 178

baby clothing 35–7
baptism *see* christening
Barbauld, Anna Laetitia 151–4
baseball 68
Bell, Lydia 166
Benn, Mrs John 7
Bennett's Academy, Winchester 166
bereavement 71–3
Berquin, Arnaud 155
birth *see* childbirth

books given to and by Jane Austen 157
boys
  clothes 37–8
  education of 91
  schools 163–5 *see also* public schools
brag (card game) 67–8
breastfeeding 8, 31–3
breeching 37–8
Bristol 49–50
brothers and sisters
  relationships between 123–6, 128–31
  separation of 136–7
brothers, Jane Austen's attitude towards 123
Buchan, Dr William 9–10, 18, 32, 33–4, 35, 46, 49, 53
Burney, Fanny 187, 212

card games 67–8
Cawley, Ann 165
Chapman, Dorothy 79
Charlotte, Queen 17, 75, 182
child mortality *see* infant mortality
childbirth 18–21
  attendance by family members 22–4
  in Austen family 22–3
  death in 15, 21
  trauma 20–1
childhood
  bereavement 71–3
  disappointment 91–3
  illnesses 45–8, 50–2
  of Jane Austen 59, 62, 165–6
  reading 156–7
Children's Friend, The (Berquin) 155
christening 26–7
Christmas Carol, A (Dickens) 103–4
Churching of Women 21–2
Chute, William John 115
classical education 166–7
clerical tutors 91
Clewes, Miss (governess) 81
Clifton (Bristol) 49, 50
clothing
  babies' 35–7

boys' 37–8
girls' 37, 38
Cole, Revd William 22
Collection of Letters, A (Juvenilia) 183–5
coming out 181–5, 187–93
Cooke, Revd Samuel 116–17
Cooper, Jane 23–4, 137, 165–6
cousins 127, 137–9
Cowper, William 167–8, 169
Craven, Charlotte 177
cricket 68

daughters and sons in a family 16
death in childbirth 15, 21
Delany, Mary 187
dentistry 54
deportment 185–6
dice 65–6
Dickens, Charles *A Christmas Carol* 103–4
disappointment, childhood 91–3
discipline, parental 101–2
dislike of own children, parental 100–1
dolls 70
dressings for children's wounds 52

Edgar and Emma (Juvenilia) 131
Edgeworth, Maria and Richard Lovell 42–3, 50, 69–71, 106–7, 148, 153–6
education
  boys' 91, 163–5
  classical 166–7
  girls' 87, 165–7
  of Jane Austen 165–6, 166–7, 174
  as play 144–5, 147
  private 172–3
  see also schools, public schools
educational toys and games 65–7
Elton, Charles Abraham 77
Emma 3–4, 13, 26, 27–9, 45–6, 46–9, 62, 66–7, 73, 85–7, 88–90, 110–13, 131, 149, 177–8, 178–80, 181, 188–9, 216
engagement, length of 214
enjoyment of children's presence, parental 109–10

Eton College 163
Evelina (Burney) 187, 212

fairy tales 147–8
families
    daughters and sons in 16
    financial pressures on 135–6
    large 130–1
family attitudes to Jane Austen 120–2
family life of Jane Austen 119–20, 136, 137
faults, inheritance of 110–13
feeding of young children 52–3
Feuillide, Eliza de *see* Austen, Eliza
financial pressures on families 135
Finch, Lady Charlotte 75–6
forceps, obstetric 18–19
fostering 34–5, 114–16, 134
Fowle, Fulwar Craven 141–2
Frederic and Elfrida (Juvenilia) 138–9
friendships 139–42
Fuller, S and J 65

Gabell, Dr Henry 170
games
    board 65–6
    card 67–8
    educational 65–7
    played by Austen family 64, 67–8
    see also sports
Gay, John 149
George III, King 17, 75, 180
ghost stories 147–8
girls
    books for 155–6
    clothes 37, 38
    education of 87
    schools 165–6, 174–80
Goddard, Dr 170–1
Godmersham, visits to by Jane Austen 39–41,
    45, 63, 120
godparents 116–17
    of Jane Austen 27, 116
Goldsmith, Oliver 147, 150, 158
Gordon, Alexander 21

governesses 74–91
Granby, Marquis of 18
Gregory, Dr John 199–200

Hall, Revd Henry 18
Ham, Elizabeth 53–4, 74, 76–8, 115, 174–5
Hamilton, Alexander 25–6, 34
Hancock, Philadelphia 24
Hanson, Clare 9
Heathcote, William 68–9, 164, 170, 171
Henry and Eliza (Juvenilia) 65, 116
history books for children 150–1, 158
History of England (Juvenilia) 158
Home, Henry (Lord Kames) 169

illegitimacy 12–13
indulgence, parental 102–8
infant mortality 16–18, 43, 44
informality of parent-child relationships,
    growth of 95–6
inheritance of virtues and faults 110–13
injustice, parental 99
'irritability' in pregnancy 9

Jack and Alice (Juvenilia) 66, 82, 157–8
jigsaw puzzles 66
Johnson, Dr Samuel 96–7, 99, 100

Kames, Lord *see* Home, Henry
kindness, parental 108–9
Knatchbull, Sir Edward 212
Knight, Charles 170
Knight, Edward 71–3, 136
Knight, Fanny 63–4, 79, 80–1, 122, 137–8,
    157, 209–12
Knight, George 38–9, 71–3
Knight, Marianne 54
Knight, William 88

La Tournelle, Mrs 166
labour pains 19–20
Lady Susan 100, 175–7
Lamb, Charles 153
large families 130

learning *see* education
Lefroy, Anna 8, 61–2, 100–1, 120, 122, 137–8, 157, 158, 208–9
Lefroy, Anne 17–18
Lefroy, Ben 209
Lefroy, Fanny Caroline 99, 101, 120
Lesley Castle (Juvenilia) 50
Lessons for Children (Barbauld) 151–4
Little Goody Two-Shoes, The History of (Newbery) 143–7, 148–9
Littleworth, Elizabeth 35
Lloyd, Eliza 141
Lloyd, Martha 36, 123, 140–1
Lloyd, Mary *see* Austen, Mary
love, marrying for 198–201, 207–8, 210–12

male midwives 19
Mansfield Park 26, 41–4, 66, 73–4, 83–4, 87, 92, 100, 110, 114–15, 117, 123–6, 127, 128–9, 134–5, 136, 171, 189–94, 195–8, 214–15, 216–17
Marlborough, Duke of 17
marriage
    intentions 193–212
    love as the motivation for 198–201, 207–8, 210–12
    parental influence on 204–7
    partner, character of a 201–3
Mathew, General 99
Mears, Martha 8
Memoirs of Mr Clifford, The (Juvenilia) 157
Meyrick's School, Ramsbury 164
midwifery 18–19
miscarriage 9–10, 22–3
moral character of women 186
Moss, William 20–1, 34, 49
motherhood
    inadequate 113–14
    surrogate 114
Mozeen, Thomas 150
multiple pregnancies 7–8
Murry, Ann 157

naming of children 26–7

needlework 71
nephews and nieces of Jane Austen
    advice to as writers 158–60
    advice to regarding relationships 209–12
    attitude towards 38–41, 61–2, 62–3, 71–3, 101–2, 109–10, 121, 122
    gifts of books to 157
Newbery, John 68, 146–7, 150, 161–2
Northanger Abbey 59–60, 68, 73, 97–9, 130, 148, 156, 187–8, 212–14

obstructed labour 18

parent-child relationships, growth of informality in 91–5
parental
    address, styles of 95–6
    affection 108–9
    discipline 101–2
    dislike of own children 100–1
    enjoyment of children's presence 109–10
    inadequacy 113–14
    indulgence 102–8
    influence on marriage 204–7
    injustice 99
    tyranny 96–9
Parent's Assistant, The (Edgeworth) 50, 106–7
parents, fictional characters as 215–17
Pennington, Sarah 199, 201
Percival, Thomas 157
Persuasion 54–8, 73, 109, 110, 113–14, 130–1, 131–2, 132–4, 139–40, 175, 181, 188, 204–5, 210, 216
playlets by Jane Austen and Mary Lloyd 36–7, 52–3
Plumptre, John 209–10, 211, 212
Porter, Agnes 50–1, 51–2, 67, 74, 78, 182–3
Practical Education (Edgeworth) 42–3, 69–71, 148, 153–6
pregnancy
    behaviour during 10–11
    multiple 7–8
    physiology of 8–9
presentation at court 182–3

Pride and Prejudice 16, 82–3, 87, 102, 108–9, 110, 130, 138, 140, 183, 187, 194–5, 201–3, 216
private education 172–3
public schools 167–72
punishment 75–6, 96
puzzle maps 66

Ranelagh 187
reading
    by Jane Austen in childhood 156–7
    primers 151–5
Reading Ladies Boarding School 165–6, 174
Regency Etiquette (Anonymous) 185–6, 193
Richardson, Samuel 31–2, 158
Rowlandson, Thomas 68
royal children 75–6

Sanditon 51, 130, 177
schools
    boys' 163–5
    girls' 165–6, 174–80
    public 167–72
    see also education
sea air, health advantages of 47, 48–9
Sense and Sensibility 9, 11–13, 24–6, 51, 65, 82, 99, 102–3, 104–6, 110, 135–6, 139, 171–2, 205–7, 215–16
servants, children's familiarity with 42
Sharp, Anne 79–80, 88
Sibbald, Susan, 84–5, 175
Sir Charles Grandison (Richardson) 31–2, 158
sisters
    isolated 132–4
    relationships between 132
sisters-in-law, Jane Austen's attitude towards 122–3
Smellie, William 19
sons and daughters in a family 16

speculation (card game) 67–8
sports
    outdoor 68
    village 68–9
    see also games
Stone, Lawrence 22
Strangways, Ladies Mary and Harriot 182–3
surrogate motherhood 114
swaddling 35–6, 36–7

table manners 42–3
Talbot, Lady Mary 19–20, 22, 50–1, 51–2, 54
teething 46
Terry, Michael 208–9
theatricals, family 63–4, 137
Thrale, Hester 187
Tilson, Mrs 7
Tonbridge School 173
toys 64–5, 69–71
Trimmer, Sarah 149, 150–1
tutors, clerical 91
tyranny, parental 96–9

Underwood, Michael 17, 35, 46

Vickers, William 157
Vickery, Amanda 21–2
virtues, inheritance of 110–13

Walter, Philadelphia 59, 119
Watsons, The 91–2, 93–4, 132, 174
weaning 33–4
Weeton, Nelly 74, 76, 78, 87
wet-nurses 31, 32
Wiggett, Caroline 115
Winchester College 170–1, 180
Wollstonecraft, Mary 8, 31, 32, 74–5, 87, 90–1, 107–8, 186–7, 200–1
worms (in children) 46
writing by children 157–62